Exceptional Children and Youth An Introduction

Edward L. Meyen
University of Kansas

LOVE PUBLISHING COMPANY
Denver, Colorado 80222

Copyright © 1978 Love Publishing Company
Printed in the U.S.A.
ISBN 0-89108-074-0
Library of Congress Catalog Card Number 78-50498
10 9 8 7 6 5 4 3 2

ACKNOWLEDGMENTS

First acknowledgment must go to the many researchers, teachers, parents, and concerned citizens who have contributed to the changing of attitudes, expansion of knowledge, and new public policies which are influencing the futures of exceptional children and youth. These changing patterns are helping to make the study of exceptional children a preferred professional goal for young people and an optimistic endeavor for the practitioner in the field.

Appreciation has been well earned by my colleagues who shared their talents and energies in producing this resource. They displayed a high degree of professionalism through their participation in a rather unusual approach to the development of a book. This book is truly a team product.

In the process of conceptualizing and producing a book of this type, numerous people make contributions. I am indebted particularly to my students, who reviewed the manuscript during its formative stages. Special mention is due Susan Elkins for editing assistance; Judy Mantle, Sherry Muirhead, Julie Neubaur, Stella Port, Bonnie Ward, and Diane Wimmer for their assistance in preparing the manuscript; and to Judy Tate for keeping me organized.

Appreciation is expressed to Stan Love, the publisher, and Carolyn Acheson, the senior editor, for their concern for quality and the personal interest they displayed in this project.

To my family—Marie, Brad, Brett, Joy, Blake, and Janelle—thanks again!

CONTENT DEVELOPERS

Nicholas W. Bankson
Boston University

Robert H. Bruininks
University of Minnesota

P. Douglas Guess
University of Kansas

R. Donald Horner
University of Kansas

Martin J. Kaufman
Bureau of Education for
the Handicapped

Alfred D. Larson
University of Kansas Medical Center

Larry J. Little
Shippensburg State College

Edward L. Meyen
University of Kansas

June B. Miller
University of Kansas Medical Center

Linda G. Morra
Bureau of Education for
the Handicapped

Carson Y. Nolan
American Printing House for the Blind
Louisville, Kentucky

Barbara Sirvis
San Francisco State University

Joseph J. Walker
Georgia State University

Grace Warfield
University of Minnesota

Richard J. Whelan
University of Kansas Medical Center

PROCESS DEVELOPERS

Reuben Altman
University of Missouri

Burton Blatt
Syracuse University

Warren E. Heiss
Montclair State College
New Jersey

John L. Johnson
University of the District of Columbia

Marian Leibowitz
Educational Improvement Center
Hightstown, New Jersey

PREFACE

The preface of a book is generally as predictable as the table of contents. The table of contents outlines the material and serves as a directory, and the preface summarizes the content in a brief but profound manner. After considerable deliberation, I decided to vary from the traditional preface style, and to offer the reader an explanation for *why* the book is being published and why a number of people have invested their talents in its development. During the planning stages, the senior developer and the publisher explored four basic questions:

1. Does the field of special education need another introductory book on exceptional children and youth?
2. If another book is needed, what features need to be added or receive additional emphasis?
3. Does the popular support for noncategorical programming for exceptional children and youth generalize to an introductory text (e.g., should the book be organized in a manner other than by areas of exceptionality)?
4. Should the book be a single- or multiple-authored project?

For the most part, introductory texts on exceptional children and youth tend to focus on an historical analysis of society's concern for exceptional children, learner characteristics, etiology, and information relating to current issues and practices. The pattern of such texts is reasonable, and the quality in general is good. The similarities and differences among the introductory texts are rather clear, but the reason why instructors prefer one over another is not as clear. Why an additional book is needed may be equally unclear—thus, this explanatory-type preface.

The decade of the 1970s is resulting in significant changes in how our judicial system perceives responsibilities of the public school for educating exceptional children. The public, through its representatives in governmental structures at all levels, is contributing to (or at least allowing) significant changes to occur; in turn, the public schools are responding. Responses of the public schools are highly visible and, in general, represent new commitments. These commitments operationalize into practices such as mainstreaming, IEPs, due process procedures, and programming for previously unserved populations such as the severely/profoundly handicapped.

From our perspective, it was considered important not only to provide a current perspective on practices evolving from events of the 1970s, but to do so in the context of instructional planning. We also believe it is essential that principles and practices emanating from the 1970s be elaborated on in an informational sense, and be an integral part of the discussion of all areas of exceptionality. Thus emerged the following features which were to collectively convince us that an additional text was needed.

- The events of the 1970s and their implications for the future should provide the primary historical reference for the text. Except for highly relevant features, readers should be referred to other sources for extensive discussions on historical precedents in the education of exceptional children and youth.
- A major chapter should be devoted to general principles of instructional planning, with specific attention to the IEP as an example of instructional planning.
- In each chapter, where appropriate, reference should be made to major concerns such as minority group childrens' special needs, implications of principles basic to PL 94-142, emerging responsibilities of regular educators, and the changing status of the handicapped in the broader context of society.
- A separate chapter regarding the severely/profoundly handicapped would be included. Because of the recency of this area as a public education concern, we believe the discussion should not be limited to a review of current special education literature, but should present a review of relevant practices drawn from other disciplines that have had a history of working with this population in non-school settings.
- Instead of presenting an exhaustive literature review, a *resource guide* would be used as a means of directing readers to additional sources of information. This is considered an important feature because of the heterogeneous nature of individuals who enroll in introductory courses.
- Descriptive information on characteristics, etiology, and trends would be included in categorical chapters but, to the degree possible, the discussion would emphasize the exceptionalities within an educational framework.

- Providing an informational source for students in introductory courses was considered as a basic objective. An equally important objective was to present the information in a readable style without reducing the substantive value of the content.
- The text would be designed as an independent resource, but also would be part of a broader set of resources. Supplemental materials —an instructor's manual, a collection of selected readings, and materials adapted for inservice use—would be developed to benefit instructors, students and inservice personnel.
- An interactive type relationship between the developer and the publisher was considered as an important element in the development process. Both shared in decisions on team member selection, design, production, and marketing issues.

The previously discussed features combined to answer the question of single versus multiple authorship. To properly cover each area of exceptionality and to sufficiently address the specific topical concerns evolving from the 1970s, a multiple authorship approach was considered essential, but possibly not sufficient. Consequently, a developmental model was designed involving 20 individuals organized into two teams— content developers and process developers; 14 individuals, in addition to myself, were selected to assume primary responsibility for preparing the initial content chapters in the various areas of specialty. Five other individuals were selected as process developers with primary responsibility for reviewing each chapter from a particular perspective. The senior developer assumed responsibility for conceptualization and co-ordination of the project.

Team members are:

Content Developers

Edward L. Meyen - An Introductory Perspective - Instructional Planning for Exceptional Children and Youth

Martin Kaufman and Linda Morra - The Least Restrictive Environment

Robert Bruininks and Grace Warfield - The Mentally Retarded

Douglas Guess and Donald Horner - The Severely/Profoundly Handicapped

Larry Little - The Learning Disabled

Richard Whelan - The Emotionally Disturbed

Barbara Sirvis - The Physically Disabled

Nicholas Bankson - The Speech and Language Impaired

Carson Nolan - The Visually Impaired
Alfred Larson and June Miller - The Hearing Impaired
Joseph Walker - The Gifted and Talented
Process Developers

Burton Blatt - Social-Cultural Implications
Warren Heiss - Language Implications
Reuben Altman - Research Implications
John Johnson - Implications for Minorities
Marian Leibowitz - Instructional Status

This development model resulted in the content chapters being reviewed by the process developers. Such an approach involves an intensive review procedure, and has the benefit of each chapter's becoming a team effort, with a number of individuals having an influence on the content and organization.

The question of chapter organization was resolved in favor of categorical chapters supplemented with generic chapters. This decision was based upon our assumptions about introductory courses. Enrollment in most introductory courses includes beginning students in special education, regular classroom teachers, and students from related fields. Introductory courses on exceptional children as described in most college catalogs emphasize the exceptional learner; they are not courses on instructional methods or assessment techniques. Although strong arguments exist for noncategorical methods texts, our impression was that an introductory text could serve students best if organized in a manner that would provide them easy access to information on areas of exceptionality. The instructor's responsibility, then, is to illustrate similarities across areas of exceptionality and to supplement the text. Such suggestions are incorporated in the instructor's manual.

This book has become more than a collection of chapters—it has become a project involving a large number of contributors. We have made major investments in coordination and editing to combine the merits of a single authored text with the comprehensive merits of a team approach. We hope we have provided a resource which adds to the array of introductory texts, a choice which under careful analysis will prove to be different, even though at first glance it may appear as a "look alike." We believe the differences are real and significant. Above all, we hope the book will be perceived by the intended readers as having been designed specifically for them.

Edward L. Meyen
1978

CONTENTS

TABLES

Exceptional Children and Youth An Introduction

1 An Introductory Perspective

Edward L. Meyen
University of Kansas

The decade of the 1970s represents an era of significant progress for handicapped persons, their families, and the community of professionals who work with them. Because of efforts of individuals and organizations, and because of growing public concern, the 1970s have been an exciting and history-changing period for those interested in the future of the handicapped. Although an understanding of how society has perceived and, in turn, served the handicapped throughout history is important, the new directions, precedents, public policies, and resource commitments which have characterized the 70s make this particular time in history an appropriate departure point for any current study of exceptional children and youth.

This book, unlike most introductory texts in the field, will not begin with an extensive review of historical events dating back to the pre-Christian era. Events and persons contributing to the current status of exceptional children and youth will be discussed when appropriate, but the focus will be on future implications of the 1970s for exceptional children and youth, and for society as a whole.

The person beginning his or her study of exceptional children today cannot experience directly the era of the 1950s or 70s. This person, however, will participate in the era of the 1980s. Because the 80s may appear at this time to be unsettled and without clear direction, an understanding of influences which brought about the changes of the 1970s may be helpful in providing a frame of reference for the future.

Education frequently is accused of being a discipline resistant to change. Parents encounter their own past teachers when visiting their children's schools; and the tenure of school administrators can span many years. Because of economic necessity, textbooks often are used beyond their intended life spans. So too, school traditions tend to endure. These circumstances confirm the suspicions of the public. Although certain examples of curriculum additions—modern math, open schools, sex education—do represent change, these innovations quickly become absorbed into the broader context of education. New ideas tend to lose their impact when confronted by longstanding, negative public perceptions toward "the system."

Developments currently occurring in the education of exceptional children, however, cannot go unnoticed. They represent changes so markedly different from the pattern established during the last 20 years that they will not be ignored. The consequences of these changes are so far-reaching that they affect not only the education of exceptional children but the future education of *all* children.

TWENTY YEARS OF CHANGE

If in 1955 you had visited a school district with an enrollment of approximately 5,000 students and asked for a tour of facilities and programs serving exceptional children, you would have been shown the self-contained special class as the most popular model for providing services to exceptional children. Children served in these classes likely would have been identified as educable mentally retarded or emotionally disturbed. Although the special education director might have referred to children with "learning problems," the director would not have mentioned resource rooms, consulting or itinerant teachers, or learning disabled children.

Questions regarding gifted or talented children would have evoked acknowledgment that such children exist, but these students would have been handled through grouping techniques by regular classroom teachers or through acceleration via promotion. You might have found a special class for the orthopedically handicapped, but no specialized programs for the severely and profoundly handicapped. Services to the visually impaired were limited then, although some of these children might have been served through cooperative programs involving two or more districts.

Speech clinicians would have had heavy case loads focusing primarily on articulation problems, and they probably devoted the first two months of each school year to screening children for hearing losses. If you had inquired about placement practices, you would have found that the school psychologist played a major role in determining eligibility. for special class placement and in recommending education programs. Parental involvement in instructional planning was limited.

Most special classes would have been located in elementary schools, or sometimes grouped in a single building. Most special class teachers used materials they created themselves or adapted from those designed for regular classroom use. You would have found students in regular classes whom the teacher had referred for special help because of suspected learning or behavioral problems but who had not been evaluated, or students who had been recommended for special class placement but were on a waiting list.

If you had examined the children in special classes, you might have found some students who had made sufficient progress to return to regular classes but, because placement decisions rarely were reconsidered, remained in special classes. A closer look at students enrolled in special classes also might have revealed a disproportionate number of minority children compared to the number of minority children in the total enrollment.

A visit to the same district today would reveal a much different situation. While general enrollment has increased probably 20 percent, the number of handicapped children in special programs has doubled. The most startling difference observed would be the presence of severely and profoundly handicapped children. Although not necessarily ambulatory or able to communicate verbally, and most having multiple handicaps, they would be engaged in learning tasks. Gone would be many of the special classes serving segregated groups of mildly mentally retarded or socially maladjusted children. In their place would be resource rooms in which the same student would receive specialized instruction for part of the day and return to the regular class for the remainder of the day. Some special classes would exist, but attendance would be limited to students unable to profit from regular class placement.

If observant, you would notice that special education teachers have access to a variety of instructional resource materials. In addition to supplemental instructional material, they now have more curriculum materials in subject matter areas designed specifically for the handicapped. You would be introduced to itinerant teachers, resource teachers, and consultants. Principals would be knowledgeable about special programs and sensitive to changes that are occurring. Programs for gifted and talented children may not yet be fully developed, but experimental options would be found in many schools.

The speech clinician, although still concerned with articulation problems, would be involved heavily in working with teachers to set up language development programs. The clinician would be devoting more time to working with teachers and groups of children than in individual therapy. The largest single group of exceptional children served would be children with speech impairments. The next largest group would be children referred to as learning disabled. You would have to look hard to find a class for the orthopedically handicapped, since most of these children are in regular classes. You would see children with vision and hearing impairments using a variety of technological aids. Many would be attending resource rooms as well as regular classes.

On almost any given day somewhere in the district, a placement or IEP conference would be held. The IEP—an individualized education program—is developed for each exceptional child through a conference which includes teachers, support personnel, and parents. Yes, parents would be involved in making instructional decisions about their children.

If fortunate enough to sit in on a conference, you would note that the person chairing the conference is careful to involve the parents in discussions, and especially in decisions about the child's plan. If you would listen carefully during the conference and eavesdrop on conversations among its members after the conference, you likely would hear terms such as full service, compliance, free and appropriate education, mandate, confidentiality, hearing officer, rights of the handicapped, advocacy, monitoring, mainstreaming, placement, and appeal.

These changes are real. State and federal legislation now mandate local districts to provide educational services for handicapped children and youth, and they must establish procedures to ensure the rights of the handicapped. Parents play a major role in the decision making process regarding program development; and school administrators, who previously delegated responsibility to special education personnel, are now much more aware of their obligations to the handicapped. Criteria for determining eligibility for specialized programs have changed, and definitions of exceptional children likewise have been revised. Changes in eligibility criteria and definitions have resulted in some children who previously were considered exceptional no longer being served through special education programs. Individuals who previously were served only by institutions or community agencies now are being served by the public schools. A new awareness on the part of all school personnel is apparent in regard to programming for exceptional children.

IMPLICATIONS OF CHANGE

Determining the implications of change is much more difficult than merely observing that they have occurred. The above comparison is presented simply to illustrate the pattern of growth in programming for exceptional children that has transpired during the past 20 years, and to provide a perspective for events occurring during the 1970s and their effect on the current status of educational programming.

Initial reactions to a comparison of past and present might suggest that:

- today's approach is good and yesterday's approach was bad
- philosophies of education have changed
- criteria for classifying children as handicapped have changed
- there are more handicapped children and youth today
- educators have a stronger commitment to meeting the needs of handicapped children and youth today than previously

- today's public is more willing to pay higher taxes to support special education programs.

Although there may be some truth to these observations, one takes a risk in placing too much emphasis on specific observations or in searching for simple explanations. Another temptation may be to explain the current level and organization of services for exceptional children by saying simply that state and federal statutes have mandated them. Such an explanation implies that the legislation was designed to correct an inappropriate approach to educating exceptional children, or that the legislative process is a quick method of bringing about dramatic change. Of course, legislation can be effective in establishing and improving human services but, in the case of recent legislation directed at exceptional children and youth, the prior history of changing conditions produced the climate for the substantive changes called for through this significant legislation.

Contrasting special education programs of today with those of the 1950s is not a case of comparing the good with the bad, nor is it an admission of pedagogical error during the 1950s. Numerous factors have interacted and acted upon the field of education, and particularly special education, to produce the circumstances of the present—and today's circumstances are truly different from those of the 50s.

The federal government has made a concerted effort to enlarge the supply of personnel trained in special education since passage of PL 85-926 in 1958. Prior to the late 1950s, few graduate training programs were available to prepare professors for training special education personnel. Not until the late 1960s and early 1970s did a sufficient number of professors with doctoral degrees from special education graduate programs become available to staff expanding university training programs. The increased supply of special education teachers and simultaneous reduction in the teacher shortage in general education allowed school administrators to be more selective in hiring teachers. Before the 1950s, administrators were not able to be as selective as they wished, because of the scarcity of certified teachers.

Today, the situation indeed is different. Moreover, the body of knowledge related to remediation and assessment has increased. While utopia does not exist, diagnosticians have access to a far wider array of instruments designed specifically for handicapped individuals. When presented with a child who is encountering serious academic or behavioral difficulties, they have access to more options and resources. Additionally, a larger pool of personnel is skilled in assessment techniques.

The Bureau of Education for the Handicapped—the unit within the federal government responsible for educational programs serving handicapped children—has evolved as a primary force in the area of research and personnel training. The BEH has become a major advocate for full services to all exceptional children and youth. This development, combined with other efforts, reflects the high level of interest by the research community in the handicapped, and adds to the climate accenting expansion of knowledge regarding the handicapped.

Another indicator of knowledge expansion relates to the number of journals and periodicals disseminating information about education or treatment of exceptional children and youth. New journals are appearing each year, targeted toward both professionals and lay persons. In fact, the increase in research has become so marked that many periodicals reject 75 to 80 percent of manuscripts received because they simply haven't space to publish all of them. The backlog of articles also is responsible for the 18- to 24-month delay many of these periodicals experience in publishing manuscripts.

Parental and special interest groups also must be considered as a potent force in change. Parent groups have a long history of establishing and advocating programs to serve the handicapped. The forerunners of many current public school programs were classes or centers operated and funded by parents. Parent and interest groups have become sophisticated in their ability to bring about change. They have developed national structures and have learned to use the legislative and judicial processes effectively. Previously, their energies and resources were restricted to the immediate need to create classes and services for their own children. Today, the concern is broader, and parents have demonstrated the ability to influence public policy.

The history of civil rights activities during the 1960s and 1970s is related closely to parent and special interest group effectiveness in influencing today's status of exceptional children. Although the benefits the civil rights movement have contributed to the handicapped are intangible, the movement must be acknowledged for establishing a general social responsiveness that has become important for the handicapped, as well as for blacks, women, and other minorities.

Growth in support service expenditures for the handicapped represents another dimension which makes the 1970s significantly different from previous decades. A study by the Rand Corporation (1973, p.124) reports a 1971 annual expenditure on programs for the handicapped of $2.36 billion by state and local educational agencies, and $314.9 million by the federal government. If all handicapped children and youth were served at the same quality level, an additional $2.5

billion would have been required in 1971. By the 1970s, the education of exceptional children and youth required major investments of public dollars. This is particularly significant in that the National Advisory Committee for the Handicapped reported in 1975 that only 55 percent of handicapped children and youth were being served appropriately.

When one becomes aware of the profound changes which have occurred in training of personnel, in growth of knowledge, technology, and program expenditures, and the increasing influence of special interest groups, one can understand more readily that philosophies of educating the handicapped, as well as criteria for classifying persons as handicapped, *can* change. One also must recognize that these changes represent the capability of professionals and society in general to benefit from experience and acquired knowledge, and to use this input as a basis for implementing changes with the intent of improving the lives of a large population of individuals.

What has occurred has been essentially a growing concern for the needs of all children and youth—in particular exceptional children—at a time when society has had not only the legislative base and knowledge, but the fiscal wherewithal as well. Beliefs about how exceptional children should be taught have changed along with views on the schools' responsibility to this population. Many children classified as handicapped today were not identified as handicapped as recently as 20 years ago, and children now considered among the responsibilities of the public schools once were considered the responsibilities of institutions or parents.

Rarely since adopting the policy of universal education have changes of this magnitude occurred in the field of education. Moreover, the next 20 years may well reflect comparable changes. The following section describes federal and state legislative provisions designed to assure an improved future for exceptional children and youth. These provisions are specific, and they are intended to maintain the progress made over the past several years.

LEGISLATIVE CONTRIBUTIONS

A review of federal legislation clearly illustrates the increased involvement of federal government during the past 20 years in developing programs and providing benefits for the handicapped. Weintraub, Abeson, Ballard, & La Vor (1976, pp. 103-111) identified 195 federal laws specific to the handicapped enacted between 1827 and the passage of PL 94-142 in 1975. Of these laws, 61 were passed in the period from March 1970 through November 1975. In 1974, 36 federal bills which directly or indirectly affected the handicapped and gifted were signed into law (La Vor, 1976, p. 96).

When federal laws are passed, they often are followed by legislation at the state level to bring state statutes into compliance with the federal law. In some cases, states are quicker than federal government to pass laws that reflect trends or the delivery of services. During the early 1970s, congressional emphasis on the handicapped was paralleled by an effort by state legislatures. Weintraub et al. (1976) reported that:

> In 1975 a survey of state law indicated that all but two states had adopted some form of mandatory legislation. The survey further revealed that 37 of the 48 states with mandatory legislation adopted their current special education legislation since 1970. These developments make it clear that state legislators are now aware that no longer can the provision of appropriate education opportunities for handicapped children be considered optional. Of note is that this period of extensive expansion corresponds with the beginning of the right to education litigative movement (p. 83).

Legislation is essential to assure that the rights of individuals will be protected, that services will be provided, and that a basis for quality control will be ensured. The enactment of legislation, however, does not guarantee that funds required to implement the legislation always will be appropriated at a sufficient level. Nor does legislation guarantee that compliance will be enforced. For example, although most states have had compulsory attendance laws for over 50 years, requiring school attendance until age 16, large numbers of handicapped children have not been in school. This was particularly true prior to the mid-1960s. Goodman (1976) estimated that one million handicapped children and youth still are excluded entirely from public school systems.

Implementation of laws governing human services is greatly dependent on clear regulations, responsive public and professional advocacy groups, and significant consequences for failure to comply. These conditions have not always existed in terms of legislation pertaining to the handicapped, but they do exist today. This is especially true with reference to advocacy groups.

Legislation serves to define public policy. Thus, persons interested in the study of exceptional children and youth must be familiar with federal and state legislation. A detailed review of legislative history is beyond the scope of this discussion, but three federal acts have significant impact on the future of educational practices and require particular attention. These laws are:

—PL 93-380, the Education of the Handicapped Amendments of 1974
—PL 94-142, Education for all Handicapped Children Act, passed in 1975
—Section 504 of the Rehabilitation Act of 1973.

PL 93-380

Public Law 93-380 was passed in 1974 to extend and amend the Elementary and Secondary Education Act of 1965. A major implication of this law for the handicapped is the statement appearing in Section 801 of Title VIII which established national policy on equal educational opportunity:

> *Sec. 801.* Recognizing that the Nation's economic, political, and social security require a well-educated citizenry, the Congress (1) reaffirms, as a matter of high priority, the Nation's goal of equal educational opportunity, and (2) declares it to be the policy of the United States of America that every citizen is entitled to an education to meet his or her full potential without financial barriers.

In the future, this section of the act may be referred to as an historical statement of public policy.

Specific provisions for the handicapped are included in part B of Section 611 through Section 621; and provisions having specific implications for educational practice are included in the amendment of Section 613 (A). Because it represents a major statement on due process procedures and serves as a basis for many of the provisions in PL 94-142, this section is reported verbatim and will be elaborated on in the discussion of PL 94-142.

> (12) (a) Establish a goal of providing full educational opportunity to all handicapped children, and (b) provide for a procedure to assure that funds expended under this part are used to accomplish the goal set forth in (a) of this paragraph and priority in the utilization of funds under this part will be given to handicapped children who are not receiving an education; and
>
> (13) provide procedures for insuring that handicapped children and their parents or guardians are guaranteed procedural safeguards in decisions regarding identification, evaluation, and educational placement of handicapped children including, but not limited to
>
> (a) (i) prior notice to parents or guardians of the child when the local or state educational agency proposes to change the educational placement of the child, (ii) an opportunity for the parents or guardians to obtain an impartial due process hearing, examine all relevant records with respect to the classification or educational placement of the child, and obtain an independent educational evaluation of the child, (iii) procedures to protect the rights of the child when the parents or guardians are not known, unavailable, or the child is a ward of the State, including the assignment of an individual (not to be an employee of the State or local agency involved in the education or care of children) to act as a surrogate for the parents or guardians, and (iv) provision to insure that the decisions rendered in the impartial due process hearing required by this paragraph shall be binding on all parties subject only to appropriate administrative or judicial appeal; and

(b) procedures to insure that, to the maximum extent appropriate, handicapped children, including children in public or private institutions or other care facilities, are educated with children who are not handicapped, and that special classes, separate schooling, or other removal of handicapped children from the regular education environment occurs only when the nature or severity of the handicap is such that education in regular classes with the use of supplementary aids and services cannot be achieved satisfactorily; and

(c) procedures to insure the testing and evaluation materials and procedures utilized for the purposes of classification and placement of handicapped children will be selected and administered so as not to be racially or culturally discriminatory.

PL 94-142

Public Law 94-142, the Education for All Handicapped Children Act of 1975, is an amendment to Public Law 93-380. It has been described as the "Bill of Rights for the Handicapped" (Goodman, 1976) because it is designed to correct inequities on behalf of the handicapped. The Act passed in the House by a vote of 404 to 7 and in the Senate by 87 to 7. This margin of support is particularly noteworthy because of the concept of perpetuity embedded in the law.

The Rules and Regulations for this Act were published in the *Federal Register* (August 23, 1977). Because the regulations provide specific directions for implementation, the reader is referred to that document as a primary reference. The law includes several definitions, priorities, and conditions which, for purposes of this discussion, will be referred to as special features.

Special Features

1. Free and appropriate public education (FAPE) is a basic requirement of the law. It means that every handicapped child and youth must be provided special education and related services at public expense.
2. Special education is defined to incorporate specially designed instruction to meet the unique needs of handicapped children. Specially designed instruction may include classroom instruction, instruction in physical education, home instruction, and instruction for hospital and institutional application. The law, in defining special education, repeats the reference to a free and appropriate public education by stating that "special education must be provided at no cost to parents or guardians."

The reference to physical education is unusual in that most definitions of special education appearing in laws and textbooks focus on education and support services but have not identified physical education as part of special education services. The intent of Congress is that physical education be provided to all handicapped children (Irvin, 1976, p. 3), and incorporation of physical education as part of the definition was a strategy of Congress to assure the provision of physical education for all exceptional children.

3. Related services include those typically referred to in the public schools as *special services* or *support services,* plus *transportation.* Inclusion of transportation in this regard is important, because in many areas handicapped children must be transported in order to receive the available services.

   Reference is made to speech pathology, audiology, psychological services, physical and occupational therapy, recreation, and medical and counseling services, except that such medical services shall be for diagnosis and evaluation purposes only.

4. Included in the definition of handicapped children are the mentally retarded, hard of hearing, deaf, speech impaired, visually impaired, severely emotionally disturbed, orthopedically impaired, other health impaired, or specific learning disabilities needing special education and related services.

5. Two priorities are specified: serving handicapped children not presently receiving an education—defined as *first priority children;* and serving children with severe handicaps within any disability who are receiving inadequate education—*second priority children.* The conditions of the law apply to all handicapped children and youth, but the priorities pertain to expenditure of funds received by districts and states through appropriations governed by the law.

6. The law specifies a federal commitment to assume fiscal responsibility for up to 40 percent of the excess costs incurred in providing a free and appropriate public education for all handicapped children. This represents a significant commitment.

7. By 1980, all handicapped children between the ages of 3 and 21 must have available to them a free and appropriate public education.

The following discussion focuses on the special features of the law, including definitions, and on three major principles inherent in the law—protective safeguards, least restrictive alternatives, and the individualized education program requirement.

Protective Safeguards

Both PL 94-142 and PL 93-380 emphasize the establishment of protective safeguards. The intent is to ensure application of due process for the handicapped. In reading the description of protective safeguards, the requirements appear to be "legal" and highly specific. Reference is made to terms such as appeal, right to cross-examine, hearings, representation by counsel, and other terms typically applied in courts of law.

Many educators have had difficulty understanding the practical implications of these requirements, as well as the rationale for their inclusion in the law. Questions have been raised as to why the handicapped should be singled out with specific protective safeguards legislated for them, when the existing due process provision should apply to all students. An examination of how the handicapped historically have been treated, however, clearly indicates that previous protective safeguards have not been applied.

The handicapped represent a minority comprised of several subgroups. Although some of the subgroups have been effective in advocating their interests (e.g., the blind, the deaf), others have not. In some cases, such as the severely and profoundly handicapped, individuals who comprise the subgroups are not capable of representing themselves. These groups must depend upon others to advocate for them. Examples of circumstances which support the need for specific laws to provide protective safeguards for the handicapped include the following:

- Many handicapped children assigned to special programs have remained in those programs throughout their educational careers. This has been true particularly of students placed in special classes for the mildly mentally retarded. The tendency has been for special education placements to be considered permanent assignments rather than short-term options designed to enhance the individual's performance and, in turn, prepare the student for return to the regular class.
- Too often, decisions of placement eligibility have been made on the basis of insufficient information or on results of inappropriate tests. Many tests discriminate against the handicapped in that the norms are not appropriate or because the handicapping condition makes the student unable to perform the task required to demonstrate test performance.
- Children with severe and profound handicapping conditions routinely have been excluded from public schools. The only options available to them prior to passage of this legislation have been public or private institutions, remaining at home, or placement in the few community-based programs which have existed for this popula-

tion. The public schools do not have a history of providing services to the severely and profoundly handicapped.

- Disproportionate numbers of children from minority groups have been placed in special education programs because their functioning level in school may have approximated that of students receiving special education. Such placement practice has ignored the cultural and educational factors contributing to their low-functioning level.
- The circumstances of care and appropriateness of training for the handicapped in institutional settings have attracted widespread attention. Many institutions have been described as overcrowded, understaffed, lacking in programming opportunities, and insensitive to patient needs. These conditions relate in large part to the failure of public agencies to commit sufficient financial resources.

PL 94-142 sets forth specific procedures which districts must carry out to establish due process. The procedures appear to be reasonable and to reflect sound programming principles. Few people disagree with the intent. Most negative reactions relate to the practical consequences of implementation in terms of all handicapped children and youth. Briefly, the procedures state that:

1. Parents must be provided an opportunity to examine all records which pertain to the school's evaluation of their child and educational decisions by school personnel affecting their child. This requirement has major implications for testing practices and for recording student information. Personnel responsible for evaluation and report preparation must be careful to give information which is meaningful to parents as well as to professionals.

2. Parents may obtain evaluations from examiners independent of the school. This requirement places schools in the position of having to support their evaluations and possibly consider evaluation data which may be contrary to their own findings. Concern has been expressed that some parents who desire an independent evaluation may find the cost involved to be prohibitive. The law is not clear about what happens if parents or guardians cannot afford independent evaluation costs. Kotin and Eager (1977, p. 20), in discussing this procedure, indicate that most states provide notice of the right to an independent evaluation but are not specific on the issue of payment.

3. Surrogate parents must be appointed if the parents or guardian of the child are not known or available, or if the child is a ward of the

state. This requirement has been in effect for some time in terms of institutionalized children who are wards of the state. The practice traditionally has been to name the superintendent of the institution as the surrogate parent. In view of the number of children involved and the administrative role of the superintendent, this practice has not been desirable.

Under PL 94-142, this practice does not meet the intent of the law (Irvin, 1976, p. 9). Persons serving as surrogate parents cannot be employees of local districts or the state educational agency. Selection and training of persons to fill the surrogate parent role are important considerations in implementing this procedure.

4. Parents or guardians must receive written notice whenever the school proposes a change in the identification, evaluation, or educational placement of their handicapped child. The requirement also applies if the school refuses to initiate a requested change. Prior to passage of PL 94-142, most states did take steps to establish regulations regarding parent consent, but these steps did not go as far as the law now mandates.

The notice must be in *written form* and in the parent's or guardian's *native language* unless this clearly is not feasible. Although many schools have followed the practice of notifying parents of placement decisions and, in some cases, evaluation, few have had experience in communicating with parents for whom English is not the primary language.

5. Parents or guardians must be provided an opportunity to present complaints in any matter relating to identification, evaluation, or educational placement of their child. Historically, parents and guardians have had the option of voicing concerns but, for the most part, they have communicated without knowing the most effective channel for expressing their views or the most appropriate source from which to seek information. Now, procedures for presenting complaints must be structured, and parents must be given information on procedures to follow.

If the due process procedures do not result in a program satisfactory to the parent or guardian, the law also allows for an impartial due process hearing. Hearings can be initiated by parents or by the school district. The hearing may be held by the local school district, an intermediate school district, or by the state educational agency, depending upon the state's laws.

Guidelines are provided on the role and selection of hearing officers, presentation of evidence, and representation by counsel. The hearing officer cannot be an employee of the child's district. Parents also have the right to appeal the hearing decision; the first level of appeal is to the state educational agency. Guidelines on the appeal process are provided.

An optional provision involves pursuing civil action through the court judicial system. Some states have a mediation process prior to the formal hearing. The purpose is to resolve the conflict if possible without a formal hearing. When successful, the meditation process saves time and expenses.

The significance of the due process procedures established by PL 94-142 is related directly to implementation and enforcement by educational agencies. Extensive planning by school personnel is necessary to efficiently implement effective procedures. Considerable and thoughtful planning also is necessary to employ the procedures in a manner which invites parental participation as equals and which encourages a cooperative relationship rather than a competitive one.

If school personnel are responsive in their relationships with parents, and if parents can be convinced of the mutual concern for establishing the most appropriate program for the child, the due process procedures should be effective and the recourse to hearings and appeals rarely would be needed. The child's best interests are served when parents and school personnel cooperatively reach decisions, and this does not mean that school personnel are always right. It does mean that all parties should attempt to use the required procedures to effect the best decisions. School districts certainly could not afford the time, funds, or personnel resources if all educational decisions pertaining to handicapped children were appealed through due process hearings.

In summarizing an extensive national review of states' responses to due process requirements of PL 94-142, Kotin and Eager (1977) state:

Another issue is whether the systems which are being adopted will provide for a sufficient equality in bargaining power between the school and the parents so the formal due process hearings will result in an accurate reflection of the merits of a case rather than a reflection of relative imbalance of power. For example, if a parent at a due process hearing is unrepresented by counsel, will the hearing be a dispute between equals? No states appear to be making any substantial effort to insure that the due process hearing is "fair" in the sense of having the opposing parties begin on an equal basis. Mere notice to the parent of the "right" to be represented is without significance unless the means to obtain counsel or an advocate is made available.

A related issue is whether the due process systems being developed will be utilized by poor and minority group parents who, traditionally, have the greatest difficulty in participating in and securing the benefits of government programs. There is very little emphasis in any of the state systems on strong efforts to insure the participation of these parents in the special education process. Greater provision for early consultation with and personal notice to parents would remedy this omission to some degree (p. 10).

The operation of due process procedures for the handicapped is new to the schools, at least in the context of requirements detailed in PL 94-142. Although the proposed rules are explicit and the law is strongly worded, one reasonably should expect that a period of time will be necessary before consistent application of the procedures will be seen. School district personnel at all levels will need to learn their roles in the school's due process system. School personnel with responsibility for the handicapped must be totally knowledgeable about the school's policies and their specific responsibilities. The policies are required to be detailed by all districts in a written plan; thus, the plan should be available to all school personnel.

Least Restrictive Environments

A unique feature of PL 94-142 (and PL 93-380) is the *emphasis on the regular class as the preferred instructional base for all children.* In contrast to most sections of the law, which set forth procedures to follow, this section intends to establish a particular philosophy or orientation toward educational programming for handicapped children and youth. Historically, handicapped children were referred *out* of regular classes, and separate programs were established in an effort to meet their educational needs. The least restrictive environment section clearly is an attempt to reverse these policies and practices which have governed educational decisions regarding programs for handicapped children and youth in the United States.

PL 94-142 and PL 93-380 state that, to the maximum extent appropriate, handicapped children, including children in public and private facilities, are to be educated with children who are not handicapped. Both laws specifically state that special classes, separate schooling, or other removal of handicapped children from the regular educational environment should occur only when the nature or severity of the handicap is such that education in regular classes with the use of supplementary aids and services cannot be achieved satisfactorily.

Although this is a strong and significant statement in terms of federal involvement in the organization of educational practices, it is not an independent effort to change dramatically what exists. The concept of the separate special class has been subjected to scrutiny since the 1930s (Pertch, 1936; Cowan, 1948; Blatt, 1958; and Goldstein, Moss & Jordan, 1965). Much has been written about the need to broaden the array of educational placement options available to handicapped children and youth. One of the more recent statements on this topic was by Dunn

(1968) in his classic article challenging the viability of the special class model. Since then, several proposed alternative models have appeared in the literature (cf. Deno, 1970; Birch, 1974; Beery, 1972; Chaffin, 1975).

The Council for Exceptional Children (CEC) conducted a survey in 1974 (prior to the legislation) which identified six states having laws that mandated placement according to the principle of least restrictive environment. An additional 10 states were providing authority for such practices through regulation. Of course, with passage of PL 94-142, all states now must comply.

Several different terms have been applied to the principle of least restrictive environment, including the *least restrictive alternative*. The most common of these terms has been *mainstreaming*. Because we are talking about a principle or philosophy which results in particular practices, rather than a set of procedures, interpretations of mainstreaming vary. Several elements, however, are common to most definitions: (1) assuming that a handicapped child can best be served through placement with nonhandicapped peers in regular class settings; (2) assigning primary instructional responsibility to regular class teachers; (3) providing support services to the regular class teacher as a means of helping the handicapped child when special assistance is required; (4) providing direct support services on a part-time basis to the handicapped child only if the regular class teacher is unable to provide an appropriate program through assistance from support personnel; (5) reserving assignment to special classes or separate programs as a last alternative; and (6) continually monitoring the child's progress, with the aim of returning the child to the regular class as soon as his or her performance suggests that such placement would be most appropriate.

Kaufman, Gottlieb, Agard, and Kukic (1975) offer the following definition of mainstreaming:

> Mainstreaming refers to the temporal, instructional, and social integration of eligible exceptional children with normal peers based on an ongoing, individually determined, educational planning programming process, and requires clarification of responsibility among regular and special education administrative, instructional, and supportive personnel (p. 35).

The primary merit of this definition is that it does not merely imply placement in regular classes. Instead, it stresses the importance of the child's current level of functioning, the child's capability for integration, and the needs for educational planning and clarification of responsibility. These are all important considerations in protecting the welfare of the handicapped individual.

A major implication of the least restrictive environment requirement for educators involves decisions pertaining to the moderately and
severely handicapped. For example, how handicapped can a child be and
still profit from placement, either full- or part-time, in a regular class?
The law does not require all handicapped children to be placed in regular
classes, but it places the "burden of proof" on the schools in justifying
placement decisions in which the handicapped child is served outside the
regular class. A district may decide that the most appropriate placement
for a handicapped child is in a self-contained special class. In such a case,
this district would claim that, for that particular child, the self-contained
class is the least restrictive environment. This points out the decision
school personnel must make when considering the needs of a handicapped child and available alternatives for services and educational
programming. Chapter 2 discusses the historical context out of which
the least restrictive environment concept has emerged.

The Individualized Education Program (IEP) Requirement

The section of PL 94-142 which has received the most support and at
the same time caused the most concern is the requirement that an
individualized education program (IEP) be developed and maintained for
each handicapped child or youth. Support for the requirement focuses on
the logic of instructional planning, and it follows that meeting the needs
of students who present complex instructional problems requires
detailed and systematic planning. The concern relates primarily to the
lack of experience by school personnel in applying procedures suggested
by the IEP requirement to large numbers of handicapped children and
youth. This lack of experience has resulted in much speculation about
the training of personnel to develop IEPs, the time required for their
preparation, and the development of procedures to evaluate and monitor the IEPs.

Instructional planning, though, is not new to educators. Thus, one
can reasonably anticipate that most districts will evolve systematic and
efficient procedures in three or four years' time which will have a
positive influence on instruction of the handicapped. To attain this level
of performance, however, will require a major investment of effort by
administrators, teachers, and support personnel.

Because this author strongly supports the concept of instructional
planning as the most effective vehicle for improving instruction for the
handicapped, a separate chapter has been included on instructional

planning. The IEP is presented (Chapter 3) in the context of a planning process and not merely a requirement of Public Law 94-142. This introduction, on the other hand, discusses IEP requirements in terms of educational and public policy implications.

The regulations of PL 94-142 are specific in describing what the IEP must include and the manner in which it must be developed; but, it does provide flexibility in formalizing implementation and monitoring procedures. The general requirement is that each state and local educational agency must ensure that an individualized education program is provided for each handicapped child designated for special education, regardless of what institution or agency will provide services for the child. If the regulations stopped at this point, most districts could comply merely by formalizing procedures they now employ to make placement decisions and to assess pupil performance. The influence of such a policy likely would not have much impact on improving instruction for the handicapped.

In an attempt to minimize the risk of such interpretations by public school personnel, however, the rules and regulations are extended by specifying requirements as to who participates in developing the IEP, the role of parents, and content requirements. Extension of the specific guidelines establishes the IEP as a precedent-setting requirement. This author was unable to identify any other federal education law which as precisely describes an educational practice or has the potential impact on instructional methods as the IEP requirement.

Because of the implications of the IEP for all school personnel, the sections of the regulations relating to participation and development of IEPs, parental participation, and content requirements will be reported, in Chapter 3, as printed in the *Federal Register* (August, 1977).

Although intended to influence instructional practices, the IEP requirement also must be perceived as a due process procedure. It can be argued that the IEP is the primary measure whereby the free and appropriate public education goal of PL 94-142 can be achieved. It provides a base of evidence upon which to make a determination of whether or not the handicapped child is being served appropriately. An examination of a child's IEP and the district's IEP procedures should clarify how instructional decisions are made, consequences of such decisions, and the specific impact of those decisions on the child's performance. Thus, in addition to being an instructional tool, the IEP becomes an accountability measure, or at least a source of data for accountability decisions.

Because the IEP process is governed by explicit guidelines, is expressed in written form, and includes evaluation procedures, some school personnel may perceive the IEP as a means for checking compliance with the law rather than as an instructional planning process to improve education for the handicapped. IEP contributions to accountability surely must be retained, but the focus should be on instructional benefits. Major efforts by principals, teachers, parents, and support personnel will be necessary to retain emphasis on the advantages of instructional planning and at the same time acknowledge the merits of accountability.

A significant long-range benefit of the IEP process will be the value derived from collecting information on student performance, in terms of long- and short-term objectives. The results should be a cumulative record of student performance based on application of instructional goals and objectives tailored to the needs of individual handicapped students. The data recorded should provide a perspective centering on curriculum and/or services, in contrast to past cumulative records which have been comprised primarily of test data and anecdotal comments. A secondary, but equally important, by-product of the process should be an increased awareness by all school personnel involved with the handicapped child as to the child's program, responses to the program, and progress patterns. The shift from placement to program concerns in itself could be the determining factor in improving instruction for the handicapped. Hopefully, all personnel will learn new skills and adjust certain behaviors as a result of their new roles in implementing the IEP requirement.

One area in which schools likely will encounter difficulty regards parent involvement in the instructional planning process. Historically, special education has elicited more parent-school personnel interaction than has regular education, but the interaction format has tended to center on placement decisions or parental requests for certain services. Such interactions often have been strained, because the school could not respond to parental requests or because parents were unwilling to agree to a placement decision advocated by school personnel.

In any event, school personnel generally have not had experience in working with parents in the context of the IEP requirement. Parents or guardians of handicapped children and youth have not been full partners in the instructional planning process, and they too lack experience in instructional planning. Since due process procedures strengthen the role of parents, districts must devise methods to involve parents in the planning process. Merely setting up procedures which comply with the law and thus allow for parental participation is not sufficient. Emphasis needs to be placed on establishing relationships which capitalize on parental involvement. Education of handicapped children is not restricted to the classroom. It is a continuous and total process which can be enhanced greatly by parental involvement.

The IEP process provides not only the reason but also the vehicle for effective involvement of parents in the education of their children. The degree to which a district is successful in establishing relationships with parents depends on the district's investment in training personnel. To effect parental participation and to improve services for handicapped students, districts must train personnel to communicate to parents that their views are respected and their participation is welcome and needed. Teachers, particularly, must give more attention to ways in which the child's education can be extended into the home.

Through the IEP, PL 94-142 could have substantial impact on the education of all students. If individualized planning is effective in improving instruction for handicapped children and youth, one can reasonably speculate that these benefits could generalize across programs for nonhandicapped children and youth. The same argument could be made about parental involvement in instructional planning. In the future, parents of nonhandicapped students possibly could organize to broaden the application of the IEP process.

Assuming that the IEP achieves the goals set forth by PL 94-142, generalization of the process to the nonhandicapped may be restricted by practical implications of time and costs. On the other hand, practical restraints may be overcome by experience in implementing the requirement for the handicapped. If the IEP requirement is successful in establishing individualized planning as a common practice, it may prove to be exceedingly important to future generations of students.

PL 94-142 is far more comprehensive than indicated by the discussion presented here. It incorporates provisions which define roles of the federal government, state educational agencies, local educational agencies, and intermediate educational agencies. It includes directives on identification procedures, fiscal responsibilities, application to private agencies, and overall implementation processes. Readers preparing themselves for professional roles in education are encouraged to study the complete rules and regulations.

Section 504: The Rehabilitation Act of 1973

Because PL 93-380 and PL 94-142 are explicitly related to education of the handicapped, many educators have tended to perceive these pieces of legislation as representing the primary legislative resources in the movement toward improving education for exceptional children and youth. In the process, the significance of Section 504 of the Rehabilitation Act of 1973 may have been overlooked. This act provides a basic source of enforcement for the other two laws.

Section 504 is the first federal civil rights law which specifically protects the rights of the handicapped. The nondiscriminatory provisions of the law pertaining to the handicapped are almost identical to the nondiscriminatory provisions related to race which are included in Title VI of the Civil Rights Act of 1964 and to Title IX of the Education Amendments of 1972.

Originally, Section 504 was restricted primarily to employment, but in 1974 Public Law 93-516 was passed, amending Section 504 to cover a broader array of services for the handicapped. *Handicapped* was defined as follows:

> For purposes of Section 504 of the Act, a "handicapped individual" is defined as "any person who (A) has a physical or mental impairment which substantially limits one or more of such person's major life activities, (B) has a record of such an impairment, or (C) is regarded as having such an impairment."

With this amendment, educational services were covered by the nondiscriminatory provisions of Section 504.

A major component of enforcement of PL 93-380 and PL 94-142 relates to the fiscal restraints imposed by Section 504 for noncompliance. Section 504 covers all services provided through agencies receiving federal financial assistance. This is explicit in the statement of purpose in Section 504:

> The purpose of this part is to effectuate Section 504 of the Rehabilitation Act of 1973, which is designed to eliminate discrimination on the basis of handicap in any program or activity receiving Federal financial assistance.

The Rules and Regulations of Section 504 are similar to those for PL 94-142 in their comprehensiveness and detail. All educators, particularly those with administrative responsibilities, should familiarize themselves with the Rules and Regulations.

Martin (1977), in referring to Section 504 and PL 94-142, summarized the implications of the laws as follows:

> Read together, these two statutes and their implementing regulations require that by September 1, 1978, each handicapped child must be provided all services necessary to meet his/her special education and related needs (p.5).

Although legislation has given visibility in the sense of permanence to changes in education and in treatment of the handicapped, the accomplishments of the 1970s have been possible only as an outgrowth of events occurring over the past 20 years. In addition to presenting a model of assessment procedures and service models, other significant issues have surfaced, including employment of nondiscriminatory testing procedures, effective placement practices, and a general movement toward establishing due process safeguards for the handicapped and their parents. While failures of the past have become issues of the present, these too must be studied in the context of an evolutionary process.

SERVICES

Central to the changes occurring during the 1970s have been the methods used in public schools to provide services to exceptional children and youth. When the special class was considered the primary means for delivering special education, placement decisions simply involved whether or not a student was eligible for special class placement. Today, the situation is significantly different. Not only do the new state and federal laws require compliance, but most local districts have realized the necessity to develop specific orientations or philosophies upon which to base the organization of their special education services.

For the most part, the major treatment form required by exceptional children is special instruction aimed at improving *academic, vocational,* or *social* performance. Some children, of course, do require other forms of assistance, such as speech or physical therapy, medical treatment, or some type of psychological counseling. Further, within the general realm of specialized instruction, a number of teaching methods, programs, approaches, curriculums, materials, and instructional technologies may be applied to modify instruction to an exceptional learner's specific needs.

Special education may be viewed from at least three primary perspectives: (1) determining the most appropriate instructional or curriculum program; (2) establishing the most accurate diagnostic base for programming; and (3) selecting the most efficient and economical administrative structure for delivering services. Obviously, the latter two relate to instruction; and instruction, to be effective, depends upon accurate diagnosis and effective administrative structures. After having reviewed a large number of public school programs over several years, however, this author believes that too many districts place primary emphasis on creating organizational structures which contribute to precise diagnosis and appropriate placement and not enough emphasis on what happens after a child is assigned to receive a particular service.

Special education is not a placement process nor is it an evaluation system, even though both are essential to quality special education services. Special education in the true sense occurs only when a child or youth receives services appropriate to his or her needs. In this context, much of what is offered in the guise of special education services is not, in fact, special education. To assume that special education occurs automatically at the time a child or youth is placed or assigned to a service may be comforting to an administrator, but such placement provides no assurances of effective special education unless those responsible for delivering the services are competent and have access to the appropriate resources.

Much of the literature published on special education focuses on *delivery models* or *organizational constructs*. The literature reveals that the trend toward mainstreaming or least restrictive environments clearly has influenced the design of service delivery models and the language used to describe them. Many models, however, could be criticized because of their abstract nature and their tendency to create "unique" terms. They also tend to focus only on mechanisms for delivery of services and not on the services themselves. This probably can be attributed to the source of such models—i.e., persons with administrative skills and/or responsibilities. The task of refining the services is the responsibility of professionals who deliver the service—e.g., teachers, therapists, clinicians, and parents.

Models and constructs or organizational structures are important, and most local special education programs are developing organizational plans to guide them in making decisions regarding handicapped children and youth. This move toward conceptualized planning is explained by Johnson (1975, p. 153), who wrote about models for alternative planning: "Today our business is not only very complex, but is also subject to the requirements of accountability—accountability for demonstrating that what we do with and for handicapped learners is productive." The employment of due process procedures, individualized planning, and the transition from a special class orientation to a least restrictive orientation certainly has complicated the role of special education administrators. These changes also have influenced the roles of teachers, other administrators, and support personnel.

One of the difficulties encountered in writing about special education services is that not only is a wide variety of service options available, but most districts tend to create their own terms for describing personnel and programs. For example, a person trained as a specialist in instructional programming for handicapped children may be called a consultant, strategist, materials and methods specialist, consulting teacher, or some other title. Common across most programs, however, is the emerging philosophy of the least restrictive alternative. If one is familiar with the general type of delivery model being used, the lack of uniformity in personnel titles is not a problem. In many ways, the creation of titles by local districts to describe their own programs has the advantage of allowing services and personnel roles to be structured to meet local needs.

The following discussion describes program options and support personnel roles in as standard a form as possible. Delivery service models which have been suggested in the literature as complying with the least restrictive alternative philosophy also will be discussed.

Special Education Services

Regular Class Placement

Placement in a regular class becomes a service option when instruction offered to the exceptional student is designed to meet the student's specific needs. Such placement assumes that the regular class teacher has received training in adapting instructional materials or in teaching methods specific to the student's needs, and that the teacher has access to necessary resource materials and consultation.

Self-Contained Special Class Placement

The self-contained special class generally is reserved as an option for students requiring full-time assignment outside the regular class. Until the late 1960s, special classes frequently were used in service delivery for the mildly handicapped. Although still a viable option for some students, the self-contained special class is not a primary option for most exceptional children.

Typically, a group of children with similar problems is assigned to a teacher who is responsible for planning and carrying out the students' educational program. The teacher may be assisted by an aide or paraprofessional, and students may receive services from other specialists. For the most part, however, their education is delivered through placement in the special class. This option is used primarily for students with moderate to severe handicapping conditions.

Part-time Special Class Placement

An option used extensively, particularly with the mildly mentally retarded, is part-time placement in a special class. This option differs from the resource room (discussed next) in that the student is part of a group during assignment to the special class and generally is assigned to the special class for at least half the school day. In the move to eliminate or reduce special classes, students likely will receive special instruction in basic skill subjects and will be integrated into regular classes for other experiences. At the secondary level, students may attend selected regular classes but receive assistance with academic and job readiness skills in the special class.

This option has advantages for exceptional children who have difficulty in working with several different teachers. It also has advantages for regular classroom teachers who have difficulty in accommodating the exceptional student's instructional needs while simultaneously meeting the needs of the larger group of nonhandicapped students. The special class teacher spends more time with the student and, consequently, is able to function in both a counseling and teaching role. In moving from full-time special classes to the least restrictive alternative model, many districts have utilized the part-time special class placement as a transition phase.

Resource Room Placement

This option is fast becoming the most popular service delivery vehicle for providing special education to the mildly handicapped. Students typically are referred to a specially trained teacher on the basis of assessed academic difficulties. The resource teacher maintains an instructional classroom in which teaching is highly individualized. The resource teacher may work with students in small groups when appropriate, but is concerned primarily with delivering remedial or supplemental instruction based on prescribed objectives for individual students. Although extensively used for mildly handicapped students, the resource room is particularly popular in the area of learning disabilities.

The resource teacher functions in a teaching role, but also frequently assumes major responsibilities in educational assessment and in developing prescriptions. An additional major responsibility of the resource teacher is to establish and maintain communication with the regular classroom teachers of students assigned to the resource room.

Placement in the resource room is intended to be short-term, and the student is returned full time to the regular class when sufficient progress is noted. For many students, however, the combination of resource room and regular class placement remains as the least restrictive alternative. Thus, not uncommonly a student may be assigned to a resource room throughout the elementary and early secondary grades.

Resource Center

A relatively recent service which is gaining popularity is the resource center. Although resource centers take varied forms, they generally are organized as a center comprised of one or two rooms and staffed by two or more teachers. Teachers assigned to the centers constitute a team capable of working with students having various handicapping conditions. Although occasionally used at the elementary level, they are found more frequently at the junior- and senior-high levels. Students are referred to the centers for specific instruction; they may be assigned for one period per day, and rarely more than three periods. Most instruction is on an individual basis, with considerable emphasis on independent work for older students.

This approach has many advantages, particularly at the secondary level, at which the centers can be presented as an instructional resource, reducing the stigma often identified with special programs. Resource centers also allow for teams of teachers to work cooperatively, making available more instructional resources for individual student needs.

The Itinerant Teacher

The role of the itinerant teacher is differentiated from that of the regular or special class teacher in that the itinerant teacher is not responsible for a classroom. Itinerant teachers provide direct services to handicapped children and youth who are assigned to regular classes or to other education settings, and provide tutorial instruction as a supplement to instruction offered by the student's regular teacher. Districts using itinerant teachers generally operate a referral system whereby teachers seeking instructional assistance for a particular student initiate a referral. This option has been used to a considerable extent in providing services for visually handicapped students. Itinerant teachers have been used to assist students in learning braille, preparing materials in braille and, in general, to provide support services in assisting the visually handicapped to maintain themselves in regular classes.

The descriptive term *itinerant* is applied to a wide range of personnel including speech clinicians, school psychologists, and social workers, in that these professionals may provide services to a student at different times. *Itinerant teacher* is used in the context of this discussion, however, to define teachers who provide direct instructional assistance to handicapped students while the student remains in the regular or special class. In other words, the itinerant teacher takes services to students, in contrast to students going out for instruction, as they do in utilizing resource room services. A positive feature of the itinerant teacher option is that, by working with the student in his or her class, these teachers are able to coordinate instruction closely with that offered by the student's regular teacher. This also allows the itinerant teacher to observe the student routinely in the natural classroom instructional setting.

The Consulting Teacher

Various titles are used by districts to describe this service option. Basically, the role of the consulting teacher is to provide consultation to teachers and other personnel involved in the exceptional child's program. This role differs from that of the itinerant teacher in that the consulting teacher does not provide direct services to handicapped children or youth except for purposes of demonstrating a technique as part of the consulting role. Most districts are careful to not assign supervisory responsibilities to consulting teachers. The intent is to make available to regular classroom teachers a person who is experienced in special education instructional techniques, who understands exceptional children, and who is skilled in the consultation process.

With the growing emphasis on enhancing the regular class teacher's responsibility in meeting the needs of exceptional children, this service option can be anticipated to increase in popularity. Certification requirements for consulting teachers or for similar roles are beginning to emerge. Early requirements typically call for a master's degree, teacher certification and/or experience in teaching exceptional children, and selected training experiences specific to the consultation process. This service model someday may become a major option as more exceptional children are retained in regular classes. The consulting teacher also might assume a role in the delivery of inservice training.

Child Study/Diagnostic/Evaluation/Prescriptive Teaching Center

No standard term has evolved to describe the comprehensive evaluation center which combines testing, experimental instruction, family counseling, and instructional planning. Such programs, however, are beginning to develop, and are comprised of highly coordinated referral, evaluation, and instructional planning services. They are designed so the student can be observed closely while responding to newly prescribed programs or services, and allow for changes to be made before a student actually is placed in the recommended program.

Such centers offer many advantages in interdisciplinary planning. They also provide opportunities for working with parents in instructional planning and in helping them better understand their child's capabilities.

Homebound Instruction

To minimize interruptions in a student's education caused by short- or long-term confinement to the home, special teachers routinely are employed by most districts to tutor homebound students. Such teachers are assigned a caseload, and visit the student in the home on a regular basis. The primary role of these teachers is to assist the child's regular teacher in preparing instructional plans which can be pursued with the homebound student on a tutorial basis. This option is intended for short-term periods of time. Under unusual circumstances, however, homebound instruction may become the student's primary source of instruction.

Hospital Instruction

Instruction for students confined to hospital settings frequently is handled in the same manner as homebound instruction. The extent of instruction offered to a hospitalized student varies according to the child's conditions. Some large children's hospitals maintain small instruction staffs in cooperation with local school districts. The goal is to help students maintain progress in school programs.

Instructional Support Services

The movement toward mainstreaming has resulted in an increased emphasis on establishing support services, to make it easier for the exceptional child or youth to remain in the regular class. Support services may be defined in different ways. They could be defined as direct services provided by specialists other than teachers (e.g., speech clinicians, school psychologists, physical therapists); or they could be defined as services beyond those provided by the regular classroom teacher. In the latter context, the resource teacher, itinerant teacher, or even special class teacher might be considered as providing support services.

This author has elected to use the term *support services* to apply to special services other than educational placement or the student's primary assignment. Obviously, a child could be assigned to a regular class and also to a resource room; in this situation, the resource room would be classified as a support service. For another student, the resource room may be the student's primary assignment. Thus, in the interest of clarification, all services which could be primary educational placements for students have been included in the previous descriptions of special education services.

The following list is restricted to services offered by specialists whose primary role is other than classroom instruction. The services will be identified by role.

School Psychologist

During the early development of special education, school psychologists provided testing services. Although they continue to assume major responsibilities in diagnosis, they also are becoming more involved in curriculum planning, consultation with teachers and parents, case management, and coordination of the IEP process. Districts frequently assign responsibility for chairing IEP conferences to the school psychologist.

Speech Clinician

More exceptional children receive speech therapy than any other special education service. The speech clinician works with children having articulation or language difficulties, as well as children with more serious speech disorders. Speech therapy services are provided in individual therapy sessions, group therapy sessions or, in many cases, through consultation with the student's teacher. Speech and language problems are common among handicapped children. For example, a mentally retarded or emotionally disturbed child may have an accompanying speech problem. Consequently, many receive speech therapy as an additional service. Some children, however, require only speech therapy and do not have other handicaps. A recent trend has been toward providing speech clinicians with more training in the area of language. Also, some school districts are beginning to employ language specialists. Although the increased emphasis on language services can be expected to continue, no pattern has been established on either the nature of the services provided or the professional training involved. The language specialist conceivably may evolve as a person trained in the combined areas of speech therapy and learning disabilities.

Physical Therapist

Physical therapists provide treatment in the general area of motor performance, upon prescription by a physician. Their services focus on correction, development, and prevention. As more programs for the severely/profoundly handicapped and preschool-aged handicapped children are initiated into the public schools, the availability of physical therapy will be furthered.

Occupational Therapist

Although occupational therapists are not employed routinely in public schools, occupational therapy is a service important to many exceptional children. Occupational therapy involves individual and group activities designed to enhance physical, social, psychological, and cognitive development. Occupational therapy is a major service provided by most rehabilitation centers. Recently, increased attention has been given to the use of occupational therapy in providing services to preschool-aged exceptional children.

School Social Worker

In recent years, the school social worker has emerged as a major resource in programming for exceptional children. These professionals provide a link between the school staff and the family. They provide a variety of case work services, including assistance in interpretation of evaluation reports and recommendations. In some districts they chair child study committees. They also provide a major resource to special educators in working with community agencies.

Examples of other support services are medical treatment, counseling, adaptive physical education, and music therapy. The total spectrum of instructional and support service options previously discussed is found in most large districts offering comprehensive special education services. These services also may be offered by private schools. If all options are to be considered in delivering appropriate programs to handicapped children and youth, most of the service options discussed will have to be made available.

One major difficulty that districts encounter in offering comprehensive services is the low prevalence of children with handicapping conditions. If districts do not have sufficient numbers of children applicable to a particular special service, they are not likely to provide the service, because of the cost involved. PL 94-142, however, will result in more districts having to provide services which they previously claimed were too expensive.

A method whereby small districts can provide comprehensive services is to combine with neighboring districts and form cooperative units. Many states have laws which require or allow for districts to form cooperatives, generally referred to as *intermediate districts* or *units*. Iowa, Wisconsin, Illinois, Texas, New York, and Michigan are examples of states having long histories of intermediate units which offer comprehensive special education services. In some cases, intermediate units have the power to levy taxes much like local districts; in other cases, member districts share the costs of services provided to individual districts. In most cases, the units are governed by boards comprised of representatives from the participating districts.

Service Delivery Models

During the early development stages of special education, public schools generally assigned administrative responsibility for services to a single administrator. This administrator may have been identified in the school organizational chart as the director of special education or special services and, in many cases, might have had additional responsibilities. As programs grew and staffs became larger, the organization was expanded to include supervisors or consultants. The early growth of public school special education was characterized by a direct effort to increase services and to build an administrative hierarchy that would not only assure provision of services but also would assure that placement responsibility and instructional decisions could be identified within reason.

During this early history, little attention was given to conceptualizing service delivery models as a basis for making instructional and placement decisions pertaining to exceptional children. Except for an occasional expression of concern that special education programs were emerging as "small empires," few questions were raised regarding the conceptual base of special education services, and little attention was given to the decision making process that resulted in students being placed in special education programs.

Events of the 1970s have had significant impact on how delivery of special education services is perceived at the public school level. No longer can we merely expand organizational structures to accommodate more services and personnel. School districts now must respond to principles underlying federal and state legislation and must comply with specific legislative requirements. This trend has stimulated considerable efforts by theoreticians and administrators to design service delivery models to aid local districts in structuring service options and making service-type decisions.

The evolving emphasis on service delivery models has been a positive process, entailing movement away from a focus on the child as the primary source of learning or behavioral problems toward including such factors as instructional environment, teaching mode, and the child's instructional history. Some authors have argued that responsibility for the child's failure rests with the school and not with the child. Lilly (1970) has proposed a zero reject model which prevents a child from being administratively separated from the regular class once he or she has been placed in the regular class. This approach forces administrators to examine instructional options within the regular class but is not fully compatible with the principle of least restrictive environment in that it does not allow for full-time placement outside the regular class. Others (Adamson & Van Etten, 1972) have taken similar positions but, when circumstances warrant, they allow for a continuum of service and provide placement in alternative programs.

Three models (Deno, 1970; Adelman, 1971; Chaffin, 1975) have been selected for discussion because of their clarity and direct application to public school settings. Each accommodates the principle of least restrictive environment. Each also takes into consideration instructional factors, in addition to student characteristics. The three models do differ in that Deno's model is comprehensive and applies to all handicapped levels, whereas the Chaffin and Adelman models are most applicable to the mildly handicapped. Conceptually, however, the models can be generalized to the more severely handicapped population. The Adelman model differs from the other two in that it is primarily a teaching or instructional model rather than a service model; but it is included to reinforce the position that true special education occurs only when remediation provided to the student is appropriate. Thus, not just the placement decision, but also remediation, intervention, and instruction are important. The Adelman model offers a helpful instructional decision making framework that can be applied in conjunction with the other models.

Deno's Cascade Model

One model frequently referred to is the cascade system proposed by Deno (1970). Figure 1.1 illustrates the hierarchy of service options offered; they range from the basic segregated model to the most integrated model. Alternatives range from Level I, which represents meeting student needs through regular class placement, to Level VII, which is described as noneducational and most restrictive. The various model levels reflect service alternatives, with larger level numbers used to identify the more segregated or restricted options. Levels also might represent characteristics of students with similar needs. *The cascade model enhances the process of matching program alternatives with student need.*

To apply the model requires that the student be served in the least restrictive environment. For example, if after careful study, a student is placed in a Level III program, his or her performance should be carefully observed. As soon as performance warrants such action, the student should be transferred to a Level II program. The goal is to potentially place all students in the regular class settings of Level I programs if they are capable of being served appropriately at that level.

However, the model does allow for students to be moved to more segregated arrangements. In this circumstance, the attitude of those making placement decisions still should be one of advocating for less restrictive placements. The model's goal is to move students upward to less restrictive alternatives. Downward moves are made only when necessary and only until the student can be returned to a higher or less restrictive placement.

Deno's cascade system appeared in 1970—early in the mainstreaming or least restrictive movement. As a conceptual model, it has become a frame of reference for local districts. Deno's discussion of the system clearly reflects a philosophy that is both compatible with public school settings and complies with the intent of PL 94-142. In describing the system, she states:

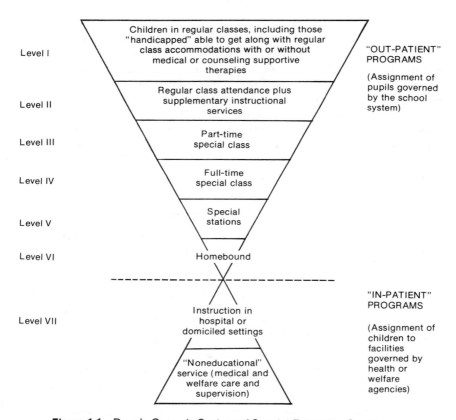

Figure 1.1 Deno's Cascade System of Special Education Service

The tapered design indicates the considerable difference in numbers of students involved at the different levels and calls attention to the fact that the system serves as a diagnostic filter. The most specialized facilities are likely to be needed by the fewest children on a long-term basis. This organizational model can be applied to development of special education services for all types of disabilities.

The cascade system is designed to make available whatever different-from-the-mainstream kind of setting is required to control the learning variables deemed critical for the individual case. It is a system which facilitates tailoring of treatment to individual needs rather than a system for sorting out children so they will fit conditions designed according to group standards not necessarily suitable for the particular case. It acknowledges that the school system is a giant intelligence test involving multiple judges who invoke highly variable criteria in making their judgments. It is designed to facilitate modification based upon changing conditions and new assumptions.

Dunn (1973) modified Deno's cascade model and directed the emphasis from levels of program options to types of exceptional pupils (Figure 1.2). He also extended the placement options from 8 to 11. Dunn's modification (inverted pyramid model) represents an improvement in the descriptions applied to placement options and in the emphasis placed on pupil characteristics. His descriptive definitions of Types I, II, III, and IV exceptional pupils add meaning to the placement options. The descriptions of pupil classifications combined with placement options result in a useful reference from which districts can structure service delivery plans and set placement criteria.

Dunn defines the four types of exceptional children as:

A Type I exceptional pupil is so classified for that segment of his school career (1) when he is enrolled in the regular program of the public day schools, (2) but the teachers in that program have failed in teaching him to such a degree (3) that special supplementary instructional materials and equipment have been made available to him and/or special education consultive services to the regular teachers who work with him; special educators are not directly teaching the child.

A Type II exceptional pupil is so classified for that segment of his school career (1) when the regular teachers have failed in teaching him to such a degree (2) that he is receiving direct instruction from one or more special educators, (3) though he continues to receive part of his academic instruction in the regular program, and (4) may be enrolled in either a regular or special class.

A Type III exceptional pupil is so classified for that segment of his school career (1) when he is receiving no academic instruction in the regular program of the public day schools, but (2) is in a separate self-contained special education day program in the local school system.

A Type IV exceptional pupil is so classified for that segment of his school career (1) when he is unable to attend any type of day school program provided by the local school system, but (2) is in a special boarding school or on hospital or homebound instruction.

Chaffin's Full-Service Model

In contrast to Deno's (1970) cascade model and Dunn's (1973) modification, Chaffin (1975) presents a model which is less comprehensive in

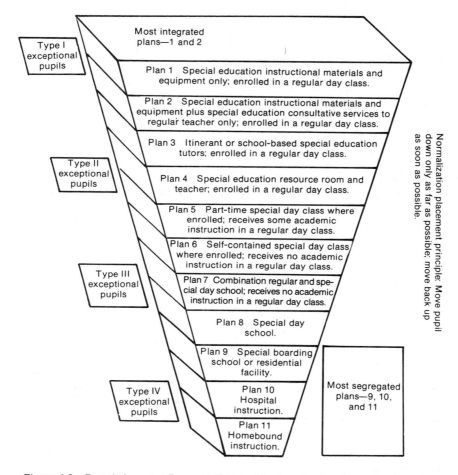

Figure 1.2 Dunn's Inverted Pyramid Model of Instruction for Exceptional Pupils

The model displays 11 major administrative plans in special education, from the most integrated to the most segregated, and from those that should serve the greatest numbers of pupils to those that should serve the least, classified for four types of exceptional children.

Note: Plan 7 could shift up one category to serve Type II exceptional pupils when such children receive part of their academic instruction in a regular day class setting, as they often do.

From: *Exceptional Children in the Schools* (second edition) by L. M. Dunn. Copyright 1973 by Holt, Rinehart & Winston. Reprinted by permission.

application but which combines direct and indirect services. It is less comprehensive in that it is intended primarily for the mildly to moderately handicapped. It also is restrictive in the range of options, since it does not include provision for special class placement, special schools, or other segregated options frequently used for the more severely handicapped.

Chaffin refers to his model as the *full-service education model* and defines full-service education as: "providing every child—gifted, average, and handicapped—with a highly individualized education program appropriate to his/her social, physical, and academic needs. Educational services are arranged in a hierarchical fashion so that they are commensurate with each child's development." Chaffin's service delivery model was developed in cooperation with a local district and employed in an elementary attendance center during its experimental stages. It was based on four objectives:

1. To provide instructional support to the regular classroom teacher;
2. To allow design of services at the building level by those who will implement them;
3. To serve the child and his or her teacher in the regular classroom, not outside of it;
4. To protect the rights of the child through an instructional-based diagnostic system and periodic review of his or her placement.

A review of the service hierarchy displayed in Figure 1.3 illustrates the emphasis on instruction rather than on placement settings. Chaffin's *basic assumption is that primary placement for the mildly handicapped is in the regular class.* This explains why the special class does not appear as a major option in the model.

Service options in Chaffin's full-service model are differentiated as *direct* or *indirect* services. Indirect service options are limited to services provided by personnel supporting the regular classroom teacher. In other words, services are not provided directly to the child but rather to the child's teacher, in an attempt to help the teacher meet the child's instructional needs. Direct services involve interaction directly between support personnel and the child. For example, the speech clinician may deliver speech therapy to the child as a direct service. The speech clinician also might work with the teacher on techniques which the teacher would apply in class as an indirect service.

Chaffin's definitions of service options are:

SERVICE HIERARCHY

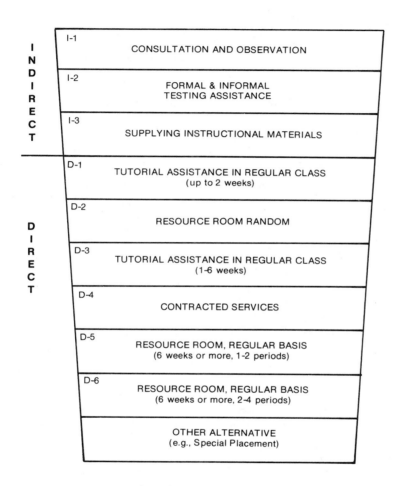

I N D I R E C T		
I-1	CONSULTATION AND OBSERVATION	
I-2	FORMAL & INFORMAL TESTING ASSISTANCE	
I-3	SUPPLYING INSTRUCTIONAL MATERIALS	

D I R E C T		
D-1	TUTORIAL ASSISTANCE IN REGULAR CLASS (up to 2 weeks)	
D-2	RESOURCE ROOM RANDOM	
D-3	TUTORIAL ASSISTANCE IN REGULAR CLASS (1-6 weeks)	
D-4	CONTRACTED SERVICES	
D-5	RESOURCE ROOM, REGULAR BASIS (6 weeks or more, 1-2 periods)	
D-6	RESOURCE ROOM, REGULAR BASIS (6 weeks or more, 2-4 periods)	
	OTHER ALTERNATIVE (e.g., Special Placement)	

Figure 1.3   Chaffin's Full-Service Education Model

From: "Will the Real 'Mainstreaming' Program Please Stand Up! (Or . . . Should Dunn have Done It?)" by J. D. Chaffin; in *Alternatives for Teaching Exceptional Children*. Copyright 1975, Love Publishing Company.

Indirect Services

I-1 Consultation and Observation: At this level of service it is assumed that the support persons have experience and knowledge which may be valuable to the regular teacher in working with children in the classroom, followed by suggestions of procedures or resources that are available to the teacher. The important concern at this level is that the help needed by regular classroom teachers comes from the experience of the support person.

I-2 Formal and Informal Testing Assistance: At this level the support person provides assistance to the regular classroom teacher in conducting the formal or informal testing that may be necessary to plan a program for the referred student. The support person does not work with the child at this level. Instead, the support person furnishes test materials or suggestions of informal means of assessment that provide both the teacher and the support person helpful information about the child.

   This level of support is intended to help the regular classroom teacher become a better diagnostician. When the teacher has obtained results of the testing, he or she communicates the results to the support person for help in program planning. This level of service is further differentiated by the amount of help the regular classroom teacher needs to administer the tests.

I-3 Supplying Instructional Resources: When the teacher and the outside support person have agreed on an instructional plan, the teacher may need assistance in locating and using the recommended resource materials. This level of support is different from I-1 in that the resource person obtains or provides explanations regarding the use of material. This level is different from I-2 in that it involves instructional rather than diagnostic resources. If a demonstration of resource material with the child is required to help the teacher implement the program, the level of service is not I-3 but, instead, a form of direct service as described below.

Direct Services

D-1 Tutorial Assistance in Regular Class (up to 2 weeks): This level of service provides for the support person to work directly with the student in the regular classroom. This service varies as a function of the needs of the child and the regular classroom teacher, but could include formal or informal evaluation, skill training in an instructional area, or helping the student learn to use prescribed resource materials. This level of service is intended to assist the regular classroom teacher in implementing a program for the student that then is continued by the teacher. Service to the child at this level is limited to approximately two weeks.

D-2 Resource Room Random: At this level of service, the *emphasis is on one specific task*. The classroom teacher sends the student to the resource room for help that cannot be provided at that particular time by the classroom teacher. This is not a continued service and is completed when the student leaves the resource room.

D-3 Tutorial Assistance in Regular Class (1-6 weeks): This level of service is different from D-1 primarily in the length of time allowed for assistance by the outside resource person. This level also is different from D-1 in that D-3 services *may involve three or more children*, whereas D-1 probably (though not necessarily) involves only one or two. As in D-1, this level of service intends that the tutorial service be maintained in the regular classroom instructional program. If it becomes apparent during this level of service that some kind of long-term support is needed to maintain the child in the regular classroom, the outside support person begins to arrange for D-4 services.

D-4 Contracted Services: This level of service can be implemented at any time during D-3. The support person and the classroom teacher evaluate (during D-3) the duration of tutorial services needed. If services in the classroom are needed for an extended period, the support person locates and trains a tutor to carry out the program.

D-5 Resource Room, Regular Basis (6 weeks or more, 1-2 periods daily): This level of service is used only when a combination of D-3 and D-4 is inadequate for instruction needed by the student. Rarely is this level used without first implementing lower level services in the classroom.

D-6 Resource Room, Regular Basis (6 weeks or more, 2-4 periods daily): Service at this level is the highest level provided within the school. Direct referral is not made at this level, but is preceded by referral to other levels of service.

Adelman's Instructional Model

The current emphasis on design of delivery system models has resulted in more attention being given to instructional models. Adelman's work is particularly significant in this area. Adelman (1970-71) has proposed a model which addresses the question of how teachers should approach instructional problems. His model differs from those previously discussed in that the emphasis is not on a service delivery system but on instructional options available to the teacher regardless of the educational setting. Changes in the learner's instructional setting are considered, but primary attention is given to the instructional *process*. In terms of instruction, Adelman's model is compatible with the inherent philosophy and practices of Deno's, Dunn's and Chaffin's service delivery models.

Adelman's model evolved from instructional concern about groups of learners classified as learning disabled, emotionally disturbed, and educationally handicapped. His behavioral classifications make the model highly applicable to most levels and areas of the handicapped. Children with learning problems are classified according to three types:

Type I: No disorder (problem results primarily from deficiencies of the learning environment)

Type II: Minor disorder (problem results from deficiencies in both the child and the learning environment)

Type III: Major disorder (problem results primarily from the child's deficits)

Such a classification system clearly acknowledges the significant differences within groups of children labeled as learning disabled, emotionally disturbed, or educationally handicapped. The heterogeneous characteristics of groups of handicapped children are important in placement and instructional decision making.

Adelman argues that a given youngster's success or failure in school is a function of the interaction between that student's strengths, weaknesses, and limitations and the specific, classroom-situational factors encountered, including individual differences among teachers and differing approaches to instruction. From this logic, Adelman developed the following position statement basic to his model.

The greater the congruity between a youngster's characteristics and the characteristics of the program in which he is required to perform, the greater the likelihood of school success; conversely, the greater the discrepancy between the child's characteristics and the program characteristics, the greater the likelihood of poor school performance.

Using the three-type classification system and the perspective of interaction between learner characteristics and classroom situational factors as the causality factor of learner success or failure in school, Adelman provides a model identified as *Sequential and Hierarchical Teaching Strategies for the Remediation of School Learning Problems.* Through the model (see Figure 1.4), he offers a two-step process to assist teachers in identifying and remediating learners' instructional needs.

An explanation of Figure 1.4 is quoted from Adelman (1970-71):

Essentially, a two-step sequential process is suggested, by which the teacher (1) establishes a personalized learning environment and then, if necessary, (2) employs up to three sequential and hierarchical remedial strategies in a sequence predetermined by the success or failure of each attempted strategy. That is, after the first step has been initiated, the teacher proceeds to the second step, for those youngsters who continue to manifest occasional to chronic learning difficulty. The three sequential and hierarchical strategies included for possible use during this instruction of prerequisites needed before school subjects can be mastered. Level A emphasizes maintaining the focus on basic school subjects. Level B emphasizes instruction of prerequisites needed before school subjects can be mastered. Level C attempts to deal with any pathological behaviors or underlying process deficits that may interfere with school learning.

No formal tests are employed to specify the etiology or level of remedial needs; assessment procedures are employed only to determine instructional needs at a particular step and level. In effect, both the youngster's type of learning problem and

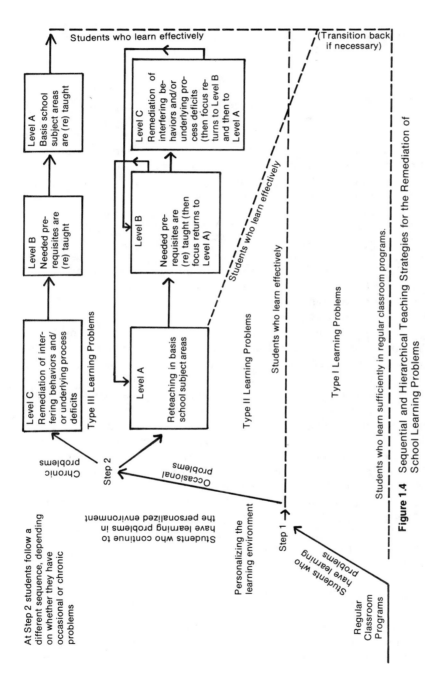

Figure 1.4 Sequential and Hierarchical Teaching Strategies for the Remediation of School Learning Problems

From: "*Learning Problems, Part I: An Interactional View of Causality*" by H. S. Adelman, *Academic Therapy*, 1970-71, 6(2), 117-123. Reprinted by permission.

the level of remedial needs are identified only after the impact of each teaching strategy becomes apparent. What is being suggested here is that the approaches be employed systematically.

Adelman's model provides an additional resource for educators responsible for designing instructional programs for exceptional children. Combined with the service delivery models of Deno, Dunn, or Chaffin, local districts have a base from which they can systematically design programs and instructional procedures focusing on service options as well as instructional processes. The models in themselves do not provide direct solutions to instructional problems presented by exceptional children, but they do provide a construct from which teachers, administrators, and support personnel can work to resolve such problems.

The emphasis on delivery and instructional models in this chapter reinforces the need for conceptual planning and illustrates the progress made in preparation planning. This does not suggest that the models discussed are sufficient, but they do provide direction for local districts as they respond to emerging federal and state legislation. The models also provide a basis from which research questions can be generated. This is particularly true of Adelman's model.

With the evolvement of instructional options designed to meet the varying needs of exceptional children and the employment of due process safeguards, administrative procedures of the past no longer are sufficient. Attention must be given to determining the exceptional child's educational needs as a prerequisite to considering available options. After the student's needs have been determined, the emphasis should shift to providing assurance that the needed services are provided. This provision may involve developing services not currently available or contracting for such services with private or public agencies.

Following the progress of the past 10 years in design of materials and development of instructional technology applicable to teaching exceptional children, districts need to construct or adopt models which provide a reference in program decision making pertaining to exceptional children. Such models, plans, or constructs must focus on both instructional and placement decisions.

DEFINITIONS AND CLASSIFICATIONS

In the past, special education literature has given considerable attention to the process of defining exceptionalities. Recently, however, the emphasis has shifted from developing definitions to focusing on the consequence of applying definitions to exceptional children. The same issues that contributed to the need for PL 94-142 can be attributed in part to the role definitions have played in educational programming for the handicapped.

In the history of general education, a developmental perspective has been possible; so third graders, fourth graders, or "normal" children do not have to be defined as such to be taught. In contrast, for the exceptional child, definitions have become central to educational placement and, in turn, to designing instructional activities. The importance placed on definitions derives from explanations which on the surface appear logical. Under careful scrutiny, however, one realizes that little has been gained from the process—at least from the perspective of improving instruction for exceptional children.

These "logical" explanations include the premises that:

1. Definitions are necessary as a basis for differentiating learners whose characteristics dictate particular instructional approaches; and
2. Definitions are necessary as a basis for communication among personnel who provide various services required for exceptional children.

These explanations are defensible. One must be able to identify learners whose learning and behavioral characteristics require differentiated instruction. Also, participants in a learner's educational program must understand the terminology used to describe the learner. What has occurred in the history of providing special education services, however, has been a compromise in the use and formulation of definitions. For example, as public schools began to develop special education services, they found eligibility criteria necessary, and definitions became the route whereby children were determined eligible or ineligible for a particular service. State laws and regulations used definitions as a basis for approving programs and children for placement in programs. The typical approach involved stating a general definition of exceptional children, accompanied by more specific definitions for each categorical area of exceptionality served by the public schools.

One can understand why eligibility criteria were necessary and why definitions of exceptional children evolved as they have. As a note of caution, however, definitions couched in the context of law or state regulations do have influence, and the definitions convey confidence to the user. If educators read in their state regulations that a child with a measured intelligence quotient below 50 is trainable mentally retarded, they believe the statement or at least adhere to the requirement in making placement decisions. During the 1950s and early 1960s many definitions incorporated in state regulations were of this type and provided specific criteria. Because eligibility criteria for placement were established as a condition for allocating financial assistance to districts for services to exceptional children, they were even more influential. The establishment of eligibility criteria by state education agencies, combined with the practice of applying such criteria as a basis for allocating supplemental financial aid to districts, has had a significant impact on public school services to exceptional children and on decisions to serve or not serve particular children.

The practice of using definitions of exceptional children as the basis for eligibility implies a number of questionable assumptions. For example, it suggests that:

1. Definitions offer information which teachers can use to design instructional programs for children whose characteristics approximate those included in the definition;
2. Definitions are predictive in designing services;
3. The label that evolves from formulating a definition is a symbol which is restricted in application to conveying the definition's meaning;
4. It is possible to describe exceptional children sufficiently to assume consistency in interpretation;
5. Either causative factors or patterns of characteristics are specific enough to allow for precise definitions.

Using definitions as statements of eligibility has had both negative and positive influences on the growth and development of educational programs for exceptional children. From the negative perspective, at least three examples can be cited. First, the eligibility-type definition provides a basis from which the regular classroom teacher can easily refer an exceptional child out of the classroom. The early history of the referral process was not necessarily oriented toward referring children for services, but rather became a practice which appeared to be aimed at referring the child out of the regular class. In too many cases, this resulted in exclusion from school.

Second, such definitions tended to emphasize limitations rather than strengths. For example, criteria which were incorporated into the definition focused on low intelligence, inability to hear or see, physical limitations, or generally unacceptable social behavior. By meeting the conditions of the definitions, the child was classified on the basis of what he or she could not do, rather than on developing the child's capabilities. Having been identified as an exceptional child, the child acquired a label which, in addition to making him or her eligible for a particular service, carried with it a negative value or stigma that frequently influenced the child far beyond the education program. The self-fulfilling prophecy of Rosenthal and Jacobson (1968), which has been criticized method-ologically, suggests that people expect children to perform in accordance with their label. If this theory is valid, teachers influence student performance by how they interpret any labels applied. The typical approach to identifying a child as "exceptional" has involved the employment of assessment techniques intended to isolate the child's deficits. The teacher then was presented with detailed negative data on the child's performance history. While one reasonably may assume that teachers' expectancy levels have been influenced greatly by the nature of information presented to them about the exceptional child, research supporting this view is inconclusive.

A third example of negative effects relates to the performance assumption which historically has been associated with most definitions of exceptional children. The tendency has been to assume that if a child is classified as exceptional, he or she not only will remain exceptional, but will always need special education services. Treatment of the educable mentally retarded prior to the 1970s is a good example. After having been identified as educable mentally retarded, these children generally were placed in a special class. After placement, consideration rarely was given to returning the child to the regular class. Placement became permanent, and so did the label.

Positive benefits derived from the definition practice have been of a general nature and not always directly experienced by individuals who have been labeled. Benefits centered on program growth because of the emphasis on establishing programs specific to categories of exceptional children. The categorical approach to defining exceptional children and programming allowed special interest groups to be specific in promoting programs, and it facilitated legislative efforts. An additional benefit derived from the visibility given to exceptional children in the broader context of education. Even though the perceptions that teachers acquired about exceptional children often were inappropriate, the design of separate programs based on assumed needs and defined character-istics did contribute to the concept of special education and helped set the stage for mandating education for all exceptional children. Even though special education services presently are undergoing a restructuring process and several significant philosophical changes are occurring relative to school responsibility, some credit for progress must be given to the categorical approach in structuring and delivering special services to exceptional children.

Problems in Defining Exceptional Children

At least two major problems are encountered in formulating definitions regarding exceptional children. First, the reason for establishing definitions of exceptional children is to create a classification system for making educational or educationally related program decisions. If the conditions which caused children to be mentally retarded, learning disabled, hearing impaired, visually impaired, physically handicapped, emotionally disturbed, gifted, or hearing or speech impaired were related to a single cause (e.g., disease) or if conditions resulted in children exhibiting highly similar characteristics and instructional needs, the task would be simplified greatly. The situation, however, is much more complex. Most of the characteristics resulting in identification of children as exceptional are acquired rather than existing at birth. Also, considerable overlap in characteristics among types of exceptional children is apparent.

Even when a group of exceptional children can be identified as having similar characteristics, educational needs among members vary extensively. In the area of the hearing impaired, for example, preciseness is possible in measuring hearing loss if a person elects to use degree of hearing loss as a major definition criterion; however, the needs of children still vary, since children of the same age and level of hearing have differing language development, academic performance, social skills, and physical development levels. Variability is even greater in other categorical areas which are more difficult to define, such as the emotionally disturbed and learning disabled.

An additional problem in defining exceptional children relates to the temporal status of the characteristics of exceptional children. Exceptional children do change, and their educational needs change accordingly. If a special education program is effective for a given child, the characteristics which make this child exceptional should change. A child with an articulation problem who receives speech therapy probably will improve to the point that the articulation problem is corrected and the child is no longer a speech impaired or exceptional child. A deaf child upon entering school may have limited language skills, but after several years in special education programs, he or she may develop effective communication skills. The hearing level may remain the same, but educational needs will have changed drastically because of the acquired communication skills. The reasons for change relate to maturation, effectiveness of educational treatment, motivation, and general environmental factors.

The lack of single causes or explicit explanations for what makes a child exceptional, combined with the variability of characteristics among children within categories of exceptionality and the changing nature of exceptional children, clarify the problems inherent in formulating definitions. Past practices in defining exceptional children have been insufficient and probably have contributed to the inappropriate placement of many children in special education programs whose needs could have been met in the regular classroom. In view of the potential negative consequences for children labeled as exceptional, the author advocates a conservative approach to definitions, eligibility, and placement.

Implications of Classifying Exceptional Children

If the problems discussed above are significant, what guidelines should school districts use in attempting to match individual children's needs with special education service options? Obviously, they must rely on some form of classification of learners by particular instructional requirements, since exceptional children do represent a population having unique instructional needs. Classifying exceptional children by broadly stated definitions is insufficient as a basis for remediating their particular difficulties. The dilemma faced by the public schools is primarily one of transition. By today's standards, past practices are unacceptable. We have the capability to implement more effective procedures, but time is required to make the transition systematically. Goldstein, Arkell, Ashcroft, Hurley, and Lilly (1975), writing in *Issues in the Classification of Exceptional Children,* clearly place the past and present in perspective.

> The classification of handicapped children for educational purposes has always been a controversial matter among educators. Recently, however, the parents of handicapped children, national and state associations of parents, and social scientists have extended the controversy—even to the point of involving the courts in efforts to arrive at actions that will be most equitable for handicapped children in public education.
>
> Essentially, the controversy over classification as a decision point in public education centers on the following questions: (1) Are the schools justified in using classification systems to deny some children access to education? (2) Are systems of classification so porous that misclassification is as possible as classification, with the result that some children are assigned to educational settings inconsistent with their

inherent capabilities and thus are denied an appropriate education? (3) Are classification criteria so flexible that available educational settings can be used as repositories for children, irrespective of the child's needs? (4) Are classification systems substituted for the real descriptors of children's characteristics to the extent that teachers and administrators are responding to labels rather than data as they portray children's educational needs?

The traditional points of departure for classifying handicapped children in education are in regard to their sensory, intellectual, physical, and behavioral status and, more recently, combinations of these. Obviously, these categories are too gross to be of any real service as indices to educational intervention today. Nevertheless, one by one they took shape over the 200 years or so that formal education has been operative in Europe and the United States (p. 6).

. . . Although some might agree that present systems for classifying handicapped children in the public schools have some value to administration in that they provide pegs upon which funding and management procedures can be hung, their value to the educational enterprises is less pronounced. Their limited relationship to teaching/learning activities, along with their ambiguities, makes possible educational practices that are unproductive and frequently unjust. To put it another way, they give minimum direction in decision making about day-to-day instructional needs of children; at the same time, they permit children who require interventions other than those typical of special education to be sidetracked into these classes. Moreover, they often are inaccurate and can be distracting and misleading to some teachers (p. 55).

Goldstein et al. recommended that "labels and systems of classification be abandoned in favor of more precise descriptions of individual children as they have implication for classroom interaction." Such a recommendation likely will receive considerable support from public school personnel. Public school administrators and special educators have experienced numerous frustrations in attempting to adhere to state and federal regulations requiring the use of labels based on definitions which are impractical, if not inappropriate, for educational decision making. On the other hand, if implemented, that recommendation could still result in the development and use of a classification system; the difference will be in the utility of the classification system for educational decisions and the lessening of the impact on the individual.

Resolving the Definition/Classification Issue

If the emphasis on defining exceptional children and in setting eligibility criteria for participation in special services shifts from general statements of definitions to an approach which emphasizes learning characteristics which are descriptive of instructional and service needs, brief descriptive statements no longer will be sufficient. Instead of relying on descriptive statements as a means for structuring a definition and/or classification system, attention will need to focus on a *process*.

The Council for Exceptional Children (1977), reporting on definitional issues, stated that regardless of the classification system used, definitions by necessity must be based on criteria designed to facilitate identification, evaluation, and educational programming and placement. This position appears compatible with that of Goldstein et al. (1975). It also is consistent with requirements of PL 94-142 regarding identification, due process, and the individualized education program. To accomplish fully the transition to specifying characteristics which provide usable indices for remediation decisions and planning and which are applied in the context of identification, evaluation and programming will require several changes on the part of those who set regulations and implement practices.

The most significant changes which could occur to resolve the definition/classification dilemma would be for public education to implement a continuum of educational and service alternatives, to individualize instruction, and to eliminate the dichotomy between serving exceptional and nonexceptional students. PL 94-142 will steer public education in this direction, but the financial provisions will continue to inhibit full accomplishment. As long as the state and/or federal government is required to reimburse or supplement local districts for the cost of providing services to exceptional children, the necessity for eligibility criteria will continue and most likely will exert undue influence on educational decisions. Only when districts are able to offer a full array of instructional and service options and are free to match those options to learner needs without regard for why the learner has such needs and whether or not they are exceptional will it be possible to minimize the assumed stigma of labels and to maximize the value derived from making decisions based on learner-specific information.

Because the special education literature continues to be based on categorical definitions, and because PL 94-142 perpetuates the use of such definitions, a discussion on descriptive definitions is included in this chapter. In an attempt to place definitions in a context of assessment, planning, and evaluation, a separate chapter on instructional planning also is included. Chapter 3 emphasizes making instructional decisions based on learner information relevant to instructional needs and minimizes the emphasis placed on categorical classifications of exceptional children. Subsequent chapters addressing specific categories of exceptionality elaborate on characteristics, needs, and programming options; attention in these chapters also will focus on definitions. This approach represents somewhat of a compromise to accommodate the state-of-the-art—it necessitates presenting information on exceptional children by categories while focusing attention on instructional planning as an indication of the direction in which we should move in the future.

Using the Term "Exceptional"

Use of the term "exceptional" is not a recent innovation. The International Council for the Education of Exceptional Children (now CEC) was founded in 1922. Baker (1953), in his book *Introduction to Exceptional Children*, stated that "exceptional" is a more inclusive term than "handicapped," since it emphasizes children at both extremes of various scales (p. 12); and went on to elaborate on application of the term to mental abilities by including the gifted and the mentally retarded within the meaning of "exceptional." This differentiation between exceptional and handicapped continues today, with *exceptional being the most inclusive, and handicapped having a more restricted meaning* (i.e., excluding the gifted).

The term *handicapped* has more meaning than *exceptional* for the lay public. The general public tends to interpret *exceptional* as applying only to the gifted. Thus, in spite of the term's long history in the context of education, use of the term *exceptional* contributes to confusion when used in the public news media. Some professionals also question the use of *exceptional* as the primary label.

Scriven (1976), in a paper presented at a conference on mainstreaming sponsored by the Leadership Training Institute/Special Education at the University of Minnesota, made some candid observations about using the term *exceptional* in the context in which it has come to be applied. He stated:

> I cannot condone the euphemistic use of the term "exceptional children" to refer to handicapped children. There are exceptional pupils whose problems we are not discussing; they happen to be the ones from whom the term "exceptional children" was stolen because of its honorific connotations. We will not help children by misrepresenting them . . . and it is a terrible foundation for such an effort to begin by misrepresenting the entire group of such children. It not only misleads the public, but does it in a way that reduces support; and it steals from the genuinely exceptional child not only a name but the support that (s)he also needs very badly indeed.
>
> It is just as much of a tragedy for a bright child to be made to hate school and study by being bored and curbed and criticized for the behaviors associated with rapid learning and searching as it is for a handicapped or slow-learning child to be treated as a morally inferior being or one that "can't be taught." (Or if not just as much of a tragedy, still a very great tragedy, especially because of the possibility of such people's producing substantial yields for the rest of society, such as a Salk vaccine.) . .
>
> The well-intentioned euphemism drifts into deception; it is a poor substitute for tackling the real problem of preventing professionals and lay people alike from treating certain students improperly. We have to learn to identify facts correctly and then to face the facts, not redescribe them.

If anglos turn out to be more avaricious than latinos, I do not want the avarice test thrown out or described as the "emolument-orientation index." If men turn out to be genetically more vicious or dishonest than women, I do not want this situation redescribed to save the feelings of men. If fairhaired, blue-eyed, overweight anglo males are highly likely to be avaricious, vicious, sadistic, and psychopathic, I do not want to be called "exceptional." I want to be recognized as a bad *prima facie* risk for positions of social leadership or, in short, a probable menace! I also would like to have the chance to show that this *prima facie* evidence does not apply to me as an individual and to be judged on my actual record, and I would hope that you would join me in that effort. But not by calling me "probably exceptional" (p. 63).

Scriven is not merely raising semantic questions. He is reminding the profession of the necessity to employ a language that *communicates*. In his paper, he goes on to cite the consequences of labels and to clarify the significant issues which have emerged specific to the status of gifted learners when the term exceptional is used as a generic term in the broader context. His criticisms are warranted to a degree. With today's knowledge, advocacy groups, and literature sources, a more appropriate and descriptive term probably could be coined. But because of the term's history and the pressing priorities of the 1970s, this may not be the time to yield to a temptation to suggest an alternative.

This topic has been presented because readers need to be aware that, while special educators may apply the term without explanation, it does not communicate the same meaning to everyone. In the reasonable future, other options probably will emerge. Criticism undoubtedly will continue, and the need to respond still will be present. The response, however, should occur only when conditions in the public schools are such that reliance on definitions for educational decisions will have lessened, and the emphasis will have shifted to matching learner characteristics to instructional procedures. By then, the need for a definition for purposes of classifying children probably will no longer exist!

Examples of Definitions

Kirk's (1972) definition of exceptional children is:

The exceptional child is defined as the child who deviates from the average or normal child (1) in mental characteristics, (2) in sensory abilities, (3) in neuromuscular or physical characteristics, (4) in social or emotional behavior, (5) in communication abilities, or (6) in multiple handicaps to such an extent that he requires a modification of school practices, or special educational services, in order to develop to his maximum capacity (p. 4).

Kirk's definition is clearly stated and reflects the literature and practices of 1972. His definition emphasizes deviation from an assumed norm or standard, and focuses attention on the need to modify school practices or require special educational services as criteria for determining exceptionalities. The definition also projects optimism in that the implied basis for classification is to enhance the individual's attainment of his or her maximum capabilities.

Definitions appearing in state regulations continue to adhere to descriptive statements similar to Kirk's definition. The CEC (1977a), in a report on definitions used by states, indicated that, "Most states utilize a similar generic definition of handicapped children which is categorical in nature." The same is true of descriptive statements in PL 94-142.

Dunn's (1963, 1973) work in defining exceptional children has been helpful. He has responded to criticism of practices occurring in the 1950s and 1960s, which centered primarily on the issues of overreferral, inappropriate placement, and placing too much emphasis on the use of tests in making placement decisions. In 1963 Dunn defined exceptional children as those:

> (1) who differ from the average to such a degree in physical or psychological characteristics (2) that school programs designed for the majority of children do not afford them opportunity for all-around adjustment and optimum progress, (3) and who therefore need either special instruction or, in some cases, special ancillary services, or both, to achieve at a level commensurate with their respective abilities (p. 3).

In the 1973 revision of his book, he offered a more restrictive definition.

> An exceptional pupil is so labeled only for that segment of his school career (1) when his deviating physical or behavioral characteristics are of such a nature as to manifest a significant learning asset or disability for special education purposes; and, therefore, (2) when, through trial provisions, it has been determined that he can make greater all-round adjustment and scholastic progress with direct or indirect special education services than he could with only a typical regular school program (p. 7).

Dunn's 1973 definition, in the opinion of this author, is a marked improvement, as well as a significant contribution to the literature. It is a conservative definition in that it introduces the concept of *trial placement* as a condition of determining exceptionality, and it calls for close monitoring of the exceptional child's program. Dunn's definition recognizes a direct relationship between the child being labeled exceptional and the superiority of the special education services over regular class placement only. These features of Dunn's 1973 definition have the effect of causing school districts to determine the adequacy of the child's education program in the process of determining whether or not the child is exceptional and in need of special education services. Although Dunn's 1973 text includes definitive chapters on categorical areas of exceptionality, his basic definition of exceptional children does not specifically refer to various categorical types.

An examination of the literature, including state rules and regulations, indicates little substantive variance in how the specific categories of exceptional children have been defined. The language used to describe the different categories varies but, in general, overall definitions have been similar. Rather than compare a selection of definitions, reference will be made here only to those definitions appearing in the *Federal Register* (August, 1977), which contains the Rules and Regulations of PL 94-142. These definitions are typical of those adopted by most states. The exception is Massachusetts, which, according to the CEC report on definitions (1977), is the only state with no definition of categories for the various handicapping conditions in its laws or regulations.

Because most school districts will attempt to comply with PL 94-142 for purposes of financial assistance, the categorical definitions promulgated by the Rules and Regulations probably will be representative of categorical definitions adopted by districts in the future. Section 121a.5 of the Rules and Regulations for PL 94-142 include the following definitions:

Sec. 121a.5   Handicapped children.

(a) As used in this part, the term "handicapped children" means those children evaluated in accordance with §§ 121a.530—121a.534 as being mentally retarded, hard of hearing, deaf, speech impaired, visually handicapped, seriously emotionally disturbed, orthopedically impaired, other health impaired, deaf-blind, multi-handicapped, or as having specific learning disabilities, who because of those impairments need special education and related services.

(b) The terms used in this definition are defined as follows:

(1) "Deaf" means a hearing impairment which is so severe that the child is impaired in processing linguistic information through hearing, with or without amplification, which adversely affects educational performance.

(2) "Deaf-blind" means concomitant hearing and visual impairments, the combination of which causes such severe communication and other developmental and educational problems that they cannot be accommodated in special education programs solely for deaf or blind children.

(3) "Hard of hearing" means a hearing impairment, whether permanent or fluctuating, which adversely affects a child's educational performance but which is not included under the definition of "deaf" in this section.

(4) "Mentally retarded" means significantly subaverage general intellectual functioning existing concurrently with deficits in adaptive behavior and manifested during the developmental period, which adversely affects a child's educational performance.

(5) "Multihandicapped" means concomitant impairments (such as mentally retarded-blind, mentally retarded-orthopedically impaired, etc.), the combination of which causes such severe educational problems that they cannot be accommodated in special education programs solely for one of the impairments. The term does not include deaf-blind children.

(6) "Orthopedically impaired" means a severe orthopedic impairment which adversely affects a child's educational performance. The term includes impairments caused by congenital anomaly (e.g., clubfoot, absence of some member, etc.), impairments caused by disease (e.g. poliomyelitis, bone tuberculosis, etc.), and impairments from other causes (e.g., cerebral palsy, amputations, and fractures or burns which cause contractures).

(7) "Other health impaired" means limited strength, vitality or alertness, due to chronic or acute health problems such as a heart condition, tuberculosis, rheumatic fever, nephritis, asthma, sickle cell anemia, hemophilia, epilepsy, lead poisoning, leukemia, or diabetes, which adversely affects a child's educational performance.

(8) "Seriously emotionally disturbed" is defined as follows:

(i) The term means a condition exhibiting one or more of the following characteristics over a long period of time and to a marked degree, which adversely affects educational performance:

(A) An inability to learn which cannot be explained by intellectual, sensory, or health factors;

(B) An inability to build or maintain satisfactory interpersonal relationships with peers and teachers:

(C) Inappropriate types of behavior or feelings under normal circumstances;

(D) A general pervasive mood of unhappiness or depression; or

(E) A tendency to develop physical symptoms or fears associated with personal or school problems.

(ii) The term includes children who are schizophrenic or autistic. The term does not include children who are socially maladjusted, unless it is determined that they are seriously emotionally disturbed.

(9) "Specific learning disability" means a disorder in one or more of the basic psychological processes involved in understanding or in using language, spoken or written, which may manifest itself in an imperfect ability to listen, think, speak, read, write, spell or to do mathematical calculations. The term includes such conditions as perceptual handicaps, brain injury, minimal brain dysfunction, dyslexia, and developmental aphasia. The term does not include children who have learning problems which are primarily the result of visual, hearing, or motor handicaps, of mental retardation, or of environmental, cultural, or economic disadvantage.

(10) "Speech impaired" means a communication disorder, such as stuttering, impaired articulation, a language impairment, or a voice impairment, which adversely affects a child's educational performance.

(11) "Visually handicapped" means a visual impairment which, even with correction, adversely affects a child's educational performance. The term includes both partially seeing and blind children.
(20 U.S.C. 1401(1), (15).)

PL 94-142 includes two definitions which historically have not been included consistently in state definitions—the multihandicapped and the deaf-blind—but PL 94-142 does not include the gifted. The gifted are not included because the legislation does not mandate programs for this category. Many states, however, are including the gifted in mandatory legislation at the state level. For example, the Kansas 1978 State Plan (1977) defines *gifted* as follows:

Intellectually gifted individuals are those who have potential for outstanding performance by virtue of superior intellectual abilities. The intellectually gifted are those with demonstrated achievement and/or potential ability. Individuals capable of outstanding performance include both those with demonstrated achievement and those with minimal or low performance who give evidence of high potential in general intellectual ability, specific academic aptitudes, and/or creative thinking abilities (p. 134).

Definitions of the Future

One is tempted to be prophetic and offer a new definition of exceptional children which might serve as a reference for the 1980s, but to attempt such a statement would be presumptuous and also would contradict the author's position that the emphasis should shift from defining the exceptional learner to establishing instructional options and matching options with learner characteristics. The author concurs with a statement which appeared in a report on definitional issues published by the Council for Exceptional Children (1977a) stating that:

Regardless of the classification system used, definitions and eligibility criteria can be operationalized only through the process of identification, evaluation, educational programming, and placement. The fluid nature of these procedures contrasts with the static nature of definitions and criteria . . . The type of personnel involved and the nature of their qualifications is considered an integral part of identification, evaluation, and educational programming. The appropriateness of a child's educational programming depends in great part on the ability of qualified personnel to operationalize definitions and eligibility criteria through established procedures (p. II.5).

This statement represents the logic for including Chapter 3— Instructional Planning—in this introductory text. This author believes that teachers skilled in instructional planning and support personnel skilled in assessment and team planning will contribute to establishing a public school climate in which effective decisions can be made, ones which match instructional options with learner characteristics. If this is established, the need for eligibility criteria (i.e., definitions as a condition for program placement) will not be necessary. Instead, a frame of reference will be offered from which one might formulate his or her own definition of exceptional children.

Rather than approach definitions of exceptional children from the learner's perspective, why not give primary attention to the array of potential instructional options that exist and the characteristics of those options which make them appropriate for exceptional children or learners experiencing serious problems in school. In describing instructional options for exceptional children, the following statement could apply and serve to define exceptional children.

> **Instructional options for exceptional children are those which require:**
> — accurate, in-depth assessment of learner strengths and weaknesses
> — intensive remediation intervention attention by specially trained teachers, support personnel, and instructional aides
> — a focus on instructional needs which require more time to remediate than routinely can be accomplished in regular instructional settings
> — precise instructional planning by teachers and support personnel
> — the use of specially designed instructional materials and/or activities
> — modifications or adaptations in the organization and/or structure of the regular curriculum
>
> **Given that instructional options meeting the above conditions are established, children and youth whose characteristics dictate the need for such instructional options would be considered exceptional.**

INCIDENCE AND PREVALENCE OF EXCEPTIONAL CHILDREN

The question of numbers has been a concern throughout the history of developing educational programs for exceptional children and youth. A review of state regulations and local district policies suggests that the field has been preoccupied with pupil-teacher ratios, case loads, identification surveys, and funding formulas based on the number served versus the number assumed to exist. The emphasis on pupil-teacher ratios and case loads has been influential in setting controls on the number of exceptional children which can be assigned to a teacher or support personnel. This practice has at least provided a degree of assurance that teachers could devote their attention to development of remediation programs and not have to direct energies to controlling the size of their classes. Although violations have occurred, the power of financial aid tied to approval requirements pertaining to class size and case loads has prevailed.

Identification Practices

Any attempt at identifying exceptional children assumes one knows the population one is seeking, that one recognizes the appropriate persons when one finds them, and that, upon identification, one is prepared to serve them. In the case of exceptional children, identification always has been a priority. Although few public schools have been able to serve all exceptional children identified, the concern for identifying all children who presumably are exceptional has been constant.

Given the current status (which is better than it has ever been) of defining exceptional children and of the technology available for screening and diagnosis, serious questions can be raised about past practices. This is particularly true when considering the lack of resources to accommodate their needs upon identification. Too often, well designed and implemented identification processes result only in labeling the child, because of insufficient programs. This has been characteristic of many districts in the past. Granted, the numbers of children on waiting lists have served as *prima facie* evidence in advocacy efforts to establish programs, but the risks of over-identification and the assumed labeling effects may have balanced out the advocacy benefits.

The resources required to carry out identification procedures without the benefit of precise criteria or adequate instruments over the years has had considerable influence on the roles of support personnel. During the 1950s and 1960s, for example, school psychologists devoted a major portion of their time to administration of intelligence tests to identify children eligible for classes serving the educable mentally retarded. More concern was placed on identification than on re-evaluation after placement. During this same time, many speech clinicians screened for speech and hearing problems from the beginning of school until the Thanksgiving break. The amount of time they were able to commit to therapy—i.e., services to children—was reduced greatly by the assignment to screening tasks.

Certainly, identification is important. How else does one determine who is in need of help? But this is also a question of perspectives. The disproportionate emphasis on identification during the past 20 years may have been detrimental when the state of readiness is considered. Little is gained if a child is identified inappropriately and labeled by an examiner lacking sufficient skill, or if the assessment instruments employed are ineffective or inappropriate. The pressures of long waiting lists may have precipitated the establishment of classes or programs beyond the fiscal or personnel resources of districts. These effects may be difficult to document, but the observations are defensible.

The purpose of these comments is not to argue against the identification requirements of PL 94-142, but rather to provide a frame of reference for cautions which need to be exercised as the field moves into a new era in identifying exceptional children and providing special education services. The circumstances are different today, but many of the same hazards exist. PL 94-142 mandates a *free and appropriate public education* for all handicapped children and youth. Most states additionally have passed legislation in support of public school programming for the gifted. Thus, upon identification, some assurance is given that appropriate services will be provided. Also, PL 94-142 requires the employment of nondiscriminatory tests, which represents another important source of assurance. The IEP processes offer further assurance that identification will not result only in the issuing of a label. Nevertheless, we still lack precision in defining who is and who is not exceptional. Although improvements have been made in training personnel skilled in assessment, room for improvement is obvious. The due process procedures, effectively implemented, will help guard against inappropriate identification of children and youth.

Numbers are still important, but in a different context. To comply with PL 94-142, school districts must identify all handicapped children and provide appropriate programs. Financial assistance also is based on numbers—which represents a hazard, but probably a necessity.

Although some states have had legislation mandating educational programs for exceptional children, and districts have developed systematic needs assessment procedures, we do not have a good data base to support estimates on the number of exceptional children. Several reasons account for the lack of accurate information on numbers. First, the tendency has been to alter eligibility criteria for particular programs. For example, if a state raises the upper limit on the IQ score criterion for placement in programs for the mildly retarded, the number of children identified as mildly retarded increases; if the criterion is lowered, the number identified decreases. The variability across states in defining categorical types of exceptional children has contributed to the problem of establishing useful data bases upon which predictions can be made regarding the number of exceptional children within a district.

Until recently, most of the data sources on numbers of exceptional children have resulted from needs assessment studies conducted in specific geographic areas. Such investigations are useful within the geographic areas studied but must be examined carefully if generalizing the results to other areas. The reason for this caution relates to circumstances which cause handicapping conditions. Historically, more children have been identified as mildly mentally retarded in geographic areas characterized by unfavorable socioeconomic conditions. An outbreak of rubella likely would increase the numbers of children with hearing problems beyond the numbers identified in a geographic area similar in size but which did not experience such an epidemic.

Even the quality and level of special education services can influence the number of exceptional children. Several years ago the author was employed in a state education agency of a midwestern state. In a review of programs for the trainable mentally retarded, one community had far more children in TMR programs than would be expected based on any known estimates. The reason related to the community's long history of operating comprehensive services for the trainable mentally retarded. The community, in essence, attracted families seeking programs for their trainable children. The result was a dramatic increase in the number of trainable children in the population of that community.

Distinguishing Between Incidence and Prevalence

The literature frequently incorporates two similar terms when describing population studies on exceptional children: prevalence and incidence. The two terms have different meanings but, unfortunately, often are used interchangably, causing confusion for the person seeking accurate information. Simply stated, prevalence refers to the number of exceptional children *currently existing*; incidence refers to the number of children who, *at some time in their life, might be considered exceptional*. Obviously, the latter figure would be much higher; it also is more difficult to substantiate.

MacMillan (1977), in differentiating the terms as they apply to mental retardation, presents a useful illustration:

> To illustrate how the two distinct statistics can be derived, suppose you wanted to know how widespread chicken pox was in your neighborhood. You could go from door to door asking three questions: (a) How many children live here? (b) How many of them have had chicken pox within the past six months; (c) How many have ever had chicken pox? With these figures totaled for the whole neighborhood, you could derive two different statistics, one for incidence and one for prevalence.
>
> To determine the *prevalence* of chicken pox in the neighborhood you would divide the total number of *b*'s (those who had chicken pox within the past six months) by the total number of *a*'s (all children living at home) and multiply the answer by 100 to express it as a percentage.
>
> Prevalence, incidentally, does not always refer to a six-month period. For instance, you could have asked instead how many children had chicken pox within a year. The important thing to remember is that prevalence refers to a specific time frame.
>
> To determine *incidence* you would divide the total *c*'s (all children who have *ever* had chicken pox) by the total *a*'s (all children living at home) and multiply the answer by

100 to find the percentage of children in the neighborhood who have ever had chicken pox. Obviously this would be a higher figure than the one you got for prevalence (p. 60).

When school districts or state education agencies conduct needs assessment surveys, they generally establish prevalence rates rather than incidence rates. In the future, as local districts and state education agencies gain experience in implementing identification requests of PL 94-142, they will find the feasibility of establishing incidence rates much easier. The obvious advantage of having established prevalence rates for the main categorical types of exceptionalities is to guide districts in determining their success in identifying exceptional children. Even with defensible prevalence rates, however, a certain amount of variance always will exist among districts which will cause differences in the prevalence figures of exceptional children across districts. Nevertheless, improved prevalence rates will be helpful to districts in making program decisions.

Prevalence Data

Gearheart and Weishahn (1976) compiled a prevalence rate table based on a composite of state and federal reports (see Table 1.1). Although the table does not include the gifted nor does it report specific

Table 1.1
Prevalence of Handicapped Children in the United States

	Percent of population	Number of children ages 5 to 18*
Visually impaired (includes Blind)	0.1	55,000
Hearing impaired (includes Deaf)	0.6 to 0.8	330,000 to 440,000
Speech handicapped	3.5 to 5.0	1,925,000 to 2,750,000
Crippled and other health impaired	0.5	275,000
Emotionally disturbed	2.0 to 3.0	1,100,000 to 1,650,000
Mentally retarded (both educable and trainable)	2.5 to 3.0	1,375,000 to 1,650,000
Learning disabilities	2.0 to 4.0	1,100,000 to 2,200,000
	11.2 to 16.4	6,160,000 to 9,020,000

*Number of children based on 1978 population estimates. It must be concluded that it is difficult to know precisely the number of handicapped students, but this table is consistent with estimates provided by government agencies, such as the Bureau of Education for the Handicapped (United States Office of Education).

From: *The Handicapped Child in the Regular Classroom* by B. Gearheart and M. Weishahn. Copyright 1976 by the C. V. Mosby Co., St. Louis. Reprinted by permission.

data on the severely/profoundly handicapped, the prevalence rates and estimated numbers of children are representative of most estimates appearing in the literature. The range in prevalence figures includes the lowest percent usually reported.

Several states required districts to conduct a census of handicapped children before passage of PL 94-142 even though no national requirement dictated this effort. Now, PL 94-142 requires that each handicapped child be identified and that districts report data on handicapped children served. Section 121a.751 of PL 94-142 states:

Sec. 121a.751   Annual report of children served—information required in the report.
    (a) In its report, the State educational agency shall include a table which shows:
    (1) The number of handicapped children receiving special education and related services on October 1 and on February 1 of that school year, and the average of the numbers for those two dates;
    (2) The number of those handicapped children within each disability category, as defined in the definition of "handicapped children" in § 121a.5 of Subpart A; and
    (3) The number of those handicapped children within each of the following age groups:
    (i) Three through five:
    (ii) Six through seventeen; and
    (iii) Eighteen through twenty-one.
    (b) A child must be counted as being in the age group corresponding to his or her age on the date of the count: October 1 or February 1, as the case may be.
    (c) The State educational agency may not report a child under more than one disability category.
    (d) If a handicapped child has more than one disability, the State educational agency shall report that child in accordance with the following procedure:
    (1) A child who is both deaf and blind must be reported as "deaf-blind."
    (2) A child who has more than one disability (other than a deaf-blind child) must be reported as "multihandicapped."
(20 U.S.C. 1411(a) (3); 1411(a) (5) (A) (ii); 1418(b).)

The reason for this requirement relates to compliance with the mandatory provision of the law requiring all handicapped children and youth to be served. The number served also provides the basis for allocating federal funds to states and local districts. Because of the financial implications, an additional element of the section warrants mention—the restriction that a child with more than one disability can be reported only once. This "nonduplicated" provision in the regulation is argued by some school administrators to be unduly restrictive. If a child needs the services of both a resource room teacher and a speech clinician, the child is receiving two services, and the costs increase accordingly. Thus, they would argue that the child in this example should be counted twice. The situation is even more pronounced in the case of the severely/profoundly handicapped, who generally need several services. The above restriction, of course, results in lower prevalence rates.

Data are not available for accurate comparisons between actual counts resulting from PL 94-142 and surveys conducted previously under similar conditions, although this will be possible in the future. Comparisons, however, can be made based on estimated prevalence data reported in previous years. The 1976 Annual Report of the National Advisory Committee on the Handicapped contains data on the estimated number of handicapped children served and not served in the 1975-76 school year (see Table 1.2).

The Bureau of Education for the Handicapped/U.S. Office of Education, in reporting 1976-77 data derived from reports received from states on implementation of PL 94-142 and PL 89-313, offers an interesting comparision (Table 1.3) with estimated data in the above report of the National Advisory Committee on the Handicapped.

The data compiled in Table 1.3 for 1976-77 include children served between the ages of 3 and 21, whereas the 1975-76 data of Table 1.2 are reported on children served between the ages of 0-19. The 1975-76 report estimated that 4,310,000 handicapped children between the ages

Table 1.2
Estimated Number of Handicapped Children Served and Unserved
By Type of Handicap (1975-76 School Year)

	1975-76 Served (Projected)	1975-76 Unserved	Total Hand. Child. Served & Unserved	% Served	% Unserved
Total Age 0-19	4,310,000	3,577,000	7,887,000	55%	45%
Total Age 6-19	3,860,000	2,840,000	6,700,000	58%	42%
Total Age 0-5	450,000	737,000	1,187,000	38%	62%
Speech Impaired	2,020,000	273,000	2,293,000	88%	12%
Mentally Retarded	1,350,000	157,000	1,507,000	90%	10%
Learning Disabled	260,000	1,706,000	1,966,000	13%	87%
Emotionally Disturbed	255,000	1,055,000	1,310,000	19%	81%
Crippled & Other Health Impaired	255,000	73,000	328,000	78%	22%
Deaf	45,000	4,000	49,000	92%	8%
Hard of Hearing	66,000	262,000	328,000	20%	80%
Visually Handicapped	43,000	23,000	66,000	65%	35%
Deaf-Blind & Other Multi-Handicapped	16,000	24,000	40,000	40%	60%

From: *The Unfinished Revolution: Education for the Handicapped* (1976 annual report by the National Advisory Committee on the Handicapped to the U.S. Department of Health, Education and Welfare/Office of Education).

of 0-19 were served. The actual count on the 1976-77 school year reported 3,721,808 children between the ages of 6 and 21 receiving special education services. The difference in age range precludes a direct comparison, but the count reported in 1976-77 clearly is lower than the estimates reported in 1975-76.

One might question the validity of the 1975-76 estimates. Another explanation (and probably more plausible) relates to the need for more systematic reporting procedures by local districts and state educational agencies. Another factor which may have contributed to the difference is the issue of the nonduplicated count, previously discussed. Most estimates of prevalence consider the need of an individual child for service as a single entity and do not take into account whether or not the same child needs more than one type of service.

An examination of prevalence data reported by the Bureau of Education for the Handicapped (1977) reveals contrasting differences among states in the percentages of children reported as receiving special education services. For example, using school ages 5-17 and the 1975

Table 1.3

Number of Children Receiving Special Education and Related Services by Reporting Category and Handicapping Condition

(1976-77 School Year)

| Handicapping Condition | Reporting Category[1] | | | Percent of Total Served |
	P.L. 89-313	P.L. 94-142	Total	
Speech Impaired	0	1,309,020	1,309,020	35.2
Mentally Retarded	131,487	840,257	971,744	26.1
Learning Disabled	0	799,593	799,593	21.5
Emotionally Disturbed	30,378	254,007	284,385	7.6
Other Health Impaired	16,107	125,449	141,556	3.8
Deaf and Hard of Hearing	27,522	62,222	89,744	2.4
Orthopedically Impaired (Crippled)	8,413	78,889	87,302	2.3
Visually Handicapped	9,925	28,539	38,464	1.0
Total	223,832	3,497,976	3,721,808	99.9[2]

[1] Children counted under P.L. 89-313 are excluded from the count under P.L. 94-142.
[2] The percentages do not total 100 because of rounding.

Note: The totals in Tables 1 and 2 vary slightly because of averaging and rounding operations in the tabulations.

From: Bureau of Education for the Handicapped/Office of Education, Washington, DC, 1977.

Table 1.4
Handicapped Children Reported for P.L. 94-142
as a Percentage of State Population

State	Percent of All Children[1]	Percent of School-Age Children[2]	State	Percent of All Children[1]	Percent of School-Age Children[2]
Alabama	4.05	5.99	Nevada	5.84	7.05
Alaska	5.85	7.24	New Hampshire	6.02	4.43
Arizona	6.19	7.74	New Jersey	5.58	7.96
Arkansas	3.58	4.98	New Mexico	3.44	4.72
California	4.61	6.75	New York	3.60	5.37
Colorado	5.29	7.30	North Carolina	4.76	7.13
Connecticut	5.60	8.13	North Dakota	3.50	5.33
Delaware	6.04	8.83	Ohio	3.95	5.99
Florida	4.99	6.38	Oklahoma	4.74	7.00
Georgia	4.77	6.85	Oregon	4.51	6.46
Hawaii	3.30	4.68	Pennsylvania	4.75	7.18
Idaho	5.13	6.93	Rhode Island	4.54	7.04
Illinois	5.25	7.84	South Carolina	6.73	9.92
Indiana	4.22	6.31	South Dakota	3.57	5.50
Iowa	4.83	7.20	Tennessee	6.85	10.05
Kansas	4.42	6.91	Texas	5.14	7.33
Kentucky	4.55	6.73	Utah	8.19	11.48
Louisiana	5.63	8.24	Vermont	2.43	3.52
Maine	6.10	8.65	Virginia	4.31	6.30
Maryland	5.56	7.94	Washington	5.47	8.11
Massachusetts	5.90	8.72	West Virginia	4.68	7.12
Michigan	4.15	6.16	Wisconsin	3.24	4.73
Minnesota	4.89	7.21	Wyoming	5.42	7.45
Mississippi	3.12	4.55	Dist. of Col.	2.52	4.31
Missouri	5.48	8.24	Puerto Rico	.82	1.14
Montana	3.03	4.35	Other*	3.82	5.25
Nebraska	4.57	6.78	Total	4.54	6.82

*American Samoa, Guam, Trust Territories, Virgin Islands

[1]Children 3 through 21 years old (1970 Census). This column is displayed on the map, Figure 1.5.

[2] Children 5 through 17 years old (1975 population estimates). This percentage indicates state status relative to the 12 percent ceiling of P.L. 94-142.

From: Bureau of Education for the Handicapped/Office of Education, Washington, DC, 1977.

population estimates, Utah reported the highest percentage of children served, 11.48. Vermont reported the lowest percentage served among the 50 states, 3.52. When the territories are included, Puerto Rico was the lowest at 1.14 percent. (See Table 1.4 for a comparison by state.)

A review of the map (Figure 1.5) reveals no particular pattern based on demographic factors. For example, the seven states reporting 6 percent or more children between the ages of 3 and 21 being served are similar demographically to many states reporting much lower percentages. The seven states reporting over 6 percent were Maine, New Hampshire, Delaware, South Carolina, Tennessee, Arizona, and Utah. Most of these states are rural and sparsely populated, but they are not substantially different demographically from New Mexico, Arkansas, North Dakota, South Dakota, or Wisconsin, all of which reported percentages less than 3.9 percent.

In view of the lack of experience in nationwide data collection using procedures required by PL 94-142, one may reasonably assume that the variance is related to local reporting procedures and to the current levels of programming for handicapped children and youth. As local districts comply with PL 94-142, both problems should be corrected.

EXCEPTIONAL CHILDREN FROM MINORITY GROUPS

Public education to date is regarded as having been generally ineffective in meeting the needs of children from minority groups. For a period of time early in the civil rights movement, the focus was on broader social issues as they affected the schools, but little attention was given to discrimination occurring in special education programs. Many of the practices employed by local districts in the referral process and placement of children in special education programs were obviously discriminatory. The view of Jones and Wilderson (1976) is representative of the criticism aimed at special education practices through the early 1970s.

From the perspective of minority group members, self-contained special classes were to be indicted on several counts, including but not limited to beliefs (a) that minority group children were overrepresented in special classes, particularly for the mentally retarded; (b) that assessment practices are biased; (c) that special education labels are stigmatizing; and (d) that teachers hold negative attitudes toward the potential of minority group children. These views, reinforced by professional special educators in some instances, have served to highlight for many minority parents and professionals the view that institutionalized racism is part and parcel of educational practice (p. 3).

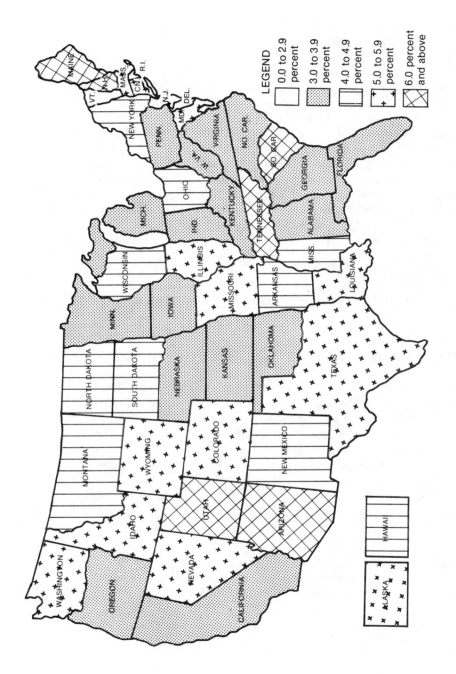

Figure 1.5 Handicapped Children Reported For P.L. 94-142 as a Percentage of All 3 Through 21 Year Old Residents

An initial response of students beginning the study of special education might be to search for an explanation to refute claims such as those voiced by Jones and Wilderson. If special education is intended to help exceptional children and youth develop to their fullest potential and to prepare them for productive lives as contributing adults, how could discriminatory practices evolve in the context of educating exceptional children? One would assume that the values and motivations of professionals making decisions on educational placement of exceptional children would be sufficient insurance to guard against practices of discrimination.

The answer to this dilemma obviously is not simple, but a plausible response centers on the influence of the school as a social institution and the status of special education during the 1950s and 1960s. Then special education was in a growth state, with major emphasis given to establishing special classes for the mildly mentally retarded. The dominant policy for dealing with children who presented management or serious instructional problems for the regular classroom teacher was to refer the child out. The result for the referred child was often a special education program and, in most cases, a special class. The situation was aggravated by regular classroom teachers' lack of understanding of culturally different children. Their perceptions of the culturally different child often were influenced by the child's language pattern, unresponsiveness to the teacher's teaching methods, low achievement, and assumed lack of interest in learning. These circumstances resulted in a high rate of minority children presumed to be in need of special education, or at least in need of being removed from the regular class.

The prevailing procedure for placement in special classes was for the teacher to initiate a referral. The school psychologist then would administer an individual intelligence test, and if the child's full scale IQ score was within a specified range set by the state, the child was determined eligible for a special class and so placed. As simplistic as this sounds, it was a general practice.

The due process procedures required by PL 94-142 did not exist. Few options were available to the child or the parents. The problem was aggravated by a lack of appropriate assessment instruments and the fact that placement in a special class tended to become a permanent assignment. Special educators were at a disadvantage in altering this practice. In most districts special education had little administrative influence, programs were underfinanced, and most public school special educators were committed to developing a broader base of special education programs.

Special educators presumably operated under the assumption that instruction offered through special classes was better for the child than that received in the regular class, where efforts were being initiated to refer the child out. Whether or not instruction was better for the culturally different child in a special class is not known—and maybe not even a relevant question. The fact remains that the culturally different child acquired an additional label which increased the problems he or she already was encountering in society. Of course, some minority group children have been appropriately placed in special classes, but the evidence is clear that generally they have been disproportionately represented in special classes, especially those for the mentally retarded.

The status of minority group children in decision making which has characterized special education placement practices in the past is illustrated clearly in the work of Mercer (1973) and Silberberg and Silberberg (1974). Mercer reported that the rate of placement of black children in special classes was three times higher than would be expected based on the proportion of blacks in the population. Jones and Wilderson (1976), in examining Mercer's data, analyzed the relationship of placements of anglos, blacks, and Mexican Americans; they found that black children were 7 times as likely and Mexican-American children 10 times as likely as Anglo children to be placed in special classes. From a different perspective, Silberberg and Silberberg observed that value judgments entered into decisions regarding the type of program offered to children with similar needs:

> If a black and a white child are not learning well, chances are that the black will be called *mentally retarded* and the white will be called *learning disabled*. The latter term has a much more positive image, suggesting that the learning disabled white child is average but needs extra remedial help to fulfill his potential. The black child is seen as inferior and needing much less of a challenge, including much less of the monies set aside for special programs (p. 56).

These perspectives acknowledge that discriminatory practices have occurred in the past and suggest that special educators, as part of a larger social institution, share in the responsibility. They imply, however, that the lack of responsiveness by special educators is due in part to the state-of-the-art surrounding special education during its early stages—i.e., the emphasis on program development, inadequate assessment measures, and general lack of administrative and fiscal influence.

In studying the relationship of special education to the broader issue of injustice for minority group children in public education, one must keep the time element in perspective. The criticisms or indictments of special education which appear in the literature generally focus on practices prevalent through the 1960s. These practices surfaced as major legal issues in the early 1970s, and in the middle 1970s were dealt with through state and federal legislative acts. Johnson's (1969) often-quoted statement appeared at a pivotal point in time:

> Special education is part of the arrangement for cooling out students. It has helped to erect a parallel system which permits relief of institutional guilt and humiliation stemming from the failure to achieve competence and effectiveness in the task given to it by society. Special education is helping the regular school maintain its spoiled identity when it creates special programs (whether psychodynamic or behavioral modification) for the "disruptive child" and the "slow learner," many of whom, for some strange reason, happen to be black and poor and live in the inner city (p. 245).

Individual special educators and professional groups in special education were overtly acknowledging discriminatory practices, and efforts to correct the situation were emerging. Unfortunately, advocating for change and setting policies and procedures is much easier than actually creating changes. The due process procedures of PL 94-142 and the influence of Section 504 of the Rehabilitation Act will have impact on the decisions and acts of individuals in the future, but this will require a process of educating teachers, administrators, and support personnel to alter the manner in which emotional and instructional needs of minority group children are met in special education programs.

Considerable progress has been made in setting the conditions necessary for change. The degree to which needs of exceptional children from minority groups are met in the future greatly depends on the efforts of special educators in:

1. Reducing the impact of labels,
2. Improving assessment instruments and procedures,
3. Preparing teachers to be responsive to the unique needs of exceptional children from minority groups, and more sensitive to their cultural heritage, and
4. Maintaining due process procedures which operationalize to protect the welfare of children.

Effects of Labels

Few topics in special education have received more attention in the literature than the effects of labels. Most special educators would agree that labels applied to exceptional children not only convey negative information about the labeled child, but tend to have a negative influence on the life of the child. Support for this position is drawn heavily from logic, observation, and from examining the progress of exceptional children, which historically has been less than justifiable, based on the investments made in special education. The degree to which insufficient progress has been due to effects of labeling versus other variables is still an open question, but, in the broader context of the exceptional child's life, a strong case can be made that the value of the label does not enhance the child's future, even though it provides the basis upon which special services are made available. MacMillan (1977), in reviewing research on the effects of labeling in the area of the mentally retarded, states:

> The evidence for and against classifying and labeling is complex and inconclusive. Although it does not demonstrate convincingly that calling attention to people with intellectual deficiencies by giving them special treatment is always a bad thing, the controversy over labeling should make us all more sensitive to its potential hazards: By labeling a person as retarded, we may place additional burdens on him that will make it more difficult for him to gain acceptance, or we may increase whatever feelings of depreciation he had without the label (p. 245).

In the case of the child from minority groups, the situation is compounded by the high probability of being mislabeled as exceptional.

Lessening the impact of labels in the future will require more than merely coming up with less noxious labels. As pointed out by Rivers, Henderson, Jones, Ladner, and Williams (1975), "New labels represent emerging forms of stereotyping, with many of the negative outcomes that characterize the older practices." What can be done is to shift from an emphasis on deficits to an emphasis on strengths in the process of assessment. This, combined with a conservative approach to placement of children in special programs and an improvement in the programs offered, could reduce the stigma traditionally identified with being labeled exceptional.

Assessment

The use of most standardized tests, particularly scales for measuring intelligence, has come under severe criticism when applied to children from minority groups. Although much of the criticism centers on the selection of items, representativeness of norms, and the influence of examiner's testing procedures, many test producers argue that many of the problems relate to tests being misused and inappropriately interpreted. Both perspectives probably are valid. The future demands improvement in design and standardization of assessment instruments and in training those who administer tests.

A more significant area of concern relates to the conceptualization of what constitutes appropriate assessment for purposes of educational programming. Assessment approaches currently receiving attention, and which hold promise, include criterion-referenced testing (Popham, 1971), domain-referenced testing (Hively & Reynolds, 1975), and pluralistic assessment (Mercer, 1975). Broadening the base of assessment approaches, improving design, and using norm-referenced tests will provide the options necessary for restructuring our assessment practices and improving instructional decisions. These changes, combined with the shift in placement and instructional decision making as a result of the IEP and due process requirements of PL 94-142, should result in more accurate placement decisions and more effective education for exceptional children from minority groups.

Teacher Effectiveness

Improvements in teacher effectiveness applied to exceptional children from minority groups must be couched in a generally improved instructional climate. This includes needed changes in assessment practices, changes in administrative and fiscal support, increased availability of instructional materials which reflect cultural differences among children, and changes in attitudes of children within the culture mix of the public schools.

At this stage in the movement toward improving instruction for children from minority groups, one cannot differentiate arbitrarily between changes needed in the behavior of teachers of exceptional children from minority groups from teachers generally. Changes must occur regardless of the minority child's educational placement or instructional needs and are applicable to all teachers and professionals within the school setting. Reference to techniques specific to areas of exceptionality will appear when appropriate in subsequent chapters.

Efforts to increase teacher responsiveness to the needs of children from minority groups have given primary attention to needs of the black child. Responses by teachers have a broad range. Some have adopted approaches which emphasize teaching coping skills. Others have emphasized intensive remediation programs. Some districts have established alternative schools. The "right" approach or the "right" emphasis remains to be determined. Johnson (1976) takes a rather strong view of the needs of black children.

The primary task for the black handicapped child is to master the skills of language, eliminate self-destructive behaviors, and to understand that he must become a source of knowledge which will improve his community. To do this, black educators must begin to embrace positively results-oriented techniques such as precision teaching with its foundation in learning theory, and become advocates for other teaching strategies which produce *academic* results in black children. The time has passed when rhetoric about "feelings" is acceptable. Discussions of process, expectations, and curriculum as a tool should continue; however, our overriding question must be: Does any of it raise achievement from where it was before the technique was applied? The major goal of any program addressed to black children must be to improve significantly the black student's ability to speak, read, write, *and think*. In the case of exceptional black children the major task is to provide them with the adaptive behaviors which will permit normalization of activities of daily living, the release of latent creativity, and provide a set of technical skills which will permit maximum independence in the community (p. 170).

One can generalize Johnson's position to the needs of all children from minority groups, including Mexican-Americans, American Indians, and Asian Americans. Having established priorities, however, doesn't answer the question of which teaching behaviors need to be changed and how the changes can be brought about. The most frequent teacher variable appearing in the literature relates to respect for individuals and their cultural backgrounds. If teachers understand a child's uniqueness, respect the child's individuality, and are familiar with the child's cultural background, they are in a better position to make instructional decisions and to establish an environment conducive to learning. To ignore the child's culture as a source of information and to make instructional decisions based only on assessment data and the child's educational history is to ignore information essential to sound instructional decisions.

To illustrate cultural differences, Pepper (1976) contrasts values of the American Indian with those of the dominant society (see Figure 1.6). Similar comparisons based on the cultural differences of blacks or Mexican-Americans also could be included. The decision to use the American Indian as an example relates only to the general lack of reference to the American Indian within special education literature.

Merely understanding cultural differences obviously is not sufficient, but it is a critical step in the process of designing instructional materials, structuring teaching activities, and maintaining rapport with students. It also provides the much needed base for research on teaching children from minority groups.

Due Process

The procedural aspects of due process in relation to PL 94-142 are discussed earlier in this chapter. The due process provisions are intended

Indian	*Dominant Society*
Wisdom of age and experience is respected. Elders are revered by their people.	Older people are made to feel incompetent and rejected.
Excellence is related to a contribution to the group—not to personal glory.	Competition and striving to win or to gain status is emphasized.
Cooperation is necessary for group survival.	Competition is necessary for individual status and prestige.
Children participate in adult activities.	Adults participate in children's activities.
Family life includes the extended family.	Family life includes the nuclear family.
Time is present oriented—this year, this week—NOW—a resistance to planning for the future.	Time is planning and saving for the future.
Clocktime is whenever people are ready —when everyone arrives.	Clocktime is exactly that.
Work is when necessary for the common good. Whatever Indian people have, they share. What is mine is ours.	Work is from 9-5 (specified time) and to obtain material possessions and to save for the future. What is mine stays mine.
Good relationships and mutual respect are emphasized.	Success, progress, possession of property and rugged individualism are valued above mutual respect and maintaining good relationships.
People express their ideas and feelings through their actions.	People express themselves and attempt to impress others through speech.
People conform to nature.	People try to dominate and desecrate nature.
Early childhood and rearing practices are the responsibility of the kin group.	Early childhood and rearing practices are the responsibility of the nuclear family.
Native religion never imposes or proselytizes.	Religious groups proselytize, coerce and impose their beliefs on others.
Land gives the Indian his identity, his religion and his life. It is not to be sold, not owned, but used by all.	Land is for speculation, for prestige, to be owned, sold, or torn up.
Going to school is necessary to gain knowledge. Excelling for fame is looked down upon by the Indian.	Going to school is necessary to gain knowledge and to compete for grades.
Indians have a shorter childhood, and the male is held to be a responsible person at the age of 16.	Childhood is extended, and the male is held to be a responsible person at the age of 21.
People usually are judged by what they do.	People usually are judged by their credentials.

Figure 1.6   A Comparison of Values

From: "Teaching the American Indian Child in Mainstreaming Settings," by F. C. Pepper, in *Mainstreaming and the Minority Child* (R. L. Jones, Editor), published by the Leadership Training Institute/Special Education, Minneapolis, 1976.

to provide protective safeguards for all children, but they hold particular meaning for the future of minority group children. If effectively implemented, they should minimize the chances of inappropriate placement and, in essence, mislabeling. They also should serve as a primary source of influence in improving instructional programming. Above all, they provide a visible target for advocacy.

The needs of exceptional children from minority groups represent a major concern for the future. Their history is linked closely with events in the history of special education which are serving to change the future of all exceptional children.

SUMMARY

Although a pattern of progress in behalf of exceptional children has been developing since the turn of the century, the decade of the 1970s clearly represents *the period of significant achievement.* Advocacy groups emerged as social and legislative forces, and rights of the handicapped became a major public issue. Questions of rights and issues related to discrimination were settled in the courts. Federal and state governments responded by passing legislation to assure the future of exceptional children and youth. The landmark pieces of federal legislation included PL 93-380, PL 94-142, and Section 504 of the Rehabilitation Act of 1973. The outgrowth of this era has influenced public education in this country greatly. The changes affect all children, as well as the roles of most educators.

The most significant effort was the mandating of a free and appropriate public education for all handicapped children. Now children cannot be excluded from school because they are "too difficult to teach" or because they require special transportation provisions to get them to school. The manner in which educational needs of exceptional children are met also is changing. The self-contained special class is no longer the preferred placement; the emphasis has shifted to the principle of least restrictive environment, with the regular class suggested as the preferred setting for most exceptional children. Public schools are expanding the array of instructional options available to exceptional children in an attempt to provide the most appropriate program and, in turn, the least restrictive alternative.

Closely related to the changing philosophy in educating exceptional children has been the establishment of due process procedures and the requirement of an individualized education program (IEP) for all handicapped children. The due process procedures offer the handicapped and their families much needed protective safeguards; the IEP is the primary vehicle for improving education for exceptional children. A particularly important element of the IEP is the required involvement of parents and/or guardians in instructional planning.

The impact of the 1970s will be far-reaching. Not only are educational practices changing, but the roles of professionals too are changing. This is particularly true in the public schools. Traditional roles of many specialists are being redefined, and new roles are being established. The allocation or, in some cases, reallocation of fiscal resources is becoming evident at the local, state, and federal levels to enhance full implementation of the legislated changes.

Paralleling the progress made through litigation and legislation, a major effort by the special education profession has been to develop instructional technology, increase the supply of trained personnel, and to validate organizational models for the delivery of special education services. Progress in each of these areas has been significant. A review of the current literature reflects advancements by local districts and state educational agencies in establishing accountability systems for monitoring offerings and effectiveness of special education services. The literature also contains examples of models or constructs such as those by Deno (1970), Chaffin (1975), Dunn (1973), and Adelman (1971) to aid districts in their instructional and placement decisions regarding exceptional children.

Definitions continue to receive attention; however, the emphasis appears to be beginning to shift from formulating definitions of exceptional children solely for serving as eligibility criteria for placement to an emphasis on establishing definitions as a basis for instructional planning. Exceptional children are defined in this chapter from the perspective of the learner, with primary attention given to appropriateness of instructional options given information based on learner characteristics. Such an approach to definitions emphasizes learner strengths as well as deficits and requires that learner characteristics be considered in an instructional context. It also minimizes the assumed negative effects of labels.

The status of handicapped children from minority groups came under careful scrutiny during the 1970s. Placement practices have been altered to correct the circumstances which resulted in disproportionate numbers of children and youth from minority groups being placed in special education programs. The needs for nondiscriminatory assessment instruments and for more consideration of cultural differences in instructional planning are emerging as major educational issues.

Accomplishments of the 1970s have made the study of exceptional children an essential element in professional preparation of all educators. No longer are the characteristics and needs of exceptional children a concern only to their parents and to special educators. School administrators' and regular class teachers now share in the responsibility for educating exceptional children. The specialness of special education is becoming more special—but hopefully less visible. For exceptional children and their families, the era of the 1970s represents an historical period. The ground rules for the 1980s clearly have been set.

REFERENCES

Adamson, G., & Van Etten, G. Zero reject model revisited: A workable alternative, *Exceptional Children*, 1972, *38*, 735-738.

Adelman, H. S. Learning problems, Part 1: An interactional view of causality. *Academic Therapy*, 1970-71, *6* (2), 117-123.

Adelman, H. S. Learning problems, Part 2: A sequential and hierarchical approach to identification and correction. *Academic Therapy*, 1971, *6* (3).

Baker, H. J. *Introduction to exceptional children.* New York: Macmillan Co., 1953, p. 12.

Beery, I. *Models for mainstreaming.* San Rafael, CA: Dimensions Publishing Co., 1972.

Birch, J. W. *Mainstreaming: Educable mentally retarded children in regular classes.* Minneapolis: University of Minnesota Leadership Training Institute/Special Education, 1974.

Blatt, B. The physical, personality, and academic status of children who are mentally retarded attending special classes as compared with children who are mentally retarded attending regular classes. *American Journal of Mental Deficiency*, 1958, 62.

Bureau of Education for the Handicapped. *BEH data notes.* Washington, DC: September 1977.

Chaffin, J. D. Will the real "mainstreaming" program please stand up! (or . . . should Dunn have done it?) In E. L. Meyen, G. A. Vergason, & R. J. Whelan (Eds.), *Alternatives for teaching exceptional children.* Denver: Love Publishing Co., 1975.

Council for Exceptional Children. *An analysis of categorical definitions, diagnostic methods, diagnostic criteria, and personnel utilization in the classification of handicapped children.* Discussion draft done pursuant to a grant from the Bureau of Education for the Handicapped, U.S. Office of Education, August 1977. (a)

Council for Exceptional Children. *Insight.* Government Report, December 1977, Volume 12. (b)

Cowan, P.A. Special class vs. grade groups for subnormal pupils. *School and Society*, 1948, *48*.

Deno, E. Special education as developmental capital. *Exceptional Children*, 1970, *37* (3), 229-237.

Dunn, L. M. (Ed.). *Exceptional children in the schools* (1st ed.). New York: Holt, Rinehart & Winston, 1963, p. 37.

Dunn, L. M. Special education for the mildly retarded — Is it justified? *Exceptional children*, 1968, *35*, 5-22.

Dunn, L. M. (Ed.). *Exceptional children in the schools* (2nd ed.). New York: Holt, Rinehart & Winston, 1973, pp. 7, 38, 39.

Federal Register (Part IV). Washington, DC: Department of Health, Education & Welfare, August 1977, *42*, (163).

Gearheart, B. R., & Weishahn, M. W. *The handicapped child in the regular classroom.* St. Louis: The C. V. Mosby Co., 1976.

Goldstein, H., Arkell, C., Ashcroft, S.C., Hurley, O.L., & Lilly, M. S. Schools. In N. Hobbs (Ed.), *Issues in the classification of children.* San Francisco: Jossey-Bass, 1975, p. 55.

Goldstein, H., Moss, J., & Jordan, L. *The efficacy of special class training on the development of mentally retarded children* (Cooperative Research Project No. 619). Urbana, IL: Institute for Research on Exceptional Children, 1965.

Goodman, L. V. A bill of rights for the handicapped. *American Education*, 1976, *12*(6), 6-8.

Hively, N., & Reynolds, M. C. (Eds.). *Domain-referenced testing in special education*. Minneapolis: Leadership Training Institute/Special Education, 1975.

Irvin, T. *Conference summary of Public Law 94-142*. Washington, DC: Littlejohn Assoc., 1976.

Johnson, J. L. Special education in the inner city: A change for the future or another means for cooling the mark off? *Journal of Special Education*, 1969, *3*, 241-251.

Johnson, J. L. Mainstreaming black children. In R. L. Jones (Ed.), *Mainstreaming and the minority child*. Minneapolis: Leadership Training Institute/Special Education, 1976.

Johnson, R. A. Models for alternative programming: A perspective. In E. L. Meyen, G. A. Vergason, & R. J. Whelan (Eds.), *Alternatives for teaching exceptional children*. Denver: Love Publishing Co., 1975.

Jones, R. L., & Wilderson, F. B. Mainstreaming and the minority child: An overview of issues and a perspective. In R. L. Jones (Ed.), *Mainstreaming and the minority child*. Reston, VA: Council for Exceptional Children, 1976.

Kansas State Department of Education. *State Plan for Fiscal Year 1978, Special Education*. Topeka, KS: Approved by State Board of Education, October 1977.

Kaufman, M. J., Gottlieb, J., Agard, J. A., & Kukic, M. D. Mainstreaming: Toward an explication of the construct. In E. L. Meyen, G. A. Vergason, & R. J. Whelan (Eds.), *Alternatives for teaching exceptional children*. Denver: Love Publishing Co., 1975.

Kirk, S. A. *Educating exceptional children*. Boston: Houghton-Mifflin, 1972.

Kotin, L., & Eager, N. *Due process in special education: A legal analysis*. Cambridge, MA: Research Institute for Educational Problems, Inc., 1977.

La Vor, M. L. Federal legislation for exceptional persons: A history. In F. J. Weintraub, A. Abeson, J. Ballard, & M. L. La Vor (Eds.), *Public policy and the education of exceptional children*. Reston, VA: The Council for Exceptional Children, 1976.

Lilly, M. S. Special education: A tempest in a teapot. *Exceptional Children*. 1970, *37*, 43-49.

MacMillan, D. L. *Mental retardation in school and society*. Boston: Little, Brown, 1977.

Martin, E. *Insight*. Reston, VA: Council for Exceptional Children, 12, December 19, 1977, p. 5.

Mercer, J. R. *Labeling the mentally retarded*. Berkeley: University of California Press, 1973.

Mercer, J. R. Cross-cultural evaluation of exceptionality. In E. L. Meyen, G. A. Vergason, & R. J. Whelan (Eds.), *Alternatives for exceptional children*. Denver: Love Publishing Co., 1975.

National Advisory Committee on the Handicapped. *The unfinished revolution: Education for the handicapped* (1976 Annual Report to U.S. Dept. of Health, Education & Welfare). Washington, DC: U.S. Government Printing Office, 1976.

Pepper, F. C. Teaching the American Indian child in mainstreaming settings. In R. L. Jones (Ed.), *Mainstreaming and the minority child*, Minneapolis: Leadership Training Institute/Special Education, 1976, p. 133-158.

Pertch, C. F. *A comparative study of the progress of subnormal pupils in the grades and in special classes*. New York: Teachers College, Columbia University, 1936.

Popham, W. J. (Ed.). Criterion-referenced measurement: An introduction. Englewood Cliffs, NJ: *Educational Technology*, 1971.

Rand Corporation. *Services for handicapped youth: A program overview*. Santa Monica, CA: Author, 1973.

Rivers, W. L., Henderson, D. M., Jones, R. J., Ladner, J. A., & Williams, R. L. Mosaic of labels for black children. In N. Hobbs (Ed.), *Issues in the classification of children*. San Francisco: Jossey-Bass, 1975, p. 222.

Rosenthal, R., & Jacobson, L. *Pygmalion in the classroom*. New York: Holt, Rinehart, & Winston, 1968.

Scriven, M. Some issues in the logic and ethics of mainstreaming. *Minnesota Education*, 1976, 2 (2), 61-67.

Silberberg, N. E., & Silberberg, M. C. *Who speaks for the child?* Springfield, IL: Charles C. Thomas, 1974.

Weintraub, F. J., Abeson, A., Ballard, J., & La Vor, M. L. (Eds.). *Public policy and the education of exceptional children.* Reston, VA: The Council for Exceptional Children, 1976, p. 103.

RESOURCE GUIDE

Issues/Policies

Jordan, J. B. *Exceptional child education at the bicentennial: A parade of progress.* Reston, VA: Council for Exceptional Children, 1976.

Jordan, J. B. (Ed.). *Teacher, please don't close the door.* Reston, VA: Council for Exceptional Children, 1976.

Meyen, E. L., Vergason, G. A., & Whelan, R. J. (Eds.). *Alternatives for teaching exceptional children.* Denver: Love Publishing Co., 1975.

Reynolds, M. C. (Ed.). *Report on the conference on special education in school system decentralization.* Minneapolis: University of Minnesota Leadership Training Institute/Special Education, 1975.

Spicker, H. H., Anastasiow, N. J., & Hodges, W. L. (Eds.). *Children with special needs: Early development and education.* University of Minnesota: Leadership Training Institute/Special Education, 1976.

Warfield, G. J. (Ed.). *Mainstream currents.* Reston, VA: Council for Exceptional Children, 1974.

Program/Trends

Bernstein, C. D., Kirst, M. W., Hartman, W. T., & Marshall, R. S. *Financing educational services for the handicapped.* Reston, VA: Council for Exceptional Children, 1976.

Blatt, B. Public policy and the education of children with special needs. *Exceptional Children,* 1972, *38,* 537-545.

Blatt, B. *Souls in extremis — an anthology on victims and victimizers.* Boston: Allyn & Bacon, Inc., 1973.

Gilhool, T. K. Education: An inalienable right. *Exceptional Children,* 1973, *39,* 597-609.

Hobbs, N. *The futures of children.* San Francisco: Jossey-Bass Publishers, 1975.

Jones, R. L. (Ed.). *Mainstreaming and the minority child.* Reston, VA: Council for Exceptional Children, 1976.

Johnson, R. A., Gross, J. C., & Weatherman, R. F. (Eds.). *The right to education mandate.* University of Minnesota: Audio-Visual Library Service, 1973.

Lippman, L., & Goldberg, I. I. *Right to education: Anatomy of the Pennsylvania case and its implications for exceptional children.* New York: Teachers College Press, 1973.

Mental Health Law Project. *Basic rights of the mentally handicapped.* Washington, DC: Author, 1973.

Wolfensberger, W. *The principle of normalization in human services.* Toronto: National Institute on Mental Retardation, 1972.

Exceptional Children/Characteristics

Blatt, B., Biklen, D., & Bogdan, R. *An alternative textbook in special education.* Denver: Love Publishing Co., 1977.

Dunn, L. M. (Ed.). *Exceptional children in the schools.* New York: Holt, Rinehart, & Winston, 1973.

Gardner, W. I. *Learning and behavior characteristics of exceptional children and youth.* Boston: Allyn & Bacon, Inc., 1977.

Haring, N. G. (Ed.). *Behavior of exceptional children.* Columbus, OH: Charles E. Merrill Publishing Co., 1974.

Haring, N. G., & Brown, L. J. (Eds.). *Teaching the severely handicapped.* New York: Grune & Stratton, Inc., 1976.

Hewett, F. M., with Forness, S. R. *Education of exceptional learners.* Boston: Allyn & Bacon, Inc., 1977.

Kirk, S. A. *Educating exceptional children.* Boston: Houghton Mifflin Co., 1972.

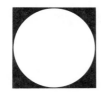

2 The Least Restrictive Environment: A Major Philosophical Change

Martin J. Kaufman and Linda G. Morra
Bureau of Education for the Handicapped

Few disciplines have experienced philosophical changes as significant as the movement toward the principle of *least restrictive environment* in educating exceptional children and youth. To many, the trend represents a reversal of practices argued for and maintained by special educators prior to the 1970s. To others, it represents gaining understanding into the *real* needs of exceptional children and youth. Evolvement of the least restrictive environment (LRE) principle in relation to other legislated practices was discussed in Chapter 1. Because it represents a philosophy of human service and thus is much more than a practice or a service option, this principle warrants particular attention by beginning students in special education.

Chapter 2 is included to lend further insight into the principle of least restrictive environment through discussion of its historical origin, its intended meaning, and implications for the futures of exceptional children and youth. Particular attention is given to specific events concerning care and treatment of the mentally retarded which have served to influence public policy in this area. The discussion of least restrictive environments builds on concepts introduced in Chapter 1 but is presented in an independent manner to accent the importance of the principle and its significance as a philosophical change from the past.

Educational placement and instructional programming for the handicapped have long been considered as highly related or even synonymous concepts—in other words, that the various educational placement alternatives for the handicapped systematically provide the necessary types of instructional programs. A growing recognition of the heterogeneity of learning needs of the handicapped, the need to provide a comprehensive continuum of services for the handicapped, and a clouding of opinion as to what should be taught to the handicapped, however, present difficulties in differentiating among alternative service programs for the handicapped. In the absence of a strong consensus on the appropriateness and effectiveness of different curricula with different handicapped children, individual teachers have too often been left to define instructional programs based on their experience, philosophies, and varying needs of children placed in their classrooms. Thus, placement and programming reveal little correspondence. In this context of clearly different educational settings and not merely as differentiated instructional programming, we consider and direct attention to the concept of *least restrictive environment* (LRE).

HISTORY AND IMPLICATIONS OF
THE LEAST RESTRICTIVE ENVIRONMENT CONCEPT

The least restrictive environment concept requires that educators specify educational goals and instructional objectives for handicapped children and youth based upon their individual needs. After the instructional program for the student has been identified, the educational setting for program implementation must be selected. This setting is to be the least restrictive—or most normal appropriate—based on the needs of the handicapped child.

The least restrictive environment is a legal concept, referred to in the courts as the *doctrine of the least restrictive alternative.* Within the courts, the doctrine of the least restrictive alternative was applied to other areas long before it was used in education. The 1918 case of *McCullough* v. *Maryland* contained the kernels from which the concept developed. In this case, which concerned the right of the federal government to establish a national bank, the court stated that regulations affecting the citizens of a state should be both "appropriate" and "plainly adapted" to the end sought. Although the exact wording has differed in court cases since then, the notion of least restrictive alternative continued to be found in cases that centered on the conflict between government interests and personal liberties.

In the case of *Shelton* v. *Tucker* (1960), the doctrine of the least restrictive alternative was applied to education. *Shelton* v. *Tucker* challenged the legality of an Arkansas statute which required every teacher as a condition of employment in a state-supported school or college, to file an affidavit listing every organization to which he or she had belonged or regularly contributed within the preceding five years. In striking down the statute, the Supreme Court stated that the statute's interference with freedom of association went far beyond what might be justified in the exercise of the state's legitimate inquiry into the fitness and competency of its teachers; "less drastic means for achieving the same basic purpose" could be found. That is, the purpose should be served with as little imposition on the individual as possible.

The late 1960s and early 1970s were characterized by a wave of litigation concerning the right of all children to equal educational opportunity. The well-known case of *Brown* v. *Board of Education* (1954) became the cornerstone for application of the least restrictive alternative to the education of handicapped children. In *Brown*, the Supreme Court established that the concept and practice of segregation has no place within public education. Following this case, nonracial educational inequities were struck down by the lower courts. According to Burgdorf (1975), the lower courts heard testimony from various professionals in the field of education who stated that separating children into isolated groups and assigning labels to them as "mentally deficient" or even "exceptional" have a stigmatizing effect upon those children. In *Wolf* v. *Legislature of the State of Utah* (1969), for example, the court ruled that:

> A sense of inferiority and not belonging affects the motivation of a child to learn. Segregation, even though perhaps well intentioned, under the apparent sanction of law and state authority, has a tendency to retard the educational, emotional and mental development of the children.

While addressing public school exclusion, *Wolf* brought together the concepts of stigma and segregation.

The case of the *Pennsylvania Association for Retarded Children* (PARC) vs. *Commonwealth of Pennsylvania* (1971) went beyond the right of children to a public school education; it expanded rights of mentally retarded children to include an equal educational opportunity and due process. This is the first case to apply the least restrictive alternative to the education of handicapped children. The court stated:

> It is the Commonwealth's obligation to place each mentally retarded child in a free, public program of education and training appropriate to the child's capacity, within the context of presumption that, among the alternative programs of education and training required by statute to be available, placement in a regular public school class is preferable to placement in special public school classes, is preferable to placement in any other type of program of education and training.

PARC was followed shortly by *Mills* v. *Board of Education of District of Columbia* (1972). In *Mills*, the court in effect ordered that the same principles espoused in the PARC decision apply to all handicapped children in the District of Columbia. These cases thus established the principle of least drastic educational placement of handicapped children. That is, given two or more alternative educational settings, the handicapped child should be placed in the most normal setting appropriate, with as little interference with the normal educational process as possible.

Further, the *PARC* and *Mills* cases implied the need for providing a continuum of alternative placements. Alternatives were stated as placement in regular public school class with ancillary services, placement in special public school classes, and other placements such as separate schools or institutions. Order of preference was specified by degree of restrictiveness or, in other words, the extent to which the educational placement alternative differed from normal placement in a regular educational class. Neither the *PARC* nor *Mills* cases stated that every child requiring special education services must receive a program in the regular classroom environment. As explained by Burgdorf (1975), "The law has never stated that equal treatment means identical treatment for different types of persons" (p.11). The law, however, does mean that "there is a presumption that children should be in regular classes" (p.14), and if they are not in regular classes, there have to be good reasons why they are not.

Following the *PARC* and *Mills* cases, the litigative movement accelerated, along with passage of state-level special education legislation. States' needs for funds to implement such legislation, as well as activities of parents and other advocates for handicapped individuals, were major factors in increasing the role of federal government in the education of handicapped children. Public Law 94-142, the Education for All Handicapped Children Act of 1975, can be viewed as the cumulative result of past state and federal legislative efforts to provide equal educational opportunities to all handicapped children.

The major objectives of PL 94-142, as discussed in Chapter 1, are to assure that all handicapped children are provided a free appropriate public education, to ensure that the rights of handicapped children and their parents or guardians are protected, and to assist states to provide and evaluate services to handicapped children. The law includes, as part of its definition of an appropriate education, placement in the least restrictive environment. Section 612 (5)(B) of the law requires each state to establish procedures to assure that, to the maximum extent appropriate, handicapped children, including children in public or private institutions or other care facilities, are educated with children who are not handicapped. Further, removal of handicapped children from the regular educational environment to separate classes, separate schools, and other more restrictive environments is to occur only when the nature or severity of the handicap is such that education in regular classes with the use of supplementary aids and services cannot be achieved satisfactorily.

While the least restrictive environment concept is clear, its implementation is not as straightforward as it might first appear. Terms such as "appropriateness," "nature or severity of the handicap," and "satisfactory education in regular classes with supplementary assistance" are subject to value judgments and thus are likely to result in different interpretations. As a starting point, one might analyze PL 94-142, its accompanying regulations, and various remarks made by Edwin Martin, Deputy Commissioner of the Bureau of Education for the Handicapped, related to implementation of the least restrictive environment provision.

Three major points can be made.

First, PL 94-142 assumes that *handicapped learners are heterogeneous in learning needs.* The implementing regulations clearly state that the least restrictive environment is to be individually determined for handicapped children. Martin (1977) amplifies this requirement.

> The appropriate educational placement for individual children remains, of course, a matter for local determination. The new policy, however, does seem to rule out blanket judgments by school officials that all children with a particular kind of handicapping condition (the educable retarded, for example) shall be educated in self-contained classrooms, or that all handicapped youngsters should be placed in special schools. Instead, separate judgments must be made for each child, and these judgments must be based on an analysis of that child's individual needs (p.13).

The need for individual determination of educational placements also would rule out blanket judgments involving the placement of handicapped learners into regular classes even though regular classes are the preferred placement. Placement in the least restrictive environment that is appropriate should be determined individually for each handicapped child.

The second point is closely related and also rests on the assumption that handicapped children are heterogeneous in learning needs. Under PL 94-142, *an individualized education program (IEP) is to be developed for each handicapped child in need of special education and related services.* The IEP, as discussed in Chapter 3, is a written document, and among its required contents are a statement of annual goals and short-term objectives for the child, as well as a statement of the special education and related services to be received by the child and the extent to which the child will participate in the regular classroom. *The IEP refers only to that portion of the child's education which can be considered special education.*

PL 94-142 regulations specify that the child's educational placement is based on his or her IEP. According to that child's needs, individual goals and objectives are specified. After the special education instructional program for the child has been identified, the educational setting in which the program will be implemented must be selected.

Martin (1977) elaborates on this process:

> First, judgments about placement must be made on the basis of the individual child, considering not only the characteristics of the educational problem involved but the specific objectives of an instructional program developed to meet that particular child's needs. The procedure calls for an evaluation of the particular needs of a given child and then the careful structure of a program with stated objectives specifically designed to meet those needs. The program in turn implies the development of a strategy—perhaps involving various instructional approaches and settings—for achieving those objectives (p.14).

The outcome of these requirements is the selection of a setting for service delivery to an individual child rather than selection of an educational program (such as an EMR program) that has goals for a theoretically homogeneous group of children. This situation perhaps stemmed from the increasing difficulty of educators to define what was "special" about special education classes. Also, focusing on individual needs resulted from recognition of heterogeneity among populations of handicapped children previously thought to be homogeneous. Finally, variations within settings in instructional programming for the handicapped make it impossible to consider educational settings and instructional programming as synonymous concepts.

The third point is that PL 94-142 implies a *continuum of settings for service delivery to handicapped children.* The continuum is hierarchical and is based on *temporal integration* or, in other words, the amount of contact the setting provides handicapped children with nonhandicapped peers. PL 94-142, of course, presents the preferred environment as placement in a regular classroom with the use of supplementary aids and/or services. The statement required in IEP documents describing the extent to which the handicapped child will participate in the regular classroom makes it evident that this placement must be considered. Although PL 94-142 does not rank other service delivery settings in increasing order of restrictiveness, other settings are identified as self-contained special education classrooms, separate day schools, and residential schools or institutions. Based upon the dimension of temporal integration, one can assume that special classes are preferable to separate day schools, and that separate day schools are preferable to residential schools or institutions. The hierarchical service delivery model further assumes that a child's degree of learning disability may be remediated and may change over time. Such change should be reflected in placements in settings over time from more to less restrictive environments.

Educational placement and instructional programming for the handicapped no longer can be considered as synonymous concepts. With development of the least restrictive concept, the heterogeneity of handicapped learners has achieved widespread recognition, and placement has become an individualized process. The goal has become that of selecting a setting for service delivery to a child which represents the least restrictive or most normal setting appropriate for the child based upon his or her individualized education program. Settings for service delivery are considered more or less restrictive based on the temporal integration possible with nonhandicapped peers. Although the regular classroom is the preferred setting and must be considered, the regular classroom setting is not the least restrictive environment appropriate for all handicapped children;

over time, however, children not in the preferred setting should be able to move from more to less restrictive environments.

PAST AND CURRENT PLACEMENT DETERMINATIONS

Many special education service delivery system alternatives were available prior to PL 94-142. These delivery systems typically are presented as continua, with settings ordered by degree of restrictiveness. Usually, the least restrictive environment on the continuum is regular classroom placement with no direct services to the child but consultation offered to the regular classroom teacher by a special education professional. The most restrictive setting usually is considered to be a residential facility which offers little or no contact with nonhandicapped peers.

Special educators have not always agreed, however, on the number of or basis for interim positions on the continuum. In addition to temporal integration, variables such as the directness, intensity, duration of the services provided, and/or the type of instruction offered have been considered (e.g., Deno, 1970; Bruininks & Rynders, 1971; Chaffin, 1975). The models by Deno (1970) and Chaffin (1975) discussed in Chapter 1 are considered as fairly representative of the models developed and increasingly implemented by our nation's schools. Only the historically major setting distinctions are discussed here. These are residential schools (including institutions), special education day schools, special education self-contained classrooms, and regular classroom plus resource room service. For each of these four settings, the historical review includes the rationale for creation of each alternative, and programming practices within each setting as they relate to the principle of least restrictive environments.

Residential Schools and Institutions

The rationale for placing handicapped children and youth in residential schools or institutions has at various times included the following explanations: (1) a need for separation from society; (2) a need for domicile living; (3) a need for intensively supervised living and/or therapeutic medical care; (4) a need for unique treatment; and (5) a need for extreme flexibility in program scheduling. The number and type of explanation varied according to the nature of the particular child's handicapping condition, and the label of mental retardation often was broadened to include individuals with emotional disturbances, disabilities, or even disadvantages.

Guggenbuhl (quoted by Kanner, 1964) is credited with the idea and practice of institutional care and training of groups of mentally retarded children in 1839. In establishing his residential institution, Guggenbuhl expressed the goal of cure or normalcy, proceeding from the conviction that "the immortal soul is essentially the same in every creature born of woman," and he aimed to "awaken the souls" of his charges (p.24). Guggenbuhl's prescribed regimen included sensory stimulation techniques, attention to diet and medical treatment as needed, and occupational training. His efforts were widely acclaimed, and his institution became the model and guide for similar establishments in Germany, Austria, Great Britain, the Netherlands, the United States, and other countries. These institutions were founded on the belief that through a segregated setting and established instructional techniques, one could create a therapeutic environment and convert the mentally retarded into useful, productive citizens who could be returned to the mainstream of society. Cure, normalcy, or at least amelioration were the intent of such early institutions for the mentally retarded.

The private institutional movement for the retarded in this country was initiated by Wilbur in 1848. Around the same time, Howe convinced the Massachusetts legislature that training and education of the "feeble-minded" was a public responsibility. Largely because of Howe's efforts, the Massachusetts legislature allotted money for a school for the mentally retarded in 1848. In 1851, New York began a state school for the retarded, directed by Wilbur, and by 1890, 14 states had similar institutions. The practice of separate facilities for the education of mentally retarded children was clearly established.

By 1885 the intent of institutional programs for the retarded had changed. Institutions were being transformed from residential schools to custodial asylums (Lazerson, 1974). This transformation was complete by 1918. Four major reasons for this shift in emphasis have been presented by historical researchers (Davies & Ecob, 1959; Kanner, 1964; Lazerson, 1974). The first reason was the growing concern for where the institutionalized could go when released. At first, the institutions returned many of their numbers to the community, but expectations for self-sufficiency often were not realized. Lazerson (1974) cites an 1872 Pennsylvania survey which reflected the growing concern for the future of those released from institutions. The survey showed that, of the 3,500 "feeble-minded" in that state, only 700 came from homes that could support them.

The second reason for the transformation of institutions was the tremendous increase in admissions. As explained by Kanner (1964), the original institutions usually had fewer than a dozen pupils, and funds were sufficient to provide quality educational programs. By the 1870s, however, occupancies were increasing into the hundreds, with many more on waiting lists. Institutions were pressured to admit many severe cases of retardation, since no suitable alternatives existed for their care, and some parents exerted pressure to take their mildly retarded children, in seeking relief from their dependency.

The *hereditarian theory* of the nature of intelligence formulated around 1880 provided a third reason for keeping the mentally retarded in custody. Theoreticians of this bent argued that if intelligence were fixed, educational instruction would be largely wasted effort and, therefore, custodial care was all that could be done for the retarded.

Fourth, pedigree studies of families such as the Jukes (Dugdale, 1877), the Zeroes (Jorger, 1905), and the Kallikaks (Goddard, 1912) led to the idea that society needed to be protected from the harm done by the presence of mentally retarded individuals in the community. Those considered "feeble-minded" came to be viewed as a menace to society. They were described, for example, as:

> . . . almost invariably immoral; most of the women bore illegitimate children; nearly all were antisocial, vicious, and criminal; they were all idle and shiftless and seldom supported themselves; they were highly dangerous people roaming up and down the earth seeking whom they might destroy (Fernald, 1923, p.211).

The only way to halt the tide of poverty, degeneracy, crime, and disease was to permanently segregate the retarded so that they "would neither contaminate others nor reproduce" (Lazerson, 1974, p.20).

Thus, residential facilities for the retarded were initially developed at the end of the nineteenth century to provide intensive educational programs, but by the turn of the century, the residential facilities had turned into basically custodial institutions. Today, institutions generally have retained their custodial function. Few individuals are placed in institutions primarily for educational purposes, and institutions are undoubtedly the most restrictive placement on the service delivery continuum. Residential schools have developed separately from institutions which do have delivery of educational programs as their primary purpose. Institutions and residential facilities both are being challenged, however, as to whether they are legitimate placements for any handicapped child, with the argument that, at a minimum, severely handicapped children should be served in community based facilities.

For example, the parents of children at Pennhurst Center in Pennsylvania filed a class action suit charging the State with segregating the retarded by delivery of separate services rather than encouraging rehabilitation in community based facilities. The U.S. District Court ruled that the State was violating the constitutional rights of retarded individuals by isolating them at Pennhurst. The decision noted that residents have not received, and are not receiving, minimally adequate habilitation, or the education, training, and care required by retarded individuals to reach their maximum development.

On the other hand, some argue that both institutions and residential schools have a purpose; i.e., institutions serve those who require mainly medical and custodial care, and residential schools traditionally have served the educational needs of children with low-incidence handicapping conditions, such as the deaf and blind. Proponents also have argued that, in addition to the difficulties encountered by rural and sparsely populated localities in providing effective educational programs to one or two handicapped learners in their areas, the residential school actually may offer these children greater educational opportunities.

A recent *New York Times* magazine article (Greenberg & Doolittle, 1977) presented the case for residential schools for the deaf. Among the arguments presented was that the residential school provided deaf role models and deaf peers as opposed to the psychological isolation encountered with hearing peers. In addition, the residential school provided more opportunities for deaf students' participation and involvement in all facets of normal school life—from the football team to the Student Council. The argument implied that, for the majority of deaf students, the residential school is in effect the least restrictive environment.

In any event, challenges to placements in institutions and residential schools surely will continue. The issue of whether these placements can be considered least restrictive environments for any handicapped child remains unresolved. Courts and litigation may finally resolve the issue.

Special Education Day Schools

The rationale for educational placement of handicapped individuals in separate day schools has at various times included the following explanations: (1) a need to serve large numbers of handicapped children; (2) a need for special curricula and environment; and (3) a need in many regions to form cooperative multi-district programs for both economic efficiency and instructional effectiveness.

During the last decade of the nineteenth century and the first decades of the twentieth century, the public schools emerged as a site for the care and education of the handicapped. As stated by Lazerson (1974), this reorientation was not a result of rejection or criticism of the custodial and segregational nature of residential institutions. Rather, it was a result of the large numbers of handicapped children, who clearly could not all be accommodated by the institutions. A major reason for the awareness of a large number of handicapped children was the development of compulsory school attendance laws. At the turn of the century, most states were moving toward compulsory school attendance, and there was increasing demand that schools take responsibility for social problems. As Lazerson stated:

> The creation of a mass educational system highlighted the problems of group and individual differences and raised in a cogent way the phenomenon of "failure," i.e., those who did not achieve despite the availability of opportunity . . . (With) the triumph of public education . . . children from inferior stock and environments, truants and incorrigibles, and those suffering from physical and mental defects were now the school's responsibility (p. 37).

Suddenly, schools were forced to deal with a wide range of abilities, without the option of automatically excluding (or letting drop out) those who did not fit into the system. The need for an alternative setting became an issue which led to establishment of special day schools.

As contrasted with residential institutions, special day schools provided an organizational mechanism for the development and provision of special curricula and instructional techniques. The day schools provided a special environment while permitting a child the advantages of remaining in his or her home and community. Originally, the special day school typically was found in large urban school districts. These districts generally had a need to serve large numbers of handicapped children—which made the provision of a special school, with a concentration of special education and related services, economically practical.

In less urbanized areas, day schools often have been established and managed by parent organizations such as affiliates of the National Association for Retarded Citizens or United Cerebral Palsy. Until recently, these private day schools have provided the only educational services for a family with a handicapped child in many communities. At present, they remain the primary vehicle for service delivery to *preschool* handicapped children.

The public special day school concept originally established in urban areas emerged in rural areas in the form of cooperative regional special day schools. These schools continue to be primary service delivery mechanisms. The Intermediate Educational Units (IEUs) in Pennsylvania and the Board of Cooperative Educational Services (BOCES) in New York are examples of current regional day schools for the handicapped. The rationale for these cooperative regional special day schools has been a need to efficiently provide comprehensive services to handicapped children where it would be extremely difficult for any single small school district to provide such educational programming and related services such as speech, occupational and physical therapy or mobility training.

Special day schools, however, currently are being challenged in light of the least restrictive environment principle. The arguments are basically the same as those presented against institutional and residential school placements; i.e., special day schools are still essentially self-contained programs for the handicapped. While they do offer more opportunity for interaction with normal peers by allowing the handicapped child to remain at home and in the community, the child has no interaction with nonhandicapped peers during the school day.

In a sense, special day school programs are in a more vulnerable position than residential schools. The rationale for placement in a residential school as the least restrictive environment often has been based on the intensity of special education and related services needed by the child, including the child's need for a 7-day-a-week, 24-hour-a-day structured program. The arguments for special public day schools have been largely economic. Thus, they are open to the charge that, given more resources in the school system, the child's instructional program could be implemented in a self-contained classroom in a regular public school, which would allow more contact or at least proximity to nonhandicapped peers.

Special Education Self-Contained Classrooms

The special education self-contained classroom has been the most prevalent arrangement used by public schools to provide instruction to the handicapped. The rationale for placement in self-contained special education classrooms typically has included: (1) a need for homogeneous grouping of handicapped children by nature and severity of the handicapping condition in order to facilitate the provision of instruction; (2) a need for flexibility in determining the appropriate level of segregation from nonhandicapped peers; (3) a need for provision of special curricula and instructional techniques for the handicapped; and (4) a need for coordinated, sequential programming.

The first self-contained class for "backward" children is believed to have originated in Providence, Rhode Island, in 1896. This class and others·established before 1915 probably contained "problem children" in general. Although the residential institution was considered the preferred placement even for the mildly retarded, the need for special classes in the public schools was accepted, as illustrated by the following quotation (Goddard, 1910) on educational placements for mildly retarded individuals:

> . . . (this) special group of children . . . requires very special attention . . . Our public school systems are full of them, and yet superintendents and boards of education are struggling to make normal people out of them. One of the most helpful things that we can do would be to distinctly mark out the limits of this class and help the general public to understand that they are a special group and require special treatment, in institutions when possible, or in special classes in public schools, when institutions are out of reach (p. 364).

By 1922, 23,000 retarded pupils were enrolled either in special day schools or classes. The special class was to be the standard environment for educating mildly handicapped children for decades to come. The educational environment for mildly to moderately handicapped children became a labeled and segregated classroom in either a special building or a regular school. Typically, the class consisted of a small group of children with a similar degree of cognitive impairment who were taught by a specially trained teacher, using methods and materials different from those used in regular classes. Segregation became an end in itself; return to the regular classroom was not a goal of the special class. The goal of education for even the mildly handicapped had shifted from the early goal of normalcy to life styles (some more sheltered and protective than others) commensurate with abilities.

School curricula for the retarded from 1930 on reflected this goal by stressing not the modification of intellectual development, but social and vocational competence (Erdman & Olson, 1966). The sensory-motor curriculum proposed by Montessori (1912), the "watered down" or modified curriculum developed by Innskeep (1926), and the unit approach presented by Ingram (1935) were supplanted by approaches that emphasized occupational and social learning. Hungerford, DeProspo, and Rosenzweig (1948), for example, developed a program of occupational education for the retarded in New York City schools, which emphasized occupational information and social placement. In the Illinois curriculum, Goldstein and Seigle (1958) stressed life situations with which the retarded would need to cope; i.e., learning to live safely, to keep healthy, to earn a living, and to manage money.

Thus, the special segregated class was perceived as providing the environmental conditions necessary to meet educational needs of handicapped children—including special curricula and teaching techniques, individual and/or small group instruction or tutoring, and relief from the competition of the regular classroom. The segregated class has been viewed as providing an environment in which activities and requirements can be geared to the child's level of functioning.

The special education self-contained classroom was the initial public school response to efforts of parent organizations to gain services for their handicapped children. Over time, however, goals of the special self-contained classroom became blurred. It was not clear whether the goals were remediation of information-processing deficits, instruction in basic skills, self-help skills, and pre-vocational training, remediation of academic and behavioral deficits, or some combination of the above. It was no longer clear whether the goal of special education in the self-contained classroom was to provide the child with a sheltered protective environment or to develop the child's level of functioning to a point at which regular classroom placement with the aid of support services was appropriate.

The question increasingly asked was: What is special about special education? The efficacy of self-contained special education classrooms was questioned (e.g., Dunn, 1968) in relation to basic skills training and the perceived social stigma to children as a result of such placement. Definitions of handicapping conditions changed, altering the types and number of children labeled as handicapped. In California, for example, legislation was passed which changed the guidelines for defining the educable mentally retarded and resulted in thousands of children being decertified as EMR and returned to regular classes. Concern was voiced for those children who had been mislabeled and had suffered a stigmatizing classification. In short, given the inability to clearly articulate the uniqueness of instructional programs available in self-contained classrooms, legal and legislative pressures have built against segregated programming.

Today, however, few would disagree that for some handicapped children, primary placement in a special education self-contained classroom is the least restrictive setting appropriate. Such primary placement does not preclude the integration of handicapped children into regular education programs for art, music, lunch, and other activities as appropriate. If, however, the self-contained special classroom is no longer a program with discernable goals, but rather a setting for implementation of a child's individualized education program, the problem remains of determining for whom and under what conditions such segregated placement is appropriate.

Resource Classrooms

The provision of special education services in resource rooms had as its underlying premises: (1) greater organizational efficiency; (2) reducing stigmatization of the handicapped child which resulted from placement in segregated special classes; and (3) emphasizing instructional remediation. Most of the conceptualizations of a continua of special education services contain options in which a handicapped child is placed in the regular classroom with supplementary services provided to the child and/or regular classroom teacher. The resource room is one common form of supplementary service model (Baarstad, 1965; Barksdale & Atkinson, 1971; Beery, 1972; Bruininks & Rynders, 1971; Ebert, Dain, & Phillips, 1970; Gardner, 1971; Hammill & Wiederholt, 1972; Hartman & Rockhold, 1973; Prouty & Prillaman, 1970; Reger, 1973). The resource room is an instructional setting which the child usually visits on a regularly scheduled, part-time basis. Generally, the child spends the rest of the day with his or her regular class.

As early as 1875, an occasional voice questioned the value of segregation for the mentally retarded. Wynter (1875), for example, argued for the benefits of mixing "imbeciles" with "sane" members of society. Through the power of imitation, she postulated, imbeciles learn from those of greater intelligence. The segregated setting, on the other hand, was viewed as intensifying idiocy. Such voices were largely drowned out, however, by the volume of voices describing advantages of the segregated environment.

Numerous studies during the late 1950s and 1960s investigated the effectiveness of special class placement as compared with regular class placement of mentally retarded children (Bacher, 1965; Baldwin, 1958; Blatt, 1958; Carroll, 1967; Cassidy & Stanton, 1959; Diggs, 1964; Goldstein, Moss & Jordan, 1965; Kern & Pfaeffle, 1962; Kirk, 1964; Mayer, 1966). Known as *efficacy studies*, these research efforts generally defined effectiveness as achievement, as measured by nationally standardized achievement tests. The efficacy studies were deficient methodologically, and the findings were equivocal. The studies did not support either regular or special classes as the most appropriate placement for retarded children. Educators such as Johnson (1962), however, used the efficacy studies to question why mentally retarded children did not clearly achieve more academically in special classes than in regular classes, when the former had fewer pupils, supposedly better trained teachers, and more financial resources available on a per capita basis.

Given the lack of evidence for justifying a delivery system that often required a teacher for every 9 to 12 handicapped children, less costly alternatives were sought. The resource room, conceptually considered to supplement regular instruction, was perceived as an efficient option for delivering special education services. This organizational arrangement, in contrast to the special class, would permit each special education teacher to instruct approximately three times as many children. In part, a misperceived cost saving caused many administrators to support the provision of this placement alternative in their schools.

Among proponents of the idea that placement in special classes led to stigmatization of the child, Dunn (1968) stated that "removing a child from the regular grades for special education probably contributed significantly to his feelings of inferiority and problems of acceptance" (p.9). Studies investigated social acceptance and rejection (Baldwin, 1958; Johnson, 1950; Johnson & Kirk, 1960), social adjustment (Ainsworth, 1959; Cassidy & Stanton, 1959; Goldstein et al., 1965; Kern & Pfaeffle, 1962; Thurstone, 1960), and self-concept (Mayer, 1966; Meyerowitz, 1962) of handicapped children in both regular and special classes. In court cases, detrimental effects of the "mentally retarded" label were cited as fact.

Data available from the studies, however, were actually anything but conclusive. In reviewing the studies concerning effects of the mentally retarded label, MacMillan, Jones, and Aloia (1974) found that the evidence presented failed to support the notion that labeling had long-lasting and devastating effects on those labeled. They concluded that, "While many accept as fact that labeling children mentally retarded has detrimental effects, conclusive empirical evidence of these effects was not found" (p. 257).

Methodological problems included the lack of control for possible devaluations of the self which occurred prior to being labeled, the appropriateness of the instruments used with mentally retarded subjects, and the comparability of responses given by mentally retarded and nonmentally retarded subjects to personality measures. Studies such as Meyerowitz (1967), however, continue to be cited as evidence that special class placement has a debilitating effect on self-image and acceptance. Thus, the belief prevailed that a placement alternative which separated the handicapped learner from nonhandicapped children for only limited periods of the school day would be less stigmatizing.

Little evidence exists concerning the relationship between amount of time separated from nonhandicapped peers and self concept or social acceptance. Some special educators have argued that the mere "pulling out" of the child from the regular class for any special education services is detrimental. Answers to these questions require further research before empirical facts can substitute for current social values and opinions.

In the resource room, a specially trained teacher may provide the child with educational and/or behavioral assessment to pinpoint problems, individualized instruction in problem areas, and special materials and activities designed to foster certain skills or alleviate certain problems. Resource room programs generally reflect an orientation that a child's participation in or rejection from the regular education program depends less on the handicap than it does on the ability to perform selected classroom tasks (Jenkins & Mayhall, 1973). The content of resource room programs usually is determined by assessing what a child needs to know and is able to demonstrate in order to function in the regular classroom. The *objective of the resource room approach is to remediate measured deficits in language/reading, arithmetic, and/or social behaviors.* The resource room teacher also may consult with the child's regular teacher concerning appropriate methods or materials for the child.

The diversity of learner needs in any school building and the limited number of placement options often available within single buildings or rural districts, however, results in optimization of classrooms and personnel—not specialization. Thus, necessity and priorities require that available personnel be used to meet children's instructional needs whether or not these needs are consistent with a conceptual model of alternative instructional settings. Consequently, some children may spend the entire day in a resource room, others may receive their entire basic skill instruction in a resource room, and still others may receive their intended supplemental instruction in the resource room.

IMPLICATIONS FOR THE FUTURE

Because handicapped children differ in the severity of their educational needs, a comprehensive continuum of educational services is needed to provide appropriate services. Current practices for alternative settings include institutions, special schools, special education self-contained classrooms, resource classrooms, plus the total spectrum of supportive services. Given the legislative, judicial, and fiscal expansion of support for special education in the 1970s, the question remains as to what trends will emerge in the 1980s. Considering the broad social and systemic changes of the 1970s, the 1980s should be a period in which attention will be focused increasingly on the nature and quality of services being provided.

During the 1980s, we believe there will be a continued need for residential/institutional programs. There will continue to be handicapped children from broken or disintegrating families for whom residential accommodations are required. Further, from a programmatic perspective though, community based programs will continue to grow, but a reexamination of how many handicapped children are needed to efficiently provide a comprehensive instructional program will need to occur. In many instances, mentally retarded and emotionally disturbed children living in an institution will increasingly attend programs in public schools while continuing to reside at the institution. This trend has been recognized and supported by federal Title I funds which provide assistance to local school districts offering services to these children. However, allowing for the rate at which communities are likely to develop and provide such services, institutional programs will be a part of the continuum of service settings available to the handicapped in the 1980s.

The current number of mildly handicapped children served in special education day schools probably will continue to decrease in the 1980s. The social and litigative pressures to implement the doctrine of least restrictive environments will create difficulty in programmatically arguing for these programs. Regional programming, however, will increase in the provision of special education and related services to the severely handicapped. We think the regional provision of related services will become increasingly apparent in the 1980s as one of the few efficient ways by which small school districts can provide occupational or physical therapy, mobility training, and so forth.

Further, the pressure for deinstitutionalization of the mentally retarded and emotionally disturbed into community based programs is predicted to result in a growth of day school programs in the 1980s. The basis for these programs already is present in the form of community mental health centers. The continued growth of programming for infants 0-2 and youth 18-21 probably will occur initially in the context of these programs.

In a hazardous prediction, the 1980s will see a continued prevalence of self-contained classrooms, but the classes will be for an ever increasing group of more severely handicapped youngsters. The self-contained classroom in which mildly handicapped children were integrated for part of the day will be difficult to discern from what we will call resource rooms in the late 1970s and 1980s. It would seem that resource rooms will continue to expand in the 1980s, but will reflect an eclectic responsiveness to building and district needs rather than conceptually oriented specialized settings. The resource room seems to be the emergence of flexible programming which was reflected in a more restricted manner in the self-contained classrooms of the 1970s.

To provide a comprehensive continuum of special education service settings consistent with the doctrine of the least restrictive environment, three major issues will have to be resolved. First, the issue of what is to be taught handicapped children must be reviewed for each category of exceptionality. A review of program content will provide a standard by which to assess the extent to which regular class programs appear consonant with the needs of a handicapped child. In addition, such an analysis would permit a determination of what commonality exists in content across categories of handicapped children. Finally, examination of not only what these children need to know but how they learn would provide the basis for clearly determining what types of alternative settings are needed and the basis for establishing discernibly different instructional treatments. The provision of alternative settings related to the various instructional treatments would be determined by factors other than just content.

A second critical issue which must be addressed in the 1980s relates to the number of children requiring services and the personnel available. The delivery of appropriate programming requires sufficient children to warrant investments in providing comprehensive services. The parallel to this issue is seen in the consolidation of school districts in regular education to permit development of "comprehensive high schools." Consolidation similarly is seen in the emerging delivery systems for special education. This premise led to establishment of intermediate educational units such as those of Pennsylvania, Iowa, and Wisconsin; and to other cooperative arrangements such as the Boards of Cooperative Educational Services in New York. This issue of sufficient children for comprehensive programming will be particularly vexing for the severely and profoundly handicapped. With the current trend toward deinstitutionalization, the level of regionalization necessary to provide appropriate programming will have to be resolved.

A final issue which needs to be addressed relates to the provision of a comprehensive continuum of special education service settings. Considering the differences in what should be taught and how, along with the need for sufficient numbers of children, an array of inter-agency relationships will be necessary. In addition to the emerging trend of multi-district cooperation for providing services, coordination of programs provided by state, county and/or city departments of education, health, welfare, and corrections will be necessary. For example, many community mental health programs for disturbed children are provided under the auspices of departments of health. Another example is the growing complexity of relationships between public and private schools. The efficient and effective provision of special education and related services will require the development of different patterns consistent with local school district needs. The form these inter-agency agreements will take is a challenge to be met in the 1980 s.

Special education will continue to progress from a period of separatism to greater assimilation into the regular education administrative and instructional organization. The 1980s will be a decade of increased pressure to be accountable for the nature and quality of services delivered, which in turn will require the expensive provision of a comprehensive array of settings. The relationship between placement and programming decisions and practices should begin to emerge in a manner that will permit articulation and justification. Resolution of these relationships will be necessary to effectively implement the doctrine of least restrictive environments.

REFERENCES

Ainsworth, S.A. *An exploratory study of educational, social and emotional factors in the education of mentally retarded children in Georgia public schools* (U.S. Office of Education Cooperative Research Program, Project No. 171). Athens: University of Georgia, 1959.

Baarstad, D.L. A resource room for the educationally handicapped pupil. *California Education,* 1965, *3* (4), 14.

Bacher, J.H. The effect of special class placement on the self-concept, social adjustment, and reading growth of slow learners (Doctoral dissertation, New York University, 1964). *Dissertation Abstracts,* 1965, *25,* 7071. (University Microfilms No. 65-6570)

Baldwin, W. The social position of the educable mentally retarded child in the regular grades in the public school. *Exceptional Children,* 1958, *25,* 106-108.

Barksdale, M.W., & Atkinson, A.P. A resource room approach to instruction for the educable mentally retarded. *Focus on Exceptional Children,* 1971, *3* (4) 12-15.

Beery, K. E. *Models for mainstreaming.* San Rafael, CA: Dimensions, 1972.

Blatt, B. The physical, personality and academic status of children who are mentally retarded attending special classes as compared with children who are mentally retarded attending regular classes. *American Journal of Mental Deficiency,* 1958, *62,* 810-818.

Brown v. *Board of Education,* 347 U.S. 483 (1954).

Bruininks, R.H., & Rynders, J.E. Alternatives to special class placement for educable mentally retarded children. *Focus on Exceptional Children,* 1971, *3* (4), 1-12.

Burgdorf, R.L., Jr. *The doctrine of the least restrictive alternative.* Unpublished manuscript, Council for Handicapped People, Columbia, SC, 1975.

Carroll, W.W. The effects of segregated and partially integrated school programs on self-concept and academic achievement of educable mentally retarded. *Exceptional Children,* 1967, *34,* 93-96.

Cassidy, V., & Stanton, J. *An investigation of factors in the educational placement of mentally retarded children: A study of differences between children in special and regular classes in Ohio.* (U.S. Office of Education, Cooperative Research Program, Project No. 043). Columbus: Ohio State University, 1959.

Chaffin, J.D. Will the real "mainstreaming" program please stand up! (or . . . should Dunn have done it?) In E. L. Meyen, G. A. Vergason, & R. J. Whelan (Eds.), *Alternatives for teaching exceptional children.* Denver: Love Publishing Co., 1975.

Davies, S.P., & Ecob, K.G. *The mentally retarded in society.* New York: Columbia University Press, 1959.

Deno, E. Special education as developmental capital. *Exceptional Children,* 1970, *37,* 229-237.

Diggs, E.A. A study of change in the social status of rejected mentally retarded children in regular classrooms (Doctoral dissertation, Colorado State College, 1963). *Dissertation Abstracts,* 1964, *25,* 220-221. (University Microfilm No. 64-4180)

Dugdale, R.L. *The Jukes: A study of crime, pauperism, disease, and heredity.* New York: Putnam, 1877.

Dunn, L.M. Special education for the mildly retarded: Is much of it justifiable? *Exceptional Children,* 1968, *35,* 5-22.

Ebert, D.W., Dain, R., & Phillips, B.N. An attempt at implementing the diagnosis-intervention class model. *Journal of School Psychology,* 1970, *8,* 191-197.

Erdman, R.L., & Olson, J.L. Relationships between educational programs for the mentally retarded and the culturally deprived. *Mental Retardation Abstracts,* 1966, *3,* 311-318. (J.H. Rothstein (Ed.), *Mental retardation: Readings and resources* (2nd ed.). New York: Holt, Rinehart, & Winston, 1971.)

Fernald, W.E. Thirty years progress in the care of the feeble-minded. *Journal of Psycho-Asthenics,* 1923-24, *29,* 206-219.

Gardner, O.S. The birth and infancy of the resource center at Hauula. *Exceptional Children,* 1971, *38,* 53-58.

Goddard, H.H. Four hundred feeble-minded children classified by the Binet method. *Journal of Psycho-Asthenics,* 1910, *15,* 17-30. (Rosen, M., Clark, G.R., & Kivitz, M.S. (Eds.). *The history of mental retardation: Collected papers* (Vol. 1). Baltimore: University Park Press, 1976.)

Goddard, H.H. *The Kallikak family.* New York: Macmillan, 1912.

Goldstein, H., Moss, J.W., & Jordan, L.J. *The efficacy of special class training on the development of mentally retarded children.* (U.S. Office of Education, Cooperative Research Program, Project No. 619). Urbana: University of Illinois/Institute for Research on Exceptional Children, 1965.

Goldstein, H., & Seigle, D. *The Illinois plan for special education of exceptional children: A curriculum guide for teachers of the educable mentally handicapped.* (Circular Series B-3, No. 12) Springfield: Illinois Department of Public Instruction, 1958.

Greenberg, J., & Doolittle, G. Can schools speak the language of the deaf? *New York Times Magazine,* December 11, 1977, p. 50.

Hammill, D.D., & Wiederholt, J.L. *The resource room: Rationale and implementation.* Philadelphia, PA: Buttonwood Farms, 1972.

Hartman, R.K., & Rockhold, A.E. Case studies in the resource room approach. *Journal for Special Educators of the Mentally Retarded,* 1973, *9,* 109-115.

Hungerford, R., DeProspo, C., & Rosenzweig, L. *Philosophy of occupational education.* New York: The Association for the New York City Teachers of Special Education, 1948.

Ingram, C.P. *Education of the slow-learning child.* Yonkers, NY: World Book, 1935.

Inskeep, A.L. *Teaching dull and retarded children.* New York: Macmillan, 1926.

Jenkins, J.R., & Mayhall, W.F. Describing resource teacher programs. *Exceptional Children,* 1973, *40,* 35-36.

Johnson, G.O. A study of the social position of mentally handicapped children in regular grades. *American Journal of Mental Deficiency,* 1950, *55,* 60-89.

Johnson, G.O. Special education for the handicapped—A paradox. *Exceptional Children,* 1962, *29,* 62-69.

Johnson, G.O., & Kirk, S.A. Are mentally handicapped children segregated in regular grades? *Journal of Exceptional Children*, 1960, *17*, 65-68.

Jorger, J. Die familie zero. *Archiv fur Rassen-und Gesellschafts-Biologie, Einschiesslich Rassen-und Gesellschafts-Hygiene*, 1905, *2*, 494-559.

Kanner, L. *A history of the care and study of the mentally retarded.* Springfield, IL: Charles C. Thomas, 1964.

Kern, W.H., & Pfaeffle, H.A. A comparison of social adjustment of mentally retarded children in various educational settings. *American Journal of Mental Deficiency*, 1962, *67*, 407-413.

Kirk, S.A. Research in education. In H.A. Stevens & R. Herber (Eds.), *Mental retardation: A review of research.* Chicago: University of Chicago Press, 1964.

Lazerson, M. *Educational institutions and mental subnormality: Notes on writing a history.* Paper presented at a meeting of the National Institute of Child Health and Human Development and the Rose F. Kennedy Center for Research in Mental Retardation, Albert Einstein College of Medicine, April 1974.

MacMillan, D.L., Jones, R.L., & Aloia, G.F. The mentally retarded label: A theoretical analysis and review of research. *American Journal of Mental Deficiency*, 1974, *79*, 241-261.

Martin, E. Mainstreaming as national policy. In P.H. Mann (Ed.), *Shared responsibility for handicapped students: Advocacy and programming.* Coral Gables, FL: University of Miami Training and Technical Assistance Center, 1976, pp. 13-15.

Mayer, L. The relationship of early special class placement and the self-concepts of mentally handicapped children. *Exceptional Children*, 1966, *33*, 77-80.

McCullough v. Maryland, 4 Wheat 316, U.S. Ed. 579 (1918).

Meyerowitz, J.H. Self-derogations in young retardates and special class placement. *Child Development*, 1962, *33*, 443-451.

Meyerowitz, J.H. Peer groups and special classes. *Mental Retardation*, 1967, *5*, 23-26.

Mills v. Board of Education of District of Columbia, 348 F. Supp. 866, 880, (D.D.C., 1972).

Montessori, M. *Montessori method*, (A.E. George, trans.) New York: Stokes, 1912.

Pennsylvania Association for Retarded Children (PARC) v. Commonwealth of Pennsylvania, 343 F. Supp. 279 (E.D. Pa., 1972), Consent Agreement.

Prouty, R.W., & Prillaman, D. Diagnostic teaching: A modest proposal. *Elementary School Journal*, 1970, *70*, 265-270.

Reger, R. What is a resource-room program? *Journal of Learning Disabilities*, 1973, *6*, 609-613.

Reynolds, M.C. A framework for considering some issues in special education. *Exceptional Children*, 1962, *28*, 367-370.

Shelton v. Tucker, 364 U.S. 479 (Ark., 1960).

Thurstone, T.G. *An evaluation of educating mentally handicapped children in special classes and in regular classes* (U.S. Office of Education, Cooperative Research Program, Project No. OE-SAE-6542), Chapel Hill: University of North Carolina, 1960.

Wolf v. Legislature of the State of Utah, Civil No. 102626 3rd Jud. Dist. Ct. (Utah, Jan. 8, 1969).

Wynter, A. *The borderlands of insanity.* London: Piccadilly, 1875.

The opinions expressed herein do not necessarily reflect the position of the U.S. Office of Education, and no official endorsement by the U.S. Office of Education should be inferred.

RESOURCE GUIDE

Issues

Ballard, J., & Zettel, J. Public Law 94-142 and Section 504: What they say about rights and protection. *Exceptional Children,* Nov. 1977, *44* (3).

Blatt, B. On the bill of rights and related matters. In R. Heinrich & S. Ashcroft (Eds.), *Instructional technology and the education of all handicapped children.* Columbus, OH: National Center on Media and Materials for the Handicapped, 1977.

Chambers, D. Right to the least restrictive alternative setting for treatment. In B. J. Ennis & P. R. Friedman (Eds.), *Legal rights of the mentally handicapped* (Vol. 2). New York: Practicing Law Institute, 1974, pp. 991-1014.

Gilhool, T. K. Education: An inalienable right. *Exceptional Children,* 1973, *39.*

Hobbs, N. *The futures of children.* Washington, DC: Jossey-Bass, 1975.

Melcher, J. W. Law, litigation, and handicapped children. *Exceptional Children,* 1976, *43.*

Wolfensberger, W. *The principle of normalization in human services.* Toronto, Canada: National Institute on Mental Retardation, 1972.

Program Implications

Bruininks, R., & Rynders, J. Alternatives to special class placement for educable mentally retarded children. *Focus on Exceptional Children,* Sept. 1971, *3* (4).

Chaffin, J. D. Will the real "mainstreaming" program please stand up! (or . . . should Dunn have done it?). *Focus on Exceptional Children,* Oct. 1974, *6* (5).

Kaufman, J., Gottlieb, J., Agard, J., & Kukic, M. Mainstreaming: Toward an explication of the construct. *Focus on Exceptional Children,* May 1975, *7* (3).

Lovitt, T. C. Mainstreaming the mildly handicapped: Some research suggestions. In R. Heinrich & S. Ashcroft (Eds.), *Instructional technology and the education of all handicapped children.* Columbus, OH: National Center on Media and Materials for the Handicapped, 1977.

Mercer, J. R. Crosscultural evaluation of exceptionality. *Focus on Exceptional Children,* Sept. 1973, *5* (4), 8-13.

National Asociation for Retarded Citizens. *The partnership: How to make it work.* Arlington, TX: Author, Sept. 1977.

3 Instructional Planning for Exceptional Children and Youth

Edward L. Meyen
University of Kansas

Teacher training programs historically have emphasized the need for instructional planning by teachers. School districts have reflected this emphasis in their policies on lesson plans, in curriculum selection and development, and in guidelines on the evaluation of teacher effectiveness. In spite of the unquestioned need for planning, however, the planning process has only begun to emerge as an effective, widespread practice.

The increased emphasis on sound instructional planning can be attributed in part to the growing concern among consumers. Parents and the public in general are beginning to raise questions about the reported decline in academic achievement, particularly in the basic skills. Initially, this concern tends to center on the curriculum, but eventually it focuses on decision making regarding individual students. At that level instructional planning becomes a major concern.

The lack of rapid progress in instructional planning has related primarily to the practical realities of the classroom teacher's role. For the most part, teachers have had to initiate, evaluate, and review student programs within the constraints of overloaded schedules, minimal planning resources or directives, and limited administrative support for planning. In the past, when administrators became concerned about the need for planning, or when parents sought information related to their children's programs, the teacher was the focal point of most of the pressure.

The special education teacher's role in instructional planning also has been affected by the above circumstances—in spite of the obvious need for detailed planning in programming for exceptional children and youth. Too often, the evidence of instructional planning has consisted of hurriedly written lesson plans limited to general goals, detailed assignments combined with anecdotal records, and history-oriented cumulative records. Such planning gives little more than nebulous directives and does not provide the resources needed for instructional decision making. As a basis for programming for exceptional children, this process is totally insufficient.

Several significant developments, however, have had a positive influence on the teacher's role in instructional planning:

1. Districts are beginning to provide release time for planning;
2. More resource personnel are available to aid teachers in making planning decisions;
3. The range and amount of materials available simplify the teacher's efforts in designing plans appropriate to the needs of their students;

4. Instructional planning is being linked with accrediting agencies as a measure of quality control; and

5. The Individualized Education Program (IEP) requirement of Public Law 94-142 represents the single most important event regarding instructional planning for exceptional children. (Later in this chapter, the IEP will be discussed as an instructional planning approach.)

Discussions on instructional planning among teacher trainers often result in the expression of differing views. Some will agree that understanding the child is most critical and that teachers who are responsive to the needs of the learner will make good instructional decisions without a technology of planning. Others place importance on knowing the subject matter; from their perspective, appropriate instructional decisions emanate from the context of what is to be taught.

Both arguments have obvious merit, but most teachers enter the profession without sufficient knowledge of the learner and without sufficient knowledge of the subject matter. Although they have learned some skills in both areas, they lack the level of expertise to intuitively make instructional planning decisions. Teachers must rely on experience to develop and improve their judgment in instructional decision making. Even experienced teachers require a planning process to assure that the varied needs of their students are met.

As more exceptional children enter the regular classes, the need for skills in instructional planning will increase in importance. The regular class teacher, in addition to encountering more children who present complex instructional demands, also will need to develop competence in areas tangential but related to instructional planning. For example, the National Advisory Council on Education Professions Development (1976) has identified the following set of skills as necessary for all teachers:

a. Teachers should understand how a handicap affects a child's ability to learn in the classroom.

b. Building on this understanding, teachers need to become competent in recognition of handicaps and prescription of learning experiences. They will need to be able to identify specific conditions and prescribe appropriate instructional experiences. The level of sophistication in this area need not be high, as expert advice and support should be available through one of many possible delivery models.

c. In conjunction with diagnosis and prescription of learning experiences, regular classroom teachers will need skills in the individualization of instruction. The variance posed by handicapped children necessitates at least some degree of individualization, requiring a familiarity with resources and instructional materials for handicapped children.

d. Teachers will need a better understanding of the emotions of handicapped children. Not only must they be able to empathize with the handicapped but they must be able to focus a part of the education experience on the child's emotional development.

e. Teachers need to develop a conceptual and practical understanding of the process of mainstreaming. Integral to this is the development of a new understanding of the role of the special education teacher as a consultant and resource person. Perhaps most importantly, teachers will need to develop competence and self-confidence in dealing with handicapped children, based upon skills developed through experience, additional in-service training, and use of support services.

f. Finally, teachers will need to be able to apply this collective understanding in their interactions with parents of the handicapped and with nonhandicapped (p. 16).

A significant problem to be faced in redirecting teacher efforts in instructional planning relates to teacher attitudes. Having become accustomed to planning under adverse conditions, many teachers perceive instructional planning as an added task neither valued by administrators nor resulting in benefits for them or their students. This attitude is reasonable in view of the circumstances under which instructional planning has been carried out in the past. A reallocation of resources and changes in attitudes of administrators is required if effective instructional planning is to be achieved.

INSTRUCTIONAL PLANNING AS A PROCESS

No single set of planning procedures applies to all instructional settings. Teachers vary in their planning preferences just as they prefer particular teaching methodologies. Differences in available resources also influence the instructional planning approach a teacher might follow. But certain general principles and planning concepts have broad application and, if followed, increase the opportunities for quality instruction. Instructional planning ideally results in providing effective instruction appropriate to learner needs. Within this context, at least four objectives specific to instructional planning are set forth:

1. To make use of available information on learner characteristics and instructional options in planning specific teaching activities.
2. To establish short-range objectives within a long-term plan that can be implemented as intended, often by persons other than the teacher responsible for the original planning.
3. To allow for collecting evaluative evidence that illustrates the pupil's cumulative performance.

4. To provide a base for instructional decisions regarding programs for individual pupils.

To be effective, instructional planning must focus on the uniqueness of the individual learner. Thus, a planning process does not substitute for the teacher's lack of knowledge about how children learn. Calder (1977) offers 11 principles for instructional decision making. These principles illustrate a range of teacher competencies which can be considered as prerequisites to effective planning.

1. The learner should possess the basic readiness skills needed to ensure some degree of success in the new task.
2. The learner should be made aware of the value and meaning of the new task.
3. The task should be analyzed to determine the difficulties that may be encountered because of any special needs of the learner.
4. The task should begin with familiar experiences and skills and progress to new experiences and skills.
5. The task should be presented in a manner that will provide the learner with a degree of success and satisfaction.
6. The task should be planned and a procedure developed for presenting it to the learner. When possible, the plan should be initiated and executed by the learner.
7. The task should include options that meet the learner's learning style.
8. The task should have flexibility and provide for differentiated assignments in order to meet the individual needs of the learner.
9. The task should be planned to provide the learner with reinforced repetition and practice to ensure retention.
10. The task should provide for constant performance evaluation by the learner, teacher, paraprofessional, or peer tutor.
11. The assignment of a new task should be the result of continuous evaluation of the learner's performance on the present task (p. 13).

In implementing these objectives and principles, a systematic approach to instructional planning clearly is required. To be maximally effective, instructional planning for exceptional children must encompass more than merely specifying objectives, initiating activities, and measuring their effects on pupil performance. Consideration also must be given to identifying behaviors that suggest learning problems and becoming familiar with procedures that bring the children to the attention of appropriate resource personnel. While these concerns are beyond the actual instructional process, they are critical to instructional planning that will result in the most appropriate educational placement for the exceptional child. For the nonhandicapped child, instructional placement decisions rarely are made, since the child merely progresses through the graded system; placement decisions are important, but they primarily serve to set the conditions for instructional decisions.

Planning Guidelines

Following are some suggestions that can serve as guidelines in the instructional planning process. They are not rules, nor do they constitute a recipe for successful instructional planning. Rather, they derive from observation of teachers engaged in successful instructional planning for exceptional children.

Systematization

The purpose of instructional planning is to assure that instructional decisions about a student's program consider all information pertaining to the learner's needs. This requires systematic planning. The relative severity of learning problems exhibited by exceptional children dictates further that planning be continuous and not occur only when the child's problem is interfering with instruction.

Detail

No plan can describe all of the skills, concepts, and information that a child will or should be taught. Even if this were possible, it would not be desirable. Learners vary in their responses to tasks, and the risk is present that a teacher may adhere to a detailed plan when evidence shows that the plan should be altered to meet the child's changing needs. Planning must allow for "on the spot" decision making.

On the other hand, sufficient planning time on the part of the teacher is important to success of the plan. Decisions must be made on how detailed a plan should be regarding skills, activities, and materials. The more serious the learner's problem, the more precise the planning required. Another major consideration pertains to whether or not persons other than the teacher will be involved in carrying out the plan. The plan should contain sufficient information to assure appropriate interpretation and implementation.

Format

The content and provisions for remediation, not the plan's organizational format, determine its appropriateness for a particular student. The organization and recording format of instructional plans, however, do influence how well planning efforts succeed. An organized plan simplifies the matching of instructional options to learner characteristics.

To ensure uniformity, districts often adopt or design a particular planning system. Some advantages accrue in having all teachers use a similar format: A uniform approach simplifies the administrator's role in evaluating the effectiveness of teacher planning; and uniformity in format enhances communication among teachers. In most cases, forms are designed to make planning more convenient and to reduce the amount of time involved.

Program Emphasis

In developing instructional plans, teachers have a tendency to refer only to the child's most immediate problems. Certainly, more specific planning is required to remediate obvious serious learning problems, but a program or curriculum emphasis also must be maintained. For example, a visually impaired child who is skilled in math may be experiencing difficulty in social studies because of slowness in reading by the braille method. Planning attention must be given to the student's needs in mathematics and other subjects, even though more short-term planning may be involved in developing the student's braille reading speed and alternatives for acquiring experiences in social studies.

Intensiveness

Once a teacher has developed a program in which a child progresses satisfactorily, the time and effort (intensity) allocated to planning can be reduced. This does not mean that the teacher stops recording plans, collecting performance data, or conferring with other teachers. It means that less detailed planning is required and more planning time can be devoted to students for whom a satisfactory plan has not yet been developed.

Because of the amount of time required in effective instructional planning, the teacher must make judgments regarding how much time to devote to planning for each student. If evidence suggests that a student is progressing satisfactorily, planning becomes less formal and the emphasis shifts to program monitoring.

Evaluation

Unless planning includes the evaluation of short- and long-term objectives, the benefits will be minimal. Because specific evaluation tasks are sometimes difficult to design and not generally available in commercial form, some teachers tend to resort to available achievement measures or other standardized tests. Although standardized tests have certain advantages, they generally are not appropriate for measuring student performance on specific tasks included in routine instructional plans.

Teachers need to carefully determine when standardized measures are appropriate and when they need to consider other options. Teachers must evaluate their instructional planning, but they must use evaluation measures that relate directly to the student's instructional program. This generally results in teachers' having to design at least part of their evaluation tasks. When incorporating evaluation tasks into instructional planning, attention must be given to the relationship of the evaluation task to the instructional activity, the time required for the teacher to design the task, the time required by the student to demonstrate task performance, and the value of the information derived in this process.

Procedures

In deciding upon instructional planning procedures, two primary factors must be considered — the impact of instructional planning on student programming, and the demands which the planning process places on teachers. The previously outlined guidelines (systematization, detail, format, program emphasis, intensiveness, and evaluation) combine to influence programming for students. But they also create time demands on teachers. If the procedures are too complex and time consuming, the teacher may not be able to plan and teach effectively. If the plan is too simple, little is gained in terms of pupil benefits.

The initial goal is to design procedures that allow for efficiency on the part of the teacher and enhance instructional decision making specific to students' needs. The ultimate goal is to employ planning procedures which result in benefits for the learner.

Teachers should assume leadership in developing planning procedures. Administrative concerns do not always contribute to teacher efficiency or pupil benefit, and administrators often answer general program questions by expanding instructional planning requirements. If program questions can be answered by an instructional planning process that does not add substantially to the teacher's workload, that process should be considered. The primary emphasis, however, should be on instructional planning for specific students, and the emphasis must be on developing *workable* planning procedures.

CONSIDERATIONS IN INSTRUCTIONAL PLANNING FOR EXCEPTIONAL CHILDREN

Some exceptional children enter school already having been identified as possessing characteristics that likely will interfere with their school performance. In general, the most serious handicapping conditions are congenital in nature and include impaired vision, defective hearing, physical problems, and multiple handicaps. For exceptional children whose problems have been identified prior to entering school, instructional planning specific to their needs can be initiated upon their enrollment. Under such circumstances, the teacher probably will have the advantage of possessing information regarding the child's preschool history.

The majority of exceptional children, however, are not identified until they encounter demands in school with which they cannot effectively cope. Although instructional planning should occur for all children, too often specific instructional planning does not occur until after a student is identified as having a problem. If the child is fortunate, a teacher will notice the child's difficulty before it becomes more serious.

Conditions resulting in the identification of a child as exceptional are numerous — social inadequacies, language skills not fully developed, academic requirements beyond the child's ability, specific learning tasks for which the child has not developed readiness, minor vision or hearing problems which previously had been unnoticed but which do affect his/her school performance. For these kinds of students, instructional planning must be broadened to include the identification of behaviors which suggest potential learning difficulties. The planning process for exceptional children must begin *before* the child has been identified as having special needs.

Suggested Planning Steps

Five sequential steps comprise the basic guidelines in planning for these children: (1) identifying potential problems; (2) initiating a referral;

(3) assessment; (4) making instructional/placement decisions; and (5) implementation.

Identifying Potential Problems

This first step actually should be preceded by a discussion on how to *prevent* children from developing learning problems. Thus, for purposes of describing a planning process applicable to exceptional children, the importance of the regular class teacher in the identification process must be stressed.

Most exceptional children are first identified as such by regular teachers who initiate a referral for assistance resulting from their concern about the child's performance. The regular class teacher is in an ideal position to observe students under a variety of circumstances. So, in addition to understanding typical patterns of child development in social, cognitive, and physical areas, the teacher must be a skilled *observer*. Even though some children are identified through planned screening procedures (e.g., vision, hearing, speech and language), teachers already should have identified behaviors suggesting possible problems in these areas.

Many techniques are available for teachers to use in identifying children with learning difficulties. These include criterion measures, informal tests, skill inventories, diagnostic tests, and observation scales. Although such testing devices are helpful, the skilled teacher also is alert to variance in pupil performance from day to day and task to task, along with other cues to inadequacies in their students' functioning.

Initiating a Referral

Although special education personnel often are involved in referrals for reevaluation or supplemental assistance for children with mild handicaps, the regular class teacher is the primary referral source. Exceptional children, therefore, often are dependent upon the regular class teacher's skill in first identifying their problem, then providing the necessary remediation or initiating a request, or referral, for assistance.

Historically, a referral for a student suspected of needing special education meant, first, removing the child from the regular class and, second, relieving the regular class teacher from further instructional responsibility. But with the current emphasis on least restrictive alternatives, mainstreaming, and integration, the referral process becomes the first step in assisting the regular teacher to meet a pupil's instructional needs. For some students, the referral will result in part-time or full-time placement outside the regular class but, more likely, the referral process will result in additional resources being made available to the regular class teacher. Resources may be in the form of diagnostic information, consultation, access to special materials or equipment, or actual assistance in teaching the child.

Once the teacher has decided to request assistance in remediating a child's problem, he or she is faced with the actualities of initiating the referral. Most districts have established referral procedures, generally involving use of a form that records the reason for referral, among other items. Through inservice training or a detailed special service manual, specific directions may be given regarding whom to contact for each of the problems encountered.

The intent of the referral process is to simplify the teacher's role and to expedite delivery of services to both teacher and child. For this reason, the typical referral form is usually brief. (Figure 3.1 provides an example). Teachers inexperienced in initiating referrals may find the form difficult to complete because they do not know what information to share and what questions will result in obtaining the proper assistance. One should remember that referral is only the first act in requesting assistance. Additional opportunities will occur for personal consultation, allowing for elaboration. This should not imply, however, that the teacher need only record a general statement about the child to suggest that testing is needed.

Moran (1976), in describing the elements of an effective referral question, states:

First, a good referral question is accompanied by all information already available to the teacher. It cannot be stressed too strongly that a teacher who refers a student must know everything that can be learned about him or her under classroom conditions before s/he should even consider referring the learner to someone else for testing.

It is totally inappropriate, for example, for a teacher to refer a student for evaluation of visual or auditory subskills involved in the reading process without simultaneously reporting to the potential examiner the student's instructional reading level, scores on skills tests in reading, and information about the student's level of vocabulary and grammar. If a teacher refers a child as a reading problem without providing the test information s/he already possesses, the teacher cannot be surprised if testing does not go beyond what s/he had already discovered. All relevant classroom test scores, behavioral observations, and reports of daily written products should be presented in summary form as part of the referral.

Second, the teacher should always report as part of a referral any intervention which s/he has already attempted with this student. For example, if s/he has conducted trial teaching of a VAKT (Visual-Auditory-Kinesthetic-Tactile) method of presenting sight words and has found it ineffective, s/he should report that

REFERRAL
FOR
RE-EVALUATION

IBAS FORM 6

TO: DATE:_____

STUDENT NAME _____   DATE INITIALLY PLACED
                                                 IN SPECIAL EDUCATION _____

CURRENT PLACEMENT   DATE PLACED _____   REGULAR TEACHER _____

PROGRAM _____   SUPPORT TEACHER _____

BUILDING _____   PRINCIPAL _____

                                                DIAGNOSTICIAN _____

REASON FOR REFERRAL:

FORMS ATTACHED

☐ SUMMARY EVALUATION REPORT   ☐ _____

☐ OBJECTIVE CLUSTER SUMMARY ASSESSMENT ☐ _____

☐ _____   ☐ _____

☐ _____   ☐ _____

COMMENTS AND SUPPORTIVE INFORMATION

PREPARED BY (SIGNATURE)   DATE

© 1975 Learner Managed Designs, Inc.
Published by **Edmark** ASSOCIATES
13241 Northrup Way
Bellevue, WA 98005   PRODUCT #143

Figure 3.1   Referral for Reevaluation

information; otherwise, s/he is likely to find that the examiner will recommend just that procedure for the learner whose visual skills are relatively weak. Any special materials or methods which have been tried, and the length of time they have been applied, should be mentioned. Also, the textbooks and supplementary materials currently being used with the student should be listed. If the classroom operation includes a system of rewards or a token economy, that information should be provided so that any recommendation for intervention would be made within that framework. If these types of information are provided, the teacher should not find, as so many have reported, that the examiner suggested interventions which have already been undertaken.

Third, the teacher must make a statement of what s/he has to know in order to instruct the student appropriately. That is, s/he has to be able to state what it is about the student that s/he cannot discover in the classroom. In the case of a reading problem, for example, s/he should be able to state that s/he would like to know whether Johnny demonstrates the subskills to profit from group reading instruction in the strongly phonics-oriented basal reader, or whether auditory skills are markedly below norms for his age. S/he may want to ask if Johnny's failure to complete written seatwork appears to be due to behavioral causes or deficient fine-motor skills. S/he may suspect that a student is unusually bright, and wants to know how far s/he should push the child to achieve and how he can best be motivated since he is not now achieving. If the question is one of placement, it should be so stated: Does Johnny require individualized instruction in a small group situation such as a resource room or self-contained special class? Is Jim a candidate for placement in an EMR classroom on the basis of his difficulty in keeping up with the lowest groups in the class? Should Sally have reading instruction in the resource room but remain in the classroom for all other instruction? (p. 8).

If the child's problem is not related to academic performance, but rather to social behavior or a physical/medical condition, the reported information will vary. But the responsibility remains to clearly communicate the nature of the problem.

In addition to communicating an interpretation of the child's problems and the expectation for assistance, the teacher has an obligation to prepare the child for referral. In some cases, the student's only experience with special personnel probably has been in a group situation.

Most districts have due process procedures that begin with obtaining permission for testing from parents. These procedures tend to be administrative and do not focus on helping the child understand why testing is necessary, or why other people are interested in his or her school performance. In any referral that results in testing, observation, or consultation with the student, the teacher should assist the student in understanding what will take place and why. The student's attitude clearly can influence test performance. Teachers should be alert to any cues that suggest a student is anxious about the test or consultation, and emphasis should be placed on helping the student in the area in which difficulty is being encountered. *The goal is to prepare the student to perform optimally under the testing or consultation situation.*

Assessment

The level and kind of assessment will vary according to the reason for referral. If the referral is health-related, the school nurse or physician may be involved. If the problem is related to hearing, speech, or language, the audiologist or speech clinician may be called in. If the reason for referral relates primarily to academic performance, the school psychologist or a person identified as an educational diagnostician may participate. Frequently, the response to a referral entails participation by several resource staff members.

Diagnostic procedures typically are employed in evaluation activities specific to academic problems. Although the diagnostic procedure used in other types of referrals will vary, the general series of evaluation activities will be similar.

The first priority of the educational diagnosis will be to clarify the reason for referral and to attempt to substantiate the existence of an instructional problem. This generally will involve a conference with the referring teacher and a review of anecdotal and related information specific to the suspected problem. The diagnostician may observe the student in the classroom, confer with parents, or consult with other resource personnel prior to determining what instructional steps to follow. *The diagnostician's objective is to determine the nature of the problem and to obtain the necessary information to prescribe an effective educational program.*

Formal testing may or may not be required. When the referral involves a child suspected of having a handicapping condition, the evaluation process frequently results in either a recommendation for the regular class teacher to use specific instructional techniques or for the student to be placed in special programs on a part- or full-time basis. In such cases, specific procedures must be applied. (A later section in this chapter describes these procedures.)

Having confirmed that an instructionally related problem exists, the diagnostician or school psychologist usually assumes responsibility for:

1. Determining what evaluation information is necessary to provide appropriate remediation;
2. Obtaining required approvals for testing;
3. Administering or arranging for administration of appropriate evaluation instruments;
4. Compiling needed information from appropriate sources (teachers, other professionals, records, and parents);
5. Observing the student in natural and structured settings;

6. Analyzing test results and data collected;
7. Organizing test results and data into a report format usable by a review committee;
8. Formulating recommendations;
9. Translating diagnostic information into information usable by teachers or parents;
10. Initiating procedures for IEP conferences, if indicated.

If a child is determined not to be handicapped, the diagnostician will work directly with the teacher in implementing the recommendations. If the child is found to have a handicapping condition, an Individualized Education Program (IEP), as required by PL 94-142, must be developed in a formal conference. The conference committee then becomes responsible for making instructional and/or placement decisions.

Making Instructional/Placement Decisions

The child's teacher continues to make instructional decisions during the time the referral is being processed, since the child is still enrolled. Because the referral process requires time, the teacher must continue to work with the student as effectively as possible. After the evaluation process has been completed, recommendations are made regarding needed changes in the student's program. These recommendations may involve the child's regular teacher using special techniques or materials, or the recommendation may entail placement in a special program on a part- or full-time basis.

The instructional/placement decision is a critical step in the general planning process. Evaluative and descriptive data specific to the child must be available if appropriate decisions are to be made. Decisions regarding instructional options and placement should be made in conference with resource persons and teachers most directly involved in the child's program. Because of the number of children referred for evaluation, time rarely permits more than one conference to make instructional and/or placement decisions on a referral — making the preceding steps exceedingly important. A clear set of directives should result from the conference, in terms of instructional methods and programming materials to be used, as well as evaluation guidelines and follow-up suggestions.

Implementation

Presumably, teacher and student both benefit from the planning process. The degree to which the teacher benefits depends in part on his or her effectiveness in the planning process. If the teacher clearly communicates information on the child's problem in the referral, is responsive in conferring with the diagnostician, and is an effective conference participant, the implementation step should prove beneficial.

The teacher initiating the referral now may have full responsibility for implementation, or the responsibility may be shared with a resource teacher or other support personnel. Under some circumstances, implementation may involve transferring the student to a special class, in which case the teacher is responsible for the transfer process. In situations where the student remains with the referring teacher part- or full-time, implementation means carrying out specific recommendations and continuing the planning process. The teacher must monitor the student's daily progress, with emphasis on *appropriateness* of the child's placement as well as *effectiveness* of the instructional techniques being employed. The teacher also must determine when additional assistance is needed and when to refer the student for reevaluation.

In addition, the teacher is responsible for maintaining student performance records. An important facet of maintaining records is to provide a *cumulative perspective* on how the student has progressed over a period of time. This allows for optimum review of how the student has responded to specific teaching techniques and materials. *Effective instructional planning depends on the availability of information on the student's performance in response to planned activities.*

IMPLICATIONS OF THE IEP FOR INSTRUCTIONAL PLANNING

The current national emphasis on instructional planning for exceptional children is directly related to requirements of PL 94-142. The law does not specify the planning process to be followed, but it does set forth detailed requirements on what should be included in an Individualized Education Program (IEP) and the conditions under which the plan should be developed. The law's intent is not to standardize instructional planning nor to promote a particular teaching methodology. The goal is to establish use of the IEP to bring about quality education for exceptional children and youth.

The law is explicit in its requirements that an IEP be developed for every handicapped child at the beginning of the school year and be reviewed annually. Once a child has been identified as handicapped, a conference must be held within 30 days for the purpose of developing the Individualized Education Program.

The IEP conference itself is equivalent to the fourth step in the above suggested sequence in instructional planning. *Preparation* for the IEP conference would include the earlier steps of identifying problems, initiating referral, and evaluation. Districts have used different terms to describe the conference. Many refer to it simply as the IEP conference; others call it the placement or Child Study Team conference (New Jersey) or the Administration Review and Dismissal (ARD) committee (Texas). (The latter is an attempt to reflect the main functions performed by conference participants.) Although school districts vary in how they arrange and conduct IEP conferences and in the design of IEPs, most have used the PL 94-142 requirements as a basic frame of reference. These requirements provide minimal standards for instructional planning, as a basis upon which to develop a systematic instructional planning process.

IEP Conference Requirements

From the perspective of team decision making, the conference concept is not new. Special educators have been using the team or conference approach to make placement decisions on exceptional children for many years. The changes created by PL 94-142, however, relate to the increased number of children involved, parent participation, and the requirements necessary for a written plan. In the past, conferences were held primarily in difficult cases or cases in which the child in question needed several special services. The number of conferences held by a staff depended upon program vacancies for children, the number of referrals, and the time available for staff conference participation. The result of most such conferences was a placement decision and general recommendations. Although parents may have been consulted, they rarely were invited to participate in the conference. Not uncommonly, the conference was lengthy or involved a series of sessions. Today, with the IEP requirement applying to all handicapped children, considerable attention must be given to efficiency in the use of time. It also means that careful decisions must be made regarding collection of data and organization of reports in advance of the conference.

School districts now are required to involve the following participants in all IEP conferences on handicapped children *(Federal Register, 8/23/77)*:

Sec. 121a.344 Participants in meetings.
(a) *General.* The public agency shall insure that each meeting includes the following participants:
(1) A representative of the public agency, other than the child's teacher, who is qualified to provide, or supervise the provision of, special education.
(2) The child's teacher.
(3) One or both of the child's parents, subject to Sec. 121a.345.
(4) The child, where appropriate.
(5) Other individuals at the discretion of the parent or agency.
(b) *Evaluation personnel.* For a handicapped child who has been evaluated for the first time, the public agency shall insure:
(1) That a member of the evaluation team participates in the meeting; or
(2) That the representative of the public agency, the child's teacher, or some other person is present at the meeting who is knowledgeable about the evaluation procedures used with the child and is familiar with the results of the evaluation.

The building principal frequently is the representative of the educational agency, but in some cases it is the director of special education or other administrative personnel. Regarding teacher participation, as many as three teachers commonly are involved. If a child is referred by a regular class teacher and subsequently is to be referred for placement in a resource room, both teachers will be involved. If the child is in a departmentalized program, each regular teacher may participate. This participation requirement strengthens the teacher's role and helps maintain an emphasis on instruction.

With reference to parent participation, districts must take extensive measures to encourage parents to participate. These considerations include scheduling the meetings at convenient times and maintaining effective communication with the parents. If parents refuse to participate, the conference can be held in their absence, but the district must be able to document its attempts to involve the parents and the latter's refusal to participate.

The decision on whether or not and how much to involve each student in the IEP conference is a difficult one. The intent is to have the child present by design, not arbitrarily. Of course, students should understand why changes are being made in their programs, but a discussion in the child's presence about his or her differences and needs for assistance is not always necessary. In the case of secondary-aged mildly handicapped students, valid reasons may exist for having the child present. Decisions regarding student conference participation probably are best made in consultation with the parents. "Other individuals" refers to speech therapists, psychologists, nurses, physicians, and other specialists whose expertise is related to the case being reviewed.

The conference's goal is to develop an IEP which is most appropriate for the student. But since time rarely permits involvement of all participants in more than one conference relative to a particular student, evaluative and related information must be available and effectively presented during the conference.

Each person involved must be prepared to participate. The person assigned to chair the conference is obligated to moderate the discussion in an objective manner and to encourage full participation. The emphasis, again, must be on developing an appropriate IEP for the student. One of the most difficult tasks faced by chairpersons of IEP conferences is helping the group reach agreement on the IEP. Two main strategies— staff preparation and communication with parents before the conference — will aid this decision making. Parents are expected to report their concerns and expectations for their child. It would be unfair to suggest that they will tend to be defensive, but in many cases they will need encouragement to participate, particularly in terms of their informative role. And school personnel lack experience in working with parents in making educational decisions, so the task may not be an easy one. Teachers, both regular and special, frequently will have the most difficult role. They must advocate the most appropriate IEP but at the same time may not have access to information acquired by the specialist until the time of the conference.

An important concern at this juncture is to guard against prematurely incorporating recommendations into the IEP merely to gain support from the parent or to reach agreement on the IEP. One must remember that the law does not hold the school liable if the child fails to achieve the IEP's objectives. Also, the risk is always present that an unreasonable expectation can emerge from an IEP conference. On the one hand, the IEP may exceed the student's capabilities or, on the other hand, the short-term objectives may exist already within the student's repertoire of skills. When participating in a conference, teachers need to keep in mind that they are responsible for implementation. If they knowingly agree to an IEP which they believe is not appropriate, they are not being fair to themselves or to the student. Although changes can and should be made when needed in the IEP after it is implemented, naturally it is best to begin with the most appropriate program possible. Teachers willing to assume advocacy roles can help guard against premature decisions in an attempt to reach agreement on the IEP. Because of the large number of conferences held and the time required to monitor IEPs, the potential hazard exists that the conference will become a routine meeting, with decisions made in advance and programs designed with such a low expectation level that the child will too easily attain the objectives — or unrealistic objectives may be included to fulfill parental expectations.

IEP Content

Because requirements regulating IEP content are clearly described, certain practices are common across most districts, although the format and scope of the IEPs vary substantially. Since most districts have not had extensive experience in applying the IEP concept, validated procedures have not been designed. Very few IEP models exist. Many districts have designed their own procedures and/or adopted available systems. In all cases, the first level of concern has been the degree to which the IEP format accommodates the required content. PL 94-142 specifies that each individualized program must include the following (*Federal Register,* 8/23/77):

> **Sec. 121a.346 Content of Individualized Education Program**
> The individualized education program for each child must include:
> (a) A statement of the child's present levels of educational performance;
> (b) A statement of annual goals, including short term instructional objectives;
> (c) A statement of the specific special education and related services to be provided to the child, and the extent to which the child will be able to participate in regular educational programs;
> (d) The projected dates for initiation of services and the anticipated duration of the services; and
> (e) Appropriate objective criteria and evaluation procedures and schedules for determining, on at least an annual basis, whether the short term instructional objectives are being achieved.

In reviewing the above content requirements, the plan clearly must be detailed; and the lack of existing resources should not be a limiting factor in recommending inclusion of the service. Teachers and support personnel should advocate for the services the student needs even if such services are not presently available. If they don't specify the services needed, handicapped children in many districts will never receive appropriate services. But if substantial delays are likely in gaining access to these services, alternatives should be considered, with the qualification that alternative services do not substitute for nor excuse the district from developing the desired services.

The IEP concept is a major improvement over most instructional planning practices and programs of the past, when planning centered on placement decisions. The improvement comes largely from requiring a written plan that includes evaluation procedures. Too often, students have been placed in programs with attention only to their eligibility. Now, equal emphasis must be given to describing specific program components. Hopefully, the IEP requirements will stimulate districts to employ systematic instructional planning procedures.

The IEP represents the primary vehicle in PL 94-142 for assuring quality education for the handicapped. It also provides a basis for assessing student performance and program effectiveness. Teachers now have support for establishing conditions conducive to planning, but they also must exercise their own professionalism to prevent the IEP from becoming a paper process which begins and ends with the IEP conference.

Suggested Steps for Developing IEPs

Although districts vary in the specific steps involved in designing IEPs, some general procedures are common to most districts. Two examples here will illustrate the IEP process. The reader is reminded that certain protective procedures apply to the IEP — e.g., parental permission for testing, and nondiscriminatory testing.

The first example directly refers to the general instructional planning steps previously described. Using these steps as a frame of reference, the instructional planning process can be related to developing IEPs. Figure 3.2 illustrates such an approach. The planning steps remain basically the same, with minor modifications to meet the unique instructional planning requirements of the IEP concept; and an additional evaluation step (6) has been included.

Step 1 *Identification of Learning Problems* remains the initial step in determining whether or not a student's problem is brought to the attention of appropriate personnel.

Step 2 *Referral* (this step remains essentially the same).

Step 3 *Evaluation* is broadened to include an extensive review of the available service alternatives required to meet the student's needs.

Step 4 *The IEP Conference* replaces the instructional placement decision step. Previously collected data and program needs are presented. A written plan is prepared.

Step 5 *Implementation* becomes a more comprehensive step in terms of the IEP, as the plan must be disseminated to all persons who will participate in the student's program. The plan is actually put into effect at this stage. Each participant is required to monitor the student's performance and to make any necessary modifications to the plan. This is the "service delivery" stage.

Step 6 *Evaluation* is repeated as a final step in the cycle. The intent is to determine student progress and the IEP's general effectiveness. During Step 3 the evaluation focus was on diagnosing the student's problem in preparation for recommending an IEP. During Step 5, the evaluation emphasis continues but focuses on achieving short-term objectives. In this step a deci-

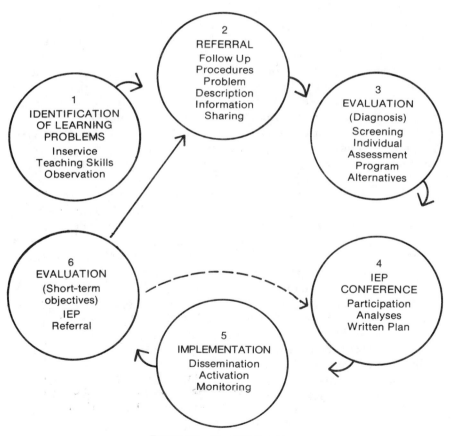

Figure 3.2   The IEP Process

sion must be made on the IEP's overall effectiveness. The decision may be to continue the IEP with minimal modification, or to initiate a referral to obtain additional evaluation services. In the latter case, Step 2's referral process will be repeated. In other cases, procedures may call for holding another IEP conference; this generally occurs when the original IEP is considered tentative and the committee desires a report at a particular time. Primarily, Step 6 is intended to satisfy the annual evaluation requirement, but in most cases evaluation should be carried out on a more frequent basis.

The flow chart in Figure 3.3 illustrates a second approach, involving a series of steps oriented to a "Placement Committee" function. This example is taken from a publication by the National Association of State Directors of Special Education (1977) designed to provide clarification on the protective procedures inherent in PL 94-142 and guidelines for developing IEPs. The steps suggested by this example center on three primary types of information — eligibility information, planning information, and placement options. These functions are similar to those described in Steps 2 and 3 of the previous example; the example in Figure 3.3 also begins with referral procedures and ends with an emphasis on evaluation (i.e., a decision or change in placement/programming). The model illustrates the kinds of decisions involved in developing an IEP and the sequence in which the decisions logically are made.

For districts to monitor the effectiveness of developing, implementing, and evaluating procedures relative to IEPs, they have become aware of the necessity to rely on specially designed forms, which may be self-designed, modified or adopted from available systems. Well designed forms allow for efficient collection and assessment of essential information without placing undue demands on teachers. Unfortunately, special education programs have a history of creating sometimes unnecessary forms that may have been *too* comprehensive. Consequently, the use of forms often is suspect. The IEP, however, *requires* a recorded plan; thus, special forms now are necessary.

The written plan serves at least three purposes: (1) It provides a permanent source of information on the student's plan which can be shared with parents, as well as with the teacher and other personnel responsible for implementing the student's program; (2) It provides a reference regarding instructional decisions made on a particular student's program; and (3) It creates a cumulative data base for future program planning for individual students. Forms are important because

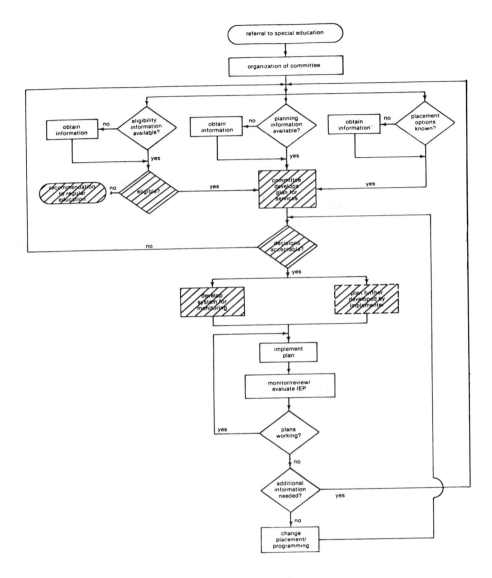

Figure 3.3 Developing the IEP

From: *Functions of the Placement Committee in Special Education: A Resource Manual*, 1976, by the National Association of State Directors of Special Education, 1201 16th Street NW, Washington, DC 20036.

districts must maintain records containing data on the IEPs — when they are developed and initiated, and evaluation data on their effectiveness. The traditional cumulative record of information ranging from test scores and anecdotal comments to attendance records is no longer sufficient or appropriate.

Designing selected forms for use in recording and monitoring the IEP necessitates an understanding of the IEP concept and the district's philosophy toward instructional planning. A system of forms can be designed which meets requirements of the law regarding IEPs but still not have a positive influence on the student's program. If attention is given only to administrative procedures or to minimal content requirements, the consequence may be a written plan which falls short of promoting quality instruction. Following are guidelines to be considered in designing or selecting forms for use with IEPs. The emphasis is on a *system* of forms rather than isolated forms for individual purposes. Particular attention has been given to suggestions which strengthen the teacher's role in the implementation stage.

Guidelines for IEP Form Design

1. *Accommodation of Full Service Information.* The forms must be designed to allow for specifying of plans for the entire range of services which a student may require. For example, a mildly handicapped student's plan may include objectives and evaluation data in the areas of academic skills, language skills, social behavior, and psychomotor tasks.

2. *Content Flexibility.* As objectives are specified, the IEP begins to include program content, but the forms themselves should not dictate the content. For example, some districts have designed forms that include skill checklists; skills considered appropriate for each student are checked, representing objectives. Such an approach is restrictive in that all skills cannot be listed. These forms also contribute to decisions which are not appropriate to the student's needs. Better, teachers should be allowed to develop specific objectives based on their knowledge of each student's needs.

3. *Emphasis on Retrieval of Program Related Information.* In designing forms, the temptation may be to request information because it is

interesting, of possible future use, or simply accessible. But the primary objective should be to elicit information related only to student program needs. Since IEPs for most students relate to educational services, the design should emphasize retrieval of instructionally related information.

4. *Effectiveness without Repeated Use.* Forms used in the implementation stage should not require constant use. If the teacher or specialist is required to record information on a regular, daily basis, or on every task in a therapy session, more time will be involved in recording than in instruction. Consideration of the teacher or other specialist's time is critical to the design of an effective system. Information must be recorded while the IEP is being implemented, but this should be accomplished without excessive time demands on the staff.

5. *Provision for Full Participation.* Most IEPs necessitate the involvement of two or more professionals (i.e., regular teachers, special teachers, and/or specialists). The system must encourage their full participation. A primary requirement is that the system provide a communication basis among participants; they should be able to exchange information on the student's performance.

6. *Utilization without Extensive Training.* This guideline is almost a commandment. If the system is so complicated or detailed that extensive training is required for its use, it likely will not be successful. Again, time is a factor. If a system is complicated, it probably will be difficult to implement. Because regular educators as well as special educators are involved in implementing IEPs, various persons must understand the system. The amount of training required to understand and use the form system should be minimal. This is not to suggest that the system should be so simple that it becomes of little value, but it does suggest that serious attention should be given to any training requirements for implementation. A good system need not be complicated.

7. *Cumulative and Program Based Qualities.* The form system must allow for collecting information on the student's program in those areas identified in the IEP. If this is accomplished, cumulative information will be available as a basis for making decisions on IEP changes. Too many form systems require only the recording of data regarding whether or not the IEP was implemented and its effects on student performance. If the goal is to improve as well as judge instruction, a more continuous approach to recording information is required.

8. *Sustaining Nature.* A major investment of time, effort, and resources is involved when a district designs or adopts a form system. Little is gained if changes routinely are made in the system after it has been initiated. Consideration should be given to reducing the likelihood of having to make changes each year. Some modifications are almost inevitable over time, and supplementary forms may be necessary additions, but to the fullest extent possible, uniformity and continuity should be maintained after a system has been initiated.

9. *Format Considerations.* Readable, understandable forms are highly desirable wherever they are used. A well-designed form is innately helpful, but someone also should be available to assist or clarify the use of the IEP system forms.

For purposes of illustration, an existing IEP form system will be discussed. The Instructional Based Appraisal System (IBAS, Meyen, 1976) represents an approach to the IEP concept, with emphasis on the instructional (i.e., implementation) stage. The instructional emphasis is compatible with the IEP's intent but probably goes beyond what is minimally necessary in terms of required accountability measures. The IBAS system is comprehensive and includes several banks; some forms intentionally are not included here (for example, parental consent forms for testing, summary forms for recording IEP conference transcripts, and parental agreement forms on which parents indicate their agreement on the IEP).

Each school should identify the functions of such standard forms and identify them with the school. In many cases, forms for these purposes could be printed on district letterhead and could include descriptive information specific to that district. The IBAS forms relate to the major elements of the IEP concept and are intended to be generalizable across districts.

Six forms comprise the IBAS system. With the exception of one form, they are completed annually or, at most, quarterly. The exception is Form 3, the Teacher's Instructional Plan (TIP) Form. Monitoring of the IEP is accomplished primarily through the routine use of this form.

Form 1 *Diagnostic Information Worksheet* (Figures 3.4-3.9)

This form is designed to assist the person responsible for diagnostic evaluation in organizing evaluation information. It is a six-page, foldout form which contains provisions for recording referral information, test data (e.g., intelligence, achievement, diagnostic), and correlated test results, informal assessments, and observations.

Side six (Figure 3.9) of the form contains a summary sheet, providing a profile for recording descriptive information, evaluation results, and summary statements based on evaluation and observations. (This form is actually a supplement to IBAS in that it is not required; it is merely an organizer for the evaluator.) The form can be shared with IEP conference participants or it can be used by the evaluator as a reference. The form is not totally appropriate for use with severely handicapped children; more appropriate data will need to be added on a supplemental form.

Form 2 *Educational Program Plan* (Figures 3.10 and 3.11)

This is the first IBAS form to be completed as part of the actual IEP. It represents the IEP's general statement and is filled out during the IEP conference. The form is printed as a file folder, allowing it to serve as a divider in the student's cumulative IEP file, as well as to store related information, correspondence, etc.

Side 1(Figure 3.10, top) contains provisions for recording and identifying student information, the placement decision, and conference team members.

Side 2 (Figure 3.11) opens up and expands to two pages to provide space for recording an assessment profile of the student's performance, observation data, analysis of skills and behaviors, suggestions on instructional strategies, and suggestions on presenting instruction, (i.e., methods and media). The Assessment Profile is the same as included in the Diagnostician Worksheet—this is done to enhance the information sharing process.

Side 3 (Figure 3.10, bottom) provides for annual goals, three-month goals, and comments. The intent is to focus the attention of conference participants on long-term goals. The reference to three-month goals is to arbitrarily suggest that, at a minimum, the general goal should be reexamined at least every three months.

By itself, this form is not an IEP, but it does stimulate instructional decisions, and it complies with most of the IEP requirements. For example, it allows for recording the student's current performance level, annual goals, educational services such as placement and media, as well as date of goals, listing of persons responsible for program plans, and additional information essential to instructional planning. It does not include short-term objectives and evaluation procedures. In fact, the form does not provide specific directions of an instructional nature. These have been intentionally separated and included on a separate form (Form 3, described below).

IBAS
DIAGNOSTIC
INFORMATION
WORKSHEET

IBAS FORM 1

☐ INITIAL EVALUATION
_____
DATE

☐ RE-EVALUATION
_____
DATE

☐ RE-EVALUATION
_____
DATE

DETAILS TO INSTRUCTORS FOR USE OF THIS FORM ARE FOUND IN THE IBAS DIAGNOSTICIAN'S MANUAL.

REFERRAL DATE _____ SCHOOL _____ GRADE _____
REFERRED BY: _____ TELEPHONE NO. _____
REASON FOR REFERRAL _____
_____
_____
_____
_____

BACKGROUND INFORMATION:

PREVIOUS TESTING

CASE # _____
PARENTS OR GUARDIAN _____
NAME _____
ADDRESS _____
SEX ___ M ___ F BIRTHDATE _____
PHONE _____ CA _____

Side 1

Figure 3.4 Diagnostic Information Worksheet
(IBAS FORM 1, Side 1)

INTELLIGENCE TEST RESULTS

GROUP

DATE	TEST NAME	COMMENTS:
RESULTS:		
INTERPRETATION:		

INDIVIDUAL

DATE	SLOSSON INTELLIGENCE TEST	COMMENTS:
RESULTS:		
CA _____ MA _____ IQ _____ PERCENTILE _____ SD _____		
INTERPRETATION:		

DATE	WECHSLER INTELLIGENCE SCALE FOR CHILDREN	COMMENTS:

VERBAL IQ _____   PERFORMANCE IQ _____   FULL SCALE IQ _____

SD _____

SCALED SCORES

INFORMATION	_____	PICTURE COMPLETION	_____
COMPREHENSION	_____	PICTURE ARRANGEMENT	_____
ARITHMETIC	_____	BLOCK DESIGN	_____
SIMILARITIES	_____	OBJECT ASSEMBLY	_____
VOCABULARY	_____	CODING	_____
(DIGIT SPAN)	_____	(MAZES)	_____

INTERPRETATION:

OTHER

DATE	TEST NAME	COMMENTS:
RESULTS:		
INTERPRETATION:		

CA

PHONE

SEX ___ M ___ F BIRTHDATE

ADDRESS

NAME

PARENTS OR GUARDIAN

CASE #

Side 2

Figure 3.5 Diagnostic Information Worksheet
(IBAS FORM 1, Side 2)

ACHIEVEMENT TESTING

DATE	TEST NAME			COMMENTS:
RESULTS:				
INTERPRETATION:				

DATE	WIDE RANGE ACHIEVEMENT TEST			COMMENTS:
RESULTS:	GRADE	STANDARD SCORE	PERCENTILE	
READING (WORD PRONUNCIATION) _____	_____	_____		
SPELLING	_____	_____	_____	
ARITHMETIC	_____	_____	_____	
INTERPRETATION:				

DATE	PEABODY INDIVIDUAL ACHIEVEMENT TEST			COMMENTS:
RESULTS:	GRADE	STANDARD SCORE	PERCENTILE	
MATHEMATICS	_____	_____	_____	
READING RECOGNITION	_____	_____	_____	
READING COMPREHENSION	_____	_____	_____	
SPELLING	_____	_____	_____	
GENERAL INFORMATION	_____	_____	_____	
TOTAL TEST	_____	_____	_____	
INTERPRETATION:				

DIAGNOSTIC TESTING

DATE	TEST NAME	COMMENTS:
RESULTS:		
INTERPRETATION:		

DATE	TEST NAME	COMMENTS:
RESULTS:		
INTERPRETATION:		

Side 3

Figure 3.6 Diagnostic Information Worksheet
(IBAS FORM 1, Side 3)

CORRELATE TESTING
(VISUAL PERCEPTION, AUDITORY PERCEPTION, LANGUAGE, MOTOR SKILLS, BEHAVIOR RATINGS)

DATE | TEST NAME | COMMENTS:

RESULTS:

INTERPRETATION:

DATE | TEST NAME | COMMENTS:

RESULTS:

INTERPRETATION:

DATE | TEST NAME | COMMENTS:

RESULTS:

INTERPRETATION:

DATE | TEST NAME | COMMENTS:

RESULTS:

INTERPRETATION:

DATE | TEST NAME | COMMENTS:

RESULTS:

INTERPRETATION:

Side 4

Figure 3.7 Diagnostic Information Worksheet
(IBAS FORM 1, Side 4)

INFORMAL WORK

DATE	DESCRIPTION OF PROCEDURES AND RESULTS

DATE	LOCATION	DESCRIPTION OF BEHAVIOR	FREQUENCY	DURATION	TYPE OF BEHAVIOR
					☐ APPROPRIATE ☐ INAPPROPRIATE
					☐ APPROPRIATE ☐ INAPPROPRIATE
					☐ APPROPRIATE ☐ INAPPROPRIATE
					☐ APPROPRIATE ☐ INAPPROPRIATE
					☐ APPROPRIATE ☐ INAPPROPRIATE
					☐ APPROPRIATE ☐ INAPPROPRIATE
					☐ APPROPRIATE ☐ INAPPROPRIATE

Figure 3.8   Diagnostic Information Worksheet
(IBAS FORM 1, Side 5)

Side 6

ASSESSMENT PROFILE

OVERALL INTELLECTUAL FUNCTIONING	BELOW AVERAGE		AVERAGE			ABOVE AVERAGE		
	WEAK		STRONG			LEVEL		
ACADEMIC AREAS ASSESSED	1	2	3	4	5	GRADE	AGE	
READING								
WORD RECOGNITION								
ORAL COMPREHENSION								
SILENT COMPREHENSION								
LISTENING COMPREHENSION								
ARITHMETIC								
ARITHMETIC COMPUTATION								
ARITHMETIC REASONING								
SPELLING								

SCREENING	VISION	DEFICIT	CORRECTED	NORMAL
	HEARING	DEFICIT	CORRECTED	NORMAL
	WEAK		STRONG	LEVEL
CORRELATE AREAS ASSESSED	1	2	3	4	5	GRADE	AGE
AUDITORY PERCEPTION							
VISUAL PERCEPTION							
GROSS MOTOR COORDINATION							
FINE MOTOR COORDINATION							
ORAL LANGUAGE COMPREHENSION							
ORAL LANGUAGE EXPRESSION							
WRITTEN LANGUAGE EXPRESSION							
SPEECH (ARTICULATION)							
SOCIAL-EMOTIONAL							

APPROPRIATE BEHAVIORS

INAPPROPRIATE BEHAVIORS

CONCLUSIONS:

RECOMMENDATION:
☐ FURTHER REFERRAL TO: _____
☐ ELIGIBLE FOR SPECIAL EDUCATION SERVICES: _____
☐ NOT ELIGIBLE FOR SPECIAL EDUCATION SERVICES

☐ SPECIAL CONSIDERATION
☐ RE-EVALUATION: (DATE) _____
☐ OTHER _____

EDUCATIONAL DIAGNOSTICIAN _____   DATE _____

ARTD COMMITTEE STAFFING DATE _____   DECISION _____   REPORT ATTACHED ☐

Figure 3.9 Diagnostic Information Worksheet
(IBAS FORM 1, Side 6)

EDUCATIONAL PROGRAM PLAN
IBAS FORM 2

PARENT OR GUARDIAN

NAME   ADDRESS   TELEPHONE

HOME LANGUAGE _____ ETHNIC _____ SEX _____

PLACEMENT

DATE	BUILDING	PRINCIPAL	GRADE

IBAS TEAM

	NAME	ROOM NUMBER
DIAGNOSTICIAN		
REGULAR TEACHER		
SUPPORT TEACHER		
OTHERS (SPECIFY POSITION BELOW.)		

© 1975 Learner Managed Designs, Inc.
Published by **Edmark** ASSOCIATES
13241 Northrup Way
Bellevue, WA 98005   Product Code #139

Side 1

INSTRUCTIONAL PROGRAM

YEAR LONG EDUCATIONAL PROGRAM DIRECTIONS

INSTRUCTIONAL GOALS FIRST THREE MONTHS _____ TO _____	

INSTRUCTIONAL GOALS SECOND THREE MONTHS _____ TO _____	

INSTRUCTIONAL GOALS THIRD THREE MONTHS _____ TO _____	

COMMENTS:

Side 3

Figure 3.10   Educational Program Plan
(IBAS FORM 2, Side 1)

NAME			EDUCATIONAL								
	LAST	FIRST	PROGRAM								
BIRTHDATE			PLAN - IBAS								

ASSESSMENT PROFILE SUMMARY OF STRENGTHS AND WEAKNESSES

OVERALL INTELLECTUAL FUNCTIONING	BELOW AVERAGE	AVERAGE		ABOVE AVERAGE	SCREENING	VISION HEARING	DEFICIT DEFICIT	CORRECTED CORRECTED	NORMAL NORMAL

ACADEMIC AREAS ASSESSED	WEAK		STRONG		LEVEL		CORRELATE AREAS ASSESSED	WEAK		STRONG		LEVEL	
	1	2	3	4	5	GRADE	AGE		1	2	3	4	5	GRADE	AGE
READING								AUDITORY PERCEPTION							
WORD RECOGNITION								VISUAL PERCEPTION							
ORAL COMPREHENSION								GROSS MOTOR COORDINATION							
SILENT COMPREHENSION								FINE MOTOR COORDINATION							
LISTENING COMPREHENSION								ORAL LANGUAGE COMPREHENSION							
ARITHMETIC								ORAL LANGUAGE EXPRESSION							
ARITHMETIC COMPUTATION								WRITTEN LANGUAGE EXPRESSION							
ARITHMETIC REASONING								SPEECH (ARTICULATION)							
SPELLING								SOCIAL-EMOTIONAL							

APPROPRIATE BEHAVIORS	INAPPROPRIATE BEHAVIORS

SKILL ANALYSIS WHEN MASTERED ✓   WHEN MASTERED ✓

ACADEMIC	✓	BEHAVIOR	✓

BASIC INSTRUCTIONAL STRATEGIES

STRATEGIES FOR MANAGING INSTRUCTION (MOTIVATIONAL TECHNIQUES, ARRANGEMENTS, PHYSICAL ENVIRONMENT)

STRATEGIES FOR PRESENTING INSTRUCTION (INSTRUCTIONAL PROCEDURES AND MEDIA)

Side 2

Figure 3.11 Educational Program Plan
(IBAS FORM 2, Side 2)

Form 3   *Teachers Instructional Plan* (TIP) (Figures 3.12 and 3.13)
This is a foldout form designed so that carbon copies can be shared. The TIP form is the major element in the IBAS approach to the IEP, representing the IEP's instructional planning and evaluation dimension. It requires the specification of objectives and, in turn, focuses evaluation on specified objectives.

Side 1 (Figure 3.12) allows for recording pertinent information. Provisions are included for:

a. Recording identification information on students, including data for starting and stopping the plan.

b. Indicating who is to receive a copy.

c. Stating instructional goals. These goals are more specific than the annual or three-month goals stated in Form 1. They are intended to identify skills, concepts, or behaviors which need immediate attention. For example, in the area of academic performance, one goal might be "to assist the student in reorganizing numbers as related to objectives up to 10"; or in the area of social behavior, a goal might be "to assist the student in discussing rather than acting out negative feelings"; in speech therapy, a goal might pertain to a particular articulation error.

d. Stating short-term objectives. The form is designed for stating a cluster of five interrelated objectives pertaining to the previously stated instructional goals. The intent is to state objectives which, if achieved, will satisfy the instructional goal. The teachers or whoever is responsible for the student's program is asked to determine the instructional goals and write the objectives. Because writing objectives is time-consuming until a person becomes skilled at the task, the IBAS includes starter banks of objective clusters. These can be used as a reference or, if appropriate, clusters of objectives can be selected from the banks and used with specific students. A cluster rather than single objectives was decided upon because most skills and concepts require that several behaviors be emphasized simultaneously.

e. Checking the student's progress. Criteria are included for checking the student's performance, the user's decisions based on student progress, and an explanation of decisions. One decision criterion relates to "carrying over" the objective. This means that the objective remains appropriate but, since other cluster objectives have been satisfied, a new TIP

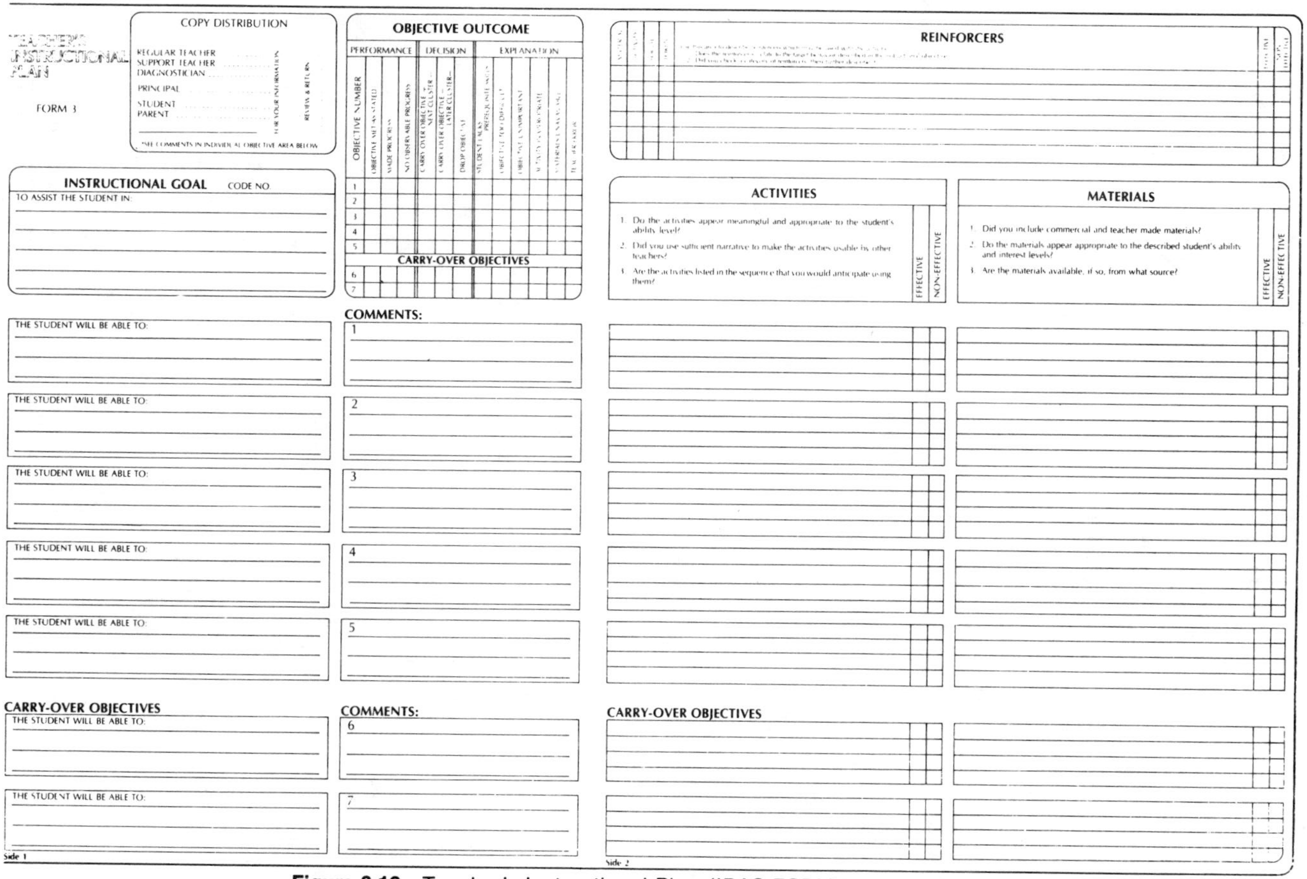

Figure 3.12 Teacher's Instructional Plan (IBAS FORM 3, Sides 1 and 2)

INSTRUCTIONS FOR USING THE TEACHER'S INSTRUCTIONAL PLAN.

A detailed explanation of the use of the Teacher's Instructional Plan is found in the Teacher's Guide.

SIDE 1 includes the instructional goal and a cluster of five instructional objectives. You may select clusters from the IBAS Objective Cluster Bank, use other curriculum objectives, or prepare new objectives following the guidelines in the Teacher's Guide.

SIDE 1 provides a place to record the objective outcome. In the three sections, you will record a choice for performance, decision, and explanation. Additional comments may be entered in the box provided next to each objective.

Indicate the distribution of each copy in the copy distribution area and if explanation is necessary for why someone is receiving a copy, fill it in on the reverse.

Check V to include in Objective Summary Assessment.

Code number of this objective.

Sequential number of objectives assigned for this student this cycle.

Example: A.31.2 is from the Objective Cluster Bank.

Example: This is the 17th objective this semester for this student.

INSTRUCTIONS (CONT'D)

SIDE 2 provides space to include a description of the instructional activities and materials you plan to use to meet the instructional objectives. The effectiveness of each activity and material should be noted by checking the appropriate column.

Reinforcers appropriate to the student reaching the objectives should be selected and recorded in the reinforcement section.

SIDE 3 provides space for a graphic illustration of the student's performance on each instructional objective. As each attempt at the objective is completed, enter the date of the session under the session number. When you have finished with an objective, after the last session indicate: "S" objective satisfied, "D" objective dropped, or "C" objective carried over. The purpose of the cluster profile is to create a record which will allow these objectives to be compared with objectives completed by the student on other T.I.P. forms.

SIDE 4 includes space for recording your comments throughout the instructional period.

NOTES

1975 Learner Managed Designs, Inc
Published by **Edmark ASSOCIATES**
11241 Northup Way
Bellevue, WA 98005

Product Code #140

Side 4

PRINTED IN U.S.A.

CLUSTER PROFILE

On last session record "S" satisfied, "D" dropped or "C" carried over

SESSION NUMBER	1	2	3	4	5	6	7	8	9	10
DATE										

SESSION NUMBER	1	2	3	4	5	6	7	8	9	10
DATE										

SESSION NUMBER	1	2	3	4	5	6	7	8	9	10
DATE										

SESSION NUMBER	1	2	3	4	5	6	7	8	9	10
DATE										

SESSION NUMBER	1	2	3	4	5	6	7	8	9	10
DATE										

CARRY-OVER OBJECTIVES

SESSION NUMBER	1	2	3	4	5	6	7	8	9	10
DATE										

SESSION NUMBER	1	2	3	4	5	6	7	8	9	10
DATE										

Side 3

INSTRUCTIONAL GOAL: TO ASSIST THE STUDENT IN: NO.

INSTRUCTIONAL AREA

DATE STARTED: / /   DATE STOPPED: / /

STUDENT'S NAME

INSTRUCTOR'S NAME

Figure 3.13   Teacher's Instructional Plan (IBAS FORM 3, Sides 3 and 4)

form can be started rather than remain on this cluster. The particular objective can be carried over to the next cluster.

f. Coding goals and objectives so that, over time, it is possible to organize the goals and objectives included in the student's program.

g. Identifying objectives which currently are considered important and worthy of inclusion in a periodic evaluation of student performance. The user marks a check in a box by the objective. Later, the checked objectives are compiled in an evaluation instrument. (Form 4 is used for this evaluation purpose.)

Side 2 (Figure 3.12) is used for recording information relating to activities and materials which the user feels are appropriate for the objective. Only brief notes are best. The idea is to cause the user to consider a wide range of activities and materials available for each objective. Teachers may not need to complete this side for each objective once the student is progressing on an appropriate instructional program.

Side 3 The Cluster Profile (Figure 3.13) is designed to help the teacher or other professionals using the form to determine the level of objectives most appropriate for the student. The user is asked to check the number of attempts required to teach each objective. No reference is made to minutes per try, nor must the recording be precisely accurate. The idea is to provide some indication of how difficult the objective was for the student.

The value of this exercise becomes apparent after several TIP forms have been used. It then is possible for the teacher or specialist to examine a series of Cluster Profiles and determine which objectives were easy and which were too difficult. If a student succeeded on one objective after the first try, it probably was too easy; if the student required eight or nine tries, it probably was too difficult. In both cases, the instruction probably was inappropriate. The user needs to examine these objectives clearly so particular elements can be identified and generalized for future objectives. No advantage is gained in specifying inappropriate objectives. The user's attention should focus on objectives at which the student succeeds in three or four tries. The Cluster Profile is a feedback source to the user and helps to assure that the student's program is maximally appropriate.

Side 4 (Figure 3.13) provides space for recording notes.

The TIP form is constructed so that after the carbons have been shared with other participants in the student's program, the person who prepared the form retains the original file copy. This form is completed for the first time during the IEP Conference. If a regular teacher and speech clinician or resource teacher, for example, are to be involved in the student's program, they each complete a TIP form and exchange copies. From that point on, each participant individually completes TIP forms, exchange copies, and retains the basic file copy. Every staff member participating in the student's program eventually accrues a cumulative record comprised of copies of the TIP forms prepared by others plus the originals they have initiated.

Every objective taught to a student need not be recorded on a TIP form but, until the teacher or specialist is certain that the student is on an appropriate program, TIP forms should be used regularly. For the first two weeks, one form per day might be used, and later the frequency can be reduced to one form per week. They should be continuous on some scheduled pattern in order to build a cumulative record on the student's progress.

Form 4 *Objective Cluster Summary Assessment* (Figure 3.14)

This form is designed as an evaluation instrument. Objectives which have been checked as important on the TIP form and require that student retention be checked are transferred to this form. This can be done on the basis of a predetermined schedule or whenever necessary to conduct a periodic evaluation of student progress. A sample of priority objectives should be recorded and an informal test designed to appraise student performance on the designated objectives. The form provides space for recording the results and thus becomes an informal achievement test tailored to to the student and the program provided the student. This approach is more valid than using a standardized test to check the student's performance on specific objectives. In brief, this is an evaluation step which provides helpful information in determining whether or not a need exists to refer the student for additional assistance or for a modification in the student's program.

Form 5 *Summary Evaluation Report* (Figure 3.15)

The objective of this form is to provide a means for periodically reviewing the student's complete program. The form constitutes an inventory of short-term objectives included in the student's per-

Figure 3.14 Objective Cluster Summary Assessment
(IBAS FORM 4)

formance. It is suggested that this form be completed every three months, but it could be done more frequently or annually. Provisions are included for recording:

a. Identification information on the student, participants in the student's program, and a brief survey of the original IEP conference;
b. Data on the number of objectives attempted and completed, plus summary data on student performance;
c. Recommendations *based* on summary evaluation;
d. Comments.

Form 6 *Referral for Reevaluation* (Figure 3.1; see page 121)

The referral form can be used at any time to request additional evaluation or assistance for the student.

IBAS was designed as an IEP system that places primary emphasis on instructional decisions after a child has been placed in a program. The TIP form, in particular, has been structured to enhance the teacher's or specialist's role in planning, evaluating, and modifying the student's program. The system allows for accounting of the experiences provided the student, review of the student's progress, and sharing relevant information among participants in the student's program. Evaluation is continuous in that decisions must be made on objectives and student performance, along with periodic and annual evaluations.

IBAS strongly suggests a team approach to implementation and IEP evaluation. The implementation team is comprised of the diagnostician or person responsible for diagnosis and the teacher/specialist involved in implementing the plan. The team is determined once agreement has been reached on the IEP at the conference. An example of a team for a student placed in a regular class but who attends an LD resource room would include the regular teacher, resource teacher, and diagnostician.

The IBAS arbitrarily operates on a 12-week cycle. Following the IEP conference, the implementation team meets at 2-, 6-, 10-, and 12-week intervals. The second- and sixth-week meetings are informal and for sharing information. The tenth-week meeting is for summarizing the student's program and planning the evaluation prior to the twelfth-week conference. Only the teacher and/or specialist are involved in the team meeting except for the twelfth-week conference, which also is attended by the diagnostician. The logic behind the twelve-week cycle is to require a decision on the appropriateness of the student's program *at least three times a year*. The number and frequency of team

Figure 3.15 Summary Evaluation Report
(IBAS FORM 5)

meetings vary according to the needs and resources of the district. (See Figure 3.16.)

Even though districts are required to hold conferences annually, for purposes of designing the IEPs and to evaluate their effectiveness, employing procedures that allow for more extensive and systematic information sharing is advantageous. Also, decisions must be made regarding appropriateness of the student's program. And a responsibility of the teacher or specialist is to monitor a student's program or refer the student for remediation when performance suggests that a change is warranted.

The IEP as an Instructional Planning Process

Implementing the IEP requirements of PL 94-142 obviously involves an instructional planning process. The question to be answered is whether or not the IEP is *sufficient* as a planning process. When compared to planning procedures employed by many special educators in the past, the IEP process represents a distinct improvement. But when contrasted with the essentials of systematic planning described earlier in this chapter, the IEP requirements are not sufficient. Bateman (1977) developed a set of instructional planning elements derived from an analysis of Peters' (1965) definition of prescriptive teaching. Bateman then compared the IEP requirements with identified elements from Peters' prescriptive teaching definition. Results of this comparison are shown on page 156.

This comparison is included as a reminder that the development of an IEP is certainly an important element in instructional planning, but that an effective process requires more. Further, Bateman does not mention relating elements which focus on conditions for planning and the leadership role of the building principal. Neither of these areas is mentioned in IEP requirements, nor are they generally referred to in discussions on instructional planning techniques, but they nevertheless merit consideration.

Certain conditions essential for effective instructional planning also are important to implementing the IEP process. In general, these conditions include:

1. Administrative support
   a. The emphasis which administrators place on instructional planning as a priority should be clearly visible to teachers;
   b. An investment should be made in resources required for instructional planning;

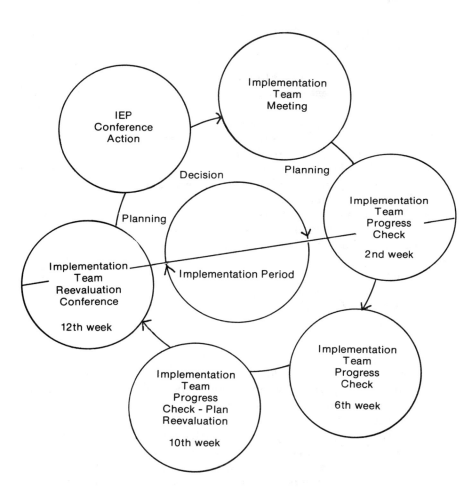

Figure 3.16 IBAS IEP Cycle

A Comparison of Elements in Prescriptive Teaching
and a P.L. 94-142 IEP

Prescriptive Teaching	IEP
Assessment of Child's Present Level	yes
Specification of Goals	yes
Specification of Objectives	yes
Specification of Teaching Tasks Inherent in Objectives	no
a. Specify how mastery will be demonstrated	no
1. Specify response requirements	no
a. Teach necessary responses	no
b. Specify antecedent events—what teacher will do	no
c. Specify required child responses	no
1. Find or develop materials and media to provide teaching format and child response practice	yes
d. Specify correction procedures	no
e. Specify consequent events	no
f. Specify evaluation procedures for each task	no
Specification of Daily or Near Daily Evaluation of Child Mastery of Objectives	annually only
Modify Tasks as Necessary	no

From: Bateman (1977, p.8).

    c. Administrators should view instructional planning from a cumulative perspective and not as something which occurs only at the beginning of the school year.
2. Definition of roles
    a. A comprehensive approach to instructional planning involves several different roles; these roles should be carefully defined;
    b. After roles are agreed upon, emphasis should be placed on each participant's understanding of his or her role in relation to the roles of others, including teachers, principals, parents, and support personnel.
3. Open communication
    a. Communication among all participants in the student's program is essential and communication procedures need not be formal;
    b. Parents and students *must* be included in the communication process.

4. Instructional planning model
   a. Teachers and support personnel should be oriented toward a model which emphasizes pupil needs, design of activities according to needs, trying out activities, evaluation of activities, and revision based on what has been learned;
   b. Establishment of the above condition likely will require inservice training.

Clearly, teachers and support personnel have fairly well defined responsibilities in the instructional planning process, but the role of the building principal has tended to vary from principal to principal. Too often, the principal has not assumed an active role in instructional planning for exceptional children. If the due process procedures, including the IEP requirements of PL 94-142, are to be appropriately implemented, the building principal must assume a leadership role in the planning process. Areas requiring the attention of building principals include:

1. Providing inservice training to teachers and support personnel;
2. Creating a building climate conducive to effective instructional planning;
3. Establishing procedures for monitoring instructional planning at the building level;
4. Assuming leadership in involving parents in the instructional planning process;
5. Providing reinforcement to teachers and support personnel for their investment in instructional planning.

SUMMARY

Instructional planning for exceptional children historically has been a concern of special educators. Until recently, however, planning has focused primarily on decisions regarding where the child will be placed for service and the type of services to be provided. Attention was given to diagnosis, but little attention was given to describing how the specific remediation needs of the student were to be met.

Now that school districts are required to develop written, individualized education programs (IEPs) for all handicapped children, instructional planning must become more systematic and specific. Instructional planning for exceptional children must be comprehensive and include data on the student's current level of performance, long- and short-term objectives, and evaluation procedures. Parental participation is an essential component.

A major change in instructional planning for exceptional children today relates to the involvement of regular educators along with special educators. In most cases, participation in instructional planning includes a regular class teacher and a special teacher; participation now is being expanded to include those teachers and specialists having responsibility for the student's program. A result of this trend is the need for systematic procedures, personnel skilled in planning, and provisions for sharing information.

REFERENCES

Bateman, B.D. Prescriptive teaching and individualized education programs. In Heinrich, R., & Ashcroft, S.C. (Eds.), *Instructional technology and the education of all handicapped children.* Columbus, OH: National Center on Media and Materials for the Handicapped, 1977.

Calder, C. R. The curriculum-instruction continuum with respect to mainstreaming of handicapped children. In Heinrich, R., & Ashcroft, S. C. (Eds.), *Instructional technology and the education of all handicapped children.* Columbus, OH: National Center on Media and Materials for the Handicapped, 1977.

Federal Register, 42 (163) August, 1977.

Meyen, E.L. *Instructional Based Approach System (IBAS).* Bellevue, WA: Edmark Associates, 1976.

Moran, M.R. The teacher's role in referral for testing and interpretation of reports. *Focus on Exceptional Children, 1976, 8* (6), 1-15.

National Advisory Council on Education Professions Development. *Mainstreaming: Helping teachers meet the challenge.* Washington, DC: Author, 1976.

Peters, L. *Prescriptive teaching.* New York: McGraw-Hill, 1965.

The IBAS forms in this chapter were provided by and reprinted with the permission of Edmark Associates, Bellevue, Washington.

RESOURCE GUIDE

Parental Involvement

Clements, J. E., & Alexander, R. N. Parent training: Bringing it all back home. *Focus on Exceptional Children,* 1975, *7,* 1-12.

Fanning, P. The new relationship between parents and schools. *Focus on Exceptional Children,* 1977, *9,* 1-10.

Kappelman, M., & Ackerman, P. *Between parent and school.* New York: Dial Press, 1977.

Kroth, R. L., & Simpson, R. L. *Parent conferences as a teaching strategy.* Denver: Love Publishing Co., 1977.

National Association for Retarded Citizens. *The parent/professional partnership: How to make it work.* Arlington, TX: NARC/Research and Demonstration Institute, 1977.

Program Evaluation

Borich, G. D. Program evaluation: New concepts, new methods. *Focus on Exceptional Children,* May 1977, *9* (3), 1-14.

Howe, C. E., & Fitzgerald, M. E. Evaluating special education programs. *Focus on Exceptional Children,* Feb. 1977, *8* (9), 1-11.

Jenkins, J. R., & Mayhall, W. F. Development and evaluation of a resource teacher program. *Exceptional Children,* September 1976.

MacMillan, D. L., & Semmel, M. I. Evaluation of mainstreaming programs. *Focus on Exceptional Children,* September 1977, *9* (4), 1-14.

National Association for Retarded Citizens. *The parent/professional partnership — Classroom programming: What should be taught?* Arlington, TX: NARC/Research and Demonstration Institute, 1977.

Yoshida, R. K., Fenton, K. S. & Kaufman, M. J. Evaluation of education for the handicapped. *Phi Delta Kappan,* September 1977.

Pupil Assessment

Heiss, W. Relating educational assessment to instructional planning. *Focus on Exceptional Children,* March 1977, *9* (1), 1-11.

Hively, W., & Reynolds, M. C. (Eds.). *Domain-referenced testing in special education.* University of Minnesota: Leadership Training Institute/Special Education, 1975.

Jobes, N. K., & Hawthorne, L. W. Informal assessment for the classroom. *Focus on Exceptional Children,* April 1977, *9* (2), 1-13.

Meier, J. *Screening and assessment of young children at developmental risk.* Washington, DC: The President's Committee on Mental Retardation, 1973.

Moran, M. R. The teacher's role in referral for testing and interpretation of reports. *Focus on Exceptional Children,* Nov. 1976, *8* (6), 1-15.

Parker, C. A. (Ed.). *Psychological consultation: Helping teachers meet special needs.* University of Minnesota: Leadership Training Institute/Special Education, 1975.

Weinberg, R. A., & Wood, F. H. (Eds.). *Observation of pupils and teachers in mainstream and special education settings: Alternative strategies.* University of Minnesota: Leadership Training Institute/Special Education, 1975.

Planning Process

Aiello, B. *Mainstreaming: Teacher training workshops on individualized instruction.* Reston, VA: Council for Exceptional Children, 1975-1976.

Deno, S. L., & Mirkin, P. K. *Data-based program modification: A manual.* University of Minnesota: Leadership Training Institute/Special Education, 1977.

Helms, D. Some perspectives on the IPI experience: Some implications for the implementation of the Education for all Handicapped Children Act of 1975. In Heinich, R. & Ashcroft, S. C. (Eds.), *Instructional technology and the education of all handicapped children.* Ohio State University: National Center on Educational Media and Materials for the Handicapped, 1977.

Langstaff, A. L., & Volkmor, C. B. *Coming back . . . Or never leaving.* Columbus, OH: Charles E. Merrill Publishing Co., 1977.

Meyen, E. L. *Developing instructional units.* Dubuque, IA: Wm. C. Brown Co., 1976.

National Association of State Directors of Special Education. *Functions of the placement committee in special education.* Washington, DC: Author, 1976.

Peter, L. J. *Individual instruction.* New York: McGraw-Hill, 1972.

Torres, S. (Ed.). *A primer on individualized programs for handicapped children.* Reston, VA: Council for Exceptional Children, 1977.

Tracy, M. L., Gibbons, S., & Kladder, F. W. *Case conference: A simulation and source book.* Bloomington, IN: Indiana Department of Public Instruction & Indiana University Developmental Training Center, 1976.

4 The Mentally Retarded

Robert H. Bruininks and Grace Warfield
University of Minnesota

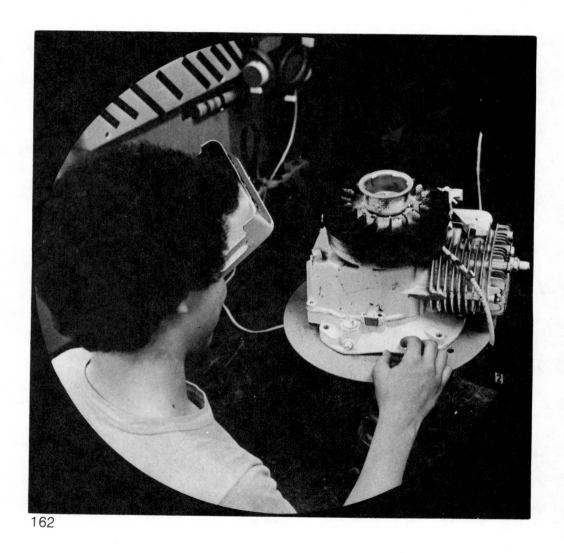

Susan. Susan is an attractive four-year-old girl whose development is considered moderately to severely retarded. Until approximately two years of age, Susan's growth was normal in the areas of speech and communication, physical and motor development, and social-emotional development. Soon after her second birthday, Susan contracted a viral disease with an accompanying high fever. Following this brief but severe illness, she displayed evidence of neurological impairment and seriously arrested development.

Her development since the illness has been slow and irregular. She continues to walk awkwardly; she has difficulty in grasping and manipulating small objects, resulting largely from deficient fine motor skills; and she has difficulty in coordinating visual perceptions with motor responses. Susan is not yet independent in toileting and frequently has accidents during the day. Although she can speak a few words and obviously comprehends many other words, her speech is limited—mainly restricted to names of familiar objects in her environment.

Susan is now enrolled in a neighborhood preschool for retarded children. Although her behavior has improved in the past six months, she often has sudden, unexpected emotional outbursts that disrupt normal classroom activities and other children. She shows little interaction with peers.

John. John is a ten-year-old boy who spends most of his school day in regular classes but received supplementary instruction for approximately two hours a day in a special education resource learning center. Until he entered school, no one suspected that John's development was in any way retarded. He appeared to develop basic movement skills at about the same time as other children his age, although he learned to talk slightly later than most children.

In kindergarten the teacher noted the difficulties that John appeared to have in making simple visual discriminations among different letters and shapes. Observations of John's lack of progress increased during the next two years in school. The first-grade teacher, although concerned over John's slow progress in comparison with his peers, thought his development in these areas was somewhat delayed but not serious enough to warrant further assessment.

During the second grade, when academic subjects such as reading and arithmetic were stressed increasingly, John's teacher became concerned about his failure to progress. Although he had developed some basic counting skills, John's reading performance was limited to recognition of a few common words. His academic achievement at the end of second grade was a grade equivalent of 1.3 on a standardized achievement test. John was referred for psychological and educational testing. The recommendation as a result of this assessment was that he be given regular tutoring to assist him in basic school subjects.

Although John encountered difficulty in mastering early elementary academic requirements, he is popular among his classmates. In playground games he is often among the first to be chosen and appears to enjoy good social relationships with other children. His physical development and motor skills are average for his age.

George. George is a moderately retarded 28-year-old man who lives in a group home with eight other mentally retarded young adults and two live-in house parents. During the day, George uses the bus to get between his home and a sheltered workshop. On workshop assembly tasks, he is slow but quite accurate in assembling the materials that require fine motor skills. He generally performs at approximately a 50 percent rate of productivity for normal workers on the same tasks.

George is well accepted by other persons in his place of residence and the sheltered workshop, although he tends to get distracted easily by fellow workers in the workshop environment, which further reduces his efficiency. His social contacts and relationships are limited largely to members of his family and persons with whom he lives and works in the group home and sheltered workshop.

George attended a special school for moderately retarded students while living at home with his parents. George can recognize common signs and reads at approximately second grade level. He also has mastered simple mathematical concepts involving use of money and telling time.

The examples of Susan, John, and George illustrate two important concepts in understanding the development and needs of retarded persons. The first is that *behavioral characteristics of retarded persons are extremely diverse and cover a wide range of performance.* Quite likely, John, although identified as mildly retarded during the school years, will cease to be thought of as retarded after he leaves school. His difficulties are related largely to the demands of learning basic school subjects. George's behavior as a young adult, however, is considered retarded by general community standards, although he appears to be making a satisfactory adjustment within his living and working environments. Susan possibly will require extensive assistance throughout her lifetime.

In these three examples, some behaviors are clearly similar to behaviors of nonretarded persons of the same age, while other behaviors are clearly below average standards for persons of the same age. These three people illustrate the wide range of human performance found among people defined as mentally retarded in our society.

The overlap in performance observed between John and his classmates illustrates a second concept about the developmental patterns of retarded persons. Although John is encountering difficulty in some school subjects, his emotional, social, and physical development are quite satisfactory and within the range expected for children his age. Overlap in the performances of mentally retarded and nonretarded persons often is observed in studies of their learning, socialization, and other characteristics. Research studies of mildly retarded children not uncommonly reveal that many retarded children achieve scores that equal or surpass the average performance of nonhandicapped children. Understanding this concept—i.e., that *performance of persons defined as retarded is not necessarily below average in all development areas*—is important in evaluating results of studies that contrast the performance of retarded and nonretarded persons.

Understanding the concepts of variability and the many behavioral similarities of retarded and nonretarded persons is important in considering much of the published research in mental retardation. With a few exceptions, however, mentally retarded persons considered on an overall group basis are developmentally below the achievement levels of nonretarded persons in most areas. Unfortunately, these common findings often lead incorrectly to the careless conclusion that mentally retarded people always perform in qualitatively different ways than nonretarded persons.

THE EXTENT OF MENTAL RETARDATION

Many individuals of all ages are identified as needing special education and a variety of community services because of mental retardation. Schools and other agencies planning such services, however have continuing problems in estimating the number of persons in need and the costs involved. An often quoted figure of three percent of the population is questionable because of: (1) changing definitions of mental retardation; (2) the uncertain status of mildly retarded individuals identified during school years; and (3) the opposition to labeling individuals considered socio-culturally retarded.

Determining the prevalence of mental retardation is further confused in that:

— Rarely can a condition of mental retardation be established without question at the time of birth. Only obviously severe damage to the neurological system can predict abnormal brain development and, even then, the ultimate degree of retardation will depend upon many other physiological and environmental factors.

— Identification of mental retardation occurs in the majority of cases soon after the child is enrolled in school, and this designation often is held only as long as the child remains in school. This circumstance leads to the reporting of more retarded persons in the school age group than in either the preschool or adult populations.

— Some confusion appears in the literature because the terms *incidence* and *prevalence* are used interchangeably, when they in fact represent two distinctly different statistics.

Incidence refers to new cases of mental retardation identified within a specific period of time (e.g., the number of children with birth defects born within one year, stated as a percentage of the total number of births). Since the figure in regard to mental retardation indicates only those infants for whom retardation can be predicted with a high degree of probability, the mildly retarded who will be identified later by schools or other agencies are not included in this count.

Prevalence is the total number of retarded persons of all ages who have ever been considered mentally retarded, as a percentage of a specified population at a given time. The prevalence figure is most useful in determining service needs.

The incidence figure is useful in other ways. It is related to prevention efforts, possible identification of new causes and, of course, to the prediction of future prevalence. A discussion of the relationship between incidence and prevalence appears in *Mental Retardation: The Known and the Unknown* (President's Committee on Mental Retardation, 1976b, pp. 8-12).

In a chapter on the prevalence and distribution of mental retardation, MacMillan (1977, p.73) suggests that the three percent figure often quoted is probably more accurate as an *incidence* (rather than prevalence) estimate. A one percent figure may reflect prevalence, because many persons are living "outside the label" during the years when they are not identified as retarded. Also, a high mortality rate in the severely and profoundly retarded groups may lower the prevalence figures at a later time.

Another source (Sontag, 1977, p. 4) gives figures based on a Census Bureau report of July 1, 1974, and states that 2.3 percent (1,507,000 persons) of the population between birth and 19 years of age are mentally retarded. This figure was determined by information from various sources, including national agencies and organizations and local directors of special education. This figure also included the mildly retarded as reported by the schools.

An additional confusing factor is the preponderance of mild retardation among subgroups of the population, especially the economically poor who are disadvantaged by effects of substandard housing and food; discriminated against because of cultural difference, ethnic origin, or race; or isolated from education and employment opportunities. Poverty has been known to have an intricate and complex relationship to mental retardation. An extensive discussion is offered in Hurley's (1970) *Poverty and Mental Retardation: A Causal Relationship.*

DEFINING MENTAL RETARDATION

The many attempts to describe and define mental retardation have led to revised definitions in an effort to reach an all-encompassing answer. Yet there is no *single* behavior which can be universally observed in all retarded persons. Historically, definitions of mental retardation have combined an emphasis on subaverage learning performance and lack of social competence. The definition of mental retardation offered by the American Association on Mental Deficiency stresses the importance of considering age-related criteria of adaptive behavior in defining mental retardation (Grossman, 1973).

Adaptive behavior is defined as the effectiveness and degree to which an individual meets age-related standards of self-sufficiency and social responsibility for his or her cultural group. As a person's adjustment is affected by intellectual ability, adaptation to one's environment is affected also by social relationships, emotional development, and the response of others to retarded persons.

These concepts are expressed in the current definition of the American Association on Mental Deficiency:

Mental retardation refers to significantly subaverage general intellectual functioning existing concurrently with deficits in adaptive behavior, and manifested during the developmental period (Grossman, 1973, p. 11).

The term *mental retardation* as used in this definition does not relate to specific etiology (cause). It is merely descriptive of current behavior and does not imply permanence of the condition. The "developmental period" is designated to be 18 years as the upper age limit. "Significantly subaverage" refers to a score on a standardized intelligence test in which an individual's score falls at least two standard deviations below the mean.

An earlier definition of the American Association on Mental Deficiency set the IQ score criterion as one or more standard deviations below the mean (Heber, 1961). Professionals still debate whether more persons should be included in the definition of mental retardation. In any case, IQ score alone does not justify a diagnosis of mental retardation. Further explicit interpretation of the terms in the AAMD definition appears in the *Manual* (Grossman, 1973) and is quoted by Robinson and Robinson (1976, pp. 30-31).

Other contemporary definitions have approached mental retardation from somewhat different points of view. Mercer (1973) looks at retardation from a social system perspective. In this interpretation, no person is considered retarded unless his or her social system has labeled him/her as such. Mercer and others have reported studies showing that many children are considered retarded by the school but not by the family, neighborhood, or any other agency (Mercer, 1973; President's Committee on Mental Retardation, 1976b).

Another view, not widely discussed but of special interest to educators, is that of Sidney Bijou (1966). Bijou sidesteps the biological or medical definitions and emphasizes individual development patterns in relation to environmental patterns of stimulation and reinforcement. This view has called attention to the learning environment in the past history of individuals and notes the deleterious effects of severely restricted conditions often experienced by handicapped children. The approach is especially relevant for educators involved in planning individualized programs for severely retarded children who have existed in sterile environments with little stimulation of any kind.

PSYCHOLOGICAL MEASURES

When psychological tests were developed early in the twentieth century, they became a relatively successful tool for predicting how well children would succeed in school tasks. A child could be compared to others of the same age, with respect to knowledge acquired (e.g., what words mean), memory, reasoning, and judgment.

The most widely used individual intelligence tests are the Stanford-Binet (most recently revised in 1973) and the scales developed by David Wechsler. The latter include the Wechsler Intelligence Scale for Children (WISC), the Wechsler Adult Intelligence Scale (WAIS), and the Wechsler Preschool and Primary Scale of Intelligence (WPPSI). Individual tests such as the Stanford-Binet and the Wechsler scales should be administered and interpreted only by qualified and experienced examiners.

Questions often are asked concerning the reliability and validity of these tests when used with retarded children. Intelligence and the many issues of testing have been discussed extensively (see Anastasia, 1976;

MacMillan, 1977). Few longitudinal studies have been conducted on the intelligence of retarded populations, but one of special interest reported that mental growth continued in the severely retarded up to age 25, and up to age 35 in many of the mildly retarded (Fisher & Zeaman, 1970). Such evidence suggests that care must be taken to not assume limits to possible continued development of retarded persons during adolescence and young adult years.

Historical accounts indicate that Alfred Binet did not set out to develop an "intelligence test." He was asked to develop a measure of educational potential among pupils in Paris schools. Binet went to the teachers for help in determining what achievements were considered important. He did not seek the causes of differences among children, although he was deeply interested in the reasons why children had difficulties in learning. (He had a personal interest because his daughter was failing in school.)

Extensive discussion of the follow-up of Binet's work by other psychologists is not possible, nor is discussion of the several revisions of Binet's first efforts and the development of new measures. In brief, overenthusiastic followers, notably Goddard, translated Binet's scales and advocated their use in classification of retarded persons. Unfortunately, Goddard (1920) suggested that heredity was the chief basis for differences in ability, a view which perpetuated an attitude of pessimism and futility in the late nineteenth and early twentieth centuries. Terman (1916) too suggested that mental retardation was inherited, that mental deficiency and moral deficiency were synonymous, and that mental growth stopped in adolescence.

Although psychological testing has been subjected to intensive study and criticism since 1960, persons who have advocated abandoning the IQ concept have not been generally supported. Emphasis in assessment has changed, however, to reflect the intelligence test as one part of the total assessment of a child's intellectual and developmental status.

Studies of mentally retarded children retested over intervals of time generally report relatively stable IQs, especially for those achieving IQ scores in the lower ranges. Some reports, however, indicate that large individual variations could be due to errors in testing, recording, or to many other influences such as environmental modification. In any case, *results from only one test should never be used to predict future performance for any individual child*, although the score obtained by a competent examiner on an individual intelligence test can contribute important information about a child.

For educators, the terms used most often to suggest the degree of students' retardation are *educable mentally retarded*, or EMR (mild), *trainable mentally retarded*, or TMR (moderate), and *severely/profoundly retarded*. A comparison of these groups with the AAMD levels as suggested in the 1973 *Manual* gives the following range of associated IQ scores.

Table 4.1
AAMD Levels of Mental Retardation

Degree of Mental Retardation	Obtained Stanford-Binet (s.d. - 16)	Intelligence Quotient Wechsler Scales (s.d. - 15)	Common Educational Terms
Mild	67-52	69-55	Educable
Moderate	51-36	54-40	Trainable
Severe	35-20	39-25 (extrapolated)	Trainable
Profound	19 and below	24 and below (extrapolated)	Severe/ Profound

Adapted from: *Manual on Terminology and Classification in Mental Retardation (Rev. ed.)*, by H. J. Grossman et al., *American Association on Mental Deficiency, Washington, DC, 1973, p. 18.*

ASSESSING ADAPTIVE BEHAVIOR

Measures of adaptive behavior depend upon judgments of persons who know the individual being tested or upon an observation by the examiner. Adaptive behavior tests have been criticized widely because they do not or cannot take into account the many varieties of cultural and geographical differences in what is considered "normal behavior." A child who never has been allowed to use a knife and fork would probably "fail" such a test item, whether or not the skill *could* have been acquired through experience.

Further, adaptive behaviors must take into account the age and physical condition of the child. One does not expect a one-year-old child to be toilet trained or capable of conversation, while an adolescent at a similar ability level would be considered incompetent and probably retarded.

Cultural values, customs, and child-rearing practices influence children's behavior patterns in ways which often make "norms" useless, both in adaptive behavior observations and standardized intelligence tests (DeAvila, 1976):

> For instance, one can understand a Latin American child's reluctance to guess at an answer to a test question when she/he has been reared within a tradition which disapproves of this type of *hablando sin saber* (speaking without knowing) (p. 95-96).

Some measures of adaptive behavior in use today are the AAMD Adaptive Behavior Scales, the Vineland Social Maturity Scale, the

Denver Developmental Screening Test, and the Apgar tests for newborns. The AAMD scales were first developed for use in institutions, but a revision is now available for use in public schools.

ASSOCIATED HANDICAPPING CONDITIONS

The condition of mental retardation is likely to be complicated by or associated with a number of additional handicaps. Educators should be prepared to take these problems into account in individual planning. A report of a nationwide survey by Conroy and Derr (1971) gives the following figures for handicapping conditions associated with mental retardation.

Table 4.2
Prevalence of Associated Handicapping Conditions
in Mentally Retarded Persons (by %)

Function	No Handicap	Partial Handicap	Severe Handicap	Description of Severe Handicap
Ambulation	57.8	32.4	9.9	Able to take a few steps with help or totally unable to walk
Upper limbs, gross motor control	57.5	34.2	8.2	Unable to hold large objects, or complete lack of muscle control
Upper limbs, fine motor control	56.1	34.9	9.0	Minimal use of hands; cannot use eating utensils
Speech	45.1	33.4	21.5	Can possibly communicate needs or wants, but uses few or no words
Hearing	85.0	11.5	3.4	Functionally or totally deaf; hearing aid partial or no help
Vision	73.3	20.9	5.9	Minimally sighted (uncorrectable or legally blind
Seizures (epilepsy, convulsions)	82.3	15.1	2.7	Severe seizures partially controlled or uncontrollable
Behavior, emotional disorders	58.1	35.7	6.3	Adjustment not possible in home environment, abnormal behavior, dangerous to self or others
Toilet training	77.5	10.2	12.3	Dependent on others, slightly toilet trained, or not trained

Note: Percentages may not add to 100 due to rounding.

Adapted from: *Survey and Analysis of the Habilitation and Rehabilitation Status of the Mentally Retarded with Associated Handicapping Conditions* by J. W. Conroy and K. E. Derr, Department of Health, Education and Welfare, Washington, DC, 1971.

As illustrated by the figures in Table 4.2, educational planning for retarded pupils can be complicated by one or several partial or severe handicaps. Difficulties in walking, gross and fine motor control, as well as emotional problems, appear in more than one-third of the group, and more than half show speech-communication problems. Some children have especially complicated conditions, because several conditions interact to make their limitations even more severe.

MENTAL RETARDATION: A SOCIAL PROBLEM

The intense interest and efforts generated by many professionals, as well as parents of retarded children and other interest groups, are reflected in the development of services, discoveries in research, and the significant increase in funds expended by federal, state, and private agencies over the past two decades. For example, in 1955, federal expenditures for services to the mentally retarded reached $15.79 million. In fiscal year 1973, the expense was estimated at $932.8 million, expended in three types of services: (1) funding direct services for retarded persons; (2) training personnel, research, construction, and coordinating agencies; and (3) "personal maintenance," or funds for maintenance and medical insurance (President's Committee on Mental Retardation, 1976b, p. 100).

A great deal of social concern is directed at the rising expense of caring for the retarded population; efforts to reduce that cost engage the time and interest of many citizen groups. The current social attitude is further directed toward obligatory provision of improved living conditions and a humane service system, along with reducing the number of persons who must depend on these services.

Two major thrusts are seen in the overall attack on reducing the social problem of mental retardation: (1) research into ways of preventing severe retardation, and (2) alleviation of conditions which affect mildly retarded persons by inhibiting or preventing their attainment of independent status as adults.

Research: Genetics

Startling breakthroughs in the field of biochemical and genetic studies have given rise to ethical dilemmas for both parents and professionals. Because it has become possible to estimate the percent of risk or the probability that a given man and woman may produce a retarded child, prospective parents may be faced with serious decisions. Thus, *genetic counseling* is one recent approach to prevention of mental retardation.

Another relatively new development is the use of a procedure known as *amniocentesis,* whereby fluid is drawn with a needle from the amniotic sac containing the fetus. Fetal cells in the fluid are cultured and analyzed to determine the fetus' chromosomal makeup. Through analysis of the chromosomal composition of a body cell, errors or so-called chromosomal anomalies can be detected.

Some chromosomal errors can be discovered in the cells of parents before a child is conceived. For example, when both parents are carriers of a defective recessive gene, as in Tay Sachs disease, there is a one-in-four chance that a diseased child will be conceived. Parents may then decide to not risk child bearing or to elect to terminate pregnancies if the fetus is found to be defective. (At present, Tay Sachs disease has no known treatment; the disease is fatal, usually within three years of life.)

Another, more frequent condition almost always associated with moderate to severe retardation is Down's syndrome. A characteristic of Down's syndrome, first demonstrated in 1959, is the presence of an extra chromosome in the human cell. This most common form, trisomy 21 (the presence of three instead of two number 21 chromosomes) is not inherited. Later, other abnormalities in the chromosomes were discovered as possibly contributing to Down's syndrome, although less frequently. Down's syndrome occurs once in every 600 to 700 live births. Risk is increased greatly for mothers over 35 years of age. Amniocentesis can be used to detect Down's syndrome in the unborn child, and this knowledge can be the basis for aborting the child, if this is acceptable to or desired by the parents.

Phenylketonuria (PKU) is an inherited condition, genetically transmitted through recessive genes. The problem results from deficiency of an enzyme needed to metabolize phenylalanine, an amino acid found in common foods such as milk. The failure to metabolize phenylalanine causes a toxic condition which damages the brain, resulting in mental retardation. The incidence of PKU is estimated as one in every 14,000 live births in the Caucasian population. Dietary treatment of newborn infants with PKU has prevented brain damage which otherwise would result in moderate to severe mental retardation. Screening infants for PKU is mandatory in most states. PKU is transmitted in the same manner as Tay Sachs disease (both parents are carriers of the defective gene).

Research centering on these conditions or diseases illustrates new knowledge which makes possible the reduction of incidence of retardation with these specific causes. Extended discussions of advances in the field of genetics and genetic syndromes related to mental retardation are presented by Robinson and Robinson (1976) and MacMillan (1977).

Research: Physical Environment

Studies of prenatal, perinatal, and postnatal conditions frequently associated with mental retardation have made information available which could substantially prevent or reduce mental retardation. Such information should be made known to all prospective parents, beginning long before children are planned. Much retardation could be prevented if certain facts were known and incorporated in health service delivery to all citizens. Examples of positive achievements include:

— Immunization against rubella and rubeola
— Use of globulin in preventing Rh sensitization
— Elimination of cretinism by supplying iodine in the diet
— Reduction of damage to newborns from oxygen deficiency and other sources of injury
— Dietary control of phenylketonuria (PKU) and other inborn metabolism errors
— Control of environmental hazards such as lead, mercury, and toxic radiation known to produce brain damage
— Expanded maternal and child health care in all sectors
— Continued widespread immunizations
— Expansion of genetic counseling centers
— Contraceptive information and improvement of techniques.

(Adapted from *Century of Decision*, President's Committee on Mental Retardation, 1976a).

Social-Psychological Prevention

Mild retardation is concentrated in the most marginal socio-economic groups. Extensive evidence now indicates that poverty with accompanying malnutrition, lack of medical and dental care, unhealthy living conditions, disrupted family life, and lack of stimulation in everyday experience combine to depress or prevent the development of "intelligence," or learning to cope with school and societal demands.

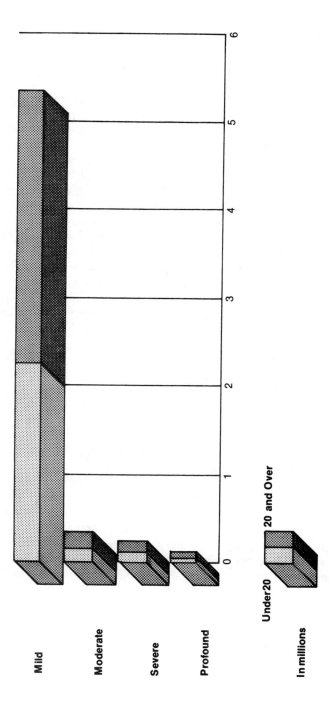

Figure 4.1 Estimated Distribution of Retarded Persons in the United States by Age and Degree

Source: National Association for Retarded Citizens

To reduce borderline and mild retardation, a massive social-political approach would be necessary to eliminate poverty—a major source of 85 percent of mental retardation. Figure 4.1 illustrates this proportion.

Experimental intervention programs with young children and their families have been studied as a means of eliminating or ameliorating retarded development in children. In many of these studies, three- and four-year-old disadvantaged children in preschool education programs with highly structured training approaches produced substantial early gains in performance that later declined after the children left the experimental treatments (Bronfenbrenner, 1974; Tjossem, 1976).

Some other evidence, however, indicates that early intervention in infancy may yield more lasting changes in language and cognitive functioning, epecially if such approaches stress helping parents to enrich interactions with their own children (Bronfenbrenner, 1974). Although studies thus far are not without methodological weaknesses, approaches to early intervention, especially those with a strong family-centered focus, appear to have some promise as a means of reducing developmental retardation in children. Bronfenbrenner (1974) has summarized and evaluated much of the available literature on the efficacy of early intervention as a means of enhancing the development of disadvantaged children.

DEVELOPMENTAL CHARACTERISTICS OF RETARDED PERSONS

Earlier, a definition of mental retardation was presented which included three concepts: (1) significantly subaverage general intellectual functioning, (2) deficiencies in adaptive behavior, and (3) the presence of discrepancies in intellectual functioning and in adaptive behavior during the developmental period of life. A person's total physical and psychological characteristics obviously are of primary concern in defining the significant deviations in growth, development, and functioning implicit in current definitions of mental retardation. Depending upon a person's life circumstances and age, development often is specified as retarded when serious deviations from expected standards occur in learning, physical growth, motor performance, social-emotional behaviors, and in receptive and expressive language skills.

Learning Characteristics

Learning may be defined as a change in behavior resulting from practice (McGeogh & Irion, 1952). Behavioral changes characterized as learning are distinguished from those due to maturation, or aging, by defining the latter as being least affected by experience and more to innate genetic factors (Breckenridge & Murphy, 1969). The concept of learning is similar to the concept of intelligence in that both attributes are inferred from observing performance.

Inefficiency and slowness in learning are invariably linked to mental retardation. No other area has produced as much recent research with mentally retarded people as that of learning and performance. By the late 1950s, only about 30 published studies had been documented of the learning performance of retarded persons (McPherson, 1948, 1958). In the 20 years from 1954 to 1974, however, the literature in this area literally exploded. Zeaman (1974) counted over 1,500 experimental studies published during this period on the learning characteristics of mentally retarded persons. The reader is directed to a number of excellent research summaries on the learning characteristics of retarded persons (Baumeister, 1967; Blake, 1976; Estes, 1970; MacMillan, 1977; Mercer & Snell, 1977; Robinson & Robinson, 1976; Routh, 1973).

Gaining an understanding of available research in this area is a formidable task, since researchers have approached the subject from a variety of perspectives. Routh (1973) has described three general orientations to studying learning among retarded persons: the *general experimental* approach, the *developmental* approach, and the *deficit* approach.

The general experimental approach assumes that retarded behavior follows the same behavioral principles that apply to nonhandicapped persons. Research stimulated by the theories and writings of B. F. Skinner, often described as operant conditioning studies, reflects the general experimental orientation. Researchers with a developmental orientation assume that retarded persons progress at a slower rate and achieve a lower developmental level than nonretarded persons. Differences in learning between retarded and nonretarded persons at various developmental levels are explained by application of additional principles (e.g., less motivation to perform). The deficit approach assumes general behavior principles but seeks to identify performance defects that are peculiarly characteristic of retarded persons or persons of varying intelligence levels. More recent work in psychological aspects of mental retardation has tended to blur distinctions among the three orientations.

Studies on the learning characteristics of mentally retarded persons usually have focused upon specific elements of the learning process. Ross (1976) has described components of the learning process in a simple hierarchical model (Figure 4.2). This model indicates that the process begins with the learner's expectations based upon previous experiences, then proceeds to actions by the learner that require selecting important features of stimulus material, organizing the material to be remembered, memorizing and recalling material, generalizing or applying what is learned to other related circumstances and settings, demonstrating through an observable performance that learning has occurred, and, finally, receiving feedback regarding the adequacy of performance so that errors can be corrected and correct performance maintained. A few selected areas of research in mental retardation illustrate some of what is known presently about the learning processes of retarded persons.

Expectancy

In the past 20 years, numerous studies have been conducted on the social learning characteristics of mentally retarded persons. Many of these studies have been based upon a theory advanced by Rotter (1954) that behavior is influenced greatly by the nature and quality of a person's interaction with the environment (Mercer & Snell, 1977). This theory is expressed by the formula, *Behavior Potential =f (Expectancy and Reinforcement Value)* (Rotter, 1975), which indicates that:

> The potential for a behavior to occur in any specific psychological situation is a function of the expectancy that the behavior will lead to a particular reinforcement in that situation and the value of that reinforcement (p. 56).

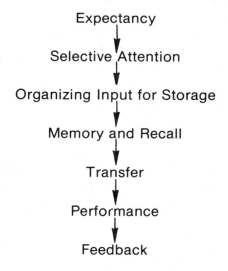

Figure 4.2   Components of the Learning Process

Common to the experience of retarded people is a history of failure, especially when faced with the demands of school learning. In light of this experience, studies, not surprisingly, have found that mentally retarded persons (1) tend to exhibit what is characterized as an *external locus of control,* in which events are perceived as unrelated to one's behavior and, therefore, beyond direct personal control, (2) tend to enter learning situations with a high expectancy for failure, and (3) tend to employ an outer-directed problem solving strategy in which they distrust their own solutions and seek excessive guidance from persons in the immediate environment (MacMillan, 1971; Mercer & Snell, 1977). Based upon these conclusions, then, mentally retarded learners often adopt orientations toward learning that aggravate their learning difficulties and make them inordinately dependent upon others for environmental cues.

Attention

Attention is considered an important part of the learning process and has received considerable stress in research on the learning processes of retarded persons. Some of the most provocative and best theoretical work in this area has been done by Zeaman and House (1963) and Fisher and Zeaman (1973). The numbers of studies related to this theoretical work are reviewed by Fisher and Zeaman (1973) and Mercer and Snell (1977).

Most of the research on attentional characteristics of retarded persons has been conducted using simple discrimination learning problems involving color and form choices. The learner in these experiments typically must select either the correct color or the correct form that is consistently reinforced over a number of learning trials. Based upon a large number of studies, Zeaman and House (1963) and others (cf. Mercer & Snell, 1977) have found that retarded subjects have difficulty selecting and attending to the distinctive features of a stimulus.

These experiments have shown that the rate of performance increase is comparable for retarded and nonretarded persons once the concept of the task is understood, but that retarded subjects take considerably longer to identify the relevant stimulus (color or form) dimensions for making the correct choice or discrimination. The precise cause of this inefficiency among retarded persons has not been clearly established, although Turnure (1970) has argued that the outer-directed orientation of many retarded persons may cause them to rely on external cues from others in solving such problems rather than focusing more specifically on the features inherent in learning tasks.

Memory and Recall

The memory and recall abilities of retarded persons have been the focus of numerous studies. One of the more influential theories in this area has been advanced by Ellis (1963, 1970). Based upon a large number of studies, Ellis and others have found that mentally retarded persons display deficiencies primarily in *short-term memory,* or the ability to retain information for short periods of time (perhaps up to 30 seconds), rather than in the ability to recall information over longer time periods. Ellis (1970) postulated that this observed deficiency in short-term memory results from a failure of retarded subjects to employ any or adequate rehearsal strategies.

Other studies have demonstrated difficulties among retarded persons in organizing lists of information (e.g., nouns on a randomly generated list) into categories for efficient recall (Spitz, 1966). In contrast, nonretarded persons as subjects in memory experiments have been found to employ spontaneously efficient organizational and rehearsal strategies that enhance organization and retention of material (cf. Mercer & Snell, 1977; Robinson & Robinson, 1976; Spitz, 1966).

More recent studies have focused upon assessing the efficacy of various strategies for organizing materials and enhancing active attempts to remember. In a series of experiments, Turnure and his associates (Turnure, 1976; Turnure, Buium, & Thurlow, 1976; Thurlow & Turnure, 1972) demonstrated that mildly retarded persons have particular difficulty in associating verbal materials (e.g., *nurse-window*) using interrogatory (why?) questions embedded in sentences but have little difficulty in associating the same verbal materials when provided greater thematic content in the form of paragraphs. Given elaborated learning conditions in which retarded subjects were asked to recall verbal pairs initially given in paragraphs, mildly retarded children approached the recall scores of nonretarded peers. Teachers frequently use such interrogatory questions with children in special education classrooms, but the questions frequently go unanswered (Turnure, 1976).

Other studies have found that performance of retarded subjects is enhanced on memory tasks when they are provided direct training in the use of rehearsal strategies, although the durability and transfer of such learning to other situations appears somewhat limited (cf. Robinson & Robinson, 1976). The noticeable trend toward assessing the efficacy of active intervention strategies in studying the learning and retention processes of retarded persons may some day yield powerful strategies for ameliorating their observed deficiencies in memory and recall.

Operant Conditioning

Perhaps no other theoretical and empirical work has directly contributed as much to the care, treatment, and training of retarded persons as research activities in the area of operant conditioning. Stimulated by the research and writings of B. F. Skinner, work on application of operant conditioning principles to the problems of retarded behavior has been prolific during the past several years.

The cardinal principle of operant conditioning is that *the strength of a response is influenced by the nature of its consequences.* Other important principles are that (1) behavior must be expressed by the person before it can be modified by environmental conditions, and (2) behavior can be shaped and maintained through carefully applied and scheduled rewards.

Various techniques for developing and maintaining desirable behaviors of retarded persons through operant conditioning have been researched in recent years. Efforts have been successful in shaping important improvements in the behaviors of retarded persons in areas of vocational performance; orientation toward performance in classroom learning tasks, language skills, toileting, and other self-help skills; and other areas of learning and adjustment (Deno, Gutmann & Fullmer, 1977; MacMillan, 1977; Mercer & Snell, 1977; Robinson & Robinson, 1976; Thompson & Grabowski, 1977). The rapidly increasing amount of research on operant conditioning offers much hope for continued improvement of teaching and training programs for retarded persons.

Implications for Teaching

Although intensive research into the learning processes of retarded persons is a relatively recent development, a number of important principles can be applied to the teaching environment (Denny, 1966; Mercer & Snell, 1977). A selective list is summarized below:

1. Conduct continuous measurement of behavior, careful analysis of learning task sequences and demands, and provide consistent application of rewards for correct performance.
2. Provide differential information regarding the quality of the learner's responses, with immediate information of results and reinforcement for correct responses.
3. Build a task sequence for learning in easy steps, basing each subsequent performance on previously learned responses.

4. Provide spaced (distributed) as opposed to highly concentrated (massed) forms of practice.
5. Provide practice beyond the initial expression of a response, and redundancy in presentation, to ensure long-term retention (over-learning).
6. Teach direct strategies for organizing and rehearsing material through labeling or associating material with pictures, events, or objects.
7. Reduce the number of irrelevant dimensions and increase the number and distinctiveness of relevant cues in stimulus materials (e.g., letters, words, forms, colors).
8. Provide realistic successes for students through specific goals and by consistently pairing specific behaviors with predictable consequences.
9. Encourage realistic goals and a style of problem solving that reduces dependency by building self-confidence and a self-directed approach to solving problems.
10. Provide models of good performance, preferably models similar to the learner's age and of the same sex.

Recent years have witnessed increased interest in the learning processes of retarded persons. Investigations are moving toward assessing the effects of directed instructional strategies and the influence of environmental conditions on learning. This trend bodes well for developing improved teaching and training techniques to enhance the learning and performance of retarded people.

Physical Growth and Motor Development

A common assumption regarding retarded persons is that they are not as deficient in physical and motor development as they are in intellectual and academic achievement. While this assumption may be somewhat applicable to mildly retarded persons, there is little actual basis for this conclusion, especially as applied to development of severely and profoundly retarded persons. Bruininks (1974) has provided a detailed summary of research in this area.

A large number of studies on the physical growth and development of retarded persons largely corroborates early findings by Tarbell (1883): Overall, mentally retarded persons are appreciably below standards for nonretarded age-mates in height, weight, and skeletal maturity. Their growth proceeds at a slower rate and continues for a longer period of time. Prolongation of the growth period for retarded persons appears related to the delayed onset of puberty. As with other indices of development, a positive relationship exists between intellectual and growth status, with mildly retarded persons least deficient in physical development. Severely retarded persons, in contrast, are distinctly inferior to retarded age-mates on indices of physical development; in fact, distributions of scores between the groups show little overlap.

Studies of motor skills development reveal a pattern similar to measures of growth for retarded persons. Bruininks (1977) compared the performances of mildly and moderately retarded pupils with age-matched nonretarded pupils on subtest, gross motor, fine motor, total battery, and short-form scores on the *Bruininks-Oseretsky Test of Motor Proficiency*. Figures 4.3 and 4.4 depict scores of the two groups of retarded pupils on subtest and battery composite standard scores, respectively.

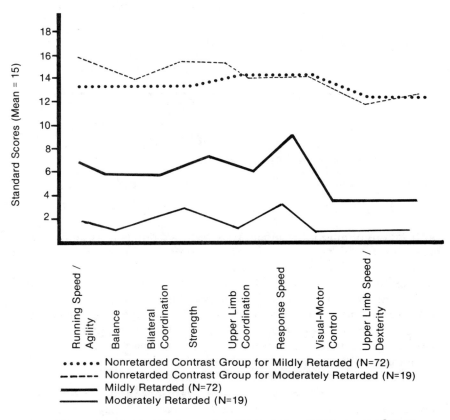

• • • • • Nonretarded Contrast Group for Mildly Retarded (N=72)
– – – – – Nonretarded Contrast Group for Moderately Retarded (N=19)
━━━━━ Mildly Retarded (N=72)
──────── Moderately Retarded (N=19)

Figure 4.3 Subtest Performance of Retarded and Nonretarded Children

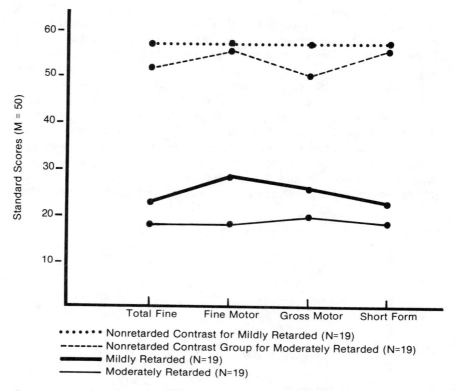

Figure 4.4   Performance of Retarded and Nonretarded on Composite Test Scores

Both groups of mildly and moderately retarded pupils were significantly below nonretarded pupils in all areas of motor proficiency; the greatest deficiencies in skill areas involved complex motor responses requiring coordination of both sides of the body in simultaneous and sequential movement patterns, coordination of visual perception with fine motor acts, precise fine motor acts under conditions of speed, and balance.

Other studies have shown a similar performance pattern in these areas, as well as deficits in the areas of muscular flexibility and endurance (Bruininks, 1974). Consistent with other development areas, severely retarded persons are most deficient in motor skills.

Though retarded persons are often deficient in motor skills when compared to nonretarded persons, such differences may in part result from limited opportunity. Widdop (1967) found that 75 percent of mildly retarded pupils in a national survey of special education programs spent less than 30 minutes per week in structured physical education programs. Furthermore, their peer group activities outside school programs are probably limited, since retarded children as a group are given lower status scores on peer relationship measures.

Despite lower achievement in motor skills and possible restrictive opportunities to develop such skills, retarded persons have shown improvement in motor proficiency following structured, short-term training (cf. Bruininks, 1974). With the obvious need for motor proficiency in occupations and tasks performed by retarded persons, one wonders why so little attention has been given to this area of development in school and other agency training programs. More recently, however, activities such as the Special Olympics are emphasizing this curriculum area for retarded pupils.

Social-Emotional Characteristics

Historically, definitions of mental retardation have presented a combined emphasis on subaverage learning performance and lack of social competence. Just as a person's adjustment is affected by intellectual ability, adaptation to one's environment also is affected by social relationships, emotional development, and responses of others.

Studies over the past 75 years or more present interesting findings on the affective characteristics and social relationships of retarded persons. Despite limitations in study design and procedures, such information is important in understanding the meaning of retardation in the context of our own society.

Peer Relationships

With the growing movement to serve handicapped persons in regular education programs, understanding peer attitudes toward retarded students has become an increasingly important consideration. Meanwhile, special educators have long accepted as axiomatic the idea that mere physical proximity of handicapped to nonhandicapped students did not necessarily lead to their desired psychological integration. Gottlieb (1975) arrived at the following conclusions in an excellent review of available studies on public, peer, and professional attitudes toward retarded persons:

1. The general public views retarded persons as severely handicapped with associated physical and emotional disabilities;
2. Mental retardation often is confused with mental illness;
3. Regardless of the educational model employed, mildly retarded children are not as socially accepted by age-mates as are non-retarded children; and
4. The less desirable peer group status of retarded children appears to be related more to undesirable social behaviors than to their learning abilities and performance.

The preceding conclusions, especially those regarding peer relationships, are supported by many studies. Understanding the real meaning and implications of mental retardation, however, is not simple. A study by Bruininks, Rynders, and Gross (1974) suggests that situational factors may affect the social status of retarded children. This study assessed the peer status of mildly retarded children who were enrolled in regular classrooms and who received supplementary instruction in resource rooms in urban and suburban schools. When rated by children of the same sex, mildly retarded children in urban schools achieved *higher* status scores than nonretarded children but, in contrast, those in suburban schools were significantly lower in social status than their nonretarded classmates. Findings of a study reported by Gottlieb and Budoff (1973) appear to confirm these results. Although the precise reasons for these surprising findings are unknown, mildly retarded children clearly are not uniformly unpopular. Indeed, many mildly retarded students enjoy high regard by peers.

As a group, mentally retarded children are less accepted than nonretarded peers in regular education settings. The most probable hypothesis is that peer relationship difficulties experienced by many retarded children are rooted in nonacademic behaviors, especially the use of verbally aggressive behaviors and (negative) reinforcement patterns toward their classmates (Gottlieb & Budoff, 1973; Hartup, Glazer & Charlesworth, 1967). Modest efforts to improve peer relationships of retarded children have met with mixed success (Gottlieb, 1975), but further effort in this area clearly is needed if attempts to integrate retarded children into regular public school programs are to succeed.

Community Adjustment

One illuminating way to gain understanding of the adaptive behavior of mentally retarded persons is through study of their adjustment as adults in community settings. Excellent published reviews of studies in this area exist (Cobb, 1972; Goldstein, 1964; Heber & Dever, 1970; Mac-Millan, 1977; McCarver & Craig, 1974). These studies generally conclude that mentally retarded persons are inferior to nonretarded persons in several aspects of community adjustment including employment records, participation in community activities, and appearance in welfare and police records. Although they do not change jobs more frequently, mentally retarded persons generally occupy positions in unskilled categories and appear to be more frequently discharged during periods of economic recession.

Studies of community adjustment are difficult to conduct, since the influence of many early factors cannot be assessed. Mild degrees of retarded development, especially, are related strongly to early conditions of poverty—conditions that again may be associated more with marginal community adjustment than with learning ability and school achievement. The conclusions of two separate reviews, based largely on the same findings, illustrate the difficulties of assessing information on the community adjustment of persons who were once identified as mentally retarded:

> In summary, the picture portrayed by recent analyses of the status of graduates of special classes, as well as persons discharged from institutions, is not a bright one at all. They appear to be at the lowest points on the scales of social and occupational adjustment (Heber & Dever, 1970, p. 404).

> The most consistent and outstanding finding of all follow-up studies is the high proportion of the adult retarded who achieve satisfactory adjustments, by whatever criteria are employed (Cobb, 1972, p. 145).

Adjustment for retarded persons (and for us all) doubtless depends upon the joint contribution of many factors. The work of Edgerton (1967) and Edgerton and Bercovici (1976) illustrates the complex nature of community adjustment. In a study of 48 persons discharged from a large institution to independent community placements, Edgerton (1967) discovered a number of persistent themes characterizing their adjustment, including (1) marginal social and economic adjustment, (2) the need for nonhandicapped benefactors to assist and maintain them in the community, and (3) a persistent orientation toward trying to pass as normal to avoid the stigma of mental retardation.

In a follow-up study approximately 12 to 14 years later, many of the original study group had changed their economic and social circumstances, and those who were found seemed less reliant on benefactors and less concerned about passing as normal. Edgerton and Bercovici (1976) stress the difficulties of predicting the future course of community adjustment of retarded persons from earlier measures.

That retarded persons experience difficulties in community adjustment is well documented, although their level of adjustment appears better than might be expected based upon measures of intelligence and achievement. To what extent community adjustment of retarded persons is rooted in learning deficiencies, poor training, environmental circumstances, or earlier environmental deprivations is unknown, although all of these factors likely interact in limiting their adjustment to life.

Emotional Disturbances

Based upon limited studies, agreement generally has been reached that a higher prevalence of behavioral disturbances exists among retarded persons than in the population as a whole (Beier, 1964; MacMillan, 1977).

Despite this relationship, the identification of mental retardation with emotional disturbance, mental illness, and criminal conduct is not justified. (Gottlieb, 1975; MacMillan, 1977). MacMillan has aptly summarized this distinction.

> The review of personality *traits* in retarded persons fail to reveal differences of kind and serves only to emphasize that the retarded are not a group apart from the nonretarded but rather part of a continuum. While there may be differences in the frequency with which the retarded exhibit certain traits, these differences can be explained by different life experiences they are exposed to . . . and certainly cannot be interpreted as characteristics inherent in mental retardation (p. 417).

SERVICES AND PROGRAMS FOR THE MENTALLY RETARDED

The history of care and treatment of retarded persons is dominated by contradictions of cruelty and compassion, neglect and concern, and isolation and integration. Systematic attempts to provide treatment for mentally retarded and other handicapped persons originated relatively late in history—primarily in the nineteenth century. Prior to 1800, opportunities for care and treatment of retarded persons were very rare (Kanner, 1964).

Although steady growth in services for the retarded has been occurring during the past 175 years, a phenomenal increase in services has transpired during the past 30 years. Much of this increased attention by government and the private sector has resulted from the energy of and pressure by parents of retarded children—largely through the impetus of the National Association for Retarded Citizens (NARC) and its affiliate state and local associations, along with a few concerned public officials.

The reader is directed to a number of scholarly treatments of this history (Kanner, 1964; Davies & Ecob, 1959; Sarason & Doris, 1969; Wolfensberger, 1976). Of particular interest is the realization that public attitudes toward mentally retarded and other less advantaged groups have had a pervasive influence (positive or negative) on definitions of mental retardation, research, and philosophies underlying organization of services at any given time. When prevailing political and social thought was idealistic and optimistic, care and treatment expanded in scope and assumed a generally progressive orientation toward habilitating and improving the lives of retarded persons. As the prevailing political Zeitgeist turned negative and pessimistic, services for retarded persons became restrictive, isolated, and less optimistic in character (White & Wolfensberger, 1969; Wolfsensberger, 1976). Table 4.3 presents a simplified summary of broad historical periods with their more distinctive characteristics.

Historical and contemporary treatment of retarded persons is better understood by analyzing prevailing social and political ideology than by depicting trends in services. Presently, service models and treatment approaches are changing rapidly, due substantially to changes in social thought and the ideology being applied to serving handicapped persons. Current trends stress approaches of social integration, individualized treatment, and accountability for results—trends that have been influenced substantially by adoption of the *normalization principle* as an underlying philosophy of services.

Table 4.3

Historical Periods in the Treatment of Retarded Persons

Period	Social-Political Emphasis	Treatment of Retarded Persons
Antiquity to 1700 Neglect and Superstition	Varied considerably depending upon the specific historical period.	Characterized by neglect, superstition, harsh and cruel treatment. Little systematic attention given to retarded people. Occasional, infrequent humane attempts at providing care.

Table 4.3 (Continued)

Period	Social-Political Emphasis	Treatment of Retarded Persons
1700-1800 Awakening Scientific and Humanitarian Interest	Dominated by political and social idealism, with an optimistic view regarding the malleability of intelligence and the importance of assuring equality of people, freedom of thought, and democratic forms of government.	Focus on improvement of the situation of retarded persons with the hope that they could achieve normal functioning and integration into society. Generally small treatment programs located in community settings.
1880-1925 Era of Pessimism and Eugenic Alarms	Emphasis on application of genetic discoveries and the theory of evolution to understanding social issues; intense economic competition and industrial development. Assumption was that mental retardation resulted from genetic influences and that retarded persons represented a threat to society and social order.	Restrictive treatment with emphasis on protecting society from retarded persons (White and Wolfensberger, 1969). Sterilization laws, isolated institutions in remote areas, and other restrictive measures prevailed. Habilitation and community integration were given much less emphasis than during the preceding period.
1930-1965 Increased Responsibility by Government	Realization, largely resulting from the Depression, that government must assume some responsibility for the welfare of less advantaged persons.	Legislation and services expanded but often were based upon restrictive forms of treatment (e.g., special settings, remotely located institutions, large facilities).
1965-present Individual and Human Rights	Growing emphasis on the rights of individuals, along with development of treatment ideologies which de-emphasize effects of labeling and provide treatment through generic services and alternative service models in settings that minimize the separateness of retarded from nonhandicapped persons.	Greatly expanded services, but under conditions of increased self-criticism and experimentation. Models of service stressing integration, individualized planning and treatment, advocacy, and accountability for decisions and programs.

The Normalization Principle

An often overlooked issue in examining the nature and structure of educational and social services is the role of ideology (Wolfensberger, 1972). Typically, services for retarded people and others with handicapping conditions are discussed with reference to the number of people served and the amount of funds expended for their support. Yet, attitudes and beliefs about the nature of mental retardation greatly influence the public policies and private actions that affect and control decisions regarding the scope, characteristics, and quality of services.

During recent years, persons interested in services for retarded persons have found the normalization principle an important philosophical concept for planning and improving services. This concept was first introduced by Bank-Mikkelsen, director of the Danish Mental Retardation Service, and Bengt Nirje, former director of the Swedish Association for Retarded Children (Wolfensberger, 1972), and has provided much of the ideological impetus behind innovative service arrangements for retarded people in Scandinavian countries.

Two definitions of the normalization principle are commonly cited. Nirje, who introduced the concept in a publication of the President's Committee on Mental Retardation in 1969, defines the normalization principle as "making available to all mentally retarded people patterns of life and conditions of everyday living which are as close as possible to the regular circumstances and ways of society" (Nirje, 1976, p. 231). To emphasize the culturally relative nature of the concept, Wolfensberger (1972) described the normalization principle as "utilization of means which are as culturally normative as possible, in order to establish and/or maintain personal behaviors and characteristics which are as culturally normative as possible" (p. 28).

If applied as a concept for planning and managing services, several corollaries of the normalization principle can be used to increase the effectiveness of services. Some of these corollaries are:

—Planning and managing services for retarded people which require attention to normative cultural patterns (Wolfensberger, 1972).

—Allowing retarded persons to experience normal routines of the day (e.g., dressing, eating in normal size groups), and normal routines of the life cycle (e.g., activities appropriate to one's age) that generally accompany increasing maturity (Nirje, 1969).

—Providing experiences with peers and the opportunity to live in a bisexual world (Nirje, 1969).

—Respecting choices and desires, and providing normal economic and civic privileges (Nirje, 1969).

—Providing education, training, care, and residential living in facilities of normal size and appearance (Nirje, 1969).

—Using generic services wherever possible, rather than separate ones (Wolfensberger, 1972).

Applying the normalization principle to planning and managing human services for retarded and other handicapped people does not imply that the nature and severity of a person's handicap should be ignored. The key phrases in both definitions of normalization are: "as close as possible" and "as culturally normative as possible." The extent to which regular opportunities and services are available to handicapped people becomes an issue for research and practice to resolve. As Wolfensberger (1972) stated, "The proposed reformulation implies both a process and a goal, although it does not necessarily imply a promise that a person who is being subjected to normalizing measures and processes will remain or become normal" (p. 28). Proponents of the normalization principle, however, assume that programs exemplifying this ideological orientation will more successfully establish and maintain the behaviors necessary for increased growth, independence, and productive living for retarded persons.

Overview of Needed Services

The impact of the normalization principle, new forms of legislation, and the results of recent court litigation have greatly changed the availability and character of services provided to retarded people. Much of the impetus for federal legislation affecting retarded persons resulted from recommendations of the President's Panel on Mental Retardation appointed by President John F. Kennedy approximately 15 years ago. Since the time of that report, several important acts have been passed that provide direct benefits to retarded people and their families.

During fiscal year 1976, the Department of Health, Education and Welfare obligated an estimated $1.9 billion in some of the following areas: preventive services, basic and supportive services (e.g., clinics, rehabilitation, long-term care), training of personnel, research, construction and income support. Far more money for these same service areas is allocated through state and local governments and private sources. In 1970, for example, Conley (1973, 1976) estimated that approximately $5 billion was spent on services for retarded people, the benefits in terms of human gains (although difficult to estimate) far outweigh the economic costs.

Services for retarded persons are undergoing rapid changes, due largely to the impact of a number of social and cultural factors (cf. MacMillan, 1977; Hobbs, 1975). Some of these influences are:

— Increased emphasis on rights of the retarded to adequate treatment in residential and training programs, adequate wages and working conditions, access to available resources and services, and avoidance of unjustified effects of labeling and discriminatory practices through testing and the inappropriate use of records. Many of these rights are now affirmed in federal legislation such as the Developmental Disabilities Act (Public Law 94-103) and the Education for All Handicapped Children Act (Public Law 94-142), through federal court decrees, and through state legislation.

— A changing ideological emphasis toward services as exemplified by the normalization principle and its application to regulations and practices affecting services (e.g., mainstreaming in public education).

— Advances in prevention (Begab, 1974) and concerns regarding right to life for severely handicapped infants.

— Increased emphasis on providing comprehensive, community-based services, especially for unserved populations such as young children and older retarded persons.

What services do mentally retarded people often need in order to fulfill the expectations implied by the normalization principle? The Developmental Disabilities Assistance and Bill of Rights Act (Public Law 94-103) cites a number of essential services for mentally retarded and other developmentally disabled citizens. Essential direct services for retarded persons are summarized in Table 4.4.

Table 4.4
Essential Services for Retarded and Other
Handicapped Persons

Category	Description

1. Developmental programs
 	
  a. Day activity
  b. Education
  c. Training
	1. Includes a variety of educational and care programs appropriate for a person's age and severity of handicapping conditions.

Table 4.4 (Continued)

Category	Description

2. Residential services
 	
  a. Domiciliary
  b. Special living arrangements
	2. Includes out-of-home living quarters: 24-hour lodging and supervision, and less supervised living arrangements for less severely handicapped persons (e.g., supervised apartment).

3. Employment services
 	
  a. Preparation
  b. Sheltered (including work activity)
  c. Competitive
	3. Includes a continuum of vocational evaluation, training, and work opportunity in supervised and independent settings.

4. Identification services
 	
  a. Diagnosis
  b. Evaluation
	4. Includes efforts to identify presence of disabilities and their probable cause(s), and to assess and plan service needs of the disabled person.

5. Facilitating services
 	
  a. Information and referral
  b. Counseling
  c. Protective and socio-legal
  d. Follow-along
  e. Case management
	5. Includes a variety of actions needed to insure that disabled persons are informed of available services, assisted in getting services, provided protection of rights and guardianship if needed, and given continued review of plans to insure that services are appropriately delivered.

6. Treatment services
 	
  a. Medical
  b. Dental
	6. Includes appropriate medical care, prosthetic devices needed for maximum adjustment, and dental care.

7. Transportation	7. Transportation to training, work, and other activities.
8. Leisure and recreation	8. Structured and unstructured leisure opportunities as needed.

Note: Much of this material has been adapted from material in the Developmental Disabilities Assistance and Bill of Rights Act.

Although not all the services listed in Table 4.4 are used by the majority of persons identified as retarded sometime during their lives, their availability is nonetheless necessary to insure that retarded and other handicapped persons enjoy sufficient opportunities for meaningful and productive lives. More severely retarded persons are likely to require all of these services at some point in their lifetimes. Mildly retarded persons, however, may need only some of them, particularly those services pertaining to education, training, and employment.

Contemporary Educational Programs

Social changes occurring since 1950 have pressed hard on traditional schools, resulting in a strong trend in current programming to reverse the past practice of segregating the mentally retarded in special settings, especially those children mildly affected. Current federal and state legislation uses the term *least restrictive environment* to suggest that the regular class offers less restriction of opportunities for learning. A corollary term is *mainstreaming,* which is defined by Birch (1974):

> Simply stated, mainstreaming is providing high quality special education to exceptional children while they remain in regular grades for as much of the day as possible (p. 2).

In actual operation, mainstreaming has been described much more extensively, indicating that it is *not* the radical act of simply returning a child to a regular class in which he or she was once failing. Rather, it is an effort to provide a child as normal an educational experience as possible, taking into account the individual characteristics of the child, and selecting the type of services along a continuum of possibilities, a "cascade" of options (cf. Deno, 1973). This range of educational offerings illustrates the movement from most restrictive settings (home or hospital) through various part-time arrangements in special locations or classes, to full-time attendance in regular classes, frequently augmented by supplementary instructional services and/or medical, counseling, or supportive therapies.

The push toward mainstreaming did not come from regular teachers, who are now responsible for testing the efficacy of the practice. In actuality, most mildly retarded pupils have never been removed from regular classes, because they seemed to be able to make some progress in learning and did not show problems in behavior. As Robinson and Robinson (1976) noted, "The children who are most likely to have been singled out for special placement are those who are difficult to handle (more often boys than girls), and who are learning little from exposure to the regular programs" (p. 379).

Following the rapid expansion of segregated special classes in the 1950s and 1960s, a burst of discontent arose from professional special educators over the failures and inadequacies of these classes. In addition, children of the economically poor, or from racial, ethnic, or culturally different families were notably over-represented in special classes. Well known special educators expressed concern.

> The conscience of special educators needs to rub up against morality . . . The *entente* of mutual delusion between general and special education that special class placement will be advantageous to slow learning children of poor parents can no longer be tolerated (Dunn, 1968, p. 22).

> Special education is helping the regular school maintain its spoiled identity when it creates special programs . . . for the "disruptive child" and the "slow learner," many of whom, for some strange reason, happen to be black and poor and live in the inner city (Johnson, 1969, p. 245).

> It is the position of this writer . . . that traditional special education services represented by self-contained classes should be discontinued immediately for all but the severely impaired . . . (Lilly, 1970, p. 43).

Major issues remain unresolved: public attitudes, fears, and outright rejection of the retarded; the problems of financing and staffing faced by public school administrators; and the necessity for re-education in teacher preparation programs (thus changing college curricula) to include *all* the children.

Regardless of the problems and expressed opposition, future programming likely will keep more mildly retarded children in regular classes. The challenge to all educators—regular and special teachers and administrators—is to improve the quality of educational service within as near normal settings as possible. Attention therefore should be focused on: (1) administrative arrangements which will facilitate increased individualization of planning, (2) development of technology and supportive aids for teachers dealing with broader ranges of ability; and (3) modification of school curricula toward greater flexibility. Further discussion of these issues is provided by Bruininks and Rynders (1971), MacMillan (1971), and MacMillan, Jones, and Meyers (1976).

Administrative Approaches

One way of adjusting to individual children's needs is to provide the regular teacher with assistance. Many such arrangements have been worked out; e.g., an itinerant or resource teacher helps the regular teacher in the classroom or by taking the child out of the regular classroom for periods of special tutoring in a resource room. Resource teachers have assumed many different roles. Direct teaching of special children, of course, is characteristic of their work, but other considerations may be equally important, such as being able to communicate well and get along with other teachers.

Even if regular class placement, adequately supported, may be considered at this time to be the most desired arrangement, it is not certain that all special classes can be abolished in the future. In any case, more extensive modification of the curriculum usually will be necessary, especially for children in the trainable or moderately retarded range of abilities. And a child who needs continued help in self-care skills such as dressing and traveling independently will need time to develop and practice such basic behaviors under guidance.

The special class may well be in a regular school building, where some experiences with normal peers will be possible, especially in nonacademic classes, making possible many diversified and constructive activities. Regular class students can be peer tutors; field trips can be shared; special students with talent can join in music, art, and recreational activities. The importance of such experience for the regular pupils is obvious; learning to recognize the needs of one's peers who are "different" should begin in childhood.

Special Schools

A frequent practice is now for several school systems to cooperate in interdistrict arrangements, often setting up large schools for the moderately or "less able" retarded. Such programs have been applied especially to secondary school-age students whose developmental levels are substantially below their age-mates. The curriculum in such special schools generally has emphasized learning of survival or coping skills such as recognizing basic vocabulary or safety words, preparing for increased independence, and employment training under close supervision.

For mildly retarded students, The Education for All Handicapped Children Act (PL 94-142) should effectively eliminate the segregation of secondary students who need no such restrictions. Individualized programs, as required by the Act, will allow most students to continue their education in community schools. The individualized plans should consider strongly the area of career preparation. The transition from school to successful employment for moderately retarded persons depends a great deal on the cooperation and communication of teachers, counselors, and other agency assistance (vocational rehabilitation) in order to match the student's capabilities to local community job opportunities.

Programs: Infancy and Early Childhood

The projects Head Start and Follow Through are examples of preschool programs intended to compensate young children for the detrimental effects of inadequate stimulation, nutrition, and health care in early years.

Public responsibility for care of infants has yet to be acknowledged generally in the United States. A few infant stimulation programs have been funded in which parents are given direct help in the nurturing of their young children. A national Home Start program could be developed to assist low-income parents in early developmental training of their children in their own homes (President's Committee on Mental Retardation, 1976b).

In perhaps 85 to 90 percent of cases, mild retardation, not involving identifiable organic or physical cause, is associated with conditions arising from the environment, poverty, racial and ethnic discrimination, and family distress (p. 80).

The issues surrounding the importance of a child's early environmental impact have not been resolved. The assertion that the first four years of life are overwhelmingly important (Bloom, 1964) is quoted frequently. Recently, this emphasis has been challenged by observations that enrichment of educational opportunities for handicapped children must be continued during elementary school years and into adolescent and young adult years as well. With improved technology, teaching techniques (e.g., contingency management) have been developed which are powerful enough to effect behavior change regardless of the individual's age, degree of retardation, or current status.

Perhaps it is well that early childhood education be evaluated carefully for cost and effectiveness. The most successful studies have shown that involvement of the families, especially the mothers, is always an important factor (Bronfenbrenner, 1974).

Longitudinal studies will help to determine the how, when, and with whom, to work for the benefit of very young handicapped children. At the University of Minnesota, a project involving young Down's syndrome children and their mothers has shown promising results (Rynders & Horrobin, 1975). Children enrolled in the program developed better expressive language skills, concept formation, and higher scores on individual intelligence tests than did children in a contrast group.

Programs: Elementary

Few carefully sequenced curricula have been developed for mentally retarded learners, and with even the best plans, the teacher's skill in adapting to the individual learner is essential to success. Teacher competency is the key, not the selected training courses or certification standards. Educably retarded students are so varied in their differences, each unique in personality and background, that they seem more heterogeneous than a group of "normal" peers. As expressed by MacMillan (1977),

The program that is offered to the EMR child has as its major goal that these children will as adults possess the skills and attitudes needed for successful living and working in the society (p. 441).

Teachers—regardless of training— must select goals appropriate for the community and the social milieu in which the EMR child will live as an adult. Parent expectations should be taken into account on choices of tasks to be learned. If factory employment is a future possibility, the skills to be learned would be different from those needed in a vegetable-growing community.

In any case, curriculum guides must be used judiciously. What is being offered to the learner is extremely important to his or her future. Time should not be wasted on irrelevant and nonessential skills. Deciding what is relevant is the task of educators.

Programs: Secondary, Vocational

All education should be, in a sense, vocational or career oriented. In the perspective of Brolin (1976), one's career encompasses the total life experience: employment, leisure time, life style, personal and social relationships.

If such a broad view is acceptable, educational objectives should be set up for children with differing ability levels but with some common interests. Comfortable living as an adult depends a great deal upon human relationships. Ability to care for one's personal needs is basic. Contributing to the environmental arrangement in which one lives is certainly desirable. Economic independence rates high in social approval, though it's not always essential for an individual's sense of worth. The goal of *maximum independence* as an adult is probably the strongest note in educational program planning, regardless of degree of mental retardation.

Educational programs for both educable and trainable retarded students should offer opportunities to practice habits to sustain good mental and physical health; to learn skills necessary for self-care and safe living; to relate to other persons for necessary help and guidance; to accept responsibility to the fullest extent possible; to give and receive affection appropriately.

As prospective employees, the retarded need to acquire habits in keeping with steady employment: dependability, promptness, courtesy, willingness to accept direction, and productivity. Such attributes have been determined to be more important than academic skills beyond rudimentary levels. A great many jobs require no reading or computation skills.

There are hopeful signs that public attitudes are changing. Recent surveys indicate that more persons are now willing to accept retarded persons as neighbors or employees. There is also a recognition that most retarded persons should not be in institutions and that many of them are able to support themselves and live independently (see Figure 4.5). With the conversion from large institutions to community living arrangements such as group homes, board and care, or foster homes, adaptations by community agencies must accommodate retarded citizens in new ways and with attitudes of acceptance. Retarded adults need more than room, board, and a job. Leisure opportunities must be available to them—parks, playgrounds, bowling alleys, theatres, evening and daytime informal classes. Boys' and girls' clubs (e.g., 4-H, Scouts), teenage activities sponsored by churches, and adult organizations ideally should be cordial to all neighbors and citizens.

Following is an excerpt from a brief biography of Mary Pate, which appeared in *Century of Decision* (President's Committee on Mental Retardation, 1976a).

> She's 60 years old and adjusting to semi-independent living in a large city. That's not easy after spending most of her life at Walden State School and Hospital.
>
> Mary Pate was institutionalized when she was five years old. The earliest records spoke in vague terms of an "irresponsible and indigent" father and mother and of four children being sent to various orphanages and state institutions. The record states that Mary was admitted to Walden because she was "an extremely slow child who is given to fits . . . a serious problem in the community."
>
> Four years ago, she was placed in a small group residence for women in a city not far from Walden. At the same time, she began work at a vocational training center. After a year and a half of life at the group residence, Mary moved into an apartment of her own.
>
> Today, Mary Pate is experiencing an array of situations—both fearful and hopeful— more complex than any she has known. Here are glimpses of Mary's present world:
>
> *Maintaining an Apartment:* "Every weekend I wash my clothes at the laundromat, and then I clean and scrub my apartment from one end to another. My landlord says nobody has ever kept it so clean."
>
> *Vocational Training:* "It's hard working at the workshop. They keep you working so fast . . . I get tired of bolting those two pieces of metal together. I wish I could work in a hospital, making beds."
>
> *Her Seizures:* "I've learned to know when they are coming on . . . when to sit down and rest . . . or lie down. I walk to the University Medical Center to pick up my pills. I never miss taking them. When I do have a seizure, I feel bad . . . like the other day when one happened while I was shopping in Kroger's. That makes me feel wrong. I've just got to be more careful."
>
> *Leisure Time:* "The people at the workshop go bowling, but I don't go. They also have dances, but they're no fun either. I'm too old for that. On the weekends I stay in the apartment and clean up. Once in a while one of the counselors and I go out to dinner. Also, I go to the First Baptist Church. I found some friends there. I was baptized. They wouldn't let me do that at the institution. They said I couldn't go under water because of my seizures. That didn't matter here. Now I'm trying to follow the rules of the baptists."

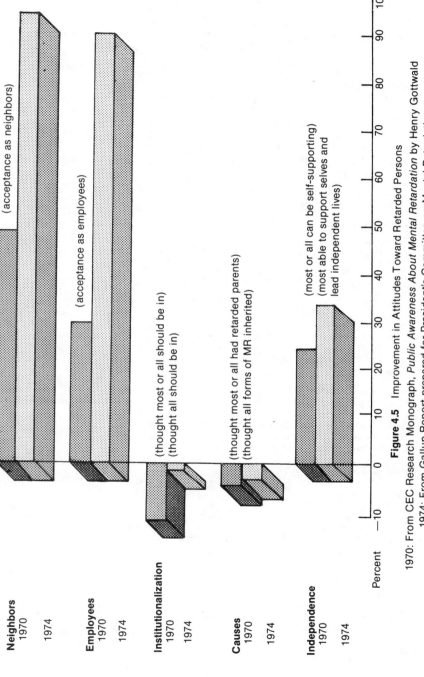

Figure 4.5 Improvement in Attitudes Toward Retarded Persons

1970: From CEC Research Monograph, *Public Awareness About Mental Retardation* by Henry Gottwald
1974: From Gallup Report prepared for President's Committee on Mental Retardation

Mary Pate has come a long way from cowering in a corner on the ward of a large institution. Now she works to master the nuances and rules of a new environment. Sometimes she has fears that the complexities of the city may be too much for her, but her own determination then becomes evident. For example, she and her community counselor were talking about the coming of the year 2000 A.D. and what life would be like for her then. Mary asked the counselor to help her figure out how old she would be. When it was clear that she would be 85, she responded, "I'd like to live until then . . . and even longer" (pp. 87-88).

Education, recreation, friends, companions and counselors—Mary Pate needs the same things you and your family need.

Residential Services

Early attempts to provide services for retarded persons often were accomplished through the development of residential institutions. As noted earlier, the character of residential programs has mirrored quite closely society's general attitudes toward retarded persons. Several excellent historical accounts of residential services for retarded persons have been published (Heal, Sigelman, & Switzky, in press; Kanner, 1964; Wolfensberger, 1976).

Dramatic and widespread changes have been witnessed in residential services for retarded persons during the past few years. The term *deinstitutionalization*, often used to describe many of these changes, generally includes three related components: (1) an alternative to admission to large publicly operated institutions through development of alternative community programs of care and training; (2) returning or releasing persons from institutions to community settings, with appropriate pre-release preparation; and (3) establishing residential living environments which provide protection of the human and civil rights of retarded persons in all settings.

Until the late 1960s, nearly 200,000 persons resided in public residential facilities. During the eight years after 1968, approximately 50,000 retarded persons were released from these facilities (Butterfield, 1976; Scheerenberger, 1976) into a variety of placements. Most persons released from these facilities were mildly and moderately retarded; consequently, nearly 90 percent of the persons currently residing in publicly operated facilities are now severely and profoundly retarded (Scheerenberger, 1976).

The position statement of the National Association of Retarded Citizens (1976) defines residential services as "some type of living condition other than individual's home" (p. 3). According to the statement, such services should:

— Provide a home environment with supervision and guidance as needed;
— Afford living experiences appropriate to the age, functioning level, and learning needs of the individual;
— Provide access to necessary supportive, habilitative, and rehabilitative programs based on a developmental model of programming; and
— Provide access to the mainstream of community life (p. 3).

Some residential facilities commonly found in the United States include:

Foster Family Care Homes.   Families living in the community take one or more retarded children or (less often) adults into their home to live as a member of the family. In most states foster homes as a whole are licensed and reimbursed for expenses, but seldom do states have special licensing or funding for families taking retarded individuals.

Group Homes.   A group home is usually a large, family-type dwelling in the community in which 6 to 15 retarded individuals live, with supervision by one or more professional staff often called house parents. Residents often participate in normal housekeeping duties. The degree of supervision and training within a group home depends upon the philosophy of the home and the abilities and needs of residents. House parents or staff people at the group home are responsible for supervising group home residents on a 24-hour, seven-day-week basis, but daytime activities such as school or work usually take place in the community, as do social and recreational activities.

Board and Care Homes.   Board and care homes are less structured than group homes. Residents sleep and eat in the home, but the family or staff operating board and care homes are not generally responsible for supervision of their residents. Thus, the retarded individual or other services such as case management must assume responsibility for finding daytime activities and obtaining any needed services.

Supervised Apartments.   Supervised apartment programs offer more independence than either group homes or board and care facilities. This service model usually consists of several apartment units occupied by mentally retarded individuals within a larger building. Staffs residing in a separate apartment unit in the same building are responsible for general supervision of apartment residents and assist them in learning skills necessary to live independently in the community.

Residential Schools.   Residential schools most often are regarded primarily as educational programs rather than as residential programs. Living arrangements vary but are often similar to dormitory arrangements. Separate staffs are usually responsible for supervising residential and educational portions of the program.

Nursing Homes.   Nursing homes generally are large community residential facilities intended primarily to serve elderly nonhandicapped individuals. However, since nursing homes provide room and board and 24-hour responsibility for serving the needs of their residents, retarded individuals often are placed in these facilities. Nursing homes usually do not provide nonmedical services for retarded individuals. In some instances, health needs of retarded people dictate that they must receive continuing nursing care, in which event a nursing home may be an appropriate placement.

Institutions. Institutions generally are the largest type of residential facility and often provide most services in a single setting. Residents typically spend their entire day on the grounds of the institution, although they may participate in recreation or education programs outside of the actual building in which they reside. Living arrangements in institutions typically are organized on a ward basis with sleeping areas and a dayroom for every 20 to 30 individuals. This model is changing as federal guidelines for funding impose standards which require more homelike living arrangements.

The number and variety of small community residential living alternatives is expanding rapidly; most of the community residential facilities have been developed since 1970 (Baker, Seltzer & Seltzer, 1974; O'Connor, 1976). One of the more innovative ventures is the Eastern Nebraska Office of Retardation (Lensink, 1976), a community service development and coordination effort that provides for residential, training, and other community living needs of retarded persons. Consistent with the principles of normalization and developmentally based services, extensive use is made of generic community services and small, homelike living arrangements.

Research on the effects of institutional living is longstanding and extensive. A number of studies provide documentation revealing that considerable variation in quality of care exists among programs (Klaber, 1969; King, Raynes & Tizard, 1971), but general agreement has been reached that commitment to an institution generally is accompanied by decline in intellectual functioning and language functioning unless the previous environment was extremely impoverished (Heal et al., in press).

Quality of care in publicly operated and privately operated facilities has not been researched extensively. The available information, though inadequate, does suggest that smaller facilities provide more adequate care than do larger ones. There is little evidence, however, that smaller facilities affect the behavioral functioning of their residents more beneficially than do the larger ones (Balla, 1976). Those facilities with more resident-oriented, as opposed to administratively-oriented, practices of care appear to provide more effective living conditions for retarded persons (King et al., 1971; Klaber, 1969).

An issue of particular concern is that of the factors contributing to admission and readmission of persons to out-of-home residential placements. Little is known regarding the reasons for admission and readmission to nonpublicly operated residential services. Scheerenberger (1976), however, does provide information concerning reasons given for readmission of retarded persons to publicly operated residential facilities. The leading cause cited by personnel in the facilities was lack of community services (52 percent), followed by community rejection and difficulties encountered by families in coping with management problems presented by their retarded children. Careful training before release from an institutional setting appears to enhance community adjustment and lessen the chances of return to the institution (Bell, 1976; Gollay, 1977).

Reasons for *initial* out-of-home placement of retarded persons to residential facilities are generally: (1) difficulty of providing adequate care within the home, and (2) inappropriate social behavior in the community (Conley, 1973; Thorsheim & Bruininks, 1977). Saenger (1960) found that severity of retardation was most frequently given by the families as the reason for initial placement of retarded children in a residential institution, followed by inappropriate conduct in the community. (The latter reason was confined primarily to reasons for placing mildly and moderately retarded persons in institutions.)

Prevention of long-term residential placement is a goal of current social policy (Kugel & Shearer, 1976; National Association for Retarded Citizens, 1976). Certain vexing problems remain, however, in implementing the social policy goal of deinstitutionalization. A number of recent studies report community opposition to establishment of group homes, poorly developed community services, poor coordination of services, and inadequate monitoring of services as major obstacles (Heal, et al., in press; O'Connor, 1976; Scheerenberger, 1976). Another significant concern is that the focus of government policy often encourages expensive forms of care. Average reimbursement for placement in a state operated institution is generally several times higher than financial support for family foster care. Few states, moreover, provide any direct support to families to alleviate additional costs of caring for retarded children. Indeed, parents even encounter difficulty in securing private health insurance coverage for retarded children (Warner, Golden, & Henteleff, 1972). Increased attention to some of these concerns is needed to achieve the expectations and realities implied by the concepts of normalization and deinstitutionalization.

LEGAL AND HUMAN RIGHTS

In recent years, the courts have been called upon to help bring about better educational opportunities for retarded children and more humane treatment for institutionalized persons. Many children once entirely excluded from schools are now receiving educational services under improved circumstances and in appropriate settings. A review of court actions brought to benefit the retarded is presented by Burt (1975).

An outstanding case of court action which recognized rights to education was the *Pennsylvania Association for Retarded Children (PARC)* v. *Commonwealth of Pennsylvania* (1972). This case was settled by a consent agreement which began a major reorganization of activities by the state to locate, assess, and evaluate every retarded child, to be followed by definite program plans for a free publicly supported education "appropriate to the child's capacity."

Another landmark case brought on behalf of children was *Mills* v. *Board of Education of the District of Columbia* (1972). In this case, the right to public education was sought for children handicapped by physical disabilities, emotional disturbance, and behavioral problems, as well as the mentally retarded.

Other issues regarding children's rights have been brought to the courts. For example, the placement of children in special classes has been attacked, as in *Diana* v. *State Board of Education* (1970). This suit was brought on behalf of Spanish-speaking children who had been labeled as retarded through use of tests which were challenged as inappropriate.

Concern for retarded citizens of all ages has been expressed in other ways as in (1) formal declarations of rights; (2) litigation in federal courts regarding the rights of retarded persons to adequate treatment, the right to reject unwanted treatment, and the right to reasonable privacy; and (3) legislative, regulatory, and agency requirements such as those contained in the Developmental Disabilities Act and Public Law 94-142 (The Education for All Handicapped Children Act). Based upon the combined impact of these forces, retarded and other handicapped persons have rights protected by law, including:

- Rights to a free and appropriate education
- Rights to adequate treatment in residential institutions
- Rights to appropriate earnings consistent with their level of productivity, in institutions and other settings which provide work opportunities

- Rights (of handicapped persons and their parents) to due process and consultation in placement decisions and other areas affecting their well-being
- Rights of access to employment, transportation, education, and the environment
- Rights to reasonable protective services.

The number of excellent discussions of these issues include those of Kindred, Cohen, Penrod, and Shaffer (1976) and Swardron (1975).

Increasingly, organized efforts are being made to provide protective services to mentally retarded and other handicapped persons. A National Center on Law for the Handicapped at Notre Dame University and a special panel of the American Bar Association, for example, currently probe legal issues affecting handicapped and disabled persons. Other legal assistance efforts provide direct representation and assistance to handicapped persons. One such approach was organized in 1973 by the Minneapolis Legal Aid Society through assistance from the Minnesota Developmental Disabilities Program. This special project, staffed by trained attorneys and legal advocates, has provided (1) consultation and direct representation to hundreds of handicapped persons, (2) training to volunteer lay advocates, and (3) assistance in drafting state statutes in such areas as zoning to prevent discrimination against community residential facilities, and a progressive guardianship law.

Other efforts outside the legal process are developing to provide volunteer advocate services to increase the participation of mentally retarded citizens in community life. These efforts generally include trained volunteers who spend time with handicapped persons in a variety of recreational and other community activities. Often, these citizen advocates or volunteers perform the role of benefactors (Edgerton, 1967) by assisting retarded persons in areas in which help is needed. The concept of citizen advocacy is discussed fully by Wolfensberger and Zauha (1973).

Emphasis on assuring and protecting the rights of retarded persons is increasingly evident in most services throughout the United States and in many other countries. Although much has been accomplished recently in this area, much remains to be accomplished to realize rights affirmed in the statement of the International League of Societies for the Mentally Handicapped (see Figure 4.6).

*   *   *   *   *   *   *   *   *   *

WHEREAS the universal declaration of human rights, adopted by the United Nations, proclaims that all of the human family, without distinction of any kind, have equal and inalienable rights of human dignity and freedom; and
WHEREAS the declaration of the rights of the child, adopted by the United Nations, proclaims the rights of the physically, mentally or socially handicapped child to special treatment, education and care required by this particular condition.

Now therefore

The International League of Societies for the Mentally Handicapped expresses the general and special rights of the mentally retarded as follows:

ARTICLE I: The mentally retarded person has the same basic rights as other citizens of the same country and same age.

ARTICLE II: The mentally retarded person has a right to proper medical care and physical restoration and to such education, training, habilitation and guidance as will enable him to develop his ability and potential to the fullest possible extent, no matter how severe his degree of disability. No mentally handicapped person should be deprived of such services by reason of the costs involved.

ARTICLE III: The mentally retarded person has a right to economic security and to a decent standard of living. He has a right to productive work or to other meaningful occupation.

ARTICLE IV: The mentally retarded person has a right to live with his own family or with foster parents; to participate in all aspects of community life, and to be provided with appropriate leisure time activities. If care in an institution becomes necessary it should be in surroundings and under circumstances as close to normal living as possible.

ARTICLE V: The mentally retarded person has a right to a qualified guardian when this is required to protect his personal well-being and interest. No person rendering direct services to the mentally retarded should also serve as his guardian.

ARTICLE VI: The mentally retarded person has a right to protection from exploitation, abuse and degrading treatment. If accused, he has a right to a fair trial with full recognition being given to his degree of responsibility.

ARTICLE VII: Some mentally retarded persons may be unable due to the severity of their handicap, to exercise for themselves all of their rights in a meaningful way. For others, modification of some or all of these rights is appropriate. The procedure used for modification or denial of rights must contain legal safeguards against every form of abuse, must be based on an evaluation of the social capability of the mentally retarded person by qualified experts and must be subject to periodic reviews and to the right of appeal to higher authorities.

ABOVE ALL—THE MENTALLY RETARDED PERSON HAS THE RIGHT TO RESPECT.

Figure 4.6 Declaration of General and Special Rights of the Mentally Retarded

SUMMARY

The term *mental retardation* evokes numerous meanings among laymen and professionals. Although misconceptions regarding its true meaning still persist, much progress has been made in the prevention of conditions which lead to retarded development in children and in the care and treatment of retarded persons. A dominant impression gained from studying knowledge in this area is that retarded persons exhibit characteristics and needs similar to those of nonhandicapped persons. While recognizing that effects of retarded development are limiting to the individual, current trends in training and care stress expansion of opportunities and integration of retarded persons into normal community activities.

Over 15 years ago the President's Panel on Mental Retardation (1962) recommended, in addition to increased efforts in research and prevention, that services be comprehensive, community-centered, and organized to form a continuum to meet the lifelong needs of retarded citizens. Despite the continuing need for services that still persists, changes in recent years offer optimism that the crippling effects of retarded development can be reduced and that vast improvements can be achieved in the lives of retarded citizens.

REFERENCES

Anastasia, A. *Psychological Testing.* New York: Macmillan, 1976.

Baker, B.L., Seltzer, B.G., & Seltzer, M.M. *As close as possible.* Cambridge, MA: Behavioral Education Projects, Harvard University, 1974.

Balla, D. Relationship of institution size to quality of care: A review of the literature. *American Journal of Mental Deficiency,* 1976, *81,* 117-124.

Baumeister, A.A. Learning abilities of the mentally retarded. In A.A. Baumeister (Ed.), *Mental Retardation.* Chicago: Aldine, 1967, pp. 181-211.

Begab, M.J. The major dilemma of mental retardation: Shall we prevent it? *American Journal of Mental Deficiency,* 1974, *78,* 519-529.

Beier, D.C. Behavioral disturbances in the mentally retarded. In H.A. Stevens & R. Heber (Eds.), *Mental retardation.* Chicago: University of Chicago Press, 1964, pp. 453-488.

Bell, N.J. IQ as a factor in community lifestyle of previously institutionalized retardates. *Mental Retardation,* 1976, *14,* 29-33.

Bijou, S.W. A functional analysis of retarded development. In N.R. Ellis (Ed.), *International review of research in mental retardation* (Vol. 1). New York: Academic Press, 1966.

Birch, J.W. Mainstreaming: *Educable retarded children in regular classes.* Reston, VA: Council for Exceptional Children, 1974.

Blake, K.A. *The mentally retarded: An educational psychology*. Englewood Cliffs, NJ: Prentice-Hall, 1976.

Bloom, B.S. *Stability and change in human characteristics*. New York: Wiley, 1964.

Breckenridge, M.E., & Murphy, M.N. *Growth and development of the young child*. Philadelphia: W.B. Saunders, 1969.

Brolin, D.E. *Vocational preparation of retarded citizens*. Columbus, OH: Charles E. Merrill, 1976.

Bronfenbrenner, V. *Is early intervention effective? A report on longitudinal evaluations of preschool programs* (Vol. II). Washington, DC: Department of Health, Education and Welfare Publication COHD 76-30025, U.S. Government Printing Office, 1974.

Bruininks, R.H. Physical and motor development of retarded persons. In N.R. Ellis (Ed.), *International review of research in mental retardation* (Vol. 7). New York: Academic Press, 1974, pp. 209-261.

Bruininks, R.H. *Manual for the Bruininks - Oseretsky Test of Motor Proficiency*. Circle Pines, MN: American Guidance Service, 1977.

Bruininks, R.H., & Rynders, J.E. Alternatives to special class placement for educable mentally retarded children. *Focus on Exceptional Children*, 1971, *3*(4), pp. 1-12.

Bruininks, R.H., Rynders, J.E., & Gross, J.C. Social acceptance of mildly retarded pupils in resource rooms and regular classes. *American Journal of Mental Deficiency*, 1974, *78*, 377-383.

Burt, R.A. Judicial action to aid the retarded. In N. Hobbs (Ed.), *Issues in the classification of children* (Vol. 2). San Francisco: Jossey-Bass, 1975, pp. 293-318.

Butterfield, E. Some basic changes in residential facilities. In R.B. Kugel & A. Shearer (Eds.), *Changing patterns in residential services for the mentally retarded*. Washington, DC: President's Committee on Mental Retardation, 1976, pp. 15-34.

Cobb, J.B. *The forecast of fulfillment*. New York: Teachers College Press, 1972.

Conley, R.W. *The economics of mental retardation*. Baltimore: Johns Hopkins University Press, 1973.

Conley, R.W. Mental retardation — An economist's approach. *Mental Retardation*, 1976, *14*, 20-24.

Conroy, J.W., & Derr, K.E. *Survey and analysis of the habilitation and rehabilitation status of the mentally retarded with associated handicapping condition*. Washington, DC: Department of Health, Education and Welfare, 1971.

Davies, S.P., & Ecob, K.G. *The mentally retarded in society*. New York: Columbia University Press, 1959.

DeAvila, E. Mainstreaming ethnically and linguistically different children: An exercise in paradox or a new approach? In R.L. Jones (Ed.), *Mainstreaming and the minority child*. Reston, VA: Council for Exceptional Children, 1976.

Denny, M.R. A theoretical analysis and its application to training the mentally retarded. In N.R. Ellis (Ed.), *International review of research in mental retardation* (Vol. 2). New York: Academic Press, 1966, pp. 1-27.

Deno, E.N. (Ed.). *Instructional alternatives for exceptional children*. Reston, VA: The Council for Exceptional Children, 1973.

Deno, S.L., Gutmann, A.J., & Fullmer, W. Educational programs for retarded individuals. In T. Thompson & J. Grabowski (Eds.), *Behavior modification of the mentally retarded* (2nd ed.). New York: Oxford University Press, 1977, pp. 235-300.

Diana v. Board of Education. C-70-37 (RFP Dist. N. Calif.), 1970.

Dunn, L.M. Special education for the mildly retarded: Is much of it justifiable? *Exceptional Children*, 1968, *35*, 5-22.

Edgerton, R. *The cloak of competence: Stigma in the lives of the mentally retarded*. Berkeley: University of California Press, 1967.

Edgerton, R.B., & Bercovici, S.M. The cloak of competence: Years later. *American Journal of Mental Deficiency*, 1976, *80*, 485-497.

Ellis, N.R. The stimulus trace and behavioral inadequacy. In N.R. Ellis (Ed.), *Handbook of mental deficiency*. New York: McGraw-Hill, 1963, pp. 134-158.

Ellis, N.R. Memory processes in retardates and normals. In N.R. Ellis (Ed.), *International review of research in mental retardation* (Vol. 4). New York: Academic Press, 1970, pp. 1-32.

Estes, W.K. *Learning theory and mental development*. New York: Academic Press, 1970.

Fisher, M.A., & Zeaman, D. Growth and decline of retarded intelligence. In N.R. Ellis (Ed.), *International review of research in mental retardation* (Vol. 4). New York: Academic Press, 1970, pp. 151-191.

Goddard, H.H. *Human efficiency and levels of intelligence.* Princeton, NJ: Princeton University Press, 1920.

Goldstein, H. Social and occupational adjustment. In H.A. Stevens & R. Heber (Eds.), *Mental retardation.* Chicago: University of Chicago Press, 1964, pp. 214-258.

Gollay, E. Deinstitutionalized mentally retarded people: A closer look. *Education and training of the mentally retarded,* 1977, *12,* 137-144.

Gottlieb, J. Public, peer, and professional attitudes toward mentally retarded persons. In M.J. Begab & S.A. Richardson (Eds.), *The mentally retarded and society: A social science perspective.* Baltimore: University Park Press, 1975, pp. 99-126.

Gottlieb, J., & Budoff, M. Social acceptability of retarded children in nongraded schools differing in architecture. *American Journal of Mental Deficiency,* 1973, *78,* 15-19.

Grossman, H.J. (Ed.). *Manual on terminology and classification in mental retardation* (rev.). Washington, DC: American Association on Mental Deficiency, 1973.

Hartup, W.W., Glazer, J.A., & Charlesworth, R. Peer reinforcement and sociometric status. *Child Development,* 1967, *38,* 1017-1024.

Heal, L.W., Sigelman, C.K., & Switzky, H.N. Community residential alternatives for the mentally retarded. In N.R. Ellis (Ed.), *International review of research in mental retardation.* New York: Academic Press, in press.

Heber, R.F. A manual on terminology and classification in mental retardation (rev.). *American Journal of Mental Deficiency Monograph,* 1961. (Supplement 64)

Heber, R.F., & Dever, R.B. Research in education and habilitation of the mentally retarded. In H.C. Haywood (Ed.), *Social-cultural aspects of mental retardation.* New York: Appleton-Century-Crofts, 1970, pp. 395-427.

Hobbs, N. *The futures of children.* San Francisco: Jossey-Bass, 1975.

Hurley, R. *Poverty and mental retardation: A causal relationship.* New York: Random House, 1970.

Johnson, J.S. Special education for the inner city: A challenge for the future or another means for cooling the mark out? *Journal of Special Education,* 1969, *3,* 241-251.

Kanner, L. *A history of the care and study of the mentally retarded.* Springfield, IL: Charles C. Thomas, 1964.

Kindred, M., Cohen, J., Penrod, D., & Shaffer, T. (Eds.). *The mentally retarded citizen and the law.* New York: The Free Press, 1976.

King, R.D., Raynes, N.V., & Tizard, J. *Patterns of residential care: Sociological studies in institutions for handicapped children.* London: Routledge & Kegan Paul, 1971.

Klaber, M.M. The retarded and institutions for the retarded. In S.B. Sarason & J. Doris (Eds.), *Psychological problems in mental deficiency (4th ed.).* New York: Harper & Row, 1969, pp. 148-185.

Kugel, R.B., & Shearer, A. (Eds.), *Changing patterns in residential services for the mentally retarded.* Washington, DC: President's Committee on Mental Retardation, 1976.

Lensink, B. ENCOR, Nebraska. In R. B. Kugel & A. Shearer (Eds.), *Changing patterns in residential services for the mentally retarded.* Washington, DC: President's Committee on Mental Retardation, 1976, pp. 277-298.

Lilly, M.S. Special education: A teapot in a tempest. *Exceptional Children,* 1970, *37,* 43-49.

MacMillan, D.L. Special education for the mildly retarded: Servant or savant? *Focus on Exceptional Children,* 1971, *2*(9), pp. 1-11.

MacMillan, D.L. *Mental retardation in school and society.* Boston: Little, Brown & Co., 1977.

MacMillan, D.L. The problems of motivation in the education of the mentally retarded. *Exceptional Children,* 1971, *37,* 579-586.

MacMillan, D.L., Jones, R.L., & Meyers, C.E. Mainstreaming the mildly retarded: Some questions, cautions and guidelines. *Mental Retardation,* 1976, *14*(1), pp. 3-10.

McCarver, R.B., & Craig, E.M. Placement of the retarded in the community: Prognosis and outcome. In N.R. Ellis (Ed.), *International review of research in mental retardation* (Vol. 7). New York: Academic Press, 1974, pp. 146-207.

McGeogh, J.A., & Irion, A.L. *The psychology of human learning.* New York: Longmans, Green & Company, 1952.

McPherson, M.W. A survey of experimental studies of individuals who achieve subnormal ratings on standardized psychometric measures. *American Journal of Mental Deficiency,* 1948, *52,* 232-254.

McPherson, M.W. Learning and mental deficiency. *American Journal of Mental Deficiency,* 1958, *62,* 870-877.

Mercer, J.R. *Labeling the mentally retarded.* Berkley, CA: University of California Press, 1973.

Mercer, C.D., & Snell, M.E. Learning theory research in mental retardation: Implications for teaching. Columbus, OH: Charles E. Merrill, 1977.

Mills v. *Board of Education of the District of Columbia.* 348F Supp. 866 (DDC), 1972.

National Association for Retarded Citizens. *Position statement on residential services.* Arlington, TX: Author, 1976.

Nirje, B. The normalization principle and its human management implications. In R. Kugel & W. Wolfensberger (Eds.), *Changing patterns in residential services for the mentally retarded.* Washington, DC: President's Committee on Mental Retardation, 1969, pp. 179-195.

Nirje, B. The normalization principle. In R.B. Kugel & A. Shearer (Eds.), *Changing patterns in residential services for the mentally retarded.* Washington, DC: President's Committee on Mental Retardation, 1976, pp. 231-240.

O'Connor, G. *Home is a good place; A national perspective of community residential facilities for the developmentally disabled, Monograph No. 2.* Washington, DC: American Association on Mental Deficiency, 1976.

Pennsylvania Association for Retarded Children v. *Commonwealth of Pennsylvania,* 343F, Supp. 279 (E.D., PA.), 1972.

President's Committee on Mental Retardation. *The 6-hour retarded child.* Washington, DC: USGPO, 1970.

President's Committee on Mental Retardation. *Mental retardation: Century of decision.* Washington, DC: USGPO, 1976.(a)

President's Committee on Mental Retardation. *Mental retardation: The known and the unknown.* Washington, DC: USGPO, 1976.(b)

President's Panel on Mental Retardation. *A proposed program for national action to combat mental retardation.* Washington, DC: USGPO, 1962.

Robinson, N.M., & Robinson, H.B. *The mentally retarded child: A psychological approach.* New York: McGraw-Hill, 1976.

Ross, A.O. *Psychological aspects of learning disabilities and reading disorders.* New York: McGraw-Hill, 1976.

Rotter, J.B. *Social learning and clinical psychology.* Englewood Cliffs, NJ: Prentice-Hall, 1954.

Rotter, J.B. Some problems and misconceptions related to the construct of internal versus external control of reinforcement. *Journal of Consulting and Clinical Psychology,* 1975, *43,* 56-67.

Routh, D.K. (Ed.). *The experimental psychology of mental retardation.* Chicago: Aldine, 1973.

Rynders, J.E., & Horrobin, J.M. Project EDGE: The University of Minnesota's stimulation program for Down's syndrome infants. In B.E. Friedlander (Ed.), *Exceptional infant* (Vol. 3). New York: Brunner/Mazel, 1975, pp. 173-192.

Saenger, G. *Factors influencing the institutionalization of mentally retarded individuals in New York City.* Albany, NY: Interdepartmental Health Resources Board, 1960.

Sarason, S.B., & Doris, J.L. *Psychological problems in mental deficiency* (4th ed.). New York: Harper & Row, 1969.

Scheerenberger, R.C. *Managing residential facilities for the developmentally disabled.* Springfield, IL: Charles C. Thomas, 1976.

Sontag, E. (Ed.). *Educational programming for the severely and profoundly handicapped.* Reston, VA: The Council for Exceptional Children, Division on Mental Retardation, 1977.

Spitz, H.H. The role of input organization in the learning and memory of mental retardation. In N.R. Ellis (Ed.), *International review of research in mental retardation* (Vol. 2). New York: Academic Press, 1966, pp. 29-56.

Swardron, B.B. *Mental retardation - the law - guardianship.* Toronto: National Institute on Mental Retardation, 1975.

Tarbell, G.G. On the height, weight, and relative rate of growth of normal and feeble-minded children. *Proceedings of the Association of Medical Officers of the American Institute for Idiotic and Feebleminded Persons,* 1883.

Terman, L. *The measurement of intelligence.* New York: Houghton Mifflin, 1916.

Thompson, T., & Grabowski, J. (Eds.). *Behavior modification of the mentally retarded.* New York: Oxford University Press, 1977.

Thorsheim, J.J., & Bruininks, R.H. Admission and readmission of mentally retarded people to residential facilities. Minneapolis: Unpublished manuscript, University of Minnesota, 1977.

Thurlow, M.L., & Turnure, J.E. Elaboration structure and list length effects on verbal elaboration phenomena. *Journal of Experimental Child Psychology,* 1972, *14,* 184-195.

Tjossem, T.D. Early intervention: Issues and approaches. In T.D. Tjossem (Ed.), *Intervention strategies for high risk infants and young children.* Baltimore: University Park Press, 1976, pp. 3-33.

Turnure, J.E. Distractibility in the mentally retarded: Negative evidence for an orienting inadequacy. *Exceptional Children,* 1970, *37,* 181-186.

Turnure, J.E. *Toward the clarification of classroom contexts: Pragmatic preliminaries to effective instruction.* Paper presented at the Annual Convention of the American Association on Mental Deficiency, Chicago, June, 1976.

Turnure, J., Buium, N., & Thurlow, M. The effectiveness of interrogatives for promoting verbal elaboration productivity in young children. *Child Development,* 1976, *47,* 851-855.

Warner, F., Golden, T., & Henteleff, M. Health insurance: A dilemma for parents of the mentally retarded. *Exceptional Children,* 1972, *39,* 57-58.

White, W.D., & Wolfensberger, W. The evolution of dehumanization in our institutions. *Mental Retardation,* 1969, *7*(3), 5-9.

Widdop, J.H. *The motor performance of EMR children with particular reference to the identification of factors associated with individual differences in performance.* Doctoral dissertation, University of Wisconsin, 1967 . (University Microfilms No. 67-12, 493)

Wolfensberger, W. *The principle of normalization in human services.* Toronto: National Institute on Mental Retardation, 1972.

Wolfensberger, W. The origin and nature of our institutional models. In R.B. Kugel & A. Shearer (Eds.), *Changing patterns in residential services for the mentally retarded.* Washington, DC: President's Committee on Mental Retardation, 1976, pp. 35-82.

Wolfensberger, W., & Zauha, H. *Citizen advocacy and protective services for the impaired and handicapped.* Toronto: National Institute on Mental Retardation, 1973.

Zeaman, D., & House, B.J. The role of attention in retardate discriminate learning. In N.R. Ellis (Ed.), *Handbook of mental deficiency.* New York: McGraw-Hill, 1963, pp. 159-223.

Zeaman, D. *Experimental psychology of mental retardation: Some states of the art.* Invited address to meeting of the Annual Convention of the American Psychological Association, 1974.

The authors wish to thank Bradley Hill and Gordon Krantz for their constructive suggestions on portions of this chapter.

RESOURCE GUIDE

Historical Information

Doll, E. E. A historical survey of research and management of mental retardation in the United States. In E. P. Trapp & P. Himelstein (Eds.), *Readings on the exceptional child* (2nd ed.). New York: Appleton-Century-Crofts, 1972, pp. 47-98.

Kanner, L. *A history of the care and study of the mentally retarded.* Springfield, IL: Charles C. Thomas, 1964.

Rosen, M., Clark, G. R., & Kivitz, M. S. *The history of mental retardation* (Vols. 1 & 2). Baltimore: University Park Press, 1976.

Family

Ingalls, R. P. The family of the retarded child. *Mental retardation. The changing outlook* (Ch. 13). New York: Wiley & Sons, 1978, pp. 313-338.

Jordan, T. E. The Family. *The mentally retarded* (4th ed., Ch. 4). Columbus, OH: Charles E. Merrill Pub. Co., 1976, pp. 107-162.

Wolfensberger, W., & Kurtz, R. A. (Eds.), *Management of the family of the mentally retarded.* Chicago: Follett, 1969.

Patterns of Development

Blake, K. A. *The mentally retarded: An educational psychology.* Englewood Cliffs, NJ: Prentice-Hall, 1976.

Ingalls, R. P. Learning and memory in the mentally retarded. Language and mental retardation. Cognitive development in the retarded. *Mental retardation. The changing outlook* (Ch. 8, 9, & 10). New York: Wiley & Sons, pp. 189-260.

Zigler, E. Cognitive developmental and personality factors in behavior. In J. M. Kauffman & J. S. Payne (Eds.), *Introduction and personal perspectives.* Columbus, OH: Charles E. Merrill Pub. Co., 1975, pp. 360-387.

Treatment

Koch, R., & Dobson, J. C. *The mentally retarded child and his family: A multidisciplinary handbook.* New York: Brunner/Mazel, 1976, pp. 157-302.

Mercer, C. D., & Payne, J. S. Programs and services. In J. M. Kauffman & J. S. Payne (Eds.), *Mental retardation. Introduction and personal perspectives.* Columbus, OH: Charles E. Merrill Pub. Co., 1975, pp. 109-136.

Robinson, N. M., & Robinson, H. B. Psychotherapy with the mentally retarded. *The mentally retarded child* (2nd ed., Ch. 19). New York: McGraw Hill, 1976, pp. 391–409.

Educational Programming

Brolin, D. E. *Vocational preparation of retarded citizens.* Columbus, OH: Charles E. Merrill Pub. Co., 1976.

Goldstein, H. Importance of social learning. In J. M. Kauffman & J. S. Payne (Eds.), *Introduction and personal perspectives.* Columbus, OH: Charles E. Merrill Pub. Co., 1975, pp. 276-311.

Kolstoe, O. P. *Teaching educable mentally retarded children.* New York: Holt, Rinehart & Winston, 1976.

Lent, J. R. Teaching daily living skills. In J. M. Kauffman & J. S. Payne (Eds.), *Introduction and personal perspectives.* Columbus, OH: Charles E. Merrill Pub. Co., 1975, pp. 246-275.

5 The Severely and Profoundly Handicapped

P. Douglas Guess and R. Donald Horner
University of Kansas

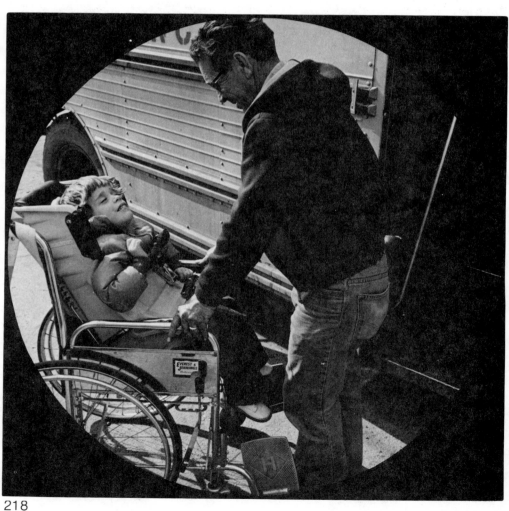

Providing public educational opportunities to the population of children and youth described as severely/profoundly handicapped is new to American school systems. In the past, education was considered unnecessary and inappropriate for these children. Often, severely handicapped children have been kept at home, isolated from the community; and they did not appear in public schools. In many instances, they have been placed in public or private institutions where they would spend their entire lives.

As a society, our treatment of institutionalized handicapped children has too often been one of neglect. Dehumanizing living conditions, lack of proper medical care, inadequate training opportunities, and other undesirable circumstances have been widely documented. In most cases, these conditions have resulted from a combination of inadequate staff, lack of knowledge, and service delivery problems common to large organizations.

Certainly, some advocates have struggled to improve living conditions for individuals residing in institutions. But even the most ardent reformers of the past would not have envisioned the current national commitment to include severely handicapped children in the mainstream of public education, a commitment which gives severely handicapped children the right to a free public school education. This development presents the field of special education with an immense challenge, as well as an opportunity to serve a population of children who have been ignored for too long.

The national commitment to provide education for severely handicapped children is the outgrowth of an interrelated series of events occurring over the past few years. When Gilhool (1973) wrote, "litigation is busting out all over," he succinctly summarized the beginning of a national movement to redefine the role of education for the severely handicapped in American society. Over the past few years, favorable court decisions have established the right to free public education for all school-aged children (Melcher, 1976). Subsequent federal legislation, primarily Public Law 94-142, has served to further the *right to education* concept identified in earlier court decisions.

A second major influence on the national commitment to provide educational opportunities for severely handicapped children originated with the U.S. Bureau of Education for the Handicapped. BEH administrators were among the first to support the right to education concept (Sontag, 1976), and they have consistently spoken out in behalf of the severely handicapped. To illustrate—BEH Director Edwin Martin (1976) made the following statement while addressing a conference for the severely handicapped attended by professional workers, parents, and citizen advocates:

> As professionals and citizens, you must help protect the rights of these citizens. You must use your courage to speak out in public and in your professional groups against such outrages. Many will not understand. They will see only a profoundly damaged organism—"a near vegetable," they might say. They will speak of higher priorities. What you know, however, is that equity for these citizens is essential to our national security. It is essential to our fidelity to our Bill of Rights. If we violate these persons, we violate our commitment to the principle which protects us all.

A third major impetus for the right to education concept has come from the active involvement of professional educators, parents, and concerned citizens through such organizations as the National Association of Retarded Citizens and the American Association on Mental Deficiency. Individuals from these organizations have banded together to further educational opportunities for the severely handicapped. Additionally, in 1974 the American Association for the Education of the Severely/Profoundly Handicapped (AAESPH) was established. The purposes of this organization are:

1. To function as an advocate organization for the development and implementation of comprehensive, high-quality educational services from birth through adulthood in the public school sector.
2. To serve as a separate entity in advocating: (a) the development of relevant and efficient preservice and inservice teacher training programs, and (b) the development of highly specialized doctoral-level teacher training, research, and instructional design personnel.
3. To develop, refine, and disseminate training packages, instructional programs, and materials.
4. To facilitate parent involvement in all program services for the severely and profoundly handicapped.

The rapid growth in AAESPH membership attests to the commitment of professional workers, parents, and private citizens to provide appropriate educational opportunities for severely handicapped individuals. A history of neglect cannot be reversed overnight; nevertheless, a commitment by members in AAESPH and other organizations clearly and emphatically signals a new era for the field of special education and the severely/profoundly handicapped—an era of both challenge and opportunity.

RIGHT TO EDUCATION PRINCIPLES

Educators have set forth two basic principles central to the goals of providing educational opportunities to all children and to the specific commitment to serve educational needs of severely handicapped children—the *least restrictive alternative* and *zero rejection* principles.

Least Restrictive Alternative

The term *least restrictive alternative* (Chambers, 1974) has been used to summarize the specific method of establishing alternative educational programs for the severely handicapped, originally ordered by judicial decisions in the so called PARC or "Pennsylvania case." *(Pennsylvania Association for Retarded Children, Nancy Beth Bowman, et al.* v. *Commonwealth of Pennsylvania, David W. Kurtzman, et. al.)* In this case, the consent agreement stated that placement in a regular public school class is preferable to placement in a special public school class, and placement in a special public school class is preferable to placement in any other type of educational or training program.

Thus, the principle of the least restrictive alternative would require that a handicapped individual be educated in a regular public school class. He or she would be placed in a special class only in cases of "compelling state interest" to do so, if specific and justifiable criteria exist for such placement, or if any arguments against such placement are allowed in a public hearing. The least restrictive alternative implies that placement of severely handicapped children in a public school is more desirable (and less restrictive) than placement in an institution.

Zero Rejection

The principle of *zero rejection* implies access to free public education for all handicapped children. The concept is best defined as the right of an individual to be "deviant" (Segal, 1972) and an affirmation of that right by society through its schools to accommodate to the child rather than requiring the child to accommodate to the school or be excluded (Lippman & Goldberg, 1973).

Both the least restrictive alternative and zero rejection principles provide the philosophy for integrating severely handicapped individuals into the mainstream of our society and, specifically, into our public education system. When interpreted, these principles lay the groundwork for giving severely handicapped individuals the opportunity to participate in the educational system and to become full citizens in our society. The extent to which these goals are realized depends heavily on our ability to prepare teachers to educate these children, to persuade members of our society that such a task is important, and to develop further the technology for effectively teaching severely handicapped students.

Numbers of classroom sites throughout the country already have demonstrated that severely handicapped children can be taught to do many of the things that were considered almost impossible in past years. Certainly, a feeling of genuine optimism exists today that in future years technology will be available to achieve even greater gains with the severely handicapped, especially through early intervention programs.

DEFINING THE SEVERELY AND PROFOUNDLY HANDICAPPED

Children with severe or profound handicaps represent an extremely heterogeneous population. This alone has created considerable confusion among professional educators in arriving at a definition of this particular population. Earlier attempts at definition have listed specific behavioral or physical conditions (Sontag, Burke, & York, 1973), such as severe or complex disabilities that restrict ambulation or locomotion by means of typical transportation modes; behavior characteristics that are injurious to self or others; hyperactivity; impulsiveness; frequently uncontrolled bowel or bladder functions; epilepsy; grossly inadequate communication skills; mixed or multiple sensorimotor disabilities.

All of these descriptions are characteristic of the behavior and conditions commonly observed in children referered to as severely or profoundly handicapped. The descriptions imply, however, that a group of children does exist that can be separately identified and labeled as belonging to a single, common category. Clearly, this is not the case. As Sontag, Smith, and Sailor (1976) pointed out, "Children with severe or profound handicaps are children who are divergent in degree, not in kind." These authors further stated that ". . . these children form an extremely heterogeneous group, composed not only of those characterized by organicity, but also of those whose serious emotional disturbance, deafness, or severe orthopedic impairment renders them functionally retarded." ("Organicity" in this quote generally refers to damage to the nervous system and, more explicitly, brain damage.)

Use of the term *functionally retarded* is significant in arriving at a workable definition of the severely and profoundly handicapped. It implies that any such definition should be based primarily on an educational approach oriented toward programmatic instruction. This seems to be the most logical direction to take in identifying severely and profoundly handicapped children; it avoids the problem of trying to diagnostically label a group of children that is not homogeneous, and it directs the educator toward a positive program of remediation and development.

Based upon this premise, Sontag, Smith, and Sailor (1976) proposed that special education be divided into three broad areas, based upon the service requirements of children: Severely Handicapped Education, General Special Education, and Early Childhood Education. Severely Handicapped Education would concentrate on basic skill development leading to pre-academic and academic work. (Later sections will describe more fully the types of behaviors among severely handicapped children which would be included under basic skill development.) General Special Education is proposed by Sontag, et. al. (1976) to include primarily the development of academic skills (e.g., reading, writing) and those pre-academic skills leading to academic work. Children needing both of the above types of service would divide their time between programs, and exceptional children below school age would enter Early Childhood Education programs in which the emphasis would be divided between Severely Handicapped (basic skill development) and General Special Education services (pre-academic instruction).

The authors (Sontag et al., 1976) also point out that teachers of the severely handicapped need to be trained in the self-help, motor, perceptual, social, cognitive, and communication skill development areas, whereas teachers of General Special Education need competencies in teaching pre-academic and academic skill areas. Whether or not one agrees with the broad instruction-oriented categories outlined by Sontag et al., these authors do propose a definition of the severely and profoundly handicapped that recognizes the heterogeneous nature of this population and the basic behavioral deficits found among them.

CHARACTERISTICS OF THE SEVERELY/ PROFOUNDLY HANDICAPPED

Use of the term *characteristics* is not intended to imply that the population of severely/profoundly handicapped children can be easily grouped into a single category. Differences in the behavior and capabilities of these individuals are extreme—in fact, we feel comfortable in stating that differences among severely and profoundly handicapped children are greater than their similarities.

Current capabilities to evaluate and assess such a heterogeneous group are extremely limited. Most of the standardized testing and diagnostic instruments are not applicable for low functioning and multiply handicapped children. A recent effort attempted to identify existing assessment instruments appropriate for use with severely handicapped children (Sailor & Horner, 1976), but many such instruments are still too gross to accurately plan educational programs for most severely handicapped children. Recently, investigators have begun to develop assessment instruments specifically for use with this population (e.g., The Pennsylvania Training Model, Somerton & Turner, 1974). Such instruments make possible a more adequate assessment of the abilities and deficiencies of severely and profoundly handicapped children.

To preface the following discussion of characteristics, we emphasize that no severely handicapped child will display all of these behavioral characteristics or physical conditions, and no two severely handicapped children will show identical behavioral or physical profiles. These characteristics, rather, should be interpreted as behaviors and conditions commonly found within this particular heterogeneous population.

In most cases we will be discussing (1) profound delayed development and (2) deviant types of development. In the former instance, severely handicapped children are observed to develop and learn at much slower rates than do their nonhandicapped peers (or even other populations of exceptional children). Typically, they demonstrate severe lags in social, intellectual, and physical development. Many severe developmental delays are caused, in part, by observable damage to the child's motor and sensory systems. In other cases, reasons for severe delayed development are less obvious. Some children may not display gross and easily identified impairments to their motor and sensory systems, but they may show profound delays in intellectual, social, and physical growth.

In addition to profound developmental delays, many severely handicapped children may exhibit "deviant" social, intellectual, and language behavior. Deviant describes behaviors not typical of normally developing children. This should not be interpreted as meaning that severely handicapped children engage in certain behaviors that normal children do not. This clearly is not the case. Basically, behaviors are labeled deviant because the severely handicapped child is doing too much of one thing, not enough of one thing, or doing something at the wrong time or in the wrong place. This will become more clear as we describe behaviors common to the severely and profoundly handicapped.

Social Development and Adaptive Behavior

This discussion centers on behaviors and deficiencies in social skills development, including social interactions with others and bizarre behaviors or mannerisms. Adaptive behavior includes self-help skill development, or those behaviors fundamental to the individual's ability to care for his or her basic needs.

Self-help

Most severely handicapped children lack fundamental self-help and survival skills. Many are not toilet-trained, and others only partially so. In some cases, physical and neurological damage to the child precludes the development of normal sphincter control. *Spina bifida* is one example of a neurological impairment in which bowel and bladder control may not be possible. In the majority of instances, however, incontinence is indicative of the profound developmental delay common to severely handicapped individuals, and especially to younger handicapped children.

Other self-help deficiencies may include the lack of ability to feed oneself, to dress and undress, to brush one's teeth, wipe the nose, comb the hair, and so on. Again, these self-help skills may be totally absent or only partially developed. In cases where self-help skills are totally absent, severely handicapped children are highly dependent on others for survival in the same way that a typical infant is totally dependent on caretakers for life-sustaining care and assistance. For many of these children, accompanying motor and sensory impairments further retard the development of self-help skills. Fortunately, numerous programs, techniques, and procedures are available to teach self-help skills to severely handicapped children so that total dependency is not inevitable. Some of these concepts will be discussed later.

Interactions with Others

Often, severely handicapped children appear to be oblivious to other persons. They neither initiate interactions with others nor respond when others attempt to interact with them. This type of behavior may be associated with either profound mental retardation or a withdrawal pattern frequently found in cases of severe emotional disturbance. To separate out the differential effects resulting from profound retardation or severe emotional disturbance among severely handicapped children is most difficult.

Severely handicapped children who do interact socially often do so inappropriately. These types of interactions may range from antisocial-appearing behaviors such as undressing in public, to the inability to recognize situations in which certain behaviors should or should not occur. Hugging and kissing strangers, laughing at the misfortune of others, or playing in the toilet bowl are examples of the wide range of inappropriate social behavior among severely handicapped children.

Again, many of these inappropriate social behaviors are directly related to overall delayed development and would not be considered as deviant behaviors in very young, typical children. Essentially, *severely handicapped children have not learned social behaviors appropriate to their age level.*

Bizarre Behavior

Severely handicapped children sometimes are observed engaging in behaviors that appear bizarre. The most common bizarre behaviors are referred to as "stereotyped behavior": seemingly purposeless motor responses or unusual body posturing. The most frequently observed type of stereotyped behavior is rocking back and forth. Others include waving the hand in front of the face, rolling the head back and forth, flicking the fingers, grinding the teeth, twirling or spinning objects, twirling the body around, or posturing the body in unusual positions. These behaviors are common among severely disturbed children, profoundly retarded children, and retarded children who are partially or totally blind.

Various theories have been offered to explain why stereotyped behaviors occur. Some experimenters (Berkson & Mason, 1964) maintain that stereotyped behavior occurs when the child is aroused, a theory that is supported by studies reporting increased body rocking among retarded children prior to meals (Kaufman & Levitt, 1965). Studies with primates also report an increase in stereotyped behaviors when monkeys were deprived of food, excited, or frightened (Levinson, 1970).

Some investigators propose that stereotyped behaviors provide a means for severely handicapped children to respond to frustrating situations (Baumeister & Forehand, 1971). Other interpretations attribute stereotyped behavior to a form of self-stimulation; according to this theory, children engage in these behaviors because they are not stimulated by the environment. This interpretation is supported by findings that two-thirds of institutionalized residents engage in some form of stereotyped behavior and that the longer an individual remains in an institution the more likely he or she is to develop such behaviors (Berkson & Davenport, 1962).

Still other researchers believe that stereotyped acts are learned behaviors (Spradlin & Girardeau, 1966) that are rewarded by the attention they receive from other persons. This explanation is supported by studies (Hollis, 1976) showing an increase in stereotyped acts when rewards (reinforcers) follow them and a decrease when reinforcers are removed.

The high occurrence of stereotyped behavior among severely handicapped children is likely attributable to more than one cause and, at present, all of the above theories have some support. Again, stereotyped behavior is not unique to severely handicapped individuals; such behavior (especially rocking) is not uncommon among normally developing infants (Lourie, 1959).

Self-injurious Behavior

One of the most difficult behaviors to understand is self-injurious behavior, in which the individual does actual physical damage to himself or herself. Fortunately, self-injurious behavior is not common among severely handicapped children. Corbett (1975) reports that some form of self-injurious behavior occurs in 5 to 15 percent of severely retarded individuals. He also states that self-injurious behavior occurs more frequently at younger ages and is observed most often in profoundly retarded and severely emotionally disturbed children.

Self-injurious behavior may take a variety of forms, including banging the head or body against hard objects, hitting, pinching, biting or scratching oneself, eye-poking, and self-induced vomiting. As with stereotyped behavior, several theories are offered to explain why self-injurious behavior occurs. Psychoanalytic theory has various interpretations for this type of behavior, including a reduction of guilt through self-inflicted pain, inverted aggression, an attempt to establish body reality, and a form of autoerotic activity.

In some cases self-injurious behavior has been found to occur more frequently in association with somewhat rare clinical syndromes. These include the Cornelia de Lange syndrome, which is also accompanied by profound mental retardation and distinctive facial and body features, and the Lesch-Nyhan syndrome, an organic condition associated with mental retardation, athetoid cerebral palsy, and an enzyme deficiency.

Other findings show that self-injurious behavior occurs more frequently in orthopedically handicapped children and in children who are both blind and retarded or deaf and retarded. Children with multiple handicaps have also been observed to engage in more stereotyped behavior. These observations lend support to both "arousal" and "self-stimulation" interpretations of self-injurious behavior, similar to the theories offered to explain stereotyped behavior.

Other theories propose that self-injurious behavior is learned by the child. In one explanation (Frankel & Simmons, 1976), the child is thought to engage in self-injurious behavior in order to reduce adult contact in high-demand situations. In other words, the child purposely engages in self-injurious behavior to avoid an unpleasant task or situation.

Another learning theory explanation of self-injurious behavior maintains that the child purposely hurts himself or herself to gain attention from adults. Results of investigation showed that adult attention served to increase self-injurious behavior in severely disturbed children, and removal of adult attention served to decrease the behavior (Lovaas, Frietag, Gold, & Kassorla, 1965).

Numerous causative factors may be recognized as potential causes of producing self-injurious behavior in severely handicapped children. As in the case of stereotyped and other behavior, brief episodes of self-injurious behaviors are not uncommon in normal infants.

Physical Development

Many severely handicapped children show pronounced delays in sensory and motor development. Multiple handicaps are common in a number of these children. The discussion in this section centers on delayed and or abnormal motor and sensory skills in severely handicapped children.

Delayed Motor Skills

Another chapter in this book focuses on children with orthopedic impairments and crippling conditions (The Physically Disabled). Thus, we will not provide an extensive description here of severe orthopedic conditions or their causes. The reader should note, though, that severe delays in motor development in combination with profound mental retardation represent a common severely handicapping condition. Many of these children do not walk by themselves and require the use of mechanical assistance in the form of wheelchairs, walkers, braces, or support canes.

On a more impaired level, other severely handicapped children have not achieved the basic milestones of motor development. They do not roll over, hold their heads up, or grasp objects. Movement of any type may be limited. Often, their muscles are contracted, flaccid, or under-developed; and abnormal body postures and reflexes caused by brain damage are common. The extent of motor involvement varies widely in severely handicapped children — ranging from those who are virtually immobile to those who have no apparent motor skill impairments.

Impaired Sensory and Perceptual Skills

Two important factors must be considered in discussing the sensory and perceptual characteristics of severely handicapped children. The first refers to *acuity;* the second refers to *perceptual* processes.

Acuity generally refers to the extent to which an individual can see or hear. Accurate assessment of the hearing and vision of many severely handicapped children has been difficult. Recent advances in techniques and procedures, however, have aided assessment of hearing abilities of severely handicapped children, and new, innovative approaches are being used to develop procedures for testing their vision. Based upon available information, we know that visual and hearing impairments are not uncommon in severely handicapped children. Some of these children have extensive visual and hearing impairments, either alone or in combination.

Perceptual processes generally refer to how well the individual perceives and interprets his or her environment. Those severely handicapped children who can see and hear normally do not necessarily perceive the world in a normal manner.

Few studies have been reported of the perceptual processes of severely handicapped children — reflecting the difficulty in conducting this type of research with this type of child. One investigation, however, has shown that severely emotionally disturbed children have more difficulty than typical children in processing input from the visual, hearing, and tactual (touching) modalities (Lovaas, Schreibman, Koegel, & Rehm, 1971). In this study, the emotionally disturbed children learned to press a bar when a light, noise, and touch were presented together, but performance in bar pressing was much poorer when each modality (vision, sound, or touch) was presented alone. In contrast, typical children performed equally well when the vision, touch, and sound were presented alone or together. A group of retarded children performed somewhere in between the emotionally disturbed and normal children.

Other Physical Conditions and Complications

Frequently, severely handicapped children have additional physical problems which affect them and their caretakers. Many have seizures ranging in severity from brief loss of contact with the outside world to major motor convulsions. In the latter case, the child usually drops to the floor, and the body undergoes pronounced jerking movements. During the seizure the child may lose bowel and/or bladder control, and there may be bubbling of saliva around the mouth. There are numerous types of seizures resulting from abnormal electrical brain discharges. Seizure activity is especially prevalent among severely handicapped children who have cerebral palsy. The severity and frequency of most seizure problems can be significantly reduced through appropriate medication. Undesirable side-effects from medication, however, may result in drowsiness and swelling of gums around the teeth.

Some severely handicapped children have medical problems other than, or in addition to, seizures. These may include frequent respiratory and ear infections, and skin rashes caused by incontinence, braces, or too much sitting or lying down.

Cognitive Skills Development

Typically, severely handicapped children do not read, write, or perform academic skills. Frequently they cannot successfully perform many of the skills necessary for reading and writing. For example, many cannot recognize or match colors, shapes, or objects. They may not be able to follow simple directions such as, "come here," or "sit down." Many cannot hold a pencil, draw a straight line, or fit puzzle pieces together. They may be unable to sort objects, point to pictures, or recognize names or pictures of familiar persons. Again, variability in cognitive skills exists among severely handicapped persons. Some of them can successfully perform many pre-academic tasks and some, with early and intensive education, have learned to read, write, and perform in other academic areas.

Language Development

Without exception, severely handicapped children will show some type of speech and language deficiency. These problems can be roughly divided into delayed speech and language, problems in speech clarity, and bizarre speech patterns.

Speech and Language Delay

One of the major problems observed in severely handicapped children is a profound delay in their speech and language development.

Many of these children cannot talk or have only limited speech, usually restricted to a few words or short phrases. Moreover, many understand very little of what is said to them. This lack of communication skills is a major concern for persons working with children who cannot express their basic needs or desires nor share with others the experiences they encounter. It is not surprising that many severely handicapped children who lack language skills may develop other, less desirable means for self-expression, such as tantrums, crying, and aggressive behavior.

On a more positive note, the past decade has shown rapid growth in design and development of procedures and programs to help severely handicapped children learn how to talk. This effort is continuing, with considerable success.

Speech Clarity

For some severely handicapped children, the problem of speech clarity will always exist. Even when they do learn to talk, others may have difficulty in understanding them. A small number of severely handicapped children may never be able to talk because of impairments to their speech mechanisms, often associated with brain damage. For these children, alternate forms of communication — communication boards or signing — are suggested.

Communication boards have a flat surface (usually a lap board) on which the child can point to pictures, words, or other symbols to indicate what he or she woud like to say. Signing is a form of communication in which the child uses his or her fingers and arms to make symbols representing the speaker's language. This form of communication often is used by deaf individuals; and more recent attempts are being made to teach signing to individuals with retardation accompanied by severe hearing losses.

Bizarre Speech Patterns

Some severely handicapped children demonstrate unusual speech patterns when they talk. What they say may be out of context or inappropriate to the situation. They may repetitiously recite nursery rhymes or commercials they hear on television. These types of bizarre speech patterns also are often found in severely emotionally disturbed children. The speech itself may be quite clear, but the content may be meaningless.

Another type of bizarre speech pattern commonly observed in the emotionally disturbed and profoundly retarded is called *echolalia*. As the term suggests, children having this speech pattern will repeat (or echo) what you say to them. Techniques and procedures are available for treating echolalic speech, and the prognosis for children with this type of speech pattern is more optimistic, with respect to developing appropriate speech, than for children who are totally without speech.

PERSONAL RELATIONSHIPS AND INTERACTIONS WITH OTHERS

Severely handicapped children have a pronounced impact on those who come into contact with them. Their obviously delayed development, the frequent appearance of unusual or bizarre behavior, and their often different physical appearance combine to make these children obvious and even frightening to those who come into contact with them. The degree to which other persons are able to understand and accept the "deviancy" associated with severely handicapped individuals is highly variable — ranging from outward expressions of revulsion, to pity, to complete acceptance. The extent to which severely handicapped children are accepted in our society will depend greatly on the ability of educators to help develop an accepting and understanding attitude by students, parents, other family members, professional persons, and the general public.

Relationships with Parents

Parental attitudes toward their severely handicapped children vary widely. A small number of parents may completely reject their children; they may seek early institutionalization and have little further contact with their children. This occurrence is, however, the exception rather than the rule. Most parents show a genuine interest in their severely handicapped children. Many will go to extremes to get proper care for them. But many parents of the severely handicapped adhere to unrealistic goals for their children. They may go from one physician or diagnostic clinic to another with the false hope that a new diagnosis will promise a "cure" for their child. One of the most difficult tasks of the classroom teacher and other related disciplines is to temper parents' idealistic expectations with the more realistic view that, "Yes, your child can be helped, but progress probably will be slow."

Sometimes parents want to help train and educate their severely handicapped child. They might ask a teacher to suggest things to do with the child at home. These requests should not be ignored. Other parents flatly state that they do not have time for home-based training. They expect the classroom teacher and other professionals to carry the bulk of education and treatment programs. They often perceive any additional responsibilities as an extra burden to the caretaking task that will take more time away from other children and family obligations.

Relationships with Siblings

Brothers and sisters of severely handicapped children will likely reflect parental attitudes. Some siblings may be overprotective of their severely handicapped brother or sister; others may be embarrassed when friends visit their home. The extent to which siblings accept a severely handicapped child is a highly complex situation intricately interwoven into family relationships, community attitudes, and the extent to which siblings have been involved in the treatment and education of the child.

Relationships with Peers

A related question is how severely handicapped children are perceived by their peers. At school, they may be subjected to ridicule if school administrators and teachers have not taken the proper steps to prepare their students to accept and understand individual differences. Some encouraging reports have come from schools in which classes for severely handicapped children are integrated into regular school buildings. Often, students from regular classes take a special interest in their severely handicapped peers; they may even be involved as tutors for these children. In schools where severely handicapped children have become an accepted part of the program, "making fun" of these children is socially unacceptable. Again, attitudes of school peers toward severely handicapped children often are reflections of adult attitudes in the school, community, and in society at large.

Self Perception

Little is known about how severely handicapped children perceive themselves. The lack of or deficiencies in communication skills among many of these children makes it difficult for others to explore their self-concepts. Those familiar with severely handicapped children, however, are aware that many of them are sensitive to the actions and behavior of people around them. They express anger, sorrow, frustration, delight, and jealousy — all typical human reactions.

An especially poignant anecdote was related to the authors about a severely handicapped boy who had profound motor impairments and was unable to talk. This boy lived in an institution for the mentally retarded. One evening staff members observed profuse tears rolling down the boy's cheeks as he watched an unhappy scene on television. Few people had realized that this youngster was capable of showing emotion, or that he could even understand a story unfolding on television.

PROGRAMMING FOR THE SEVERELY AND PROFOUNDLY HANDICAPPED

Before their right to education was affirmed, severely and profoundly handicapped individuals had only three broad program options: They could remain at home with their parents, who had to assume the role of teacher along with parent; they could be placed in a residential institution where the emphasis was largely custodial; or, if more fortunate, they could be enrolled in a program sponsored by an agency such as a local association for handicapped individuals. Any of these options often imposed limitations leading to an increased handicapping condition.

Up to the present time, public school special education programs have been designed primarily for mildly and moderately handicapped children. Those responsible for student placement in special education programs often have excluded severely handicapped children on the assumption that their handicapping conditions are so pronounced that they will never benefit from public education. Severely and profoundly handicapped children have been considered uneducable. As a result, limited information is available on what such individuals can accomplish. But when educational programming for the severely and profoundly handicapped has been attempted, the most effective approach to date has been a behavioral one, even though promising adaptations of Piagetian developmental psychology to education of the severely handicapped are now appearing in the literature (c.f., Stephens, 1977).

The behavioral approach is characterized by: (1) assessment of the current performance level across development areas; (2) clear specification of each behavior to be learned as an instructional objective; (3) the ordering of each behavior into a curriculum sequence; (4) explicit specification of the instructions to be provided by the teacher; (5) precise use of feedback, correction, and reinforcement techniques; and (6) systematic use of measurement and evaluation procedures.

Among severely handicapped individuals, uneven development across cognitive, social and motor areas is commonly found. Identification of areas of strength, as well as those in which performance is weak or nonexistent, has enormous implications for programming. The intervention procedures used with weak or nonexistent behaviors are different from those used with stronger behaviors. Until recently, educational intervention with severely handicapped individuals focused mainly on teaching the acquisition of basic skills. Currently, however, considerable attention has been directed toward teaching strategies that focus on developing proficiency, efficiency, maintenance, generalization, and application of existing skills to new situations.

Teachers of the severely handicapped must now learn methods that promote the generalization of skills across tasks, settings, and persons. Procedures used to teach *acquisition* of a skill (such as putting on a sock) change when the instructional objective is to demonstrate *proficiency* of that skill to a specified criterion. The procedures change again when the instructional objective calls for the *generalization* of that skill with, say, (1) different socks, in different settings, and when occasioned by different persons, and (2) application of components of that skill to putting on gloves, pants, shirt, etc. The procedures change once again when the instructional objective calls for *maintenance* of the skill over time.

Teachers of the severely handicapped understandably may wonder where to begin an educational program when faced with the vast array of physical, behavioral, and learning deficits present in these children. The past experience of other teachers offers little opportunity. Until recently, classrooms for the severely handicapped have been few in number and isolated in institutions. There have been even fewer homebound and public school programs. Thus, the burden of educational programming still rests heavily on the individual teacher.

To develop an effective educational program, knowledge of typical, or normal, development patterns is critical. Without such knowledge, it is difficult to identify, target, or pinpoint the behaviors that should become the focus for instructional objectives. Considerable data have been collected on normal development; this information is indispensable to teachers of the severely and profoundly handicapped. It is also important to focus on adaptive behavior (behavior that increases the effectiveness with which an individual copes with the natural and social demands presented by the environment — home, school, and community setting).

The range of individuals designated as severely retarded is so great that a teacher probably does not know what behaviors to expect from the child entering his or her class, where to begin the programming effort, or what instructional objectives can reasonably be attained over the school year. It is unrealistic for a teacher to offer an educational program designed for "trainable" level students. It may even be unrealistic for a teacher to follow an educational program designed for another group of severely handicapped children. Although many educational programs are available for other less handicapped individuals, few programs have been developed for use by teachers of the severely and profoundly handicapped. Most of the commercially available materials that might be revised for use with the severely handicapped teach skills that have limited or no functional value for these individuals.

Systematic instructional procedures and comprehensive instructional sequences must be developed as essential components of individualized education programs for the severely handicapped. Although a few handicapped individuals may learn without the benefit of systematic instruction, generally we need to build much more systematization into instruction of the severely handicapped. The more handicapped the person, the less he or she is able to pick up the instructional cues provided naturally by the environment.

The teacher must employ precise and frequent measurement to determine (1) adequacy of the rate of progress, (2) the point at which one task is learned and the next may be started, and (3) procedures that are most effective with the least expenditure of time and energy.

The procedures and skills which teachers have used for the mildly and moderately handicapped will have to become more sophisticated in order to be effective with the severely handicapped. Most special education teachers are not trained to teach such skills as self-feeding, toileting, dressing, and walking. The need for additional applications of operant technology to behaviors for educating the severely handicapped is acute. Applications should include built-in measurement systems so the progress of children within an educational program can be objectively determined.

In the past, severely handicapped children have not been offered an opportunity for formal education until after age five, if at all. By that time, the child's behavioral repertoire often contains a variety of unacceptable and difficult to manage behaviors. Previous attempts to educate older severely handicapped individuals, using ineffective intervention strategies, generated considerable pessimism. The finding from a number of efforts in that regard that most severely handicapped children can benefit from early educational intervention is beginning to counter some of this pessimism. We now recognize that previous errors must be reversed and that educational programs used in the past must be broken down into smaller steps. We now take the position and must demonstrate unmistakably that severely handicapped individuals can learn. The following is a review of selected programs and training techniques that have been used successfully with severely handicapped persons.

Teaching Motor Skills

Some severely handicapped children exhibit little self-initiated motor behavior because of severe abnormal neurological conditions. For such individuals, the Bobaths (1964) have developed treatment procedures that rely on inhibiting abnormal patterns of muscular coordination and facilitating the normal patterns needed for functional skills.

Normal muscular coordination, for children who are spastic, is believed impossible if tonic reflexes are active (i.e., if the muscle contracts strongly with attempted movement). Such spasticity must be prevented during treatment, by using techniques that reduce tightness of the muscles.

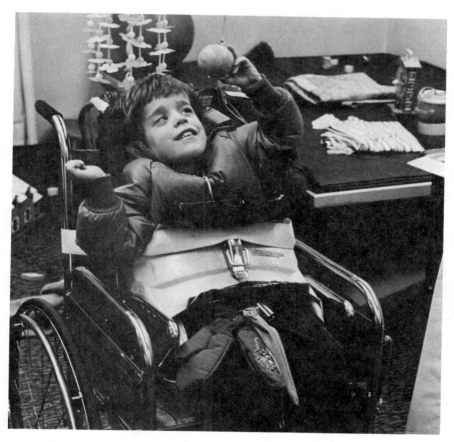

The procedures used by the Bobaths assume that changing part of the abnormal movements at the most important points can reduce spasticity throughout the body. The points are called *key points of control*. In the main, these are *proximal* (near the center of the body) and include the neck, spine, shoulder, and pelvic areas. Some reduction of spasticity also is believed possible through the use of *distal* (away from the center of the body) key points such as toes, ankles, fingers, and wrists.

Several patterns that inhibit spasticity have been described in detail (Bobath, 1967). The techniques assume that the child with spasticity has to learn to use the muscles in different ways and in different combinations, and can do this only when the spasticity has been reduced. Through proper positioning procedures, the teacher can facilitate normal movement by the child, with a normal amount of effort.

Individuals with severe motor handicaps often spend their lives in bed or in a wheelchair because they have not been exposed to an effective program designed to teach ambulation. Numerous treatment programs have been designed to teach severely handicapped children to walk. For example, Wilson and Parks (1970) presented a method of teaching ambulation that was reported to have been successful with 8 of 12 profoundly retarded young children. The method includes: (1) use of a hobby horse that moves up and down, left and right, forward and backward, and forces the compensatory movements required to maintain balance, (2) use of a "kiddy car" to help achieve laterality (differentiation of the sides of the body) and increased muscle strength, (3) use of weights attached to the ankles and wrists simultaneously with the other equipment, to further strengthen the muscles, (4) use of a "stomach board" to build neck and trunk muscles and force the child to resist gravity, (5) use of a "walker" to teach the student that moving his or her feet can make the body move in an upright position, (6) use of foam strips, carpeting, and other textured surfaces for rolling, to teach coordination and control of head, trunk and limbs, (7) use of a large, partially deflated plastic beach ball, upon which the student is placed on either the back or abdomen and rolled forward and backward, to promote relaxation, postural adjustments, and the development of spatial relationships, (8) being walked with help (including moving the student's feet if necessary) after the student can stand and support his or her weight, (9) being walked on a mattress to promote balance, and (10) using a tricycle to establish the alternating pattern necessary for walking and also to loosen tension in the knees.

Chandler and Adams (1972) report a procedure by which a multiply handicapped eight-year-old boy became an independent walker following a 28-day training program. Initially, he would walk only if placed on his feet and assisted. The procedure consisted of nine daily one-minute trials in which any increase in the number of steps over the number previously taken resulted in 30 seconds of music from a portable radio. On the eleventh day of training, the radio was turned on as soon as the child started walking and showed evidence of balance control. When the child lost control of his balance or used the wall for support, the radio was turned off. The procedure of "radio on" for walking and "radio off" for nonwalking was followed for 13 days. In addition, chocolate candy was provided each time the base rate was exceeded by at least one step. After 28 days, independent walking continued throughout each training session, even though systematic use of reinforcers was withdrawn. The boy also began to walk without support at home and in the classroom.

Horner (1971) developed an intervention procedure designed to teach use of crutches. The student was a five-year-old, severely handicapped boy with extensive paralysis of the lower extremities as a result of a spina bifida condition. Prior to training, the student had learned to sit without support, pull himself to his knees while holding onto a crib rail, and get into a creeping position; his means of locomotion was pulling himself across the floor with his arms. Before learning to use crutches, the student was taught to pull himself to a standing position, support his weight with his arms, and move forward using parallel bars for support. During this phase, two stools were placed within the parallel bars, approximately two feet apart, so that the student and teacher sat facing each other.

The first step in the procedure required only that the seated student grip the left parallel bar with the left hand and the right parallel bar with the right hand. Each successful trial was reinforced with a tablespoon of rootbeer. After criterion was reached on this step, the second step required that the student pull himself to a standing position, using the parallel bars for support, and maintain that position long enough to consume the rootbeer. Subsequent steps required that the student take three, five, and finally 10 steps before receiving the rootbeer. The student had to achieve success on at least 23 of the 25 daily trials in each of three consecutive sessions before training was advanced to the next step.

The second phase, actually establishing use of crutches, was divided into 10 steps. At first the crutches had to be secured to the student's hands with elastic bandages to prevent him from throwing them. The first step required that the student place the crutches on dots placed on the floor in front of the stool on which he was seated. Rootbeer was provided each time he placed the tips of both crutches on the appropriate dots. The second step required that he swing his body into an erect position while supported by the teacher. On the third step the teacher provided support only for the initial movement off the stool. Once the student had learned to achieve a standing position independently, the next step required that he learn to place the crutches forward. At first the teacher placed his hand on the student's back to assist in balance. The remaining steps gradually increased the complexity of the tasks, until finally the student was able to complete 12 cycles of balancing, placing crutches forward, swinging his feet forward, balancing, etc. The use-of-crutches sequence was trained in 120 sessions.

In the final phase the student was taught to use the crutches in his natural environment. He was permitted immediate access to meals, play, school, therapies, and bus rides if he walked to those activities using his crutches. With only an occasional exception, he walked to and from all programs and activities within 15 weekdays after treatment.

Teaching Self-Help Skills

Self-feeding

Intervention procedures designed to establish proper self-feeding skills among severely handicapped individuals have been directed at reducing the guidance provided by a teacher as the student progresses. In one method the teacher holds the child's hand initially and gradually moves the point of guidance up the arm toward the shoulder. A second method separates the self-feeding sequence into a series of steps and systematically eliminates the specific guidance actions provided on previous steps.

Berkowitz, Sherry, and Davis (1971) described a procedure using this second method. The procedure was broken down into the following seven steps: (1) The teacher placed a spoon in the student's hand, held the student's hand around the spoon, and totally assisted the student in completing the self-feeding cycle from plate to mouth and back to plate; (2) The teacher repeated Step 1, except that the student's hand was released near the end of the cycle approximately two or three inches below the student's mouth to set the occasion for student initiated movement of the spoon for the two or three inches into the mouth; (3) The teacher repeated Step 1 except that the student's hand was released when approximately six inches from the student's mouth; (4) The teacher repeated Step 1, except that the student's hand was released at plate level after the food was scooped; (5) The teacher repeated Step 1 except that the student's hand was released at plate level before the food was scooped; (6) The teacher repeated Step 1 except that the student's hand was released after the teacher guided it only two or three inches away from the mouth; (7) The student completed the entire self-feeding cycle without teacher guidance.

On the first training day, the teacher trained on Step 1 at all three meals. Step 2 was introduced at the first meal on the second day. Each additional step was introduced upon successful performance of the prior step for an entire meal. Occasionally, performance was so poor that the teacher had to revert to an earlier step and reestablish it. Two groups of seven boys ranging in age from 9-17 years with social ages of 1.3-1.7 years as measured by the Vineland Social Maturity Scale were trained. The first group learned to use a spoon over a period of time ranging from 2 to 21 days. The second group required 13 to 60 days. Ten of the original 14 maintained the use of a spoon over a 41-month follow-up period. The other four maintained the skill for 23 to 35 months.

In some situations profoundly handicapped students who initially learn appropriate self-feeding skills fail to use them after training is discontinued. O'Brien, Bugle and Azrin (1972) reported a program in which a six-year-old profoundly handicapped girl was taught to eat properly with a spoon through a six-step manual guidance procedure. But after training, the student failed to use the spoon; instead, she grasped the food with her hands, closed her hands compressing the food, then opened her hands and brought the food to her mouth, usually with considerable spilling. To promote the use of the spoon, an interruption-extinction procedure was initiated. When the student attempted to use her hands instead of the spoon, the teacher stopped the student's hand before it reached her mouth and, if required, removed any food present on the hands. This procedure was applied over 14 meals. After nine meals, correct eating was occurring nearly 100 percent of the time. This continued as long as the interruption-extinction procedure was in effect. When the interruption-extinction was discontinued, proper eating dropped to nearly zero. When the procedure was reintroduced, proper eating returned to the previous near-perfect level. This example indicates that some students may require a maintenance procedure such as interruption-extinction to ensure the continuation of skills acquired through training.

Many profoundly handicapped individuals have demonstrated unmanageable behaviors that impede progress in self-feeding and make training efforts appear so futile that they often have been discontinued. Azrin and Armstrong (1973) developed a program that (1) would be applicable to the profoundly handicapped, (2) could produce results in days rather than weeks, (3) would result in proper eating after training was completed, (4) would produce mealtime behavior that was indistinguishable from that of normal individuals, and (5) would be more effective than the unstructured methods often used to teach self-feeding.

Of the 22 students in the program, none could dress or bathe without help, only one could speak, one was confined to a wheelchair, one was deaf, one partially blind, and two had partial paralysis of one side of the body; 18 were on medication for problem behavior. In addition, they had been judged so incompetent at self-feeding and so dangerous to themselves that knives and forks had not been provided; their only eating utensil had been a spoon.

The program had the following 18 components: (1) Instead of three large meals a day, the regular portions were divided into "mini-meals" and served hourly throughout the day; (2) Rather than total guidance of initial use of utensils, a graduated guidance procedure was used in which the teacher never provided more assistance or resistance than was necessary to ensure a correct response; (3) Each utensil was introduced separately, and only food appropriate for that utensil was provided until the use of each utensil was mastered; (4) The standards of eating excellence (lack of spilling, etc.) were increased gradually; (5) The students were required to keep their free hand in their lap (unless both hands were required, as in cutting) to reduce the probability of grabbing food; (6) Manual guidance rather than verbal coaxing was used to reduce the amount of attention paid to inappropriate behavior; (7) All attempts to get food into the mouth by means other than a utensil were physically interrupted; (8) Distractions were minimized by conducting training at times other than regularly scheduled meals, with only the student and those involved in that student's training present; (9) Manual guidance was gradually faded to a gentle touch at the student's hand, then moved up the arm to the forearm, elbow, upper arm, shoulder, and upper back, maintaining as light a touch as possible unless more guidance was required; (10) Generous social reinforcement was given to bridge the gap between early components of the self-feeding chain (grasping the spoon, loading the spoon, etc.) and ingestion of the food; (11) A variety of social reinforcers (hugs, facial approval, various verbal praise statements, etc.) was used; (12) Once use of a particular utensil was demonstrated, the student was required to correct errors such as spilling by wiping up the spill and to correct throwing of utensils by retrieving the thrown utensil, etc.; (13) Practice of the correct form of response after correction was promoted (e.g., when food was spilled due to overloading of the utensil, the student was given several practice trials in loading small amounts); (14) More than one trainer assisted (if the student was difficult to manage) in prevention of errors; (15) Progression was from simpler responses such as use of napkin, glass, and spoon to complex responses such as use of knife and fork in combination for cutting; (16) Continuous feedback was given during training, describing to the student what was happening and praising positive effort; (17) All eating occurred only during training sessions in order to avoid reestablishing incorrect responses; (18) After the use of each utensil was mastered, all the foods necesary for use of each utensil were made available at each meal.

All students taught using the intensive mini-meal procedure learned correct mealtime behaviors within a 12-day period. (In contrast, only 36 percent of students taught with the control procedure had learned these behaviors at the end of 18 days of training.) Follow-up measures taken every four weeks showed the behaviors were still maintained 28 weeks later. The students had an average of 9 percent errors on their meals. To put this figure in perspective, the percentage of error for employees eating the same meals averaged 8 percent.

Dressing

Martin, Kehoe, Bird, Jensen and Darbyshire (1971) reported an educational intervention in which 11 severely retarded girls ages seven to twenty were taught to put on underpants, brassiere or undershirt, socks, shoes, and sweater. They also were taught to lace their shoes and to tie a knot and bow. Each of the tasks was broken down into a series of steps; each step had to be performed to a predetermined criterion before the next step was taught. In most cases training occurred on one item at a time.

The acquisition of each task was evaluated by a four-point rating scale. A "1" indicated that the student performed the task after receiving one verbal instruction to do so. A "2" indicated that the student required additional verbal prompting to perform the task. A "3" indicated that the student required partial manual guidance to perform the task. A "4" indicated that the student required complete physical guidance to perform the task. The teaching time required to reach a "1" rating ranged from an average of 23 minutes over an average of 3 sessions for putting on an undershirt to an average of 15 hours and 45 minutes over an average of 36 sessions for lacing and tying a shoe on the foot. In most cases the performance obtained by a student during training generalized to appropriate nontraining situations.

Karen and Maxwell (1967) reported an educational intervention designed to teach a seven-year-old severely retarded boy to button his shirt. The procedure employed a specially designed vest that had a one-inch button at the top. Below this was a three-fourth-inch button, followed by a one-half and finally a one-fourth-inch button. After demonstrating proper buttoning, the teacher began the training by pointing to the one-inch button and verbally instructing the student to button it.

Any attempt at buttoning received praise and an M & M candy. After attempts were consistent, reinforcers were given only if the button was placed at least part way through the buttonhole and, finally, only if all the way through. When the student consistently buttoned the one-inch button, training was shifted to the one-half-inch button. When the one-half-inch button was mastered, the one-fourth-inch button was trained. Finally, the student learned to button the buttons on his own shirt. Independent performance was maintained after four trials on the one-half-inch button and eight trials on the one-fourth-inch button.

Grooming

Treffry, Martin, Samels and Watson (1970) presented an educational intervention designed to teach severely retarded girls to wash and dry their hands and faces. The task initially was broken down into a 12-step procedure and performance was evaluated on a five-step rating, ranging from excellent (told only once to wash hands and face) to very poor (given total physical assistance in washing hands and face). Training occurred one step at a time, and the student was guided through the remaining steps. As each step was mastered, the student was required to perform it independently in subsequent sessions, and training commenced on the next step. In teaching each step, the teacher simultaneously told the student what to do and manually guided the proper performance.

Over trials, manual guidance gradually was reduced until only verbal prompts were necessary. Inappropriate responses to verbal prompts or resistance to physical guidance were followed by a sharp "no" and a 15-second time-out. When the program was started, none of the students could perform the task without some physical guidance. Nine weeks later, 7 of the 11 students could completely wash and dry their hands and faces. The percentage of "1" ratings for all students on all steps increased from 16 percent during baseline to 71 percent during the ninth week.

Horner and Keilitz (1975) developed an educational intervention designed to teach handicapped individuals to brush their teeth. Although the procedure originally was used with mildly and moderately handicapped individuals, it is applicable to the severely handicapped as well. The procedure for brushing the teeth was broken into 15 instructional steps. All 15 steps were trained at each session. A four-stage instructional procedure was used during training: (1) no help, (2) verbal instruction, (3) demonstration plus verbal instruction, and (4) physical guidance plus instruction. For each step, the teacher provided no help for approximately 5 seconds, giving the student an opportunity to perform the step without assistance. If the student failed to initiate a response within the 5 seconds, a nonspecific verbal prompt (e.g., "Go ahead" or "What's next?") was given. If the student made an inappropriate response (e.g., made faces in the mirror, licked the toothpaste tube, etc.) or attempted another toothbrushing step, the trainer provided immediate verbal instruction for that step.

Verbal instruction for each step consisted of a short imperative statement describing the expected behavior (e.g., "Wet the toothbrush"). If the student responded correctly, reinforcement was provided, and training of the next step in the sequence was initiated with no help. If the student failed to initiate a response within approximately 5 seconds, verbal instruction was repeated. If the student made an inappropriate response (e.g., sucked on the faucet, blew bubbles into the cup of rinse water, etc.), attempted another toothbrushing step out of sequence, or failed to initiate a response within approximately 5 seconds of the second presentation of verbal instruction, demonstration plus verbal instruction was initiated. This included another presentation of the short imperative statement while simultaneously demonstrating the expected behavior. Demonstration consisted of pointing or directing the student's responses and/or modeling the expected behavior. For example, when a teacher said, "Put the cap on the toothpaste," he or she might point to the cap and then to the toothpaste tube, followed by moving the hand in a circular motion as if screwing the cap on the tube. If the student performed the step correctly within about 5 seconds of demonstration plus verbal instruction, reinforcement was provided, and training of the next step was initiated with no help. No correct response within that time limit resulted in repetition of the demonstration plus verbal instruction.

Failure to respond to the repetition or the occurrence of inappropriate behavior resulted in application of the fourth and final stage of instruction — physical guidance plus verbal instruction. This stage consisted of the teacher's verbal instructing, along with physically assisting the student in initiating the desired behavior but permitting the student to complete it on his or her own. Completion of the step according to the behavioral definition was reinforced and followed by beginning the training of the next step, with no help. Failure to complete the step correctly resulted in repetition of physical guidance plus verbal instruction. If an error in performance or failure to complete the step occurred after repetition of physical guidance and verbal instruction, training of that step ceased and the training of the next step in the sequence was initiated with no help.

All 15 steps were performed independently on two of three consecutive sessions by 6 of the 8 students trained; the number of sessions required to establish this level of performance ranged from 18 to 30. The remaining 2 students had failed to reach this criterion after 36 and 25 sessions; training was terminated for these students as a result of departure of the student teachers.

Toileting

Many educational interactions with severely handicapped students have been designed to teach appropriate control of urination and/or defecation. Early procedures relied mainly on increasing the positive consequences for appropriate toileting behavior and the negative consequences for inappropriate toileting behavior. Recent procedures have used electronic devices to signal appropriate and inappropriate eliminations so they could be consequented quickly. Procedures also have employed high intake of liquids to increase the frequency of urination.

One of the early reports was that of Giles and Wolf (1966). Five severely handicapped students were selected for training on the basis of baseline data that indicated a zero frequency of eliminating in the toilet. The students ranged in age from six to eighteen years. Since simultaneous development of bowel and bladder control was believed too complicated a program, bowel control was developed first. The procedures were individualized for each of the five students.

For example, one student was to be positively reinforced for remaining seated on the toilet. For the student to remain seated long enough to be reinforced, it was necessary to tie him in the toilet training chair. Reinforcers consisted of items such as baby food, ice cream, jello, and social praise. The first three sessions were characterized by tantruming and crying, but bringing another student into the training session had a quieting effect. Tantrums and cries subsided, and the student even imitated the appropriate behavior of the second student. Suppositories and milk of magnesia were used to control the occurrence of defecation so it could be rewarded; these were discontinued when the student began to initiate elimination. Appropriate bowel elimination was reinforced with food. Both bowel and bladder elimination were consistently self-initiated by the end of the third week of training.

At this point, the student was taught to lower his pants before sitting on the toilet. A one-hour shaping session established this behavior. Food reinforcers were gradually reduced during the fourth week, and eventually discontinued. Appropriate elimination continued throughout the final three weeks of the intervention. Variations of these procedures were used with the other four students with similar success.

Azrin, Bugle, and O'Brien (1971) and Mahoney, Van Wagenen and Meyerson (1971) have developed electronic moisture detecting devices that signal the onset of urination. The device developed by Mahoney et al. consists of a double pair of rubber pants containing a switch that activates a battery powered audio-oscillator isolated between the two pairs of pants. Urine passing through a funnel-like device activates the audio-oscillator and produces a loud tone. The two devices developed by Azrin et al. are referred to as "pants alert" and "potty alert." The pants alert consists of two metal snaps attached about one and one-half inches apart to a pair of cotton training pants. The snaps are connected to an enclosed circuit box suspended from a belt placed around the child's waist. When urine begins to soak into the cotton, current from a battery is conducted from one snap to the other and powers the tone-producing oscillator. The potty alert operates on the same principle except that the device is placed inside the bowl of a potty chair and produces a different sound.

Azrin et al. (1971) used the devices described above to toilet train four profoundly handicapped girls aged three to six years. First, a two-week baseline was conducted during which the students wore an inoperative pants alert device and were placed on a potty chair (also inoperative) for five minutes every two hours. This traditional toilet training procedure resulted in wet pants an average of three to six times per day for the students. During training with the device, the students were given a glass of water every half hour to increase urination. They were placed on the toilet every half hour to provide more opportunities for urinating in the potty chair bowl. The teacher provided praise, a hug, and a bit of candy each time the signal was activated by urine collecting in the toilet bowl. When the tone was produced by urine collecting in the pants, the teacher delivered a single spank on the buttocks and withdrew attention for 10 minutes. Verbal instructions and manual guidance followed by verbal praise were used to teach the student to lower and raise the pants and to sit on the potty chair. The procedure resulted in rapid (less than a week) acquisition of proper elimination of urine.

Teaching Social Skills

One of the characteristics of the severely handicapped that clearly distinguishes them from less handicapped individuals is deficient social behavior. Social interaction skills are critical in that they are prerequisites to the learning that takes place through spontaneous imitation of appropriate behavior modeled by others. Despite the importance of such skills, the application of intervention procedures in teaching social interaction skills to severely handicapped individuals has been limited.

Whitman, Mercurio, and Caponigri (1970) developed a procedure for teaching two social interaction tasks (ball-rolling and block-passing) to two severely handicapped children. The ball-rolling task was taught by first seating the two students on the floor about three feet apart. The teacher then verbally set the occasion for rolling a ball back and forth between them. Successful performance (one student rolling the ball to the other and the other rolling it back) was assisted through manual guidance and reinforced with M & M candy and praise. The block-passing task was taught the same way except that the students were seated adjacent to each other. On the first day of teaching, reinforcement followed every successful performance. As training progressed, reinforcement was provided less often, until only every 30 back-and-forth rolls of the ball or passes of the block were followed by reinforcement.

After 20 days of training, two additional students were entered in the program. One was introduced to the ball-rolling task and the other to the block-passing task. A total rolling or passing response was expanded by one; i.e., the first student rolled the ball or passed the block to the second, the second to the third, and the third back to the first. Manual guidance was used to assist correct performance by each of the two new students. Reinforcement was given to each of the students in the trio following every complete response on day 21 and gradually decreased to once for every 15 responses by the end of training.

Before, during, and after training, measurements were taken on the amount of time spent in social interaction (defined as one student's behavior becoming mutually or reciprocally involved with a second student's behavior). Ratings were taken during two 15-minute periods each day, while the students were involved in free play. During the training phase, measures were taken at times other than when actual training was occurring. Prior to training, one student averaged only .3 minute of social interaction per 15-minute session, and the other student had 0 minutes of social interaction. This increased to an average of 4.3 minutes per 15-minute session for one student and 1.8 for the other during (but measured outside of) the training phase. After training was complete, post-training measures of social interaction declined to 2.6 minutes per 15-minute session for one student and 1.2 minutes for the other.

This study showed that reinforcement procedures can be used to at least temporarily increase social interaction outside of social interaction training even though systematic use of reinforcement is not operative outside the training situation. Generalization of social interaction extended toward students not included in training and to tasks other than the ones trained.

Another element of social behavior often lacking in the severely and profoundly handicapped is *play.* In the absence of play and similar social behaviors, severely and profoundly handicapped children often develop bizarre stereotyped behavior (i.e., repetitive body movements such as rocking, head rolling, hand waving, etc.). Flavell (1973) found that teaching three severely handicapped boys to play with specific toys decreased stereotyped behaviors. Play with a toy was developed by having the teacher initially guide the student's hand in appropriate manipulation of the toy. Approximations of appropriate use were reinforced with praise and a bite of ice cream or a piece of candy. Physical assistance in manipulating the toy was gradually discontinued as the students learned to imitate the appropriate use.

This educational intervention demonstrated that appropriate play can be developed. The maintenance of such play may be possible if toys can be found or designed that provide "natural" reinforcers for severely handicapped individuals. Most toys are designed for nonhandicapped children and require an existing, more sophisticated behavioral repertoire on the part of the child to use them appropriately. Even nonhandicapped children fail to sustain their play with most toys. Deficiencies in the reinforcing power of toys to sustain play is even more pronounced in those who are severely and profoundly handicapped.

Teaching Pre-Academic Skills

One of the behavioral deficits that characterize the severely and profoundly handicapped is a lack of certain prerequisite skills that precludes appropriate responses to academic tasks. One such skill is *attending*. Martin and Powers (1967) offered an operant analysis of attending. They stated that attending behavior is a function of a history of reinforcement having been available for such behavior and having not been available for behavior incompatible with attending. Deficiencies in attending result when reinforcement is contingent upon behavior incompatible with attending, and when attending behavior goes unreinforced.

Brown and Foshee (1971) developed an educational intervention designed to increase visual attending. The individual training aspect of this intervention appears to be appropriate for increasing the attending behavior of the severely handicapped. Plates from the *Peabody Picture Vocabulary Test* (Dunn, 1965) were used as stimuli. Some of the plates were used as attending stimuli, and others were used as training plates. One of four pictures from each of the attending plates was enlarged, placed on poster board, and displayed in the classroom. Attending was assumed to have occurred if a student could identify which one of the four pictures from the attending plates had been on display. Baseline measures taken prior to training indicated that very few of the stimuli (displayed plates) were identified correctly.

Attending training consisted of putting one enlarged picture from a training plate on display, taking students individually to a training area, and setting the occasion for identifying the picture that had been on display. Each time a displayed picture was correctly discriminated from three others over a series of training plates, the student was reinforced by being allowed to select one of a variety of reinforcers. This procedure was repeated for three weeks. When the baseline procedure was repeated with new plates, the students significantly increased the number of pictures correctly identified as having been on display. This performance was maintained during a short follow-up.

Another behavior that is an important prerequisite to the presentation of academic tasks is *sitting*. Many of the instructional strategies presented by a teacher depend upon the student maintaining a sitting position. Often, the failure to maintain such a position is incompatible with the delivery of effective instruction.

Twardosz and Sajwaj (1972) developed a procedure designed to increase sitting by a hyperactive handicapped student. Prior to the educational intervention, the student spent most of his time either squirming on the floor or jumping around the room. After baseline measures of sitting and the behaviors described, the student was placed in a chair at a table with other students, praised, and given tokens for remaining seated. At first the teacher praised the student and delivered a token (an X on a card hung on a string around the student's neck) approximately once every 10 seconds. This level of attention was gradually reduced to about once per minute. When he left his seat, the teacher ignored him until he came near the table. The teacher quickly took him by the hand, praised him for returning, and guided him onto his chair. Later, he had to touch the table or chair before the teacher prompted sitting.

The student's rate of sitting at the table rose from zero during baseline to a median of around 60 percent of the half-hour measurement periods. The percentage of time engaged in appropriate behavior (i.e., use of toys) while at the table also increased. The important point in this intervention is that the procedure, initiated as part of an ongoing classroom program, significantly increased the student's appropriate classroom behavior and decreased his inappropriate behavior with only a slight increase in time required by the teacher.

A third category of behavior critical to the education of groups of severely handicapped students is *following verbal instructions*. If the only instructional procedure a teacher can use is physical guidance, instruction, even in small groups, is not feasible.

Scheuerman, Cartwright, York, Lowry, and Brown (1974) developed an educational intervention designed to teach basic direction-following skills to young severely handicapped students. The program had three phases; each phase increased the complexity of instructions to be followed. Students had to complete one phase before training commenced on the next. The first phase taught the students to follow one component—"local" directions (e.g., "stand up"). The second phase taught one component—"distant" directions (e.g., "go to door"). The third phase taught two local components (e.g., "sit down, raise hand"). The directions to be taught were carefully selected. In Phase 1 simple body movements were selected, because the students had learned the prerequisite discrimination of body parts. Phase 2 directions were designed to teach the students to proceed to school room locations where the students were most often referred during the school day (e.g., the door, coatroom, wastebasket, etc.). Phase 3 directions were designed to teach how to follow a sequence of directions and relied on the directions learned individually in Phase 1.

The directions were taught in a group setting with the students seated in a semicircle facing the teacher. The procedure consisted of the teacher providing the verbal direction and reinforcing the student with praise and a consumable reinforcer (piece of food or sip of liquid) if the direction was followed. An incorrect response was followed by "no," a repetition of the direction, a demonstration of the correct response, and another repetition of the direction. A correct response at this point was followed by a praise comment. If the student failed to imitate the demonstration, the direction was repeated and the student was physically guided through the correct response. A correct response at this point was also followed by a praise comment. On subsequent trials the teacher gradually decreased the amount of physical assistance until the student was responding to the demonstration; the demonstration then was gradually phased out. This procedure was continued until each student correctly followed each of five randomly presented, one-component local directions.

The "distant" directions in Phase 2 were taught in the same manner, except that a student teacher or another student who could follow the distant direction provided any needed demonstrations. Phase 3 directions were taught in the same manner as Phase 1, except sets of first two, then three, and finally four two-component directions were taught at a time.

All 12 students learned to follow the one-component local and distant directions. Five of the 12 also learned two sets of two-component directions, three students learned three sets, and four mastered four sets. Although no direct measures were attempted of the extent to which training generalized to nontrained directions, teachers and parents both reported that several students were following even more complex directions than the ones trained.

Teaching Communication Skills

The development of language is extremely important to people, so any individual having pronounced delay in speech development and grossly inadequate ability to comprehend the speech of others has a profoundly handicapping condition. During the 1970s a number of investigators have turned their attention toward such individuals and have demonstrated some successful interventions in specific areas of language development. The main approaches to language development have been linguistic and psycholinguistic, in which language is viewed as an innate capacity and is taught in the same sequence in which it is believed to evolve in normal individuals. Another approach—a remedial one—views language as being learned in the same manner as other behavior and focuses on the remediation of specific language deficits.

One program based on the psycholinguistic approach has been developed by Miller and Yoder (1974). Program content was based upon data derived from studies of the language development of normal children. For the program to be applicable, the student must have no physical impairment of the speech mechanisms (larynx, tongue, palate, etc.), be able to produce sounds that at least approximate single words, and be able to imitate behaviors modeled by a teacher.

The goal of the Miller and Yoder approach is to teach as many semantic functions as possible. These functions are identified by observing the student in his or her environment and training those functions that occur most frequently. Training is designed to establish meaningful expression of the function. This is accomplished by associating the semantic function with its label and teaching the student to reproduce the label in the presence of the semantic function being taught. After this, other familiar experiences that express the same semantic function are gradually introduced. As the student begins to express these semantic functions spontaneously, the utterance is expanded to express functions such as *agent + action + object* (e.g., boy kicks ball), *agent + action + location* (e.g., daddy goes work), or *agent + object + location* (boy ball home).

A program developed by Stremel and Waryas (1974) is also based on psycholinguistic theory. The training closely follows a normal developmental language sequence and provides specific procedures. The program has three main parts; (1) early-language training, (2) early-intermediate language training, and (3) late-intermediate language training. The point of entry of a student into the training sequence depends upon the extent to which certain behaviors are already present in the student's repertoire. Before students can enter the first part of training, they must demonstrate that they attend to the teacher, follow simple instructions, and can identify at least 10 pictures or objects. With this kind of entry requirement, the program obviously is not suited for those with profound language handicaps. A student must possess at least a rudimentary linguistic repertoire.

The first, or early-language, phase initially teaches the student to express a wide range of nouns and verbs, then teaches *noun + verb* (e.g., Mommy go) and *verb + noun* (e.g., want cookie) combinations. Later in this phase, grammatical structures are expanded to include pronouns, adjectives, prepositions, and who/what/where questions. Both receptive and productive uses of these grammatical structures are trained.

In the early-intermediate training phase, the student's use of basic grammatical structures is expanded, and productive and receptive uses of auxiliary verbs, negatives, and possessives are taught. The late-intermediate phase continues to build the student's grammar and use of syntax by teaching such forms as plurals and noun/verb tense agreement.

Bricker, Dennison, and Bricker (1975) have developed a language training program that takes what they refer to as a *constructive-interaction-adaptation* approach. The program combines psycholinguistic, operant, and Piagetian approaches. Early forms of behavior such as visual tracking and grasping are viewed as a basis for later language development. If students lack such prerequisite skills, they are taught prior to language training. The program includes 24 training phases subsumed under one of five headings: attending skills, imitation, functional use, comprehension, and production. Many of the training phases can be taught concurrently. The program includes assessment guidelines to enable the teacher to place the child in the most appropriate training phase. The program provides suggested training activities rather than a rigid structure so a variety of training can occur in as wide a range of situations as possible to maximize learning opportunities.

Kent (1974) has developed a language acquisition program for severely handicapped individuals—one of the few programs that provide training procedures for students with complete lack of speech and language. The program has three sections: (1) pre-verbal, (2) verbal-receptive, and (3) verbal-expressive. The pre-verbal section is designed to develop the attending and motor imitation skills considered prerequisite for performance in later program phases. The student is first taught to sit in a chair. After this effort has been successful, any stereotyped or interfering behaviors such as rocking or hand waving are reduced through a procedure known as *overcorrection* (Azrin, Kaplan, & Foxx,

1973). The student then is taught to look at objects or the teacher's face in response to the imperative statement "look at this" or "look at me." In the final phase of this section, the teacher establishes motor imitations by modeling the behavior and instructing the student to "do this."

The verbal-receptive section is designed to develop a comprehensive receptive language repertoire. This is accomplished by teaching the child the motor responses taught in the first section with only a verbal instruction from the teacher. The student is gradually taught to point to body parts and objects and to perform certain actions in response to simple instructions (e.g., to sit down when asked verbally to do so). These instructions are gradually expanded until such behaviors as "make a circle" (with a felt tipped pen) and "make a tower" (with blocks) are taught.

The first phase in the verbal-expressive section starts with the shaping of single word utterances through modeling and imitation. Gradually, the single-word utterances are taught in response to the presence of an object or picture with such questions as, "What is this?" or "What is in the box?" A modified version of the program also is available in a nonoral format for use with the hearing impaired and deaf.

Guess, Sailor, and Baer (1976) have developed a language intervention program based on a learning theory account of language development. The total program is divided into 60 training steps. Each of the steps reflects the authors' emphasis on the importance of language use as a means of controlling the student's environment, and that the process of language acquisition is most effective when that acquisition results in the functional use of language. For example, teaching students to ask, "What's that?" when confronted by specific environmental events for which they have no label can result eventually in more effective control of their environment. Asking such a question generalizes to other unlabeled environmental events outside the teaching situation.

The steps in the first part of the program have been organized according to five dimensions: reference, control, self-extended control, integration, and reception. The *reference* dimension is designed to teach words as symbols for persons and things in the student's environment. The students are taught to label (name) 16 common objects selected by the teacher. The *control* dimension is designed to teach the students to make requests. For example, the teacher presents a glass of milk and says, "What want?" The student is taught to reply, "Want milk," and in a later step is taught to reply, "I want milk."

The *self-extended control* dimension is designed to teach the student to ask questions. When the teacher shows the student a novel item, the student is taught to ask, "What (is) that?" The *integration* dimension is designed to teach the student to respond with the appropriate label when presented with objects already learned and to seek information via question-asking when presented with a novel object. Later, the student learns verbal response sequences that resemble conversational speech. For example, the student might be shown a cookie and asked, "What is that?" The child should say "cookie." The teacher then might say, "What do you want?" whereupon the student would say, "I want cookie" and be given a piece of the cookie.

The *reception* dimension corresponds to those skills taught during speech production procedures. For example, Step 2 teaches the student to point to those items trained productively in Step 1. Step 7 provides another example. In this step the student is taught to say "yes" or "no" in response to such questions as, "Is this a ball?"

The program assumes that students have acquired verbal imitative skills prior to beginning the program. Once a student is considered a candidate for training, a "skill test" is given to determine the appropriate entry point into the program. The authors have provided guidelines designed to promote the generalization of language skills acquired through training to other than the training situation.

Carrier and Peak (1975) have developed a nonspeech communication system called *Non-Slip* (Non-Speech Language Initiation Program). The program is designed specifically for severely and profoundly handicapped students. Instead of teaching in the speech modality, students are taught to manipulate plastic symbols representing articles, nouns, verbs, and prepositions. In order to learn the communication system, a student first has to learn a number of prerequisite behaviors including picking up plastic symbols and placing them on a wooden tray; and discriminating the various shapes, the five colors, the differences between symbols with one and two stripes, and the matching of identical symbols, pictures, and objects. Teaching these prerequisites may represent as difficult a training task as teaching the communication system itself.

Once the prerequisites are learned, the students are systematically taught to string seven symbols together in a specific sequence on the tray. The seven-component sequence consists of an *article + noun + verb auxiliary + verb + preposition + article + noun*. After the sequence has been mastered, the students learn that each space in the sequence represents a class that can be filled by any one of the symbols from the set representing article, noun, second article, second noun, and so on. The students learn that specific symbols represent specific articles, nouns, etc.

The program eventually leads to such events as a teacher displaying a picture of a boy on a chair, with the student constructing with symbols the sentence, "The boy is sitting on the chair." The ultimate aim is for the student to be able to communicate events arising from the environment such as, "The teacher is coming to the cottage." Preliminary results from experimental use of the program have revealed students learning to produce in actual speech the words represented by the symbols. Further research currently is under way to determine the generality of this phenomenon and the variables controlling it.

CONTRIBUTIONS FROM OTHER DISCIPLINES

Fulfilling the needs of and hopes for the severely handicapped necessarily involves the participation of numerous other disciplines from the social, behavioral, rehabilitation, and medical fields. This interdisciplinary participation is needed initially for assessment of the severely handicapped child, leading to recommendations for treatment, education, and training. Following assessment, other disciplines should become actively involved in carrying out the planned educational, medical, and recommended rehabilitation programs. For optimal benefits to the child, each discipline should work in close cooperation with one another in a total team effort. The following discussion outlines some of the contributions involved in evaluating, educating, and treating severely handicapped children, thus providing the classroom teacher and the child's parents with a cadre of professional expertise.

Contributions from Medicine

Physicians have an important role in initial assessment of the severely handicapped child, especially when health-related problems are prominent. The physician must, of course, prescribe and evaluate a proper medication regimen for the child when seizures and other medical conditions need attention. Specialized medical personnel are also important. Consultation and corrective surgery may be required from the orthopedic surgeon. An ophthalmologist may be needed for consultation with visually impaired children. Psychiatric assistance may be of help to some severely handicapped children with emotional disturbances.

Contributions from Allied Health Personnel

A number of direct service disciplines perform duties under a physician's supervision. Many of these may be capable of making significant contributions in the treatment and training of the severely handicapped, and especially to those with physical impairments. Prominent among this group are physical and occupational therapists. They often work directly with the classroom teacher in carrying out prescribed exercises to improve the motor skills of some severely handicapped children. Physical and occupational therapists are also instrumental in helping design or locate specific adaptive devices to help the severely handicapped individual function better. These devices include special types of feeding equipment, apparatus for improving muscle control and balance, and adaptive equipment for improving the ability to move about.

Nursing personnel may also play an important role in the education and treatment of the severely handicapped. They often administer needed medication, provide emergency treatment if necessary, and perform other routine medical duties necessary for proper health maintenance. In some cases, nursing personnel may be asked to assist in special feeding problems that occur among a small number of severely handicapped children.

Similarly, nutritional and dietary personnel often are called upon to help plan the best diet for severely handicapped children, including special diets for children who have difficulty in chewing and swallowing.

Contributions from Speech Pathology and Audiology

Audiologists often are called upon to test the hearing of severely handicapped children. In some cases, they assist in prescribing a hearing aid and make the necessary follow-up contacts to assure that the hearing aid is being properly used and maintained. Speech clinicians have an invaluable role in the education of severely handicapped children, since most of these children have speech and language problems. Speech clinicians assess the child's speech and langauge abilities and make recommendations for remedial training. In many cases a speech clinician works directly with the severely handicapped child. In other instances the speech clinician directly assists the classroom teacher in selecting and carrying out specific speech and language training programs, either for individual children or groups of children.

Contributions from Psychology

Routinely, psychologists are called upon to assess the intellectual abilities of severely handicapped children and make recommendations to the classroom teacher based on their findings. Psychologists have also provided an important direct service contribution. They frequently are called upon to help select or design specific training programs, ranging from teaching self-help skills to the elimination of undesirable behavior. Psychologists have been especially instrumental in developing behavior control procedures and teaching programs for severely disturbed and profoundly retarded children.

Counseling psychologists may also provide assistance to parents of severely handicapped children. Vocational counselors often are asked to assist in the work placement and training of older severely handicapped individuals.

Social workers often provide the direct link between classroom teacher and parents or guardians of severely handicapped children. Social workers assist parents in coping with family problems that may arise in association with severely handicapped children. They frequently assist the parents and classroom teacher in obtaining specialized consultations or care and proper placement of the child in a school or other setting. Sometimes the social worker is the one person who reports directly to the parents concerning the child's progress.

Contributions from Related Disciplines

Several other professions and disciplines contribute to the treatment of severely handicapped children. Dentists and/or orthodontists may provide corrective treatment for teeth and gum problems. Recreational therapists can give recommendations for play time activities and the use of leisure time for older severely handicapped persons. Music therapists can work with severely handicapped children to develop appropriate means of expression, body awareness, and rhythm. Genetic counselors may be asked to talk with parents regarding conditions in which severely handicapped children are the result of an inherited genetic abnormality. Ministers, priests, and rabbis may be asked to discuss with parents religious implications and feelings associated with severely handicapped children.

Implications for Teacher Training

The extensive number of disciplines required for proper education and treatment of the severely handicapped presents a unique problem in personnel preparation. The full range of disciplines optimal for education and treatment of severely handicapped children is not available in rural and sparsely populated areas. Yet, classes for severely handicapped children are rapidly increasing in smaller cities and towns throughout the country. Teachers for severely handicapped children are being recruited to serve these classes. Accordingly, teacher training programs in the severely handicapped field must be comprehensive to adequately prepare teachers to fulfill some of the services that may not be provided by other disciplines in some areas.

Teachers of the severely handicapped must be prepared for competencies in many areas additional to teaching pre-academic and academic skills. They must be trained to follow techniques and procedures used by physical therapists, occupational therapists, and speech therapists. They must be acquainted with parent training techniques, able to serve as "public relations" personnel, and well-versed in legal rights of the handicapped. These teachers must know how to provide first aid, control hyperactive children, conduct educational evaluations, transfer children to and from wheelchairs, use adaptive devices, teach children to eat, dress, go to the toilet, and so on. In essence, teachers of the severely handicapped need to possess many of the skills which, traditionally, have not fallen under the name of education.

To prepare teachers for these competencies, many teacher training programs for the severely handicapped provide interdisciplinary instruction. Most often, they offer a heavy practicum orientation which offers direct work with professionals from other disciplines—an opportunity to learn many skills that can be used later, as a teacher for severely handicapped children. This is not to imply that teachers of the severely handicapped can do the actual work of other disciplines. It does imply, however, that teachers of the severely handicapped can carry out some functions of other disciplines with minimal supervision.

SUMMARY

Education and training for severely handicapped children is relatively new to the field of special education. Much is yet to be learned about the severely handicapped and the types of programs and procedures needed to allow these individuals to become more productive and useful members of our society. Intervention strategies reported to date strongly indicate that the task can be accomplished. Certainly, technology is emerging to teach the severely handicapped many more skills than thought possible. But developing new teaching procedures and programs for these individuals is only part of the task. Much more needs to be done in the home, school, and community to provide an atmosphere that accepts these children as individuals with the right to an education. As a free society, we must adhere to the principle that educational opportunity for all children is an inalienable right.

REFERENCES

Azrin, N.H., & Armstrong, P.M. The "mini-meal"—A method for teaching eating skills to the profoundly retarded. *Mental Retardation*, 1973, *11*, 9-13.

Azrin, N.H., Bugle, C., & O'Brien, F. Behavioral engineering: Two apparatuses for toilet training retarded children. *Journal of Applied Behavior Analysis*, 1971, *4*, 249-253.

Azrin, N.H., Kaplan, S.J., & Foxx, R.M. Autism reversal: Eliminating stereotyped self-stimulation of retarded individuals. *American Journal of Mental Deficiency*, 1973, 241-248.

Baumeister, A.A., & Forehand, R. Effects of extinction of an instrumental response on stereotyped body rocking in severe retardates. *Psychological Record*, 1971, *21*, 235-240.

Berkowitz, S., Sherry, P.J., & Davis, B.A. Teaching self-feeding skills to profound retardates using reinforcement and fading procedures. *Behavior Therapy*, 1971, *2*, 62-67.

Berkson, G., & Davenport, R.K. Stereotyped movements in mental defectives: I. Initial survey. *American Journal of Mental Deficiency*, 1962, *66*, 849-852.

Berkson, G., & Mason, W. Stereotyped behaviors of chimpanzees: Relation to general arousal and alternative activities. *Perceptual and Motor Skills*, 1964, *19*, 635-652.

Bobath, B. The very early treatment of cerebral palsy. *Developmental Medicine and Child Neurology*, 1967, *9*, 373-390.

Bobath, B. & Bobath, K. The facilitation of normal postural reactions and movements in the treatment of cerebral palsy. *Physiotherapy*, 1964, *50*, 246-262.

Bricker, D., Dennison, L., & Bricker, W.A. *Constructive-interaction-adaptation approach to language training* (Mailman Center for Child Development Monograph Series No. 7). Unpublished manuscript, University of Miami, 1975.

Brown, L., & Foshee, J. G. Comparative techniques for increasing attending behavior of retarded students. *Education and Training of the Mentally Retarded*, 1971,6, 4-11.

Carrier, J.K., & Peak, T. *NON-SLIP (Non-speech language initiation program)*. Lawrence, KS: H & H Enterprises, Inc., 1975.

Chambers, D. Right to the least restrictive alternative setting for treatment. In B.J. Ennis & P. R. Friedman (Eds.), *Legal rights of the mentally handicapped* (Vol. 2). New York: Practicing Law Institute, 1974, 991-1014.

Chandler, S. S., & Adams, M.A. Multiply handicapped children motivated for ambulation through behavior modification. *Physical Therapy*, 1972, *52*, 399-401.

Corbett, J. Aversion for the treatment of self-injurious behavior. *Journal of Mental Deficiency Research*, 1975, *19*, 79-95.

Dunn, L.M. *The Peabody picture vocabulary test*. Circle Pines, MN: American Guidance Service, Inc., 1965.

Flavell, J.E. Reduction of stereotypes by reinforcement of toy play. *Mental Retardation*, 1973 *11*, 21-23.

Frankel, F., & Simmons, J. Self-injurious behavior in schizophrenic and retarded children. *American Journal of Mental Deficiency*, 1976, *80*, 512-522.

Giles, D.K., & Wolf, M.M. Toilet training institutionalized, severe retardates: An application of operant behavior modification techniques. *American Journal of Mental Deficiency*, 1966, *70*, 766-780.

Gilhool, T.K. Education: An inalienable right. *Exceptional Children*, 1973, *39*, 597-609.

Guess, D., Sailor, W., & Baer, D.M. *Functional speech and language training for the severely handicapped: Parts I and II*. Lawrence, KS: H & H Enterprises, Inc., 1976.

Hollis, J. Steady and transition rates: Effects of alternate activity on body-rocking in retarded children. *Psychological Reports*, 1976, *39*, 91-104.

Horner, R.D. Establishing use of crutches by a mentally retarded *spina bifida* child. *Journal of Applied Behavior Analysis*, 1971, *4*, 183-189.

Horner, R.D., & Keilitz, I. Training mentally retarded adolescents to brush their teeth. *Journal of Applied Behavior Analysis*, 1975, *8*, 301-309.

Karen, R. L., & Maxwell, S.J. Strengthening self-help behavior in the retardate. *American Journal of Mental Deficiency*, 1967, *71*, 546-550.

Kaufman, M.E., & Levitt, H.A. A study of three stereotyped behaviors in institutionalized mental defectives. *American Journal of Mental Deficiency*, 1965, *69*, 467-473.

Kent, L. *Language acquisition program for the severely retarded.* Champaign, IL: Research Press, 1974.

Levison, C. The development of headbanging in a young Rhesus monkey. *American Journal of Mental Deficiency*, 1970, *75*, 323-328.

Lippman, L., & Goldberg, I.I. *Right to education: Anatomy of the Pennsylvania case and its implications for exceptional children.* New York: Teachers College Press, 1973.

Lourie, R.S. The role of rhythmic patterns in childhood. *American Journal of Psychiatry*, 1959, *105*, 653-660.

Lovaas, O.I., Frietag, G., Gold, V.J., & Kassorla, I.C. Experimental studies in childhood schizophrenia: Analysis of self-destructuve behavior. *Journal of Experimental Child Psychology*, 1965, *2*, 67-84.

Lovaas, O.I., Schreibman, L., Koegel, R., & Rehm, R. Selective responding by autistic children to multiple sensory input. *Journal of Abnormal Psychology*, 1971, *77*, 211-222.

Mahoney, K., Van Wagenen, R.K., & Meyerson, L. Toilet training of normal and retarded children. *Journal of Applied Behavior Analysis*, 1971, *4*, 173-181.

Martin, E. On education for the severely/profoundly handicapped and Justice Douglas (Review). *The American Association for the Education of the Severely/Profoundly Handicapped*, 1976, *1*, 105-114.

Martin, G.L., Kehoe, B., Bird, E., Jensen, V., & Darbyshire, M. Operant conditioning in dressing behavior of severely retarded girls. *Mental Retardation*, 1971, *9*, 27-30.

Martin, G.L., & Powers, R.B. Attention span: An operant conditioning analysis. *Exceptional Children*, 1967, *33*, 565-570.

Melcher, J.W. Law, litigation, and handicapped children. *Exceptional Children*, 1976, *43*, 126-130.

Miller, J.F., & Yoder, D.E. An ontogenetic language teaching strategy for retarded children. In R. Schiefelbusch and L. Lloyd (Eds.), *Language perspectives: Acquisition, retardation and intervention.* Baltimore: University Park Press, 1974.

O'Brien, F., Bugle, D., & Azrin, N.H. Training and maintaining a retarded child's proper eating. *Journal of Applied Behavior Analysis*, 1972, *5*, 67-72.

Pennsylvania Association for Retarded Children, Nancy Beth Bowman, et. al. v. *Commonwealth of Pennsylvania, David H. Kurtzman, et. al., E. D. Pa., Civil Action No. 71-42 (1972), 334 F. Supp. 1253 (1971).*

Sailor, W., & Horner, R.D. Educational assessment strategies for the severely handicapped. In N. Haring & L. Brown, *Teaching the severely handicapped* (Vol. 1). New York: Grune & Stratton, 1976.

Scheuerman, N., Cartwright, S., York, R., Lowry, P., & Brown, L. Teaching young severely handicapped students to follow verbal directions. *Journal of Special Education*, 1974, *8*, 223-236.

Segal, S.S. *No child is ineducable.* Oxford: Pergamon Press, 1972.

Somerton, E., & Turner, K. *Pennsylvania training model: Individual assessment guide.* King of Prussia: Regional Resources Center of Eastern Pennsylvania for Special Education, 1974.

Sontag, E. Zero exclusion: Rhetoric no longer (Review). *The American Association for the Education of the Severely/Profoundly Handicapped*, 1976, *1*, 105-114.

Sontag, E., Burke, P.J., & York, R. Considerations for serving the severely handicapped in the public schools. *Education and Training of the Mentally Retarded*, 1973, *8*, 20-26.

Sontag, E., Smith, J., & Sailor, W. The severely/profoundly handicapped: Who are they? Where are we? *Journal of Special Education*, 1976.

Spradlin, J.E., & Girardeau, F.L. The behavior of moderately and severely retarded persons. In N.R. Ellis (Ed.)., *International Review of Research in Mental Retardation* (Vol. 1). New York: Academic Press, 1966.

Stephens, B. A Piagetian approach to curriculum development. In E. Sontag, J. Smith, & N. Certo (Eds.), *Educational programming for the severely and profoundly handicapped*. Reston, VA: A Special Publication of the Division on Mental Retardation, The Council for Exceptional Children, 1977, 237-249.

Stremel, K., & Waryas, C. A behavioral-psycholinguistic approach to language training. *American Speech and Hearing Monographs*, 1974, *18*, 96-124.

Treffry, D., Martin, G., Samels, J., & Watson, C. Operant conditioning of grooming behavior of severely retarded girls. *Mental Retardation*, 1970, *8*, 29-33.

Twardosz, S., & Sajwaj, T. Multiple effects of a procedure to increase sitting in a hyperactive retarded boy. *Journal of Applied Behavior Analysis*, 1972, *5*, 73-78.

Whitman, T.L., Mercurio, J.R., & Caponigri, V. Development of social responses in two severely retarded children. *Journal of Applied Behavior Analysis*, 1970, *3*, 133-138.

Wilson, V., & Parks, R. Promoting ambulation in the severely retarded child. *Mental Retardation*, 1970, *8*, 17-19.

RESOURCE GUIDE

Historical Information

Lippman, L., & Goldberg, I. I. *Right to education: Anatomy of the Pennsylvania case and its implications for exceptional children.* New York: Teachers College Press, 1973.

Luckey, R. E., & Addison, M. R. The profoundly retarded: A new challenge for public education. *Education and Training of the Mentally Retarded,* 1974, *9,* 123-130.

Roos, P. Severely and profoundly retarded students — past and future. In *Educating the 24-hour retarded child.* Arlington, TX: National Association for Retarded Citizens, 1975, pp. 5-8.

Schupper, W. V., Wilson, W. C., & Wolf, J. N. Public education of the handicapped. In E. Sontag, J. Smith, & N. Certo (Eds.), *Educational programming for the severely and profoundly handicapped.* Reston, VA: Division on Mental Retardation/Council for Exceptional Children, 1977, pp. 6-13.

Family

Bicknell, F. Parental involvement in the education of the "24-hour retarded child." In *Educating the 24-hour retarded child.* Arlington, TX: National Association for Retarded Citizens, 1975, pp. 121-131.

Kenowitz, L., Gallagher, J., & Edgar, E. Generic services for the severely handicapped and their families: What's available? In E. Sontag, J. Smith & N. Certo (Eds.), *Educational programming for the severely and profoundly handicapped.* Reston, VA: Division on Mental Retardation/Council for Exceptional Children, 1977, pp. 31-39.

Kozloff, M. A. *Reaching the autistic child — A parent training program.* Champaign, IL: Research Press, 1973.

Menolascino, F. J. Understanding parents of the retarded — A crises model for helping them cope more effectively. In F. J. Menolascino & P. H. Pearson, *Beyond the limits — Innovations in services for the severely and profoundly retarded.* Seattle: Special Child Publications, 1974, pp. 172-209.

Patterns of Development

Bijou, S. W. A functional analysis of retarded development. In N. R. Ellis (Ed.), *International review of research in mental retardation* (Vol. 1). New York: Academic Press, 1966, pp.1-20.

Bricker, D. D., & Iacino, R. Early intervention with severely/profoundly handicapped children. In E. Sontag, J. Smith, & N. Certo (Eds.), *Educational programming for the severely and profoundly handicapped.* Reston, VA: Division on Mental Retardation/Council for Exceptional Children, 1977, pp. 166-176.

Cohen, M., Gross, P., & Haring, N. G. Developmental pinpoints. In N. G. Haring & L. J. Brown (Eds.), *Teaching the severely handicapped* (Vol. 1). New York: Grune & Stratton, 1976, pp. 35-110.

Haring, N. G., & Cohen, M. Using the developmental approach as a basis for planning different kinds of curricula for severely/profoundly handicapped persons. In *Educating the 24-hour retarded child.* Arlington, TX: National Association for Retarded Citizens, 1975, pp. 42-70.

Treatment

Bricker, D., Bricker, W., Iacino, R., & Dennison, L. Intervention strategies for the severely and profoundly handicapped child. In N. G. Haring & L. J. Brown (Eds.), *Teaching the severely handicapped* (Vol. 1). New York: Grune & Stratton, 1976, pp. 277-299.

Forehand, R., & Baumeister, A. A. Deceleration of aberrant behavior among retarded individuals. In M. Hersen, R. M. Eisler, & P. M. Miller (Eds.), *Progress in behavior modification.* New York: Academic Press, 1976.

Guess, D., Sailor, W., & Baer, D. M. *Functional speech and language training for the severely handicapped* (Parts 1 and 2). Lawrence, KS: H & H Enterprises, Inc., 1976.

Guess, D., Sailor, W., Keogh, B., & Baer, D. M. Language development programs for severely handicapped children. In N. G. Haring & L. J. Brown (Eds.), *Teaching the Severely Handicapped* (Vol. 1). New York: Grune & Stratton, 1976, pp. 301-324.

Kauffman, J. M., & Snell, M. E. Managing the behavior of severely handicapped persons. In E. Sontag, J. Smith, & N. Certo (Eds.), *Educational programming for the severely and profoundly handicapped.* Reston, VA: Division on Mental Retardation/Council for Exceptional Children, 1977, pp. 203-218.

Robinault, I. P. *Functional aids for the multiply handicapped.* Hagerstown, MD: Harper & Row/Medical Department, 1973.

Striefel, S. *Managing Behavior 7 — Behavior modification: Teaching a child to imitate.* Lawrence, KS: H & H Enterprises, Inc., 1974.

Watson, L. S. *How to use behavior modification with mentally retarded and autistic children: Programs for administrators, teachers, parents, and nurses.* Libertyville, IL: Behavior Modification Technology, Inc., 1972.

Educational Programming

Anderson, D. R., Hodson, G. D., & Jones, W. G. (Eds.). *Instructional programs for the severely handicapped student.* Springfield, IL: Charles C. Thomas, 1974.

Bijou, S., & Wilcox-Cole, B. The feasibility of providing effective educational programs for the severely and profoundly retarded. In *Educating the 24-hour retarded child*. Arlington, TX: National Association for Retarded Citizens, 1975, pp. 9-25.

Brody, J. F., & Smilovitz, R. (Eds.). *APT: A training program for citizens with severely or profoundly retarded behavior*. Spring City, PA: Pennhurst State School and Hospital, 1974.

Brown, L., & York, R. Developing programs for severely handicapped students: Teacher training and classroom instruction. *Focus on Exceptional Children*, 1974, *6* (2), 1-11.

Larsen, L. A. Community services necessary to program effectively for the severely/profoundly handicapped. In E. Sontag, J. Smith, & N. Certo (Eds.), *Educational programming for the severely and profoundly handicapped*. Reston, VA: Division on Mental Retardation/Council for Exceptional Children, 1977, pp. 17-30.

McCormack, J. E., Chalmers, A. J., & Gregorian, J. K. *Systematic instruction of the severely handicapped — Teaching sequences*. Medford, MA: Massachusetts Center for Program Development and Evaluation, 1976.

Smith, D. D., Smith, J. O., & Edgar, E. B. Prototypic model for the development of instructional materials. In N. G. Haring & L. J. Brown (Eds.), *Teaching the severely handicapped* (Vol. 1). New York: Grune & Stratton, 1976, pp. 155-176.

Somerton, E., & Meyers, D. G. Educational programming for the severely/profoundly mentally retarded. In N. G. Haring & L. J. Brown (Eds.), *Teaching the severely handicapped* (Vol. 1). New York: Grune & Stratton, 1976, pp. 111-154.

Sontag, E., Burke, P. J., & York, R. Considerations for serving the severely handicapped in the public schools. *Education and Training of the Mentally Retarded*, 1973, *8*, 20-26.

Williams, W., Brown, L., & Certo, N. Components of instructional programs for severely handicapped students. *Theory into Practice*, 1975, *14* (2).

6 The Learning Disabled

Larry J. Little
Shippensburg State College

Children who fail to learn in spite of diligent efforts to teach them are a concern of both parents and teachers. The literature documents numerous efforts by professionals to understand the nature of various learning handicaps and to develop treatment programs during the past century. Despite this concern for children with learning disorders, however, most programs and services for exceptional children have been directed primarily toward children with more visible learning handicaps.

By the late 1950s, considerable research had provided a basis for establishing public school programs for the mentally retarded, emotionally disturbed, physically handicapped, visually handicapped, and hearing handicapped; but many children with less visible handicaps still were not being served adequately by programs and services to fit their needs. Children in this unique group did not appear to be mentally retarded, emotionally disturbed, sensorially handicapped, or environmentally disadvantaged; yet, they demonstrated a variety of learning problems that resisted the best attempts at educational remediation. Knowledge and expertise offered by the schools clearly were inadequate.

Parents of children with learning problems sought help from a variety of sources. Often, chance or accessibility determined which professions were called upon for assistance. Some children were taken to pediatricians, generating subsequent concern among a number of specialties in the medical profession. Drawing from knowledge of neurophysiology in attempts to understand learning disorders, physicians used terms such as *brain damaged, brain injured,* and *neurologically impaired.* These terms soon came to represent a new category of exceptionality.

Other parents sought help from psychologists, who incorporated their frame of reference in attempting to understand learning disorders. New terms such as *perceptual handicap, attentional disorder,* and *hyperactivity* were commonly adopted in describing the learning disorders of the children.

Some children were seen by speech and language specialists whose orientation focused on the acquisition and use of oral language as a basis for other kinds of learning. From their study, terms such as *childhood aphasia, dyslexia, dysgraphia,* and *receptive* and *expressive language disorder* came to be associated with this population of children.

Although the focal points of study varied among disciplines, an implicit set of assumptions developed concerning what was *not* the cause of these learning difficulties. The cause was not mental retardation, sensory impairment, emotional disturbance, motor impairment, or environmental disadvantage. The disorder was assumed to be associated with a dysfunction in the central nervous system that reduced the learner's efficiency in mastering specific kinds of information and tasks that most children learned with little difficulty.

The contributions of medicine, psychology, and language have been of major significance in providing essential information to build new theories to understand how disruptions in the learning processes have interfered with learning specific tasks. But, as Lerner (1976) pointed out, the *educator* has the primary responsibility for teaching these children. Emerging theories must be translated into action for teaching children who can learn but whose disorders require a knowledge of *how* they learn, in order to present information in a way they can understand.

Specialists from various disciplines began seeing similar behaviors among children with learning disorders, but integration of this information clearly was needed because (1) each discipline emphasized different aspects of learning according to its own professional bias, and (2) each discipline was describing its observations in terms common to its own theoretical perspective. The resulting confusion in communication was staggering. The impact of the semantic confusion among professionals was felt acutely by both parents and teachers. Translating knowledge into action for teaching was difficult when the same child may have been described as dyslexic by one specialist, perceptually handicapped by another, and aphasic by a third. And the reader of such information encountered similar variance in terminology, resulting in further confusion.

DEFINING THE LEARNING DISABLED

In response to the increasing knowledge about learning disorders advanced by various disciplines, efforts were made to develop a comprehensive definition with appropriate terminology to identify this population for the purpose of providing educational services. The National Advisory Committee on Handicapped Children (1968) developed a definition which was presented to Congress; this description subsequently has become the basic definition for federal support of teacher training programs in regard to these children, and for support of programs for delivering services.

Children with special learning disabilities exhibit a disorder in one or more of the basic psychological processes involved in understanding or using spoken or written languages. These may be manifested in disorders of listening, thinking, talking, reading, writing, spelling, or arithmetic. They include conditions which have been referred to as perceptual handicaps, brain injury, minimal brain dysfunction, dyslexia, developmental aphasia, etc. They do not include learning problems which are due primarily to visual, hearing, or motor handicaps, to mental retardation, emotional disturbance, or to environmental disadvantage.

This definition is significant for several reasons. First, it established the term *learning disabilities* to denote this newly identified group of exceptional children. Second, it implied that the learning problem may result from a central nervous system *dysfunction*, rather than brain damage. Circular and often unfruitful efforts to establish the absence or presence of brain damage now could be eliminated. (This is especially important, since a child's eligibility for educational services from the LD specialist often was contingent upon a medical diagnosis of brain damage.) Third, it recognized that learning may be disrupted by any one or a combination of learning dysfunctions. For example, one learning disabled child may have perceptual difficulties; another may have difficulty with memory for certain knowledge or information; still another may have difficulty with abstract thinking involving the ability to group and classify experiences.

The dysfunction feature of the definition provided the basis for directing attention toward identifying a particular child's strengths and weaknesses and assessing the school curriculum in terms of those strengths and weaknesses (i.e., which particular tasks by their nature require the learner to possess certain strengths? Does a child possess the strengths demanded by that task? If not, can we alter the task so the child can learn the task with his or her existing strengths?). Fourth, disabilities were associated with educationally oriented tasks in basic academic areas, and a basis was established for exploring the interrelationships among oral language comprehension and usage, reading, writing, spelling, and arithmetic.

Although this definition has been adopted widely throughout the United States, it has not been unchallenged. Criticism has been voiced by Hammill (1976) on several counts. One regards the difficulty of identifying and assessing basic psychological processes in an educationally relevant way, and questions the assumption that psychological processes can be reduced to discrete functions, measured with reliability, and related in a direct causal fashion to specific learning disabilities.

Hammill also challenges the assumption that only children whose intelligence is within the normal range can be identified as having a learning disability, thereby excluding those who have intelligence scores well below average. Intelligence tests commonly used to assess children's IQs are loaded heavily with items that measure a child's past learning. If a child demonstrates that he or she has learned a substantial amount of information, the inference is that this child has at least average intelligence. If a child fails to demonstrate substantial evidence of past learning, he or she may be assumed to be mentally retarded but not learning disabled, because the score is below normal range. The circularity in this thinking is evident. If a child has a learning disability that interferes with learning certain information and that information must be demonstrated as an indication of average intelligence, can we safely assume that demonstration of at least average intelligence as measured psychometrically is a valid criterion for determining whether or not a learning disability exists?

The exclusionary clause which states that the learning disability is not primarily due to mental retardation, emotional disturbance, or environmental disadvantage is questioned. Hammill suggests that our present psychometric procedures are grossly inadequate in leading to such clear-cut differential diagnoses.

The usefulness of the current definition of learning disabilities is limited for the practical implementation of procedures that clearly identify children with learning disabilities and the generation of subsequent remedial teaching procedures appropriate to the needs of individuals within this population. Nevertheless, the definition does provide a common ground for professionals to begin testing the validity of assumptions about the nature of learning disabilities. Efforts continue to refine and clarify the nature of learning disabilities. As with building any body of knowledge, developing and testing new hypotheses contributes to new theory. As more theories of learning disability are generated, the bases for refining the definition, as well as the principles of remedial instruction, will be broadened.

Perhaps one of the major challenges in operationalizing the definition of learning disability is the tacit assumption that a learning disability is a uniform, discrete entity which either exists or doesn't exist. The naive observer sometimes fails to recognize the dynamic nature of the human organism and may ask, "What test do you use for a learning disability?" The diverse nature of learning disabilities is expressed by Johnson and Myklebust (1967) in the statement that the basis of homogeneity in the learning disabled population is *a learning deficit in the presence of adequate intelligence.* The group is heterogeneous in that it exhibits a wide variety of disabilities. To articulate a concise definition of learning disabilities is virtually impossible, since the disability may be manifested in highly dissimilar ways among children.

PREVALENCE OF LEARNING DISABILITIES

The number of children who have learning disabilities varies according to the stringency of criteria used to determine this disability. In a screening of 2,800 third- and fourth-grade children, Myklebust and Boshes (1969) found that between 7 and 8 percent of the children in the study group had learning disabilities. The National Advisory Committee on Handicapped Children (1968) estimated that between 1 and 3 percent of the school population have learning disabilities.

In any event, one typically might expect two or three children in any regular classroom to have a learning disability requiring individual assessment and intervention for the child to profit from the classroom experience. Learning disabilities appear to occur at a ratio of about 8 or 9 boys to 1 or 2 girls.

Many people have expressed concern about the invention of a new category of children—the learning disabled—who, until the past few years, appeared not to exist or existed in far fewer numbers. At least two factors may help explain this concern. First, we have become more proficient in identifying the nature of children's learning difficulties; fewer academic failures are attributed to "laziness" or statements like, "The child isn't very smart." Second, due to advances in medicine, a number of children today are surviving high-risk perinatal conditions which often resulted in their death 20 years ago. These children, who are now surviving in greater numbers, include those with residual central nervous system dysfunction. They are in regular classrooms, and their less intact learning abilities may be more dependent upon appropriate teaching strategies than is true for most children.

ETIOLOGY

Theoretical points of view regarding etiology (or cause) of learning disabilities are as varied as the types of disabilities themselves. Numerous theoretical positions have been stated and some research has been done, but many questions remain unanswered. Preliminary research findings suggest that multiple factors may interact to cause difficulty in the learner's attempts to achieve academically—no one-to-one cause-

and-effect relationship can be designated between any single factor and subsequent learning disability.

Perinatal Stress

Medically oriented research has pursued the possible impact of stressful factors upon growth and development of an infant during the perinatal period. Through clinical observation, in retrospect, Pasamanick and Knoblock (1960) hypothesized that neurological damage during the prenatal period is a potent source of neuropsychiatric disorders. They reported that examination of maternal and newborn records of 1,151 children exhibiting deviant behavior revealed a significantly greater incidence of maternal complications during pregnancy and prematurity than was exhibited by the control group.

These findings stimulated other research focusing on the nature of the relationship between perinatal factors and subsequent learning disorders. The effects of toxemia, diminished oxygen supply, prematurity, drugs as toxic agents, and smoking are but a few of the factors considered as maternal stress factors on the unborn infant. Although the definitive nature of these factors cannot be demonstrated in terms of specific psychometric and educational deficits (Colligan, 1974), interference with development of the unborn infant logically may predispose the child to greater difficulty in some areas of learning.

Closely related to this area of study is the effect of fetal malnutrition. Birch (1971) has postulated that during critical phases of cell division in the developing fetus, malnutrition may cause a permanent reduction in number of cells in the central nervous system. The reduction in quantity of brain cells is considered permanent, thus limiting brain function for later learning.

Biochemical Disturbances

Biochemical dysfunction of the body has been hypothesized as a causative factor in learning disabilities (Feingold, 1975a; 1975b). Hyperkinesis has been postulated as being related to the foods we eat. Further, it has been stated that certain children experience adverse reactions to specific chemicals present in synthetic colors and flavors. Feingold believes that these chemical food additives contribute to hyperactivity and learning disabilities. As a treatment, Feingold advocates removal of foods which contain additives, thereby removing the source of biochemical imbalance which causes learning disorders. This hypothesis has received widespread attention through the news media, but research to support the hypothesis is lacking. In a comprehensive review of the data regarding this issue, Spring and Sandoval (1976) conclude that food additives plausibly may contribute to hyperactivity in some children, but no substantial base of research has been developed to warrant wide acceptance of this theory.

A second hypothesis suggests that learning disabilities may result from inability of a child's bloodstream to synthesize normal amounts of certain vitamins (Cott, 1972). Subsequent treatment consists of massive doses of vitamins to provide optimum concentrations of substances normally present in the human body. In an experimental study, Kershner, Hawks, and Grekin (1977) have investigated the effects of massive vitamin (megavitamin) treatment for children with learning disabilities. Results from their study offer no support for use of massive vitamin treatment with learning disabled children in an effort to improve their functioning on a variety of intellectual, perceptual, academic achievement, and behavorial measures.

Eye Function and Learning Disabilities

Considerable attention has focused on the relationship between ocular (eye) mobility and learning disability, particularly by the field of optometry. Faulty eye movements have been suggested as interfering with the learner's intake of information, thereby reducing learning efficiency. This position has been refuted by ophthalmologists (Lawson, 1968; Goldberg & Arnott, 1970) who have stated that ocular movement does facilitate learning, but that learning is accomplished in the brain and not in the eyes. The study by Goldberg and Arnott showed that the degree of reading comprehension determined the eye movements rather than eye movements themselves producing comprehension of reading material. Research offers no support for the practice of training the child's eye movements as a general means of correcting a learning disability.

TWO PHILOSOPHIES OF LEARNING DISABILITY

The Developmentalist Position

The developmental point of view is based on the premise that children develop physically, intellectually, socially, and emotionally at a predetermined rate. The environment may affect or modify a child's rate of development, but it cannot be *significantly* altered (Ames, 1968). This position suggests that learning disabilities are artifacts of our insensitivity to a child's behavioral capabilities at any point in development, in relation to curricular demands placed upon the child. Ames suggests that children should not begin a formal academic program until they have developmentally mastered behaviors upon which academic learning is contingent. She further states that learning disability is primarily the result of "over placement" of the child in a curriculum—i.e., introducing tasks before the child is developmentally ready.

The Behavioral Point of View

Professionals who hold the behaviorally oriented point of view of learning reject the concept of deficient processes on the basis that processes cannot be observed, only inferred. Behaviorists emphasize environmental variables that are observable, measurable, and subject to alteration. The focus is not on the learner's altered neurology, but on environmental conditions in relation to the individual. Throne (1973) states that the learning disabled child may actually learn differently than typical children and, therefore, needs a different environment. Learning success then depends upon development of an appropriate learning environment, not upon altered neurology.

From the behaviorist point of view, related concepts and terms have arisen, such as *teaching disability* rather than learning disability (Bateman 1973). Engelmann (1969) states that children can learn if they are taught in a way appropriate for them. He criticizes those who blame the child for a learning failure, rather than critically examining teaching procedures to determine how they can be made more appropriate for the child.

CLASSIFICATION OF LEARNING DISABILITIES

To better understand the many ways in which learning disabilities may be manifested among children and the interrelationship among various disabilities, one must examine disabilities according to some type of construct or classification system. This is not to suggest that learning should be relegated to discrete categories but, for purposes of discussion and understanding, certain classifications will be viewed here.

Disorders of Verbal and Nonverbal Learning

Johnson and Myklebust (1967) have suggested that learning disabilities may occur in the area of verbal learning or in the area of nonverbal learning. Verbal learning disabilities are manifested in the broad areas of oral language comprehension, oral language usage, reading, and writing. Nonverbal learning disabilities are manifested as disturbances in time orientation, spatial orientation, directionality, picture interpretation, music and rhythm, and social perception. Some learning disabled children have difficulty within some or all of the verbal areas; other learning disabled children have difficulty primarily with nonverbal learning; still others may be affected in both learning areas.

Verbal learning disabilities have been a major concern to educators because proficiency in reading, writing, and spelling is stressed during the primary school grades. Reading and writing are necessary skills for more advanced learning at the secondary school level.

On the other hand, nonverbal learning disabilities often have been neglected, perhaps because they have not been understood as well or their importance has not been recognized as influencing the overall learning of children, or a combination of the two. Myklebust (1975) has discussed the nature of various nonverbal learning disabilities and suggested that the basis for verbal learning may be dependent upon adequate nonverbal learning to a greater degree than we have recognized. For example, if a child cannot perceive or distinguish relative sizes of comparative objects at the concrete level, he or she may have a limited basis for understanding verbal symbols such as "big, bigger, biggest" or "smaller than, larger than."

Disorders of Input and Output

Another helpful construct for classifying learning disabilities distinguishes between disorders of input or disorders of output (Johnson & Myklebust, 1967). Many children with learning disabilities have difficulty in following a class discussion because they don't readily comprehend certain key words in the discussion or do not understand complex sentences. Other children comprehend oral discussion well but have difficulty in formulating their ideas into good sentences; knowledge may be masked by an inability to express it orally. Others may comprehend class discussion and be able to express their ideas eloquently, but can't read. Still other children may have good language skills, read and comprehend sufficiently, but are unable to express their ideas in written form. These situations apply to the classification of learning disabilities according to input or output of information.

Disorders within Specific Learning Modalities

A third concept applied to the understanding of learning disabilities is that of sensory or perceptual modalities through which learning occurs. Wepman (1968) states that, among the normal population, individuals vary in their preferences for the way they learn. Some learn best by hearing; others learn best by seeing; still others learn best through the sense of touch and movement. He proposes that differential levels of functioning among perceptual modalities in an individual account for the relative ease with which that person learns certain kinds of tasks. If one's auditory perceptual modality develops irregularly, one may have difficulty with processing spoken language; if the visual perceptual modality is similarly delayed, one will have problems with reading.

This construct has served as a basis to identify deficient modality functions within the learning disabled population so that: (1) the deficient modalities can be remediated through specific teaching exercises; (2) educational instruction can draw upon the stronger modalities of the learner; or (3) a combination of teaching strategies can be directed to the intact modality while remediating the deficient one.

Learning disabilities also have been considered as disorders of specific functions in the broad areas of perception, memory, thinking, or perceptual motor integration (Johnson & Myklebust, 1967; Lerner, 1976).

Disorders of Perception

Perception may be defined as the ability to recognize and make sense of sensory stimulation, whether it be visual, auditory, or haptic (Lerner, 1976). Johnson and Myklebust (1976) state that adequate interpretation of sensory information is necessary for the learner to remember clearly and use the information for higher levels of thinking.

Visual perception is related integrally to a child's attempts to discriminate forms, letters, words, and numerals. Difficulty in visual perception may interfere with judgments about nonverbal shapes and figures, thus limiting the child's use of picture cues as a learning aid. Visual perceptual difficulties also may limit the child's recognition of letters and words, making reading difficult. *Auditory* perceptual disturbance, on the other hand, may affect numeral interpretation primarily. *Haptic* perceptual disturbance may limit children's ability to process information through the sense of touch, such as in the child who is described as "tactilely defensive" (Ayres, 1973).

For example, a ten-year-old boy was described as emotionally disturbed mainly because of his frequent fights. After examining the boy and the situations which precipitated the fighting, it was realized that he had extreme difficulty in interpreting anything that touched his body unless he could see it simultaneously. He responded to touch as a shock and immediately turned and hit whomever had touched him. The occupational therapist began to work with him to teach how to interpret numerous tactile experiences while looking at them. The therapist gradually increased the repertoire of touch experiences before asking the boy to interpret them with his eyes closed. Meanwhile, the classroom teacher placed his seat at an angle in the front corner of the room so anyone approaching him was within peripheral view. When the class formed a line to leave the room, the teacher placed him last in line to reduce incidents of bumping against other children.

Lerner (1976) stresses that perception is a learned skill and that instruction can be altered to facilitate perceptual development. Frostig (1972) suggests that teaching of perceptual skills can be incorporated into almost any lesson or activity. Thus, for learning disabled children who have perceptual disturbances affecting certain kinds of tasks, instruction can be altered to minimize the perceptual difficulty and make learning those tasks less difficult.

Disorders of Memory

For this discussion, memory is considered as either short-term or long-term. Many children with learning disabilities have difficulty holding an image in mind long enough to associate it with another image or to make a judgment about it. Short-term memory is essential to the task of retaining a sound in mind while associating it with a picture of a letter. Almost any system of reading instruction assumes some ability to associate (and remember) sounds with words or letters, particularly a phonic approach to reading. For some children, the ability to remember sound-symbol correspondences is particularly weak, making reading difficult.

Memory is also vital in learning oral language. Children must hold sounds, words, and even sentences in mind long enough to reproduce them or to abstract the rules necessary for generating their own sentences. Wiig and Semel (1976) suggest that memory is integrally related to learning specific features of oral language; i.e., short-term memory deficits may interfere with remembering sequences of sounds within words, and long-term deficits may hinder recall of words for spontaneous use.

Visual memory for letters and words is necessary in learning spelling and written language. To write words, one must remember how letters look. For words that are not spelled the way they sound, one must remember the appearance of the entire word. The child whose visual memory for letters and words is weak thus may be limited in the use of written language. For the child whose visual memory for nonverbal material is limited, the ability to remember visual details of the environment or picture material may be reduced. Therefore, performance in visual arts may be poor, because the child doesn't remember details of objects or pictures adequately to draw them.

Inadequate memory for motor patterns may present difficulty to a child who is asked to reproduce certain patterns for copying letters, numerals, or even gross motor patterns necessary for games and sports. As one studies the tasks that daily confront every school child, memory clearly is required in some form and to varying degrees in every task. For children with learning disabilities, memory disturbances may critically affect their performance on certain or various kinds of tasks. As Chalfant and Flathouse (1971) have pointed out, when a child is suspected of having memory deficits, one must ask how his or her memory varies in relation to (1) the nature of the various tasks, (2) how the tasks were presented (auditory, visual, haptic), (3) the child himself or herself, and (4) the type of response required of the child on each task (recognition, recall, reproduction in graphic form, etc.).

Disorders of Thinking

Thinking disorders represent another behavior facet of the learning disabled. Although cognitive or thinking functions are not easily studied apart from perception, memory, language, social, and motor learning, some learning disabled children exhibit unusual or even bizarre thinking patterns, while other skills may be largely intact. The early work of Strauss and Lehtinen (1947) documented evidence of "peculiarities in thinking, reasoning, and concept formation deviating markedly from the normal" (p.54) in spite of normal intelligence.

An earlier study by Strauss and Werner (1942) required both typical and learning disabled children to examine a group of 56 objects and then arrange them in groups according to some common aspect. The typical children tended to group objects of a common function (e.g., bed, chair, and table as furniture), but the learning disabled population tended to sort objects according to unusual and often irrational principles. The examiners summarized the thinking patterns demonstrated by the LD population as: (1) sorting objects according to form or color (pencil and lipstick, or a silver whistle and a silver coin); (2) sorting objects according to an unessential detail (sandpaper and matchbook cover because of the sandpaper glued to the matchbook); (3) sorting objects on the basis of some perceived, vague similarity of function (a stamp and a razor blade because the blade can be used to cut out the stamp); or (4) sorting on the basis of relationship in a hypothetical situation (whistle and sunglasses because one may find them both on a policeman).

Similar observations are frequent in situations when LD children are asked to describe the relationship between objects. They often are bound to the more observable and concrete characteristics of the objects. When asked to tell how a rabbit and a guinea pig were alike, one eleven-year-old boy said, "You can pick them up, you can feed them, and you can put them in a cage." He failed to grasp other more sophisticated attributes of the animals, such as class, form, or function.

Children who are rigid and inflexible in their ability to perceive relationships among experiences are disadvantaged when asked to make judgments and understand relationships at the even more abstract level required for language facility, mathematical reasoning, and reading comprehension. Myklebust, Bannochie, and Killen (1971) suggested that learning disabled children with cognitive disorders need instruction that provides *simultaneity*; i.e., the child is given clear-cut and, whenever possible, concrete examples of a concept, which maximizes the probability of learning the correct concept.

For example, if attempting to teach the concept of "red" as a color, one presents a series of concrete objects simultaneous to the verbal presentation of the word "red." ("This is red"—simultaneous to showing a red apple. "This is red"—simultaneous to showing a red pencil. "This is red"—simultaneous to showing a red block. "This is red"—simultaneous to showing a red pen. "This is *not* red"—simultaneous to showing a green apple.) The objects that share the attribute "red" present as concretely as possible the common feature that distinguishes them as having the attribute of "redness." The presentation of a green apple as a negative example of "redness" provides the cue that leads to development of the abstract concept that "red" is a particular color shared by many objects and is not the name of the object itself. Engelmann (1969) discusses many examples of concept teaching in his writing.

Although perception, memory, and cognitive thinking cannot be separated as discrete functions, one should be aware that, among the learning disabled population, some children do not manifest particular deficiencies in perception or memory; yet, their thinking is rigid and concrete. Some can perceive and recall words but fail to comprehend the meaning of the printed passage. Others may recognize numerals and be able to follow rote computational patterns in arithmetic without understanding the meaning of those processes. These children may learn basic skills at a rote level in the primary grades but experience greater difficulty as they advance into higher grades where reasoning and critical thinking are demanded to a greater extent.

Disorders in Perceptual-Motor Learning

Perceptual-motor disturbances as a dimension of learning disabilities have been studied by Getman (1965), Kephart (1967), Barsch (1967), Ayres (1973) and others. Perceptual-motor learning involves integrating perceptions with motor activity, and subsequently using the integrated motor activity to monitor and correct these perceptions. In kicking a ball, a child *feels* the body motion as the ball is kicked, is aware of the body as the ball lifts into the air, *sees* the ball in relation to the kick, and *hears* the ball land. Through practice, the child comes to coordinate all of these perceptions into an integrated, smooth, rhythmic activity.

Such learning is important to the child's mastery over environment and the ability to manipulate it. Kephart (1967) stresses the importance of a child's mastery over space and time as a crucial prerequisite to dealing with symbolic learning (language, reading, arithmetic). This position has resulted in the frequent assumption that perceptual-motor disturbances are causes of learning disability rather than its correlates, and this assumption has led to remedial teaching programs which have stressed the development of perceptual-motor skills with the notion that other problems (e.g., reading, spelling, arithmetic) would disappear after the child had developed adequate perceptual-motor skills. Such practices have been questioned (Hammill, Goodman, & Wiederholt, 1974). Training in perceptual-motor skills likely is most effective in developing motor skills necessary for acceptance in the child's peer group and not as a substitute for academic instruction.

EDUCATIONAL PROGRAMMING CONSIDERATIONS

The construct of verbal and nonverbal learning disorders is useful in discussing educational programming considerations, although the reader is reminded that no student should be perceived as fitting into a defined category and each is unique in the challenges he or she presents. Nevertheless, the following discussion pinpoints specific areas of disability to which teachers should be alerted in understanding, identifying, and assisting students within their realm of responsibility.

Verbal Learning Disabilities

Verbal learning disabilities may be considered as problems in the areas of oral language comprehension, oral language usage, reading, spelling, written language, and arithmetic.

Disabilities in Oral Language Comprehension

To profit from classroom instruction, the learner must be able to understand and comprehend oral language. The learner is surrounded by a continuous barrage of verbal language throughout the school day. It may take the form of storytelling, classroom discussion, oral directions, asking questions, and so on. Language comprehension problems of some learning disabled children have been recognized as an integral part of their disability, if not the basis for it (Johnson & Myklebust, 1967; Lerner, 1976; Wiig & Semel, 1976).

Language comprehension problems vary in both nature and severity. The degree of comprehension difficulty may range on a continuum from mild to severe. The most severely disabled youngsters may fail totally to understand spoken language and thus behave similarly to children who are deaf. Other children may fail to comprehend the significance of certain classes of words; e.g., they may comprehend nouns but have difficulty with certain verbs that denote tense. For example, a child may comprehend the sentence, "I ate two cookies," but fail to comprehend the sentence, "By tomorrow, I *will have eaten* four cookies." Other children may fail to grasp the significance of linguistic markers that denote meaning critical to understanding conversations, stories, or directions—for example, the marker *s* which signals plurality, *ed* which signals past tense, or *er* and *est* which signal comparative features of objects or experiences.

Studies by Wiig and Semel (1973, 1974) showed that learning disabled children and adolescents have significantly more difficulty than typical children in comprehending sentences that require logical operations such as, "The elephant sat on the mouse. Who was on the bottom?" "Give another name for your mother's father." Semel and Wiig (1975) also found that learning disabled children performed significantly poorer than their normal counterparts in comprehending and expressing sentences designed to assess comprehension of specific language features. Clinical examples of learning disabled children's difficulty with multiple word meanings are numerous. For example, the rigid semantic meaning boundaries established by some children create difficulties in interpreting shifts in word meanings according to context. A child may comprehend the meaning of the word *run* as an active verb in, "I can *run*," but fail to comprehend easily the meaning of the word *run* in other structures and contexts such as, "He hit a home *run*"; "I need to *run* by the store and pick up a few things"; or, "He had a *run* of bad luck."

Other children have difficulty in comprehending question forms, particularly questions prefaced by *who, what, why, where,* and *when.* Some children fail to interpret the kind of information denoted by the particular *wh* word and subsequently do not process the sentence accurately. An eleven-year-old boy, after hearing a story about pioneers, was asked, "Why did pioneers use conestoga wagons in their travels westward?" The boy elaborated for several minutes on pioneer life, hazards encountered by the pioneers, and so forth. When interrupted and instructed to answer the question, he couldn't do it. He had failed to comprehend the specific nature of the question, although he understood key words which stimulated a considerable amount of spontaneous language about the subject.

Other children may comprehend simple, straightforward sentences when presented one at a time, but fail to comprehend one sentence embedded within another. For example, a child may understand, "Gary lives next door" and, "He has a broken arm," when presented as two distinctly different sentences. However, the child may fail to comprehend the same phrases in the sentence, "Gary, the boy with the broken arm, lives next door."

Children's ability to comprehend spoken language often is taken for granted, and teachers may fail to realize that several children in the classroom might have difficulty understanding certain features of what is said. Children with these difficulties may appear confused when given oral directions, or they may give the impression of being bored or inattentive during a class discussion, or they may depend upon watching other children to determine what the group has been instructed to do. Teachers should be perceptive and alert to such behaviors so these conditions may be identified and remediated through teaching strategies which may include repeating oral directions in a simpler form and/or simultaneously demonstrating them.

Disabilities in Oral Language Usage

Some children master oral language comprehension at a high level and yet have marked difficulty in using oral language to express their wants and ideas. These children may present a variety of problems which affect their classroom performance.

Johnson and Myklebust (1967) have described children who are knowledgeable of word meanings but cannot readily retrieve specific words for spontaneous oral usage. A mother of a five-year-old boy who has severe language usage problems related an example of how her son relied on gestures and pantomime to communicate. The mother said that when she asked her son what he had for a snack in kindergarten each day, he immediately responded by drawing a picture of it in the air and, in one case, "shaped his two forefingers and two thumbs into the perfect shape of a pretzel." In another instance, when a squirrel had been hit by a car in front of his house, he ran in and banged one fist against his other hand, screeched, and fell to the floor to communicate the happening to the family.

Some less severely disabled children may have difficulty with spontaneous recall of words, which results in vague, diffuse oral language use. One nine-year-old boy, when asked to tell what *nuisance* meant, paused for awhile and after much thought said, "Well, you know, it's like, uh . . . well, when she, when, uh, well, it's like when Aunt Helen comes." He knew the meaning of the word *nuisance* but had extreme difficulty in finding the language to convey that knowledge. Such children often rely on gestures, pantomime, or use their hands to illustrate concepts while they attempt to talk.

Numerous studies have reported the nature of language usage problems among learning disabled children. Wiig and Semel (1975) found that, when compared to normal learners, learning disabled children (1) had greater difficulty in giving correct word definitions orally; (2) were less quick and accurate in naming verbal opposites and pictorial presentations; (3) produced more agrammatical sentences and grammatical sentences of shorter length; and (4) had longer response lags when asked to produce sentences orally. They suggest that these findings are associated with delays in cognitive processing and production of semantic units, as well as reduced ability to retrieve verbal labels and syntactic structures.

In a study of learning disabled adolescents, Wiig and Roach (1975) found that the learning disabled population, when compared with normal peers, had greater difficulty in tasks that required immediate recall of sentences varying in meaning and sentence structure. The learning disabled subjects repeated significantly fewer sentences verbatim than their normal counterparts. They appeared to rely heavily on meanings within the sentences to aid their recall. The greatest difficulty appeared to be in recalling sentences that contained a minimum of cues to meaning (semantic) or sentence structure (syntactic). The implications of these findings are important when we consider the extent to which normal language structure is stressed for adolescents in public speaking or as a basis for writing down thoughts and ideas.

In a study of the use of morphological rules in language production, Wiig, Semel, and Crouse (1973) found that learning disabled children gave significantly fewer correct responses than demonstrated by the typical population in denoting third-person singular (she walk*s*), singular and plural possessives (the boy's club versus the boys' club), and adjectival inflections (quick - quick*er* - quick*est*). The results led to the conclusion that learning disabled children were delayed in their ability to produce specific features of oral language.

Moran and Byrne (1977) found that learning disabled children also had fewer correct responses in a test to elicit future, present, and past tense markers for 50 verbs across 10 categories. Although the authors noted differences in performance between the two groups in favor of the normals, they limited their interpretations because of a lack of normative data for the normal children above age seven.

Some children demonstrate intact oral language usage clinically but have trouble constructing sentences when asked to use words and phrases that require complex structure. For example, one thirteen-year-old boy used grammatically intact sentences in conversation, but his language seemed similar to that of a younger child. When asked to incorporate the word *why* in a sentence, he responded, "Why did I come here what for?" His response to the request to use the word *herself* in a sentence was, "Herself will be late."

Children who have usage problems often restrict their language to simple structures they can generate and thus may go undetected in the classroom. They also may fail to participate in class discussions because the demands on their ability to formulate oral language are too great. Teachers must be alert in identifying children who comprehend oral language at a significantly higher level than they are able to produce it.

The teacher's role is significant in remediation of specific disabilities. When one pinpoints a particular difficulty, instruction can be incorporated readily into regular teaching strategies. For example, when Johnny asks, "How we go?" the teacher may unobtrusively reflect the question orally as, "How do we go?" before responding to the intent of the question. Or, when Mary says, "He runned over my bicycle," the teacher may reflect the correct form in a recognition or clarification response such as, "He ran over your bicycle?"

Although language problems are viewed as an integral part of many learning disabilities, understanding the nature of these problems is hindered by at least three factors: (1) the lack of valid language norms for children and adolescents; (2) the complex nature of language problems exhibited by learning disabled children (Wiig & Semel, 1975); and (3) the unknown interactional effects between language disabilities and other disorders of learning. Although research efforts continue, a vast frontier of knowledge remains to be discovered about language problems of the learning disabled.

Disabilities in Reading

Reading failure among children is probably the most common cause of teacher concern. This failure may be attributed to a number of external reasons including poor instruction, lack of interest and motivation, and limited opportunity. These possible causes should be investigated before instituting any remedial procedures.

The field of learning disabilities, having emerged from the study of brain injury, has focused attention on those reading disorders associated with central nervous system dysfunction (Lerner, 1975), often excluding reading problems associated with emotional disturbance, mental retardation, sensory handicaps, or environmental deprivation. The learning disabled child's reading problems traditionally have been analyzed by assessing strengths and weaknesses in underlying processing abilities (perception, memory, etc.) upon which reading skills are contingent. The function of the learning disability teacher is to assess the child's language abilities, auditory and visual perception skills, and memory functions so that a diagnosis of the reading disorder can be made and followed by a plan of clinical instruction to correct the disability.

The study of reading disorders associated with central nervous system dysfunction from a medical orientation accounts for the term *dyslexia* being used in many references to reading disorders. Much of the literature discusses directional orientation confusion, visual memory functions, auditory and visual modality impairments, and cerebral dominance problems as correlates, if not indeed causes, of reading disability (Money, 1962).

Johnson and Myklebust (1967) address two types of reading disorders among the learning disabled population—those associated with *visual processing* and those stemming from disturbances in *auditory processing*. Reading disorders of a visual nature are characterized by: (1) visual discrimination difficulties and confusion of similar letters and words; (2) slow rate of perception; (3) letter and word reversals and inversions; (4) difficulty in following and retaining visual sequences; (5)

associated visual memory problems; (6) inferior drawings; (7) difficulty in visual analysis and synthesis; (8) marked inferiority of visual skills in relation to auditory skills on diagnostic tests.

Remedial teaching procedures are based on the premise that stronger auditory skills should be emphasized during the initial phase of instruction, so the children can learn to identify and associate the words they hear with the words they see. Remediation of visual skills is stressed simultaneously with the emphasis on auditory reading instruction. The primary concern is both for achievement in reading and for remediation of the deficient processes considered necessary for reading.

The second type of reading disorder discussed by Johnson and Myklebust (1967) is associated with deficits in the auditory processing skills which underlie reading. These deficiencies are characterized by: (1) associated auditory discrimination and perceptual problems which hinder the use of phonetic analysis; (2) difficulty in separating words into their component phonemes and syllables or in blending them into whole words; (3) difficulty in spontaneous recall of the sounds associated with letters or words; (4) disturbances in auditory sequencing; and (5) a general preference of visual activities over auditory tasks (e.g., the child may prefer to look at a picture story sequence rather than listen to the story read orally). Johnson and Myklebust (1967) have generated principles of teaching reading to children with auditory processing problems, including the suggestion that the initial instruction phase should stress visual recognition of whole words, along with clinical teaching to strengthen auditory abilities necessary for subsequent word analysis.

For the past 10 years, studies of reading disorders among the learning disabled population have examined the nature of abilities within the various perceptual modalities that account for the learning disability (Voort & Senf, 1973; Kershner, 1975; Koppitz, 1975; Badian, 1977); the validity of differentiating modalities for testing and remedial teaching (Ringler & Smith, 1973; Camp, 1973; Larsen, Rogers, & Sowell, 1976; Arter & Jenkins, 1977); and the teaching efficacy for various modalities (Silberberg, Ivensen, & Goins, 1973; Wilson, Harris, & Harris, 1976).

Although individual studies often contradict one another, two generalizations have emerged from the above studies. First, no single, discrete process or skill is solely responsible for reading disability. Rather, reading is a complex process involving the simultaneous interaction of perceptual, memory, language, and cognitive functions. Any search for common, isolated factors in reading disability assumes a naive and simplistic approach to learning.

Second, remedial training of selected processes as measured on psychometric instruments results in some improvement of the processes assessed by that instrument. There is little evidence, however, that improvement of that process transfers to increased competence in academic areas. The statement has been made that if you want a child to learn how to read, teach him *reading*, not visual or auditory exercises to improve processes that supposedly underlie reading.

A growing awareness of the relationship between language competence and reading ability is reflected by Lerner (1976) Wiig and Semel (1976), and Wallach and Goldsmith (1977). The linguistic aspect of reading has been pursued by a number of researchers including Ruddell (1970) and Wardhaugh (1969). The total psycholinguistic view of reading is proposed by those who perceive reading as the active process of reconstructing meaning from language represented by printed symbols (Smith, Goodman, & Meredith, 1970; Smith, 1971). Emphasis is placed on discovering how readers respond quickly and accurately to many cues in language (knowledge of sentence patterns, linguistic markers that signal meaning, melody pattern, etc.) rather than on isolating words or patterns of letters on the printed page. This view of reading primarily focuses on the reader's implicit knowledge and facility with oral language rather than on discrete and often nonmeaningful elements of perceptual processing that are assumed to underlie reading disorders.

This point of view is congruent with that of Johnson and Myklebust (1967); i.e., comprehension of the printed word depends upon the reader's ability to comprehend first the spoken word form. If a child has difficulty comprehending certain oral language structures, he or she will have difficulty comprehending the printed form.

As an example, a fifth-grade boy scored at the second-grade level on a silent reading comprehension test given in his school. After working with the boy for several days, school personnel became aware that he was comprehending significantly better than his test score indicated. Examination of the reading test administered by the school showed that of 50 questions used to measure reading comprehension, 41 were questions prefaced by *wh* words. Personnel had noted earlier during the language evaluation that the boy exhibited difficulty in oral language comprehension, particularly with *wh* questions. Since he was unable to comprehend the question forms orally, he had no basis for comprehending the questions in written form. The boy then was administered a reading comprehension test in which he was able to select a picture that best described the story he read, and the resulting score was near grade level. The conclusion is that the boy's reading comprehension of some sentences was hindered by his failure to comprehend them first orally.

Relationships between certain language abilities and reading mastery have been noted in various studies. Vogel (1974) found that disabled readers were deficient in recognizing melody patterns that signal declarative and question forms in oral language. This supports the earlier finding of Clay and Imlach (1971) that efficient readers clearly demonstrate a greater degree of proficiency in using stress, pitch, and juncture in oral reading. Also, Vogel (1977) has reported more recently that disabled readers are significantly poorer than normal readers in their knowledge of rules governing the combination of the smallest units of meaning (morphemes) into words. The questions remain: To what extent does the good reader use knowledge of certain features of oral language in reconstructing meaning while reading; and how do disabled readers differ from normal readers in this dimension? While the exact nature of language deficiencies among learning disabled children still is unknown, the research strongly suggests that a relationship does exist between language abilities and reading proficiency.

When examining the relationship between language disabilities and reading disorders, one must guard against simplistic interpretations that lend to belief in a one-to-one correspondence between specific language disabilities and reading disorders. Such interpretations lead to the development of superficial remedial techniques which fail to recognize the dynamic nature of the language system (both oral and written). We cannot afford another era of instructing underlying language abilities based on blind faith that reading abilities will improve as a result.

Children fail to read for many reasons. Children with learning disabilities may have:

1. Oral language comprehension problems which interfere with their ability to derive meaning from the printed word form;
2. Difficulty with visual skills for discrimination of letters and word forms;
3. Difficulty in auditory discrimination analysis and synthesis necessary for the mastery of phonic skills;
4. Disturbances in recognizing the equivalence between the spoken and printed language forms; or
5. Some combination of these.

When we view the varied nature of reading disorders among the LD population, clearly no one method of reading instruction is appropriate for all. Rather, one must take inventory of each child's strengths and weaknesses directly related to the reading disorder and use that inventory as a basis for making clinical teaching decisions regarding the most suitable strategy or method.

Disabilities in Spelling

To understand the varied sources of difficulty in spelling among learning disabled students, one must examine the integrities required for spelling proficiency. To spell words meaningfully, the child first must be able to read them. This should not suggest that teaching of spelling be abandoned for the child with a reading disorder, but rather that teaching specific spelling words should not be attempted until the learner can recognize and read them meaningfully.

Students must be able to hear sounds and syllables within words if they are to analyze words auditorially and set them up in a sequence to guide written spelling. Children who have difficulty in breaking whole words into individual sounds or syllables may have difficulty in producing the written form of words. Their repertoire of functional integrities for spelling is limited. These children may rely solely on memorizing the visual form of words—which severely limits spelling proficiency.

The proficient speller also must be able to remember how the letters and words look in order to generate the written form on paper. Sounding out the parts of words in order to spell them is not enough. One must remember the visual image of the letters and word parts in order to write them. The child whose visual memory for letters and words is weak may be compelled to spell words the way they sound, with little regard for their visual form. These children have particular difficulty with words that do not have a high degree of sound-letter correspondence (e.g., through, know, reign).

Spelling words in the written form also assumes integrity in the fine motor skills necessary for grasping a pencil and forming letters in a correct motor sequence. Some disabled children may be able to recognize the correct written form of a word but have extreme difficulty in executing the motor movements necessary to write the word. Their written production may be so poor that spelling ability is masked by illegible writing.

With an understanding of the varied sources of difficulty that may interfere with spelling, the astute observer in the classroom may be able to identify the general nature of children's spelling difficulties. Spelling words then can be organized consistent with the learning principles most appropriate for individual children. Johnson and Myklebust (1967) set forth some principles aimed at differential teaching approaches based on the nature of the spelling deficit. First, children should be able to read words fluently before they are asked to spell them. Second, words should be separated into those that have fairly consistent sound-symbol correspondences (phonetic words) and those which have no consistent spelling rules (nonphonetic words).

Teaching phonetic spelling words emphasizes strengths in the child's association of written letters or syllables with the oral word form. *The ultimate goal is for the child to listen to a spoken word, auditorially analyze it into its parts, and then write it.* Nonphonetic words are taught by a *whole word approach.* The words are presented as wholes, followed by omission of letters in various positions within the words. Students are asked to supply the missing letters until they gradually learn to write the whole word from memory.

Some children, however, may be unable to demonstrate competency in spelling because they cannot read. Others may have adequate reading skills but be unable to spell words in the written form for a number of reasons already discussed. Our appreciation of children with spelling difficulties broadens when we analyze the nature of the spelling task in terms of the patterns of strengths and weaknesses of each child. With this appreciation, efforts to individualize in the classroom become easier.

Disabilities in Written Language

The use of written language requires many abilities. One first must have acquired proficiency in understanding *spoken* language, as well as proficiency in *reading.* The writer must *formulate ideas* in his or her mind and *sequence* those ideas in a *logical order.* Then the writer must *translate ideas into words* and *arrange these words into sentences.* In attempting to place sentences into the written form, one must be able to generate grammatically intact sentences, remember visual forms of letters and words, and translate the visual images into motor patterns necessary for forming the letters on paper. Because of the complex nature of and many component abilities required by the writing task, a number of different disabilities may interfere with learning to use written langauge.

Johnson and Myklebust (1967) distinguish among written language deficiencies as those associated with oral language comprehension, oral language usage, reading problems, and more specific disorders of written language. Children who have a narrow understanding of spoken language or who have limited language usage are highly restricted in communicating through written language. Their written language may reflect the way they hear language or the way they speak. The following note from a fourth-grade girl to her teacher reflects her oral language in writing:

My sister she needs help to becource she is in speshul head and she cate wirt in cersy.

Or, written language may be deficient because of reading difficulties. One must be able to read the printed word before producing it in the written form. If written language is deficient because of a lack of prerequisite language and reading skills, those skills must be developed before instruction in written language is stressed. In the classroom, instruction priorities must be sequenced to ensure a good basis of oral language understanding, usage, and adequate reading skills before expecting a student to master written language.

Even if oral language and reading abilities are intact, other kinds of disabilities may affect competency in written language (Johnson & Myklebust, 1967). Disturbances in visual-motor integration may impair a child's ability to perform the motor movements necessary to form letters and words. The child may know what he or she wants to say but cannot express it in writing. The learner may not be able to remember what the letters and words look like in order to write them. The child with a deficiency in visual memory for words and letters may be incapacitated when trying to express ideas. The child whose written language is impaired because of poor visual memory generally can copy letters and words if they are shown, whereas the child with a visual-motor integration disability usually is not helped by being shown a model of the letter or word.

Some children have adequate visual-motor integration and visual memory but have trouble ordering words into grammatically acceptable sentences for writing. Their difficulty is in sentence construction and organization. Their ideas may be intact, but their ability to use rules of sentence organization and punctuation is weak. The following story written by a ten-year-old boy illustrates difficulty in sentence construction:

> He is playing with the toys. He likes to play because he likes to play a lot. He is play on the table because. He is playing a the tabe because it smooth. Ther men and girl and boy and laty.

Remedial instruction for written language depends upon the nature of the disability. The aim of instruction for the child with difficulty in visual-motor integration is to help him or her develop the motor patterns necessary for forming the letters to spell words. The child whose writing is impaired because of inability to remember what letters look like needs assistance in facilitating the ability to recall images of words and letters. Children whose written language is marked by sentence construction and punctuation errors need instruction in learning to monitor their written language for such errors. The chapter, "Disorders in Written Language," in Johnson and Myklebust (1967) is a valuable source of specific teaching procedures for various types of written language disorders.

The prospect of teaching a child with poor written language skills becomes less overwhelming if it is approached by examining the particular difficulty of the individual child. Depending upon the nature of the disability, progress as a result of remedial instruction will vary from student to student. Some children may need to demonstrate their knowledge through informal oral testing during the period in which written language instruction is in progress. Some children will continue to have difficulty in mastering written language skills in spite of excellent oral language and reading abilities. Some always may be limited in their mastery of written language, and subsequent adjustments should be made in their curriculum to compensate for the written language inadequacy.

Perhaps one of the most important concepts teachers should remember is that frustration with a child's poor written work is not nearly as intense as the personal frustration of the child. A teacher must perceive students from the point of view that they can do some things better than other things, and failure to respond in certain learning areas may be more a matter of *can't* than *won't*.

Disabilities in Arithmetic

Children with disabilities in language acquisition and reading frequently have accompanying deficiencies in mathematics. Such disabilities may be attributable to many causes, but this discussion focuses only on those associated with learning disabilities.

Students with disturbances in sense of quantity at the experiential level are distinctly disadvantaged in mastering quantitative concepts represented symbolically by numerals. A fifth-grade girl was referred for help because of a severe arithmetic problem. She had average intellectual ability, and demonstrated reading at a middle fourth-grade level. Her math achievement was determined at second-grade level. In spite of three summers of remedial math instruction, she had learned most of her addition and subtraction facts at only a rote level. She knew almost no multiplication or division facts. She revealed a poor grasp of the principle of *conservation of matter*. She was unable to recognize the same mass when it was altered in appearance but not quantity. This clearly began to relate to why she had failed to grasp the concepts of multiplication or division. Meaningful mastery of those processes assumes an understanding of shifts of quantity at an abstract level—i.e., 2 x 4 is the same as 1 x 8 or as 4 x 2. After one has gained an abstract understanding of numbers, or a quantitative sense, one can perform these operations meaningfully at an abstract level.

Johnson and Myklebust (1967) describe a number of characteristics associated with children who have disturbances in quantitative thinking, including:

1. Inability to establish one-to-one correspondence at a concrete level;
2. Inability to count meaningfully;
3. Inability to associate the spoken form with the correct printed numeral;
4. Inability to learn the cardinal and ordinal systems of counting;
5. Inability to visualize clusters of objects within a larger group;
6. Inability to grasp the principles of conservation of quantity;
7. Inability to perform arithmetic operations;
8. Inability to understand the meaning of the process signs;
9. Inability to understand arrangement of numbers on a page;
10. Inability to follow and remember the sequence of steps to be used in various mathematical operations;
11. Inability to understand the principles of measurement;
12. Inability to read maps and graphs; and
13. Inability to select principles for solving problems in arithmetic.

The above characteristics represent a wide range of behaviors, but they often appear as clusters of related difficulties in learning disabled children, and suggest an underlying and pervasive disturbance in quantitative judgment. The primary principle of instruction for these children is to aid understanding and interpretation of comparative quantities at a concrete level so mental manipulation of numerical quantities can be developed later at an abstract level (Johnson & Myklebust, 1967).

Although a disturbance in quantitative thinking may be a chief factor in the arithmetic disability of many learning disabled children, other disturbances may interfere with the acquisition of math skills. Children who have language comprehension difficulties may have trouble with words having meanings unique to math (e.g., carry, set, series) or in comprehending question forms such as, "Who has the most clay, Mary or Ann? Why?" To respond to these questions, the child must be able to interpret question forms.

Reading disabilities may interfere with arithmetic mastery of story problems; and visual perceptual problems may interfere with numeral interpretation (e.g., reversing 6 and 9, or 17 and 71). Children who have perceptual-motor problems may have difficulty in copying numerals and maintaining adequate spatial orientation on the printed page. They may be able to conceptually comprehend math concepts but have trouble in writing numerals and maintaining organization on paper.

The child whose difficulty in math stems from confusion of word meanings needs instruction in learning the multiple meanings of words and how specific meanings relate to math. The child whose math difficulty is primarily in reading story problems needs assistance with reading when the assignments involve reading. Children who have perceptual problems that interfere with copying numerals or spacing numerals in written computation need assistance in structuring their work on the printed page. One must analyze the nature of the arithmetic problem beyond a simple analysis of error patterns, in order to determine the most appropriate instruction principles for a child's particular disability.

Nonverbal Learning Disabilities

The assessment and remediation of learning disabilities have centered primarily on verbal disabilities involving the understanding and use of spoken language, reading, spelling, and written language. More recently, attention has been directed toward nonverbal learning disabilities, which include almost any other skill not involved in understanding and using spoken or written language (Myklebust, 1975).

Spatial orientation represents the ability to identify one's location or position in relation to other features in the environment. A stable sense of orientation in space at an abstract level is essential to the internal awareness of directions, distance, and location necessary to guide movement within the environment. A solid grasp of spatial orientation prevents one from being helplessly lost.

Consider a child, Jim, who does not have a grasp of where he is spatially in the environment. He is a fourth-grader in an expansive, modular elementary building. Jim is sent to the library to return a book or carry a message to the office. He lacks an overall map of the building in his mind to guide his movement through the building to his destination and to return to the classroom. Consequently, Jim has to rely upon peering into every classroom, hoping to see a familiar group of faces or his teacher. His internal abstraction of where he is in relation to other points has failed him. He has to depend on a trial-and-error search. This child may be thought to be dawdling or meddling in the building, but in reality he is depending on a reduced set of cues to direct his movement.

Another closely related disturbance is that of *directionality*, or the internal sense of right and left. In moving through the environment, everyone makes countless moves that require unconscious decisions regarding choice of direction. In turning a door knob, in responding to the verbal direction to "turn left" or "raise your right hand," or in letter and numeral writing, the unconscious sense of direction is required.

Disturbances in *time orientation* represent another dimension of nonverbal learning disabilities. The normal maturation process includes development of an internal or abstract sense of time (Bateman, 1969). Adults generally are in touch with and can estimate how long they have been sitting in a meeting, how much longer until dinner, or how many days or months until a certain holiday without consulting a clock or a calendar. Most of us have an internal or intuitive sense of time. Time orientation is important in estimating and budgeting output and effort when deadlines are involved. Teachers often give deadlines along with assignments, saying, "You have 15 minutes to complete your arithmetic problems" or, "You have two weeks to write the book report." These deadlines lack specific meaning for a child who has a limited sense of time. Behavior may be characterized by tardiness, disorganization, and confusion.

An eleven-year-old boy enrolled in a learning disabilities summer practicum. The Fourth of July was to occur on Friday that year, which meant that classes would be in session only four days that week. On Monday morning Doug announced that, "I won't be in school tomorrow," because the family was going on vacation. Since his parents had agreed that Doug would attend the class daily and had not informed school personnel about an impending vacation, the teachers waited to see if Doug would appear on Tuesday. He did arrive on Tuesday and again announced that he "won't be coming tomorrow" because the family would be leaving for vacation. The same incident occurred on Wednesday and on Thursday. He did go away with his parents Friday for the three-day holiday weekend and was back in class the following Monday. Upon talking further with Doug and his parents, the teachers found that he had failed to develop a mastery of judgment regarding time. To Doug, "tomorrow" indicated any of several days after today. "Next year" represented anything beyond the next few weeks. He also used "last year" indiscriminately to describe his trip to Denver six months earlier and his trip to Disneyland when he was seven years old.

Clearly, disturbances in spatial orientation, directionality, and time orientation limit one's ability to respond to demands of the environment. One must consider the cues needed by particular children to aid them in developing such mastery. Use of an hourglass, three-minute egg timer, and kitchen timer is helpful for children who have faulty abstractions of time. They need concrete cues to make time less abstract. Children with spatial orientation difficulty may need to be made aware of visual markers, or even landmarks, to facilitate their independent movement through the environment. Children who are directionally confused may need visual markers such as arrows to provide cues to making decisions about direction.

Social perception disturbances present one of the least understood problems of students. Social perception disturbance in a person has been defined by Johnson and Myklebust (1967) as one's inability to understand the social environment, particularly in terms of self behavior in response to it. With normal development, a child begins to comprehend the nature of various situations and to adapt behaviors according to salient cues within a situation. Children learn that one set of behaviors is acceptable in church, another set acceptable in the classroom, and another set at the playground. Individuals having social perception difficulty fail to read and integrate relevant cues in a situation and to respond appropriately to those cues.

One fourteen-year-old girl with normal intelligence was referred for evaluation because of learning and behavior problems. Her parents and teachers reported unpredictable behaviors. She often behaved impulsively and did things to horrify people around her. She would on occasion dart through a rack of dresses in a department store (once turning the rack over), touch all the pieces of pie and cake in a cafeteria line, making indentations, talk aloud in church, snuff candles because she was fascinated by them, and engage in many other such activities described by her parents. The most remarkable feature was that the girl didn't perceive the inappropriateness of her behavior and was devastated when punished. She didn't appear to understand why peers avoided her.

Bryan (1977) investigated the comparative abilities of normal and learning disabled children to judge affective states of a female actress expressing positive and negative affects. Children were shown film clips, without audio cues, of the actress interacting with children and were asked to interpret emotional expressions. Learning disabled children were found to have more difficulty in interpreting subtle communications in affect than did normal children. These findings support the hypothesis that learning disabled children's social adjustment problems may arise from difficulty in comprehending nonverbal communication rather than stem from academic failure.

The above findings suggest a basis for parents and teachers to assist children who seem to have difficulty in interpreting nonverbal behavior. This assistance may mean interpreting for a child the effects of certain behaviors and other people's responses. Such interpretation can provide information from which children having social perception limitations can learn to adapt their behaviors in relation to human responses.

Behavior Disorders Associated With Learning Disabilities

Among the population of learning disabled children, some are impulsive, easily distracted, and excessively active. Many children in the general population may be considered highly active, but the behavior of those who are hyperactive appears qualitatively different from that of the normally active child. This hyperactive behavior is marked by its situational inappropriateness in learning (Connors, 1971).

The relationship between hyperactivity and learning disability is poorly defined, primarily because of (1) lack of agreement among observers in operationally defining hyperactivity, and (2) the absence of research regarding hyperactivity as a dimension of learning disabilities (Hallahan and Cruickshank, 1973).

Cruickshank (1967) distinguishes *motor hyperactivity* (excessive motor activity) from *sensory hyperactivity* (impulsiveness and inattention) and suggests that the two may occur jointly or separately. Clearly, behavior marked by excessive running around the room is different from the inability to sustain attention for a task at hand, but either type of behavior likely will restrict the learner's involvement in academic tasks, thereby reducing learning and achievement.

Many points of view can be heard regarding the concept of hyperactivity. Keogh (1971) discusses three hypotheses about the nature of hyperactivity and its relation to learning disorders. The first hypothesis is that hyperactivity may be associated with neurological impairment as the basis for learning and behavior disorders. The assumption of organic dysfunction generally is held by medically oriented researchers, with subsequent emphasis on the use of stimulant medication for treatment. The effectiveness of medication in managing hyperactivity varies. In a review of research reported by Freeman (1966), medication was found to improve *learning* in one-third of the studies, and medication improved *behavior* in nearly one-half of the studies.

The inconclusive results of research are not surprising in view of the difficulty presented in defining and measuring hyperactivity. Keogh (1971) suggests that the view of hyperactivity as a manifestation of neurological impairment may be valid for some children, but it is not a comprehensive explanation for the learning problems of all hyperactive children.

A second hypothesis regarding hyperactivity suggests that the child may be neurologically intact but the nature and extent of motor activity interferes with accurate intake of information (Keogh, 1971). During the information-seeking phase of learning new information, excessive motor activity may interfere with the learner's clear grasp of information, thus reducing learning efficiency. Based on this hypothesis, strategies to reduce the amount of motor activity during instruction may involve application of behavior modification techniques to decrease motor activity during critical phases of instruction, while simultaneously reinforcing attending behavior.

Studies in which hyperactivity has been managed through the use of behavior modification techniques have been reviewed by Prout (1977). He concludes that while results are equivocal, the use of behavioral and operant techniques has considerable potential for reducing hyperactive behavior. He also suggests cautious interpretation of reported success with behavior modification, in view of the persistent difficulty in defining hyperactivity and the inadequate research designs used in the reported studies.

A third hypothesis discussed by Keogh (1971) is that hyperactive children have rapid or impulsive decision-making processes, resulting in hasty responses before examination of an adequate amount of information upon which to base the proper response. This hypothesis again does not assume a neurological deficit. Rather, speed of response is viewed as a behavioral dimension that may be subject to behavioral alteration. Palkes, Stewart, and Kahana (1968) report success in training hyperactive boys to use self-directed verbal instructions to "slow down" while working on assigned tasks. This view of hyperactivity, based on speed of response, provides a framework for using behavioral techniques to delay the learner's response and simultaneously increase the amount of information the child is gathering, thus increasing the likelihood of a proper response.

Keogh and Margolis (1976) suggest that the construct of attention may be analyzed further in terms of particular children. Some children may have difficulty in coming to attention, and others may have difficulty primarily in seeking adequate information upon which to base a decision. Still others may have difficulty in sustaining attention for a prolonged period of time. Remediation for children may vary according to the specific nature of the attentional problem.

No one hypothesis or point of view is sufficient for the broad classification of hyperactivity and its effect on learning. Nevertheless, each alternative view provides a basis for intervention that may be effective for some children within the broader group. Research must be sustained to delineate the significant features of each child's behavior and point to appropriate individual intervention strategies.

DIAGNOSIS AND REMEDIATION

As the field of learning disabilities has evolved during the past 15 years, various approaches have emerged as to diagnosis of learning disabilities. Bateman (1967) has discussed several approaches to the diagnosis of children with learning problems. The first has been described as an *etiological* approach. The emphasis is on the cause of the disability and tends to focus on the assignment of children to diagnostic categories rather than providing instructionally relevant information. Statements representing this etiological approach may be, "severe learning disability due to probable anoxia sustained at the time of birth" or "hyperkinetic syndrome associated with central nervous system dysfunction." The etiological approach is useful primarily in identifying factors associated with learning disabilities so that subsequent preventive measures can be implemented.

Although the etiological approach was the focal point for medically oriented researchers, it had major shortcomings for the educator, who needed more information about how a child learns specific information. This need generated what Bateman (1967) termed the *diagnostic-remedial approach* as a means to identify "how to teach" as well as "what to teach." Diagnostic procedures were implemented in an effort to identify strengths and weaknesses of the learner in terms of preferred modality for learning, as well as pattern of perceptual and cognitive abilities. Upon gathering this information, a profile of strengths and weaknesses could be examined in order to plan educational remediation for the deficient educational skills. The decision might then be either to teach through the strengths or to train the weaknesses to become functional avenues for learning.

Results of the diagnostic-remedial approach introduced an era of what commonly is called *process training*, or *ability training*. The thrust of diagnostic efforts was toward identifying discrete elements of the learning processes, measuring them so the deficient ones could be identified, and providing remedial programs to strengthen the weak processes. This approach assumed that learning processes could be identified, remediated, and made functional so the child could profit from classroom instruction. Diagnosticians commonly administered a battery of tests to assess auditory and visual perceptual skills, and recommended that a child be given a set of training exercises to correspond to items failed on the diagnostic battery. In practice, the training exercises usually were in no way similar to academic tasks the child was failing and which had originally caused the child to be referred for evaluation.

The practice of identifying and training deficient processes assumed to be directly responsible for academic learning has been questioned on a number of points (Larsen & Hammill, 1975; Hammill & Larsen, 1974; Larsen, Rogers, & Sowell, 1976). The first point questions the validity of the assumption that learning processes can be reduced to discrete, independent functions for measurement. Second, reliable psychometric instruments are not available to measure such functions. Third, evidence is lacking to show that processes can be trained or remediated. Fourth, substantiating a rather simplistic cause-and-effect relationship between specific process deficiencies and failure in other academic subjects has not been validated.

Another approach to diagnosing learning disabilities has been through use of *criterion-referenced measures*. A criterion-referenced test is a usually informal measure designed to identify specific knowledge a child has learned and knowledge that hasn't been learned. The child's performance is not compared with performance of a norm group. Criterion-referenced measures range from a simple assessment of alphabet letters a child can name and not name to a more elaborate, comprehensive assessment such as the Brigance Diagnostic Inventory of Basic Skills (1976).

The child's performance is not measured in grade scores or age scores. Rather, an inventory of skills and knowledge is recorded so instruction can be directed toward teaching skills not yet learned. Criterion-referenced testing deals with observable behaviors rather than inferred processes upon which academic learning is assumed to be dependent. Criterion-referenced testing has attempted to move diagnosis closer to teaching processes, but it carries the risk that remedial instruction for the learning disabled child will become simply a redundant course of remediation in which the child is taught basically no differently than in the pre-testing period.

Any plan of diagnosis must integrate information about:

1. Skills a child has mastered;
2. Under what conditions the child is able to demonstrate those skills;
3. Skills the child has failed to master;
4. How conditions of unmastered tasks can be altered so the child can demonstrate mastery;
5. Observations of performance that can be used to generate principles of instruction to enable the child to use strengths to learn functional knowledge and skills more efficiently.

For example, a nine-year-old boy with good intellectual ability and adequate hearing and vision was referred to the learning disabilities teacher for evaluation because he was functioning poorly in reading, spelling, and written language. An IQ assessment revealed that he had high average abilities on both verbal and nonverbal tasks. He was able to comprehend spoken language, and his oral language usage was adequate. Academic achievement tests showed reading and comprehension at a low second-grade level. An inventory of sight words revealed which of the basic sight words he had learned and which ones needed to be taught. An inventory of phonic knowledge showed limited knowledge about sound-symbol associations. His classroom teacher stated that he was taught reading by using a combined sight word and phonic approach, so the evaluators assumed that he *had* been exposed to phonic skills. Then, why had he not learned phonic skills necessary for independence in reading?

In attempting to assess the prerequisite skills necessary for phonic mastery, a standardized test for auditory discrimination was administered; and the boy missed 50 percent of the discriminations. The test required him to discriminate differences between highly similar word pairs spoken by the examiner. During the testing, the child was seated with his back to the examiner and could not see the examiner's mouth. Following administration of this test, an administration of a similar set of word pairs was conducted informally, this time with the child facing the examiner. On the informal administration he again missed 50 percent of the word pairs. The examiner noted that the child closed his eyes tightly while listening to the word pairs. A third informal administration with another set of word pairs followed. This time the child was asked to watch the examiner's mouth to determine if he could "see a difference" in words as he listened to the word pairs. If the child could be trained to "see" such differences, one might hypothesize that he could be alerted to look for differences visually while the teacher was instructing with a phonic approach.

This example illustrates initial use of a standardized auditory discrimination test, in which the child failed to perform at a level similar to his age norm group. Rather than recommending training exercises to remediate auditory discrimination, a similar form of the task was presented under different conditions (child facing the examiner). Conditions were altered to determine the criteria under which the child could perform the task. Since his performance under this condition did not improve, the criterion of this task was varied along another dimension; he was instructed to combine visual cues to strengthen auditory discrimination. Since this approach appeared to aid his performance on the auditory discrimination task, one might hypothesize that he could be taught to *hear* differences more efficiently when he was instructed to *look* for differences simultaneously. This hypothesis for this child should be tested in the teaching phase to determine whether or not the specific alteration in instruction will prove useful to the child.

Because of the broad range of disabilities within the learning disabled population, no singular approach to diagnosis and remedial instruction is adequate. Rather, support is growing for the concept of *integrating* the knowledge about a child's processing strengths and weaknesses in providing instruction for the academic skills we wish to teach (Siegel, 1972). Lerner (1976) suggests that the learning disabilities teacher needs to have a broad repertoire of clinical teaching skills:

1. Task analysis of the learner involves specifying how a particular child functions—the things the child can and cannot do—modality-processing areas of strengths and weaknesses and attitudes and emotions as they affect learning.
2. Task analysis of the curriculum involves knowing the content of developmental skills and the hierarchy of components needed to perform such skills.
3. Relating the curriculum task to the learner involves the ability to coordinate data gathered from analysis of the learner with analysis of curriculum skills to be learned.
4. Making appropriate clinical decisions involves the ability to decide ways of using this information to bring about improvement in the child (pp.111-112).

This integrated approach to diagnosis and remedial instruction requires that the learning disabilities teacher have in-depth knowledge about the psychology of learning in normal children, knowledge about the impact of various disabilities on learning certain kinds of information, and thorough knowledge about the curricular content and demands of the entire school. Only with this information can the learning disabilities teacher work effectively with both the child and the regular classroom teachers.

DELIVERY OF EDUCATIONAL SERVICES

Several models have been developed to provide educational services to children with learning disabilities. These include the self-contained class; the resource room; and the itinerant teacher program.

The Self-Contained Special Class

One of the earliest models was the self-contained special class. Classes typically have consisted of between 6 and 12 children with learning disabilities. The learning disabilities teacher has been responsible for the total education of these children, including remedial teaching in their deficit areas. The intended purpose of the self-contained class is to provide intensive teaching in small groups for most of the school day, but this approach has presented several problems.

First, children often have been transported out of their home school community into a strange new school, promoting a feeling of alienation from their peers. Second, enrollment in a special class fulltime sometimes has placed a stigma on the children; they often have been labeled as "dummies" or the "retards." Third, removing children from the regular classrooms severely restricts their exposure to models of normal behavior which are crucial for social learning.

Also, grouping 10 children with learning disabilities implicitly assumes that their learning disabilities are similar. Experience indicates that this is not true. Among a group of 10 children, one may have a severe language comprehension problem affecting reading, writing, and spelling. Another may have adequate language comprehension but demonstrates a problem in the use of oral language. A third child may have good language comprehension and usage but has a reading disorder associated with an inability to integrate sounds and letters. A fourth child may have a reading comprehension problem plus a severe written language disorder. Another child may have adequate reading decoding and comprehension skills but is disabled in quantitative thinking, which interferes with spatial orientation and time judgment, math, and writing. Obviously, one teacher cannot deal effectively with the varied learning disabilities of all 10 children in the group. And no time remains for art, music, social studies, and other areas. As one teacher has said:

> At the end of the day, I stop and think about how much time I spent with each child, and it's not enough . . . . I know that each child needs it and yet I can't give it . . . there's not enough time . . . I try to teach in the basic areas of language, reading, written language, arithmetic, but I feel that they've all been cheated because they're all so different . . . they need so much more than I can give them . . . . They need individual teaching every day.

A final problem inherent in self-contained classes is that of reentry into the regular classroom. After a child has been removed from the regular classroom (and often from the home neighborhood school), communication between the special class teacher and regular classroom teachers is restricted. A student reentering the regular classroom does so with a new and distorted identity.

While the intent of self-contained classes may be noble, the results to the child seldom have been fruitful. Experience often has demonstrated an increase in behavior problems among learning disabled children grouped together, combined with a growing sense of alienation and a loss of self-esteem. Self-contained classes often are more administratively expedient for schools than they are instructionally sound for children.

The Resource Room

An alternative approach to self-contained classes is the resource room (Hammill & Wiederholt, 1972). The resource room is a center within the school and is well equipped with varied instructional

materials. It is supervised by a teacher highly trained in psychoeducational assessment and clinical teaching. Children with learning disabilities retain their assignment in the regular classroom and come to the resource room for remedial instruction for a part of their day only. This means that children can be divided into small groups for instruction appropriate to their disability, while the remainder of their day is spent in the regular classroom with peers.

For example, the resource room teacher may work for 30 minutes with three children who have similar language comprehension problems. At the end of that period, two of those children then may work with headphones at a language center to reinforce language instruction, while the teacher works with the remaining child plus two more who have just come in for remedial instruction in arithmetic. The day may continue with the fluid movement of children in and out of the resource room according to their needs for remedial instruction. (No assumption is made that the resource room teacher can provide a developmental curriculum in all areas, in addition to remedial instruction for children with learning disabilities.)

The resource room model has many strengths. First, the child does not lose identity with the normal peer group which is essential to a child's social learning. Second, the child's instructional needs are more likely to be met through a resource room teacher's flexibility in grouping children according to common needs. Third, loss of self-esteem and a growing sense of alienation from peers are less likely to occur. Fourth, the child is not deprived of learning in a developmental curriculum in the regular classroom (including social studies, art, music, etc.). Fifth, since the child never has been totally removed from the regular classroom, the reentry problem is eliminated. Sixth, the flexible scheduling permitted by a resource room allows for the concept of learning disabilities services to be delivered to other children, regardless of categorical labels.

The resource room teacher must be skilled not only in assessment and remediation but also in interpersonal communication with parents, other teachers, and members of other disciplines. The resource teacher's role is a multiple one. He or she must be able to diagnose, teach, integrate information from numerous disciplines (speech and language, reading, psychology, neurology, etc.), and serve as an advocate for children's rights to education.

The Itinerant Teacher

A third model for providing educational services is that of the itinerant teacher. The itinerant teacher may function in a capacity similar to that of the resource room, but may be responsible for serving two or more schools. The itinerant teacher may provide educational consultation to the classroom teacher and assistance to children with mild learning disabilities. The itinerant teacher may assist in preventing some children with milder disabilities from becoming behavior problems or from falling farther behind in academic learning.

A school system likely would benefit from having a wide array of educational services for children with learning problems. Just one type of service probably would not provide the flexibility and comprehensive services needed to serve children whose disabilities may range from mild to severe.

Program Services Appropriate to Age Level

Programs for the learning disabled vary with the learner's age and development. Preschool programs primarily center on the early identification of children with potential learning problems (Lerner, 1976). These programs usually include schoolwide screening of preschool children, intensive diagnosis, and compensatory programs aimed at developing learning abilities and skills necessary for success after entry into formal schooling.

Programs for primary and elementary age children vary considerably. The thrust of most programs, however, is to develop deficit language skills (including reading and written language) and skill in arithmetic. The emphasis has been on consideration of learning processes in the acquisition of academic skills (i.e., the perceptual, memory, and cognitive functions involved in reading, spelling, and arithmetic).

Programs for secondary-age children with learning disabilities have been relatively late in developing. The implicit assumption that learning disabilities can and should be remediated at the elementary school level has not enhanced development of programs at the secondary level. Nevertheless, experience has shown that, even with the best remedial instruction, many students with learning disabilities will continue to need remedial assistance and adjustments in curriculum throughout their school life. The major components of an educational program for the secondary-age student with learning disabilities have been summarized by Goodman and Mann (1976), in stating that a secondary learning disabilities program:

— is a basic education program focusing on skills in the basic areas of math and language arts.
— does not include process-based training; i.e., the emphasis is on formal academic teaching and vocational training rather than the training of perceptual and memory skills in an isolated sense.

— embodies the concept of mastery learning. Subject matter is broken down into a number of smaller learning units with the objectives defined for the mastery of each unit.
— emphasizes curriculum and curriculum management. Curriculum is defined as a cohesive and comprehensive approach to instruction in a given content area as opposed to the teaching of splinter skills.
— achieves a balance between academic and career education. Although remediation of specific deficits is a primary goal of elementary school learning disabilities programs, the secondary program must achieve a balance between continued academic instruction and the learner's preparation for post-high school pursuits.
— is an integrated program, operating somewhere between the poles of total commitment and total integration. The program is "integrated" in that each student spends part of the school day in regular and special classes.

The basic skills emphasis in curricula for learning disabled students at the secondary level is supported by Zigmond, Silverman, and Laurie (in press). Fifteen-year-old students who barely can read at a second grade level must use their limited remaining time in school to gain the basic academic skills needed for independent living in a literate society.

Several colleges and universities have developed programs for adults with learning disabilities. These types of programs are for students who may have strong intellectual abilities but whose accompanying disabilities create problems in learning in the usual sense (as in writing notes from lectures, extensive reading, lengthy written assignments, and use of oral language in public speaking). Lerner (1976, p. 47) cites a list of colleges and universities offering programs for the learning disabled.

During the past 15 years, public school programs for the learning disabled have been expanding rapidly. Some of these have been token programs; quality of services varies widely. Perhaps, development of public school programs before college and university teacher training programs were available to prepare teachers adequately in the area of learning disabilities has contributed to the uneven quality of public school programs (Cruickshank, 1977).

ORGANIZATIONAL SUPPORT

Two primary organizations are of major significance in the field of learning disabilities. The Association for Children with Learning Disabilities (ACLD) is a parent-sponsored organization dedicated to the support of programs and services for children with learning disabilities. The ACLD grew out of grassroots efforts by local parent groups committed to creating an awareness among educators, legislators, and various professionals concerning the unique needs of learning disabled children. The ACLD and its local chapters have had a major impact on the public schools in that the schools have come to recognize their responsibility to provide educational programs for children with learning disabilities. ACLD membership is open to professionals, parents, students, and anyone interested in supporting services for the learning disabled. The association also publishes *Newsbriefs*, a monthly publication, to disseminate information regarding current issues affecting the education of and services for learning disabled children.

In 1968 the Division for Children with Learning Disabilities (DCLD) was established within the Council for Exceptional Children. The DCLD is a professional organization of 10,000 members, and assumes responsibility for developing policy, ethics, and standards for the governance of professional issues related to learning disabilities. DCLD publishes *The Learning Disability Quarterly*, a forum for educational articles and research focusing on the direct application of teaching procedures for children with learning disabilities. Membership is open to members of the Council for Exceptional Children (CEC) who have specific interest in or responsibility for learning disabled children.

The *Journal of Learning Disabilities* is a privately produced monthly publication. It is not affiliated with a professional organization but provides a printed medium for publication of research related to learning disabilities.

SUMMARY

With passage of Public Law 94-142 in 1975, the U.S. Congress has supported an adequate education for all handicapped children. Three features of this law are particularly relevant to the learning disabled.

First, since the bill allows only two percent of the school-aged population to be designated as learning disabled, the definition of learning disability must be narrowed. If the two percent limit is maintained, only those children with severe learning disabilities will be eligible for service, and the remaining children will either have to be served by specialists in remedial reading and language pathology or receive no special assistance with their learning disabilities. In any case, personnel responsible for assisting children with learning disabilities is of utmost concern.

While children in need should not be kept waiting during the debate of "who should be teaching what to whom," certain qualifications and standards must be upheld by the helping professions. As emphasized throughout this chapter, learning disabilities are manifested in many forms—as language disabilities that disturb reading and written language and as disabilities in nonverbal learning that may have a pervasive effect on social learning as well as verbal learning. The teacher or helper of a learning disabled child must achieve a solid grasp of the interrelated nature of verbal and nonverbal learning, as well as the interrelationships among oral language, reading, and written language. And the teacher must be adept at sequencing and teaching skills necessary for the child to function across the entire school curriculum.

Second, the mandate for nondiscriminatory testing necessitates use of measurement techniques that do not discriminate against the child with cultural or language differences. This focus hopefully will stimulate close scrutiny of assumptions concerning the integrities of children when we use *any* standardized measure. We must not become so dependent upon formal tests that we fail to realize the impact of a language, cultural, or racial difference, as well as that of a language disability, on a child's test performance.

The third aspect of PL 94-142 warranting close scrutiny relates to the statement that "placement must be in the least restrictive environment"—with "least restrictive" often interpreted to mean education in regular classes with normal peers. Although this point clearly is directed at the frequent placement of children in self-contained classrooms where learning and participation with normal peers is limited greatly, the reverse concept of mainstreaming must be examined cautiously (Cruickshank, 1977). To place a learning disabled child in a regular class where the disability will be further debilitating is foolish.

For example, the child who has difficulty in spatial orientation and directionality in conjunction with gross and fine motor coordination problems easily can become the subject of ridicule and failure if integrated into a regular physical education class. That child's needs for physical education are vastly different from those of peers who may be ready for highly coordinated physical activities and competitive sports. The learner who has problems in oral language usage may be devastated in a high school public speaking class. *Mainstreaming must be carried out carefully and selectively, and only after matching the learner's strengths with those demanded by the curriculum* (Little, 1977).

Learning disabilities of children and youth have generated interest and concern among specialists in various disciplines, along with parents of these children. The thinking arising from this base is divergent, with a resulting proliferation of hypotheses about learning disabilities, their causes, and how they should be treated. Even more hypotheses need to be generated to further the body of knowledge as a foundation for helping these students. At the same time, a major responsibility remains with educators to structure the most effective learning experience possible for learning disabled children and youth within the schools.

REFERENCES

Ames, L.B. Learning disabilities: The developmental point of view. In H. R. Myklebust (Ed.), *Progress in Learning Disabilities* (Vol. 1). New York: Grune & Stratton, 1968.

Arter, J. A., & Jenkins, J. R. Examining the benefits and prevalence of modality considerations in special education. *Journal of Special Education*, 1977, *11*, 281-298.

Ayres, J. A. *Sensory integration and learning disorders*. Los Angeles: Western Psychological Services, 1973.

Badian, N. A. Auditory-visual integration, auditory memory, and reading in retarded and adequate readers. *Journal of Learning Disabilities*, 1977, *10*, 108-114.

Barsch, R. H. *Achieving perceptual motor efficiency* (Vol. 1). Seattle: Special Child Publications, 1967.

Bateman, B. Three approaches to diagnosis and educational planning for children with learning disabilities. *Academic Therapy*, 1967, *2*, 215-222.

Bateman, B. *Temporal learning*. San Rafael, CA: Dimensions Publishing Co., 1969.

Bateman, B. Educational implications—minimal brain dysfunction. In F. F. De La Cruz, B. H. Fox, & R. H. Roberts (Eds.), *Annals of the New York Academy of Sciences*, 1973, *205*, 245-250.

Birch, H. G. Functional effects of fetal malnutrition. *Hospital Practice*, 1971, 134-148.

Brigance, A. *Inventory of basic skills*. Newton, MA: Curriculum Associates, 1976.

Bryan, T. H. Learning disabled children's comprehension of non-verbal communication. *Journal of Learning Disabilities*, 1977, *10*, 501-506.

Camp, B. W. Psychometric tests and learning in severely disabled readers. *Journal of Learning Disabilities*, 1973, *6*, 512-517.

Chalfant, J.C., & Flathouse, V.E. Auditory and visual learning. In H.R. Myklebust (Ed.), *Progress in Learning Disabilities* (Vol. 2). New York: Grune & Stratton, 1971.

Clay, M.M., & Imlach, R.H. Juncture, pitch, and stress as reading behavior variables. *Journal of Verbal Learning & Verbal Behavior*, 1971, *10*, 133-139.

Colligan, R. C. Psychometric deficits related to perinatal stress. *Journal of Learning Disabilities*, 1974, *7*, 154-160.

Connors, K. Recent drug studies with hyperkinetic children. *Journal of Learning Disabilities*, 1971, *4*, 476-483.

Cott, A. Megavitamins: The orthomolecular approach to behavioral disorders and learning disabilities. *Academic Therapy*, 1972, *7*, 245-258.

Cruickshank, W. M. Hyperactive children: Their needs and curriculum. In P. Knoblock & J. L. Johnson (Eds.), *The teaching-learning process in educating emotionally disturbed children*. Syracuse, NY: Syracuse University Press, 1967.

Cruickshank, W. M. Myths and realities in learning disabilities. *Journal of Learning Disabilities*, 1977, *10*, 51-58.

Engelmann, S. *Conceptual learning*. San Rafael, CA: Dimensions Publishing Co., 1969.

Feingold, B. F. Hyperkinesis and learning disabilities linked to artificial food flavors and colors. *American Journal of Nursing*, 1975, *75*, 797-803. (a)

Feingold, B.F. *Why your child is hyperactive*. New York: Random House, 1975. (b)

Freeman, R. D. Drug effects on learning in children: A selective review of the past thirty years. *Journal of Special Education*, 1966, *1*, 17-44.

Frostig, M. Visual perception, integrative functions and academic learning. *Journal of Learning Disabilities,* 1972, *5,* 1-15.

Getman, G. N. The visual-motor complex in the acquisition of learning skills. In J. Hellmuth (Ed.), *Learning Disorders* (Vol. 1). Seattle: Special Child Publications, 1965.

Goldberg, H. K., & Arnott, W. Ocular motility in learning disabilities. *Journal of Learning Disabilities,* 1970, *3,* 100-102.

Goodman, L., & Mann, L. *Learning disabilities in the secondary school.* New York: Grune & Stratton, 1976.

Hallahan, D. P., & Cruickshank, W. M. *Psychoeducation foundations of learning disabilities.* Englewood Cliffs, NJ: Prentice-Hall, 1973.

Hammill, D. D. Training visual perceptual processes. *Journal of Learning Disabilities,* 1972, *5,* 552-562.

Hammill, D.D. Defining learning disabilities for programmatic purposes. *Academic Therapy,* 1976, *12,* 29-37.

Hammill, D.D., Goodman, L., & Wiederholt, J.L. Visual-motor processes: Can we train them? *Reading Teacher,* 1974, *27,* 469-486.

Hammill, D. D., & Larsen, S. C. The relationship of selected auditory perceptual skills to reading ability. *Journal of Learning Disabilities,* 1974, *7,* 429-436.

Hammill, D.D., & Wiederholt, J.L. *The resource room rationale and implications.* King of Prussia, PA: Buttonwood Farms, Inc., 1972.

Johnson, D.J., & Myklebust, H.R. *Learning disabilities: Educational principles and practices.* New York: Grune & Stratton, 1967.

Keogh, B. K. Hyperactivity and learning disorders: Review and speculation. *Exceptional Child,* 1971, *38,* 101-109.

Keogh, B. K., & Margolis, J. Learn to labor and to wait: Attentional problems of children with learning disorders. *Journal of Learning Disabilities,* 1976, *9,* 276-286.

Kephart, N. C. Perceptual motor aspects of learning disabilities. In Frierson & Barbe (Eds.), *Educating Children with Learning Disabilities.* New York: Appleton-Century-Crofts, 1967.

Kershner, J. Visual-spatial organization and reading: Support for a cognition developmental interpretation. *Journal of Learning Disabilities,* 1975, *8,* 30-36.

Kershner, J., Hawks, W., & Grekin, R. *Megavitamins and learning disorders: A controlled double-blind experiment.* Unpublished manuscript, Ontario Institute for Studies in Education, 1977.

Koppitz, E. M. Bender Gestalt test, visual aware digit span test and reading achievement. *Journal of Learning Disabilities,* 1975, *8,* 154-157.

Larsen, S. C., & Hammill, D. D. The relationship of selected visual perceptual abilities to school learning. *Journal of Special Education,* 1975, *9,* 282-291.

Larsen, S. C., Rogers, D., & Sowell, V. The use of selected perceptual tests in differentiating between normal and learning disabled children. *Journal of Learning Disabilities,* 1976, *9,* 85-91.

Lawson, L. J. Ophthalmological factors in learning disabilities. In H. R. Myklebust (Ed.), *Progress in learning disabilities* (Vol. 1). New York: Grune & Stratton, 1968.

Lerner, J. W. Remedial reading and learning disabilities: Are they the same or different? *Journal of Special Education,* 1975, *9,* 119-131.

Lerner, J. W. *Children with learning disabilities.* Boston: Houghton Mifflin, 1976.

Little, L. J. *Critical factors in the selective mainstreaming of children with learning disabilities.* Paper presented at the Pennsylvania Division for Children with Learning Disabilities Annual Conference, Norristown, 1977.

Money, J. *Reading disability: Progress and research needs in dyslexia.* Baltimore: The Johns Hopkins Press, 1962.

Moran, M. R., & Byrne, M. C. Mastery of verb tense markers by normal and learning disabled children. *Journal of Speech & Hearing Research,* 1977, *20,* 529-542.

Myklebust, H.R. *Progress in learning disabilities* (Vol. 3). New York: Grune & Stratton, 1975.

Myklebust, H. R., Bannochie, M. N., & Killen, J. R. Learning disabilities and cognitive processes. In H.R. Myklebust (Ed.), *Progress in learning disabilities* (Vol. 2). New York: Grune & Stratton, 1971.

Myklebust, H.R., & Boshes, B. *Minimal brain damage in children* (Final Report, U.S. Public Health Service Contract 108-65-142 to U.S. Department of Health, Education, and Welfare). Evanston, IL: Northwestern University Publications, June, 1969.

National Advisory Committee on Handicapped Children. *Special education for handicapped children*, 1st annual report. Washington, DC: U.S. Department of Health, Education & Welfare, January 31, 1968.

Palkes, H., Stewart, M., & Kahana, B. Porteus Maze performance of hyperactive boys after training in self-directed verbal commands. *Child Development*, 1968, *39*, 817-826.

Pasamanick, B., & Knoblock, P. Brain damage and reproductive casualty. *American Journal of Orthopsychiatry*, 1960, *30*, 298-305.

Prout, H. T. Behavioral intervention with hyperactive children: A review. *Journal of Learning Disabilities*, 1977, *10*, 141-146.

Ringler, L. H., & Smith, I. L. Learning modality and word recognition of first grade children. *Journal of Learning Disabilities*, 1973, *6*, 307-312.

Ruddell, R.B. Language acquisition and the reading process. In H. Singer (Ed.), *Theoretical models and processes of reading*. Newark, DE: IRA, 1970.

Semel, E.M., & Wiig, E.H. Comprehension of syntactic structures and critical verbal elements by children with learning disabilities. *Journal of Learning Disabilities*, 1975, *8*, 46-51.

Siegel, E. Task analysis and effective teaching. *Journal of Learning Disabilities*, 1972, *5*, 519-532.

Silberberg, N. E., Ivensen, I. A., & Goins, J. T. Which remedial reading method works best? *Journal of Learning Disabilities*, 1973, *6*, 547-556.

Smith, E. B., Goodman, K. S., & Meredith, R. *Language and thinking in the elementary school child*. New York: Holt, Rinehart & Winston, 1970.

Smith, F. *Understanding reading: A psycholinguistic analysis of reading and learning to read*. New York: Holt, Rinehart, & Winston, 1971.

Spring, C., & Sandoval, J. Food additives and hyperkinesis: A critical evaluation of the evidence. *Journal of Learning Disabilities*, 1976, *9*, 560-569.

Strauss, A.A., & Lehtinen, L.E. *Psychopathology and education of the brain injured child*. New York: Grune & Stratton, 1947.

Strauss, A. A., & Werner, H. Disorders of conceptual thinking in the brain injured child. *Journal of Nervous & Mental Disorders*, 1942, *96*, 153-159.

Throne, J. M. Learning disabilities: A radical behaviorist's point of view. *Journal of Learning Disabilities*, 1973, *6*, 543-546.

Vogel, S.A. Syntactic abilities in normal and dyslexic children. *Journal of Learning Disabilities*, 1974, *7*, 47-53.

Vogel, S.A. Morphological ability in normal and dyslexic children. *Journal of Learning Disabilities*, 1977, *10*, 35-43.

Voort, L. V., & Senf, G. M. Audio visual integration in retarded readers. *Journal of Learning Disabilities*, 1973, *6*, 170-179.

Wallach, G. P., & Goldsmith, S. C. Language based learning disabilities: Reading is language, too. *Journal of Learning Disabilities*, 1977, *10*, 178-183.

Wardhaugh, R. *Reading: A linguistic perspective*. New York: Harcourt, Brace & World, 1969.

Wepman, J. M. The modality concept. In H. K. Smith (Ed.), *Perception and Reading: Proceedings of the Twelfth Annual Convention of the International Reading Association*, 1968, *12*, 1-6.

Wiig, E.H., & Roach, M.A. Immediate recall of semantically varied "sentences" by learning disabled adolescents. *Perceptual & Motor Skills*, 1975, *40*, 119-125.

Wiig, E. H., & Semel, E. M. Comprehension of linguistic concepts requiring logical operations by learning disabled children. *Journal of Speech & Hearing Research*, 1973, *16*, 627-636.

Wiig, E. H., & Semel, E. M. Logico-grammatical sentence comprehension by adolescents with learning disabilities. *Perceptual & Motor Skills*, 1974, *38*, 1331-1334.

Wiig, E. H., & Semel, E. M. Productive language abilities in learning disabled adolescents. *Journal of Learning Disabilities*, 1975, *8*, 578-586.

Wiig, E. H., & Semel, E. M. *Language disabilities in children and adolescents.* Columbus, OH: Merrill Publishing Co., 1976.

Wiig, E. H., Semel, E. M., & Crouse, M. A. The use of English morphology by high risk and learning disabled children. *Journal of Learning Disabilities*, 1973, *6*, 457-465.

Wilson, S. P., Harris, C. W., & Harris, M. C. Effects of an auditory perceptual remediation program on reading performance. *Journal of Learning Disabilities*, 1976, *9*, 670-678.

Zigmond, N. K., Silverman, R., & Laurie, T. Competencies for teachers of secondary students with learning disabilities. In L. Mann & L. Goodman (Eds.), *Adolescents with learning disabilities*. Boston: Houghton-Mifflin, in press.

RESOURCE GUIDE

Historical Information

Hallahan, D. P., & Cruickshank, W. M. *Psycho-educational foundations of learning disabilities.* Englewood Cliffs, NJ: Prentice-Hall, 1973.

Wiederholt, J. L. Historical perspectives on the education of the learning disabled. In L. Mann & D. Sabatino (Eds.), *The second review of special education.* Philadelphia: Journal of Special Education Press, 1974.

Family

Baldauf, R. J. Parental intervention. In H. R. Myklebust (Ed.), *Progress in learning disabilities* (Vol. 3). New York: Grune & Stratton, 1975.

Beers, K. H., & Beers, J. I. Parents, professionals and public policy. In S. A. Kirk & J. M. McCarthy (Eds.), *Learning disabilities: Selected ACLD papers.* Boston: Houghton-Mifflin, 1975.

Briard, F. K. Counseling parents of children with learning disabilities. *Social Casework,* 1976, 581-585.

Buscaglia, L. F. Parents need to know: Parents and teachers work together. In S. A. Kirk & J. M. McCarthy (Eds.), *Learning disabilities: Selected ACLD papers.* Boston: Houghton-Mifflin, 1975.

Patterns of Development

Bryan, T., & Bryan, J. H. *Understanding learning disabilities.* New York: Alfred Publishing Co., 1975.

Brutten, M. Characteristic symptom patterns of learning disabled adolescents. An address to the symposium *Youth in trouble: The learning disabled adolescent* (B. Kratoville, Ed.). San Rafael, CA: Academic Therapy Publications, 1974.

Connolly, C. Social and emotional factors in learning disabilities. In H. R. Myklebust (Ed.), *Progress in learning disabilities* (Vol. 2). New York: Grune & Stratton, 1971.

Gordon, S. The psycho-sexual identity problems of adolescents with learning disabilities. An address to the symposium *Youth in trouble: The learning disabled adolescent* (B. Kratoville, Ed.). San Rafael, CA: Academic Therapy Publications, 1974.

Poremba, C. The adolescent and young adult with learning disabilities: What are his needs? What are the needs of those who deal with him? *International approach to learning disabilities of children and youth.* Tulsa: The Association for Children with Learning Disabilities, 1967, pp. 142-148.

Treatment

Connors, C. K. Drugs in the management of children with learning disabilities. In L. Tarnapol (Ed.), *Learning disorders in children.* Boston: Little, Brown, 1971.

Forman, P. M. Pharmacological intervention. In H. R. Myklebust (Ed.), *Progress in learning disabilities* (Vol. 3). New York: Grune & Stratton, 1975.

Myklebust, H. R. Nonverbal learning disabilities: Assessment and intervention. In H. R. Myklebust (Ed.), *Progress in learning disabilities* (Vol. 3). New York: Grune & Stratton, 1975.

Perlman, S. M. Intervention through psychological and educational evaluation. In H. R. Myklebust (Ed.), *Progress in learning disabilities* (Vol. 3). New York: Grune & Stratton, 1975.

Educational Programming

Hammill, D. D., & Bartel, N. R. (Eds.). *Teaching children with learning and behavior disorders.* Boston: Allyn & Bacon, 1978.

Meisgeier, C. A review of critical issues underlying mainstreaming. In L. Mann & D. Sabatino (Eds.), *The third review of special education.* New York: Grune & Stratton, 1976.

Pihl, R. O. Learning disabilities: Intervention programs in the schools. In H. R. Myklebust (Ed.), *Progress in learning disabilities* (Vol. 3). New York: Grune & Stratton, 1975.

Wiederholt, J. L., Hammill, D. D., & Brown, V. *The resource teacher: A guide to effective practices.* Boston: Allyn & Bacon, 1978.

7 The Emotionally Disturbed

Richard J. Whelan
University of Kansas Medical Center

Children who are troubled and cause trouble for parents, brothers and sisters, teachers, peers, and others with whom they interact may be diagnosed as *emotionally disturbed*. They are in conflict with self and others. The diagnosis is a behavior description as well as a label, although other labels—*educationally handicapped, behavior disordered, behavior disabled*, or *personally* and *socially maladjusted*—may be applied, depending upon the region or state. These terms are used almost interchangeably, although *behavior disorder* is the term used most frequently by educators.

Emotional disturbance in children is noncategorical in that it can happen to the rich, poor, gifted, retarded, majority, and minority. It does not honor boundaries or lines that distinguish one individual from another or one group from another. But those who are poor, are otherwise handicapped, and are discriminated against for various reasons are especially at risk for the development of behavior patterns eventually classified as deviant (Goulder & Trybus, 1977; Jones, 1976; Kauffman, 1977; Morse, 1977). While emotional disturbance is thought to be a separate entity from other conditions of pain, individuals with emotional anguish transcend all other categorical labels.

This discussion is about children whose behavior variance exceeds the tolerance or understanding level of people with whom they are in contact and, more specifically, what happens to them in classroom learning environments. And it gives ideas on how instructional practices can be means to the end of helping these children achieve ways to effectively function and participate in our society.

PERSPECTIVES

In what manner must children behave before they are labeled as emotionally disturbed? Behaviors range from almost total withdrawal to highly visible aggressive or hostile patterns. A child may exhibit behaviors predominantly at one end of this spectrum or the other; or both withdrawal and aggressive behaviors may be observed in the same child at different times, depending upon the circumstances prior to the observed behavior.

In what context or situation does behavior described as emotionally disturbed occur? In some cases, behavior considered to be deviant or reflective of emotional damage may occur only in a specific classroom and not in other situations such as the home, playground, community center, or even in another classroom located within the same school. At the other extreme, deviant behavior in a child can be observed in all environments where the child functions.

What role does the environment play in emotionally disturbed behaviors? As two contrasting examples, suppose one child who has lived in the same community setting since birth develops behavior patterns that are incompatible with the standards of the community. May one assume that the child has been exposed to experiences which evoke acceptable behavior but, for reasons unknown, has not really acquired it? Another child has performed and related well in a familiar environment but, when placed in a new situation with unfamiliar requirements, is now experiencing repeated failures. The second child's behaviors, exhibited as attempts to cope with the present failures, may be similar to those exhibited by the first child.

Although the second child may be thought by some to be emotionally disturbed, this child probably is reacting realistically to unrealistic expectations and may not be considered accurately as emotionally disturbed. The first child indeed may have emotional problems which need to be solved.

A simple analogy of the second child phenomenon occurs when one cannot speak or comprehend the language of a new geographic location. A period of learning and adjustment, often accompanied by stress and anxiety, is necessary before adequate performance can be attained. Unless the newcomer is accepted with patience, understanding, empathy, and support in the new setting, unusual, even deviant, behavior may be adopted as a coping mechanism.

Cultural Considerations

Educators must give precise and consistent attention to children from family cultures different from those represented by the school. This aspect, of course, deals with the perception, understanding, acceptance and, indeed, the celebration of differences. The circumstances surrounding these cultural considerations are unique to the United States. They pertain to the "melting pot" hope and philosophy of strength through diversity. Unfortunately, the melting pot may have been transformed into an amorphous mush in which differences among people are discouraged and diminished to some point of conformity. The end result is equivalent to the scientific term *entropy*, a condition which associates sameness with chaos. This is contrasted to the strength which can be found in differentiation and distinctiveness (Wiener, 1954).

Ideally, the melting pot concept should have been translated into a stew in which all of the various ingredients are identifiable but compatible, and are relished for their uniqueness, individual worth, and value in contributing to the good of the whole. In reality, however, attempts to sustain cultural integrity (while not entirely unsuccessful) have not been without cost to communities, schools, and individuals. Indeed, many cultures have lost their past or concealed it with a veneer of the present, in order to acquire economic and political power which would eventually allow them to *be*, rather than to become what they were not.

Not all immigrants have traveled the upward path to success. The first immigrants — Native Americans, Mexican Americans, and blacks — have found the path filled with many obstacles. Only recently have many of these obstacles been removed by litigation and legislation. Now, new thinking must follow the legalisms before the melting pot concept, the intrinsic strength of the nation, can be realized at its best.

Minority Considerations

Problems arise when one group in society seeks to impose its standards on another, a situation which usually stems from the fear of differences. A related problem develops when various groups must interact but the interaction is strained by mutual fear, distrust, and bias—all resulting from a failure to understand and accept individuals as individuals rather than stereotypical generalizations. This is the root cause of a disproportionate number of children from minority groups having been placed in special education settings.

Different experiences are necessary to learn different skills; and discrepancies between previous experiences and present expectations often remain unrecognized—leading to child failure and teacher failure. Child failure, moreover, often is misinterpreted and aggravated through inappropriate labeling, such as "mentally retarded" or "emotionally disturbed," covering up the actual teacher failure. This pattern occurs more often with minority children who, for a variety of reasons, bring to school different competencies from those assumed to be acquired by children of school age and which are deemed necessary prerequisites to learn reading, writing, and ciphering. This form of instructional failure, resulting from the inability of educators to recognize the strengths intrinsic to differences, and to use them effectively in planning learning experiences, is inexcusable. Differences, if considered wisely, can function to benefit learning. As Johnson (1976) stressed, the goal of academic and social competence is viable for *all* children, whether or not they be different when compared to the majority. If educators really espouse the value of individual differences and individualized instruction, these beliefs can be translated into successful results.

Other Social Considerations

Some children, no matter what their background, are at risk for becoming identified as disturbed, disabled, or handicapped. A hearing loss, for example, represents a disability which occurs without regard to cultural or minority factors. The same may be true for any handicapping condition. The disability label, however, must be a valid reflection of a true condition and not one attributed to reasons unrelated to the presence or absence of the handicapping condition.

Identification of a disability, moreover, should not (although it often does) carry with it the comparisons of inferior-superior or stigma-status. Rather, it intends that children in need should have the need met if they are to contribute fully as important members of society. But, traditionally, certain individuals within a group structure have been shunned because their behaviors exceed the bounds of their group's criteria for normality. Some behaviors may lead to a child's total exclusion from a group. Rhodes (1977) and Szasz (1974) discuss such exclusion as a reflection of the inner turmoil within the so-called "normal" group, and that this turmoil is too painful to confront. Being too distressful, it is displaced upon those who show deviation, a process known as *projection* (Freud, 1913/1950), thus providing justification to purge or extrude the different from the undifferent.

Educators must be aware of these powerful, intrapersonal inner processes when attempting to help others who are dealing with their own painful realities. The prevalence of pain (emotional disturbance) is one out of one, and the condition of normality is none out of none, an illusion (Rhodes, 1977). Recognition of one's own reality as well as the reality of those needing help should enable educators to better plan programs to help children help themselves become more satisfied and competent as participants in society.

IDENTIFICATION OF EMOTIONAL DISTURBANCE

Failure to recognize behavioral differences as welcome and positive elements which should be encouraged and enjoyed may lead to errors in the identification of children as handicapped. Children who are thought to be handicapped, but are actually only different from some arbitrary standard, may suffer by being placed in learning situations totally unsuitable to their real needs when, in fact, they may need only recognition and acceptance of their differences, plus changes in instructional strategies, to achieve success. Errors in placement decisions have been difficult to reverse; this is a primary reason why corrective action by the legal system has become necessary in recent years (Whelan & Jackson, 1971).

Diagnostic or identification procedures must be accurate if handicapped children are to obtain the needed educational resources, both human and material. Identification of obvious physical disabilities (e.g., in vision or hearing), while by no means easy, can be done accurately by competent professional examiners. However, when diagnostic efforts are directed at establishing the presence or absence of mental disorders (emotional disturbance), the processes are less clear. This is due, in part, to the confusion between physical illness and mental illness, and the tendency to treat both as the same when they are not (Szasz, 1974).

Historically, provision of educational experiences for the emotionally disturbed has followed the lead of mental health professionals who usually use terms associated with psychiatry—e.g., neurotic, psychotic. Since psychiatry is a branch of medicine rather than education, educators often have misinterpreted the true meanings of psychiatric terms. If the labels derive from the medical discipline, it follows that observed deviance must be symptomatic of an unobservable cause just as a high temperature is a symptom of an inflamed appendix. Therefore, when educators are informed that a child is "neurotic," and that the recalcitrant behaviors observed are caused by trauma during infancy, they are still left with the task of how to help the child learn more appropriate behavior patterns in a classroom. Help with this task is rarely forthcoming from only the diagnostic label.

Educators have reacted to this frustration by blaming the medical model for not providing explicit formulas for classroom-based intervention. In actuality, the culprit is not medicine or the medical model. To paraphrase a popular quotation, we have met the culprit, and it is us. The medical model is simply the application of the scientific method, a process which most children learn during their elementary school years. That method requires accurate observation of behavior and the application of knowledge to relate it to antecedent and subsequent events. It is applicable to educators along with physicians and psychiatrists.

The major problem, then, is not the medical model but the failure to distinguish differences between diagnostic issues unique to medicine as contrasted to those unique to education. Figure 7.1 graphically

	MEDICINE	EDUCATION
False Positive	NOT SIGNIFICANT	SIGNIFICANT
False Negative	SIGNIFICANT	NOT SIGNIFICANT

Figure 7.1 Comparison of Diagnostic Issues Confronting Medicine and Education

displays these issues. A positive result from a diagnostic process indicates the presence of a disease in medicine, or a disability of academic and/or social behaviors in education. A false positive, therefore, is a circumstance in which the individual really is not diseased or disabled. Negative denotes the absence of disease or disability. A false negative represents a situation in which an individual with a real disease or disability is considered to be free of the condition.

For medicine, the false positive does not present a significant issue. If, for example, a tuberculin skin test shows a reaction, additional tests can be administered to confirm or disconfirm the diagnosis. On the other hand, false negatives are a serious problem. If a skin test produces no reaction but the individual really does have tuberculosis, the needed treatment may be delayed until it is too late.

As shown by the Figure, the opposite holds true for education. False positives represent the most potentially serious problems for educators. This cell in the figure reflects the problems which arise when, for instance, a child is educationally diagnosed as emotionally disturbed because of observed behaviors which have not been perceived correctly as being associated with an inability to comprehend standard English. Other false positives occur when an examiner does not properly understand the cultural background of a child. For example, a child's failure to establish eye contact with an adult may be assumed to reflect autistic-like behaviors; however, if the child is a Native American from a certain tribe, casting the eyes downward when addressed by an adult is a sign of respect. The child is responding adaptively; the examiner is not; and the child is misdiagnosed.

Enough of these situations have occurred that some parents and child advocacy groups have begun to push for the three L's—leverage, litigation, and legislation—on behalf of appropriate educational diagnoses and placement of handicapped children (Whelan & Sontag, 1974). Finally, false negatives are rarely a problem for educators. Children who are truly handicapped are not often diagnosed as nonhandicapped.

Educators, as professionals, have the knowledge and skill to formulate precise diagnoses and to construct instructional programs based upon them. They need not blame medicine for the problems unique to education. A reduction in the frequency of false positives will enable educators to devote the scarce resources to those who are definitely in need—handicapped children.

EDUCATIONAL DESCRIPTIONS

Rather than present traditional psychiatric definitions of emotional disturbance, the focus will be on several that are most relevant to educators. Definitions, of course, do not solve problems, nor do they necessarily predict the precise instructional strategy which will be best for a given child.

At best, definitions are descriptors of observed behaviors. The word *autistic*, as used by Kanner (1943), refers to a rather specific set of behaviors which must be observed before the definition is applied. Rather than verbalize the entire set, a single descriptor is more convenient. As long as agreement exists on the label's meaning, it can function as a brief communication. It is a description of observed behaviors.

Definitions or labels are troublesome, however, when they are used as explanations rather than as descriptions of behavior. For example, a child must display certain behaviors before it is appropriate to apply the term "autistic." But if asked *why* the behaviors are peculiar and the response is, "because the child is autistic," a valid descriptive label becomes an invalid explanation. Knowledge is lost rather than gained, and confusion is needlessly inserted. Using descriptions as explanations—reification—is a dangerous process in that it often is used to explain instructional failures: "I can't teach this child because he is autistic." The proper statement in this case should be, "Under the conditions I have arranged, this child has not acquired the skills important for his academic and social progress." This positive approach employs the ecological notion of the relationship between child and learning environment and reduces the danger of assuming that the exhibited problems reside wholly within the child rather than in the interrelationship between child and environment. Indeed, the environment may not provide the necessary supports for enabling the child to progress in adaptive development.

In view of the problems associated with definitions, a behavior description approach is more feasible. One way to describe behavior disorders or emotional disturbance from an educational perspective is to include its effects upon others as well as the child, by asking three questions (Pate, 1963):

1. Does the child's behavior place disproportionate demands upon the teacher and other school personnel?
2. Does the child's behavior interfere with the educational progress of the peer group?
3. Does the child's behavior become more disorganized and irrational over time?

If the answer to all three questions is yes, a rationale for changes in instructional procedures has been established. The three questions cannot be used to make a diagnosis of emotional disturbance. But a diagnosis of emotional disturbance is not necessary before educational changes can be made, and, further, a diagnosis would be inappropriate solely on the basis of affirmative responses to the questions. If the child is emotionally disturbed, the answer to all three questions will be yes, but, conversely, yes answers are not sufficient to arrive at the identification of emotional disturbance; conditions other than emotional disturbance may function to elicit yes answers too. However, the information gained by application of these three questions can be used for further investigation which may or may not confirm a diagnosis of emotional disturbance. Even if that diagnosis is eventually made, its usefulness will be only in assigning extra resources consistent with and contingent upon proper identification of a handicapping condition. The fact remains that developing, implementing, and evaluating an instructional program is by

far the most important and difficult activity. A child's behavior, be it destructive, withdrawn, or both, can take a great amount of teacher time. If a child exhibits two or three temper tantrums each day, the teacher has to deal with them. In so doing, other children are deprived of the time they need from the teacher. But the most significant question is the third. If progress is not observed, conditions impinging upon the child obviously must be modified.

A more precise educational description of behaviors exhibited by emotionally disturbed children is provided by Bower (1969), based upon his extensive research in identifying children with emotional or behavioral disorders. According to Bower, emotionally disturbed children exhibit certain behavior patterns which deviate markedly from expectations, and persist or are consistently displayed over a substantial period of time. These behavior patterns include:

1. Absence of knowledge and skill acquisition in academic and social behaviors not attributed to intellectual capability, hearing and visual status, or physical health anomalies.
2. Absence of positive, satisfying interpersonal relationships with adults and peers.
3. Frequent instances of inappropriate behavior episodes which are surprising or unexpected for the conditions in which they occur.
4. Observable periods of diminished verbal and other motor activity (e.g., moods of depression or unhappiness).
5. Frequent complaints of a physical nature, such as stomach aches, soreness in the arm and general fatigue.

Of the five criteria, the first is often the initial indication that a child may be troubled, and it is a sign which teachers can easily observe. A child who is struggling and using energy to cope with inner and external turmoil has little energy left for acquiring successful coping skills. Criterion two is also readily observable; social behaviors directed at others typically are harsh and unkind, or may be marked by avoidance of others whenever possible. Regarding the third criterion, a teacher may be baffled when a child launches a physical and verbal attack upon another child or adult for no apparent reason or precipitating cause. With reference to criterion four, even the most consistently, overtly hostile child will experience periods of low behavioral output. This may be observed in slowness of walk and movements, a look of sadness, speaking without affect, and reflected in the content of assigned school work. When the veneer of artificial toughness is dropped, a frightened, confused child—one who is vainly reaching out for help—appears.

Along with teachers, school nurses often are involved in circumstances related to criterion five. In a study designed to check the accuracy of the previous statement, the author asked a school nurse to count the frequency of visits by children to the school's infirmary. Independently, the teachers in the same building were asked to rank order pupils in overall adjustment. The children who ranked lowest predictably had the most frequent visits to the school nurse. (As a note of caution, physical complaints in every instance should be checked; a complaint may have a valid medical basis and, if neglected, could lead to more serious problems.)

The five-point educational description of emotionally disturbed children can be useful to teachers for the purpose of identifying those who may need program modifications. These points also may be useful in evaluating the effectiveness of a modified program. If skills are acquired, relationships improve, behavior outbursts recede, depression is diminished, and physical complaints are real rather than contrived, an instructional program may be judged as appropriate and effective.

One other aspect of Bower's criteria needs amplification. Criteria three, four, and five may reflect strategies for avoiding and escaping from the lack of competencies associated with achieving success in criteria one and two.[1] That is, failure in skill acquisition, plus not being able to relate to others in a positive fashion, is a painful state of affairs which may lead to avoidance behavior styles. To avoid a reading lesson which invariably leads to failure, a child may have a temper tantrum, withdraw from interaction, or complain about a headache. Such avoidance behaviors are signals to a teacher to review instructional procedures. Are expectations for reading compatible with the child's competence level? Does the child have the necessary skills to relate to others? If not, the child's program must be changed.

After a rather comprehensive review of many educational descriptions, Kauffman (1977) has formulated a brief description of children with emotional disorders:

> Children with behavior disorders are those who chronically and markedly respond to their environment in socially unacceptable and/or personally unsatisfying ways but who can be taught more socially acceptable and personally gratifying behavior. (p.23).

In this description, focus is directed at behaviors which are not consistent with current societal standards. Second, the description infers that children may be aware that not all is well internal and external to selves. Third, and most important, it conveys the positive expectation that emotionally disturbed children can be helped through appropriate instructional practices. Kauffman's expanded description also presents information regarding the settings in which emotionally disturbed children, depending upon the seriousness of their condition, can be served (e.g., regular classroom, resource room, special class, residential treatment).

When all of the educational descriptions are analyzed, it becomes apparent that the behavior displayed by emotionally disturbed children is characterized by excesses and deficits (Whelan & Gallagher, 1972). Behavior excesses are those actions which the child displays to an inordinate degree—too many tantrums, too many fights. Deficits are behaviors which the child does not exhibit, or does so to a much lesser extent than the norm—too few appropriate social contacts, too few assignments completed. A listing of behavior excesses and deficits

---

1. This analysis was suggested to the author by Dr. Richard L. McDowell, Professor of Special Education, University of New Mexico.

observed in a child can illuminate and provide targets or objectives for instructional activities.

Educational descriptions are useful for circumscribing problems that require solutions. They form the foundation for subsequent development of instructional programs. They also contribute to the criteria used to evaluate effects of instructional procedures and programs (i.e., does the description change in a positive direction as a function of what is done to, with, and for a child with emotional disturbance?).

PREVALENCE

Estimates of prevalence of emotionally disturbed students in the classroom vary from a conservative 2 percent to a recently reported 20 percent of the student population (Kelly, Bullock, & Dykes, 1977). The variance in estimates can be ascribed to differences in descriptions used to identify this group of handicapped children. The 2 percent estimate considers only the more seriously involved children, and the 20 percent figure includes the full range of behavior disorders (severe, moderate, mild) requiring differential levels of intervention. For the teacher, one child in a classroom may be enough to worry about. Prevalence estimates however, are needed to plan programs on district, state, and national levels, and to allocate human and fiscal resources for their operation. In this context, the emotionally disturbed, using the conservative 2 percent prevalence estimation, are believed to comprise the most underserved group of handicapped children (Dodge, 1976).

CAUSATION FACTORS

Responses to the question of cause are varied and complex, too much so for the scope of this discussion. However, behaviors which deviate substantially from the norm do not occur in a vacuum. Causation, or etiology, of emotional disturbance usually involves the interaction of multiple factors rather than a one-to-one relationship between single cause and single effect. Behaviors exhibited by emotionally disturbed children are typically chronic (persist over time) and acute (deviate to the point of attracting attention from others).

The search for causes involves the identification of two general factors, predisposing and precipitating. *Predisposing factors* are conditions which may increase the probability of developing behavior disorders. A child who has never been allowed to develop skills for independent functioning may be predisposed to problems when placed in a classroom in which expectations to plan and work alone are high. *Precipitating factors* are the immediate stresses or incidents which function as a trigger for maladaptive behaviors. Using the example of an overly dependent child, if the mother suddenly dies, the child is left with little support—a condition that may elicit a panic reaction of withdrawal from or attacks upon the environment. Predisposing and precipitating factors usually operate in tandem. For example, most children, if given sufficient support, can manage the grief of a parent's death; they eventually adjust and continue to progress.

The causes of various classifications (e.g., transient, neurotic psychotic) of emotional disturbance may be divided into two major categories, biogenic and psychogenic. *Biogenic* refers to the physical, biological, and hereditary insults that function to diminish an individual's capability to cope with environmental demands. *Psychogenic* is used to describe internal conflicts raging within a child and the relationship of these conflicts to external, complex, environmental events.

Biogenic factors usually are more evident in the severe classifications of emotional disturbance. The presence of a genetic correlation has been noted for many years; the risk of becoming psychotic is greater for those who are genetically related to a person diagnosed as psychotic. Eysenck (1961) and Kauffman (1977) describe this relationship in some detail.

A note of caution is indicated here, to forestall what may be erroneous conclusions. If one identical twin is schizophrenic, the other's risk of becoming schizophrenic is high. It is about 90 percent if the twins are not environmentally separated, and the risk drops to about 75 percent if they are separated. This difference may be attributed to environmental influences. The caution is that the risk estimates are correlational, not causal. If schizophrenia were postulated to be caused by a recessive gene, for example, it would follow that all children of two schizophrenic parents would be schizophrenic. This does not occur. The risk, while high, is about 39 percent (Eysenck, 1961). Apparently, other complex factors, including family situations and child rearing practices, operate along with genetic factors in determining outcomes. Another question is, if two schizophrenic parents provide a highly pathological environment, why don't more than 39 percent of the children develop schizophrenia? This field of research is indeed complex, but its importance is great, as it has implications for prevention of emotional disturbance.

Psychogenic factors are those associated with the relationship between child and environment over time. The search for psychogenic causation of emotional disturbance involves careful study by mental health professionals for the full range of emotional disorders, mild through severe, and covers an individual's infancy, early childhood, late childhood, and adolescence. These time periods are used only for convenience in developing an interpersonal history; the periods overlap and are interwoven with each other. The study ranges from comprehensive analysis of events occurring over a period of years to the intensive study of immediate situations. If a child suddenly exhibits maladaptive styles of coping behaviors, the search for cause may be confined to the present or immediate past; but if troublesome behavior has developed gradually to the point that it increasingly attracts the attention of others, the search may probe for traumatic experiences in both the distant and recent past.

Etiology is a complex subject. Rarely does an investigation reveal a one-to-one effect between specific cause and specific behavior. Etiology is as varied as the varieties of behavior displayed by children diagnosed as emotionally disturbed. Rhodes (1972) has developed a significant analysis of the many factors associated with causes of emotional disturbance, one that reviews the various theories or approaches to determining etiology.

Educators, while realistically concerned with understanding the causes of behavior, also must realize that whatever the etiology, the responsibility for arranging productive learning environments remains constant. A child with biological insults must be taught just as responsibly as one who has experienced psychological trauma. However, better understanding of the conditions can lead to development of learning strategies directly related to the correction of factors which evoked maladaptive behavior patterns in the first place. Understanding serves as a foundation, a rationale, for approaching solutions to problems that children present to educators.

Two divergent approaches to understanding the origins of emotional disturbance have been selected for illustration (Figure 7.2). This schematic is vastly simplified here. The two selected approaches are highly complex and require extensive study for complete understanding. Nevertheless, the figure is designed to point out some contrasts and similarities between two different approaches to understanding the origins of emotional disturbance.

An *intrapsychic approach* (at times referred to as psychoanalytic) seeks to understand etiology through an intense examination of the inner turmoil reflected by the observable behaviors. The *behavioral approach*, an accumulation of several learning theories, searches for the understanding of cause by observing the relationship among the complex environmental events that elicit and maintain deviant behavior.

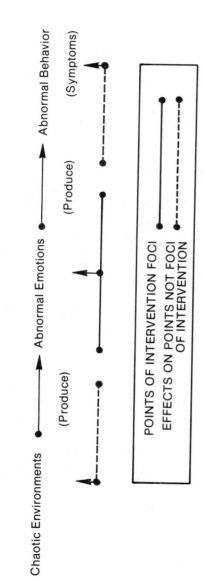
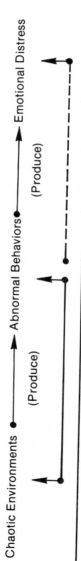

Figure 7.2 Simplified Schematic of Two Approaches for Explaining the Origins of Emotional Disturbance

The commonality between the two approaches is the *chaotic environment.* Chaotic environments are characterized by (1) incorrect and inconsistent behavior expectations, and (2) incorrect and inconsistent application of behavior events.

Incorrect and inconsistent behavior expectations are those that are too high or too low, and are too variable in the manner presented. For instance, a child may be expected to perform considerably beyond capability at one time, yet kept from performing at another time by being forced into a dependency relationship. Behavior events refer to the consequences that follow behavior. A child may be punished severely, out of proportion, for the same act which is praised at another time. In other words, the child is confronted by confusion and chaos, a situation of uncertainty in which sustained, adaptive growth potential is seriously diminished.

In the intrapsychic approach, chaotic environments are believed to produce abnormal or damaged emotions; i.e., the child's inner life is so disorganized that accurate perceptions and functional cognitive strengths are absent. These abnormal emotions logically produce or are reflected by the resulting observable, abnormal behaviors (symptoms). Abnormal behavior, thus, is a reflection and functional result of damage to the emotions. It also provides a tactic to relieve the distress and anxiety caused by abnormal emotions. One way to manage the fear of uncertainty, for instance, is to become extremely compulsive and "busy" via the bizarre actions of counting, pointing, and chanting rituals. This activity keeps anxiety at a tolerable level, but at the expense of adequate solutions to daily tasks of living.

Intervention or therapeutic efforts concentrate upon changing the inner turmoil or abnormal emotions. If the inner self can be strengthened, one can build a predictable environment from chaos. And, since the symptoms reflect the abnormal emotions, they will disappear when intervention is successful in changing the emotions.

Contrasted to the intrapsychic, the behavioral approach focuses intervention efforts upon abnormal behaviors and the chaotic environments that produce them. In other words, if individuals learn abnormal behavior, they may learn adaptive behavior, through rearrangement of the environment. A child who behaves in ways that bring negative attention from others is assumed to feel emotional distress or pain. At some level, the child realizes that deviant behavior is neither gratifying nor helpful. Emotional distress reflects evaluations placed on experiences. A child who fails a reading lesson feels less worthy as a result of that experience, despite the external bravado of not caring, which is displayed to cover up the pain.

Emotional distress also functions to provide a negative anticipatory set for entry into future interaction. If learning interactions are associated with failure, motivation to exhibit behavior (abnormal) that avoids interaction is strengthened. If the child and those who assist in changing environments and behaviors are successful, emotional distress is changed to emotional happiness (a condition reflecting positive evaluations of experience) and an eagerness to approach future positive interactions (Whelan, 1977).

Whatever etiological understanding and its associated intervention strategies professionals prefer, they must realize that children are not interested in theories. The theory which most successfully leads to alleviation of pain and to personal and interpersonal feelings of accomplishment is the ultimate validation. One approach may work better in dealing with inner turmoil. Another may work better with a child in conflict with the environment. Either way, the child must be the winner, not the theory. Only when children win can the professionals win too. The search for etiology leads to classification of children and their behaviors. That search has a profound influence upon children, resulting in proper assistance or in victimization through error (Hobbs, 1975).

BEHAVIOR COPING STYLES

The ways children devise to cope with internal and external chaos are as varied as the number of children who display them. Kauffman (1977) has classified coping styles or behavior patterns into four facets. The first includes the common dimensions of undifferentiated responses to stimuli—distractible, hyperactive, and impulsive behaviors. The second facet is directed aggression against self and others. A third facet describes children who cope by withdrawing from intervention and regressing to immature styles (e.g., tantrums, extreme dependence). The fourth facet represents behavior which violates a code of behavior prescribing the differences between right and wrong.

As indicated previously, behavior coping styles are usually of two types, excesses and deficits. Excesses are the behaviors that parents, teachers, and peers would like to reduce or eliminate. Deficits are behaviors that children fail to display or do not have in their repertoire at a level commensurate with expectations or capabilities. Deficit and excessive behaviors are children's ways of avoiding circumstances associated with pain and failure and of coping with problems from within and without, problems for which they very much need assistance.

Excessive and deficit behaviors can be further delineated into academic and social behaviors. In a study (Whelan & Gallagher, 1972),[2] school teachers were asked to list specific behaviors which they believed interfered with children's adjustment. As anticipated, boys exceeded girls by a ratio of 4 to 1 for the behaviors listed by the teachers. Over 50 percent of the behaviors listed were social, usually excessive, and 37 percent were academic, usually deficit.

Examples of social behaviors were disruptive talking without permission, being out of seat, touching, hitting, pushing, tripping, squirming, thumb sucking, and low frequence of social interaction (deficit). Academic behaviors involved incomplete work, late completion

---

2. This study was completed at a mental health workshop organized by Dr. Richard J. Whelan, University of Kansas; Dr. Patricia A. Gallagher, University of Kansas; Dr. Judith Grosenick, University of Missouri-Columbia; and Dr. Roger Kroth, University of New Mexico.

of work, inaccurate work, slowness, and sloppiness. Of the behaviors listed, 57 percent were targeted for decreasing (excesses) and 43 percent for increasing (removing the deficit). Thus, behaviors which children display as coping devices are readily recognized by teachers as needing special instructional strategies and tactics.

Coping styles adopted by children usually can be identified as one of three types. Type 1 is demonstrated by the child who can succeed, but will not invest energy in task completion. The teacher's expectations for performances are realistic, but the child's avoidance behaviors are so well established that discrimination between realistic and unrealistic requests to become involved with a task is not operational. The probability of pain through failure is just too high to risk.

The Type 2 child accepts an assigned task, but either doesn't complete it or makes many errors. Again, this coping style functions to avoid personal investment. To invest and still fail is a proposition too devastating to risk. This coping style is not characterized by the verbal and physical hostility inherent in refusal to try as is the case with Type 1. Rather, the Type 2 child can avoid the painful consequences of inappropriate aggression by placidly using up allotted task time in a nonproductive fashion. For both types, though, the result is the same, another failure.

The Type 3 child is described as having given up, characterized by the absence of behavior, a withdrawal from fighting expectations, or even the semblance of attempting to meet requests for performance. The child can be described as having resigned from the environment. All three types demand considerable teaching expertise to change the pattern of failure to one of success, but the Type 3 child presents the greatest challenge to those who hope to help children.

Children's ways of managing or coping with internal and external conflicts may not be consistent. For one situation, the style may be aggression. For another circumstance, the style may be withdrawal. For yet another situation, the child may feign compliance but remain unproductive as far as improving competencies for dealing with expectations. Emotionally disturbed children's past history is laced with many failures, all due to the inability of the environment to sustain acquisition and maintenance of increasingly complex styles needed for successful coping. The chaotic environment, until it is changed, functions to strengthen the very behaviors which interfere with the development of personally satisfying and gratifying behavior coping styles.

EDUCATIONAL STRATEGIES

Educators must deal with the behavior copying styles which emotionally disturbed children exhibit. To do so, the pattern of failure must be changed to one of success. When adults intervene to help, they must convince children that it is not another form of rejection (Long, 1974), an event they have experienced so many times during their lives.

Years ago, the field of educational planning, implementation, and evaluation for emotionally disturbed children was rife with theoretical ferment, unchanging positions, and failure to address the real issues— ensuring that children become winners (Morse, Cutler, & Fink, 1974). In retrospect, that ferment probably was desirable to the extent that the issues were defined and, therefore, could be resolved. As Morse (1977) points out, advocates of supposedly divergent theoretical positions are now finally beginning dialogues leading to mutual understanding. Children's needs are not being sacrificed for the protection of theoretical turfs.

This is not to imply that all is well in the education of troubled and troublesome children. It is not. There is much to be done and much to learn from the best teachers of all, the children. Their responses to what professionals say and do are the best guide to evaluate the success or failure of educational strategies.

The instructional procedures described have and are being used by competent teachers of emotionally disturbed children. They are descriptive rather than prescriptive. That is, their functional use requires intensive study and supervised practice and should be applied only when those circumstances prevail. These descriptions hopefully will motivate those with a commitment to the education of handicapped children, particularly the emotionally disturbed, to undertake the arduous, yet fulfilling journey of preparing to teach these children with so many unmet needs.

Educational Environments

Not too many years ago, schools routinely excluded children with problems. Emotionally disturbed children were in the sphere of agencies other than schools. They either remained at home or were placed in residential centers for custodial purposes. If education and other therapeutic services were provided, they were the exception rather than the rule. But as educators became more involved in and responsible for the emotional well being of children, programs gradually were initiated by the public schools. At first, these programs consisted of special day schools and isolated special classes, a giant step at the time, but one that seems small from the present day frame of reference.

Progress in providing programs based upon children's needs has been fraught by a pattern of "advance two steps and retreat one." Progress has been slow, but steady. Educators finally are starting to match "say" with "do" behaviors. We realize that children come to school as individuals and, therefore, require individualized planning. This concept is paramount to the emotionally disturbed who present variable quantities and qualities of diverse needs, all of which require differentially planned educational environments.

Figure 7.3 displays an administrative design for providing educational services directly related to children's needs. The services are referred to Facilitative Education Programs (Whelan, 1972) to emphasize the goals of child progress—every child a winner. These programs are designed to provide functional assistance and services for children who have not progressed as anticipated in areas of academic and social behavior development within their current learning environments. Such programs provide facilitative learning experiences for children whose progress in academic and social behavior has been limited by the nature of past and present learning environments, and attempt to change that history by facilitating acquisition of academic and social behaviors necessary for realistic and desirable progress.

Facilitative learning environments offer many options for children to receive the needed opportunities for learning and growth, both academically and socially. Placement according to individual needs is the critical factor. Another critical element is the freedom of movement among placements, again based upon the unique requirements brought by children to instructional organizations.

Coordinated and concerted use of community resources is vital for the successful operation of facilitative education programs. Emotionally disturbed children, perhaps more than any other handicapped group, require the best efforts of a multidisciplinary team if they are to be the beneficiaries rather than the victims of the caring professions. Psychiatrists, social workers, and clinical psychologists comprise the staffs of mental health and guidance centers—community resources which must be called upon by educators in planning assistance for children and their parents. Unless services are coordinated through effective communication, parents and children will be caught in unnecessary professional conflict, a burden they should not be expected to carry.

Developing and operationalizing administrative program arrangements, though important, represent the beginning of the beginning

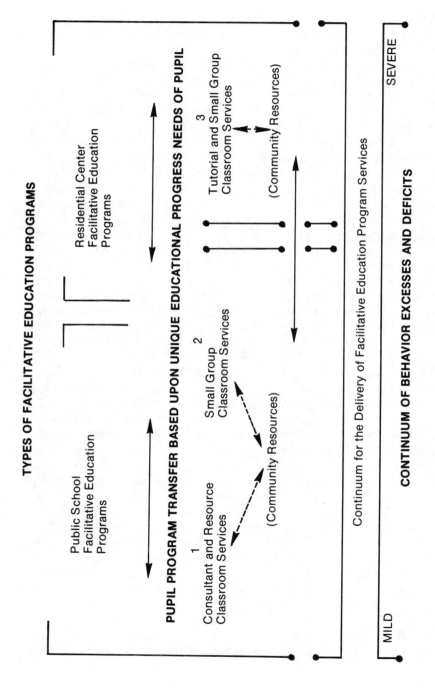

Figure 7.3 Schematic of Facilitative Education Program Services

rather than the end. What goes on within these arrangements is the most important consideration. Unless child-helper interactions are filled with warmth, understanding, and supportive firmness when children's internal controls fail, goals will not be accomplished. It is not enough to establish ends; means must be arranged to reach them.

Establishing Child-Teacher Relationships

Rothman (1977) has written a soul-searching and emotionally wrenching book which should be required reading for all teachers who aspire to help children learn, especially teachers of the emotionally disturbed. Rothman makes the point that teachers should not aspire to win status by dominating children. Teacher status is enhanced when the learning styles of children are recognized and responded to by differential teaching. Teachers win when children win. Rothman pleads the case for inner examination of motivation, as well as the external trappings of professional identification. If teachers have experienced past hurt, they all too easily (based on unawareness) transfer that hurt on to children under the guise of instruction. Long (1974) refers to this phenomenon as negative environmental practices, the tendency to respond in like manner to responses from others directed at self (e.g., aggression is met with aggression).

Few would challenge the assertion that a teacher is effective only after mastering how and what to teach. Teachers, like administrators, must be adept at arranging means to ends. They must know how to involve children in establishing ends and the means to reach them. They must establish a child-teacher relationship for the purpose of enhancing academic and social growth in the children for whom they are responsible. Role and relationship are intertwined, mutually interdependent; one cannot exist without the other. Interestingly, emotionally disturbed children are extremely perceptive, a skill learned from their prior devastating experiences with supposedly helpful adults. They can "smell out" incompetence, the absence of caring, and the true motivations of their professional helpers. An ineffective teacher does not establish positive relationships with children, and in the absence of positive relationships, desirable learning does not occur.

What are the requirements for building a positive relationship with emotionally disturbed children? Morse (1976) believes that two affective elements are essential: differential acceptance and empathic relationship.

Differential acceptance is the ability of teachers to receive large doses of hate, aggression, and hostility without reacting in kind to the children who transmit them. These behaviors are accepted for what they are—expressions of pain and anguish from the many hurts previously inflicted. Accepting behavior should not be confused with condoning it. Indeed, to do so would be a disservice to children. Differential acceptance means understanding without condemning. A child who destroys property in angry frustration can be understood, but the teacher need not approve of the destructive act.

The author once said to a child who was tearing up a book, "You know, it is OK to be angry, but I will not let you destroy the book. We can work together to deal with your anger." The child responded, wide-eyed, "I didn't know that. I thought that being angry was bad." From that point on, the child did not destroy any instructional materials, and gradually, through modeling, learned to manage and express anger in productive ways, a step toward achieving the goal of self-control. To allow a child to act out every impulse in a destructive manner is to fail the child, and when that happens, the teacher fails too. After all, emotionally disturbed children, by their very label, are unable to set a viable self structure. They must depend for awhile upon the external structure provided by others for support in dealing with inner feelings and outer expressions of them.

The *empathic relationship* requires that teachers develop the ability to discover clues, other than verbal ones, which children provide as mirrors for their inner states of being. The author, during a therapeutic camping experience, responded to the nonverbal cues of a child who did not want to camp overnight. The child's verbal behavior contained statements such as, "It's baby stuff to camp. Who needs it?" This particular child, however, was really afraid of being assaulted by other children during the night and wanted to avoid this incorrectly perceived risk. To argue logically about issues of safety, being good to get out, and so forth, would have been futile. Rather, this child was told that an assistant was needed to set up tents and build a good campfire. The child responded to this approach, discovered that assaults did not occur and, just to make sure, kept the fire roaring all night. With each subsequent camping experience, the reluctance to participate diminished, and the child actually began to enjoy camping. Anxiety, the anticipation of aversive events, was displaced by joy, the anticipation of pleasurable events, by using the empathic relationship.

Once teachers have learned to use differential acceptance and empathic relationship skills, positive interpersonal interactions with emotionally disturbed children can be established. Brendtro (Trieschman, Whittaker, & Brendtro, 1969) has further described the goals of developing a positive interpersonal relationship. Figure 7.4 is a modified schematic of the structural components intrinsic to the relationship

CHILD NEEDS	TEACHER ROLE
1. To develop responsiveness to instructions and consequences.	1. Expectations and corrective feedback source.
2. To develop analytic and synthetic insight.	2. Communication facilitation source.
3. To develop identification and imitation adaptive behavior styles.	3. Functional model source.

Figure 7.4 Structural Components of a Facilitative Interpersonal Relationship

building process. The process includes children's needs and teachers' role in meeting them. Because of their past failure-oriented history, emotionally disturbed children are not responsive to teacher's requests for certain behaviors and do not seek out their approval. In fact, approval often has the opposite effect; i.e., the responding ceases when it is approved by a teacher.

Teachers, by building trust and being supportive of children's efforts, gradually become valued sources of expectations and corrective feedback. Whenever possible, teachers should encourage children to talk about their feelings, an appropriate mode as contrasted to destructive acting out of feelings and impulses. Talking leads to insight, and often leads to changes in behaviors: "Yes, there is a better way to express anger than tearing up a book. Here are some alternatives." This is analogous to the "light bulb" over a cartoon character's head: "Now I understand. I see it all now."

The teacher also must be a functional model source. The word *functional* is stressed because if what the teacher models does not work for the child, the relationship will be impaired. Modeling an appropriate response to frustration will be adopted by a child if it functions to enhance adaptive behaviors, ones leading to success and satisfaction.

Describing child-teacher positive relationships, of course, is much easier than establishing them. Hard, dedicated work is required by both teachers and children. Many ups and downs will occur along the way, but progress will become apparent with sustained effort.

Relationship establishment usually passes through several stages (Haring & Whelan, 1965). The first is *orientation* or, as some teachers describe it, the honeymoon. This stage is in evidence when children first enter a placement. They try to appear well controlled, although obviously this is done at great cost, a veneer. This stage may last for several weeks. As the children become more comfortable and discern that the teacher will not destroy them, the second stage ensues. This is called *shaping* or *reality testing*. The children start to display the behaviors that originally led to their placement. Limits and teacher patience are tested frequently. Will the teachers "say and do" behaviors match? If the match is consistent, the third stage, *cognition*, is reached. During cognition, children begin to internalize the external environmental supports. They can verbalize them but cannot always match their behavior with the acquired insights.

The last stage, *integration*, is characterized by consistent matching of insights with observable behaviors. Children have put them together in a truly functional style of coping with daily living, including its joys and hurts. Now though, the joys are much more frequent than the hurts. Based upon guaranteed success, provided by teachers, children now approach problems with motivation to solve them for the intrinsic pleasure associated with achieving. They become motivated by the opportunity to attain, rather than motivated by the avoidance of failure. The changed motivation is reflected in their changed behavior coping styles.

Instructional Considerations

As indicated previously, the building of relationships is concurrent with providing successful learning experiences, both in the academic and social behavior areas. The concept of structure (Haring & Phillips, 1962; Hewett, 1968) provides the philosophical milieu in which relationship and instruction are combined to help emotionally disturbed children enjoy success and win. Structure is based upon the assertion that when a child succeeds in a task within an environment which facilitates success, academic and social behavior progress occurs. More specifically, *structure* is defined as behavior change procedures designed to specify and clarify the interactions among environmental events and behaviors, and the arrangement of environmental events to promote specified behavior changes (Whelan & Gallagher, 1972).

Structure also includes the precise use of behavior analysis as a measurement tool rather than an intervention method. That is, the effectiveness of a life-space interview (Morse, 1976) can be determined by applying the measurement procedures of behavior analysis. It is neutral, adaptable to intervention procedures associated with a wide array of theoretical positions.

Scientific validation of an intervention program requires (1) specification of behavior to be changed, (2) observation of the behavior before intervention, (3) during the intervention, and (4) after the intervention. This procedure can be used with intrapsychic and behaviorally derived intervention through precise, though not complex, measurement procedures.

An example of this validation procedure is displayed in Figure 7.5. The behavioral descriptions, distractions (excitement) and group contagion are associated with an intrapsychic orientation (Redl & Wineman, 1957). "Hurdle help," an intervention technique, is just one of many suggested by Redl and Wineman for teachers to use in instructional environments for emotionally disturbed children. Clinically, it has been noted that when one child becomes excited or distracted, other children may respond in the same manner; one child's behavior is contagious for other children. As shown in Figure 7.5, a one-to-one relationship between the number of distractions and the number of contagions is not the case, but the two tend to go together. Hurdle help was applied only to the child with distractions. During intervention, the other children did not receive hurdle help. In the figure, behavior of the child who received hurdle help with a task is indicated by open circles. Total number of group contagions is illustrated by the closed circles. Hurdle help obviously had an effect in decreasing individual distractions and group catagions. Also, when hurdle help was terminated, distractions and contagions began to increase again. This is a sign that hurdle help was removed too soon; the natural or intrinsic consequences of completing a task successfully were not internalized sufficiently to remove the external support of hurdle help.

One other point needs to be made in regard to the figure. It functions to verify the "ripple effect" (Kounin, 1977). Ripple effect describes what happens to other children as a result of observing what happens to another child. Even though the group was not involved in the prescribed intervention, the number of contagions was diminished.

Thus, structure and behavior analysis provide for a match between

DISTRACTIONS O/ CONTAGIONS ◐

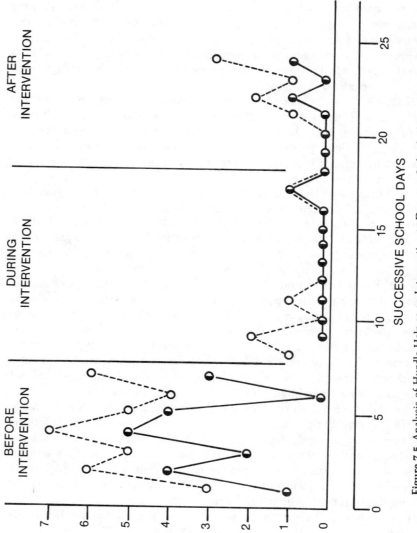

Figure 7.5 Analysis of Hurdle Help as an Intervention to Decrease Individual Distractions and Group Contagion

children's needs and the procedure used to meet them. By measuring the effects of hurdle help, for example, a teacher can determine if it works. If it does not, a match is not made, and other procedures need to be applied.

The concept of structure and measurement can be applied to academic behaviors as well as social ones. Figure 7.6 displays the result of one such brief intervention. Note that after the car was assembled, the word recognition scores remained high. Internal gratification associated with successful task completion became strong enough to maintain the behavior. This study is one example of how a teacher might relate to a Type 1 child through the precise use of motivation. It is also an example of how a teacher can become a source of expectations and consequences—one component of establishing a positive child-teacher relationship. A Type 2 child requires intensive materials presentation arrangements and brief tasks in order to achieve success. External motivation, although important, may be of only secondary importance. The Type 3 child probably will require precise planning of task presentation, and careful, consistent use of appropriate environmental consequences. Whatever the type of child encountered, *the most critical factors involve effective use of instructional materials, motivation, external and internal, and interpersonal relationship strength.* All must work together for the benefit of children.

Gallagher (1970) has developed the application of structure beyond that contained in its brief definition. She provides several guidelines for classroom instructional procedures:

1. Initial instruction is focused upon the individual child; group instruction is introduced as children are ready to progress through its use.
2. Classroom physical arrangements are changed from individual task areas to include cooperative group problem solving areas.
3. Prescribed times for task completion are changed to flexible time periods for the completion of long-term individual and group projects.
4. Student participation in planning tasks is gradually introduced.
5. Teacher supervision of classroom activities is partially replaced by children's self supervision.
6. Extrinsic consequences for task completion are replaced by intrinsic feelings of self worth that accompany success. Achievement and self esteem go together.
7. Initial placement of children for special educational services is on a full-time basis. As the children progress, they are phased (mainstreamed) into activities with peers (e.g., regular classroom).

These seven steps, or guidelines, are selected examples of the elaboration which Gallagher has proposed to make the structured approach even more useful to teachers. The approach has been used to teach emotionally disturbed children positive, creative behavior coping styles (Gallagher, 1972). Implementing the guidelines is much more difficult than verbalizing them. It requires many teacher hours of individual and group planning. The guidelines follow very closely the notion that

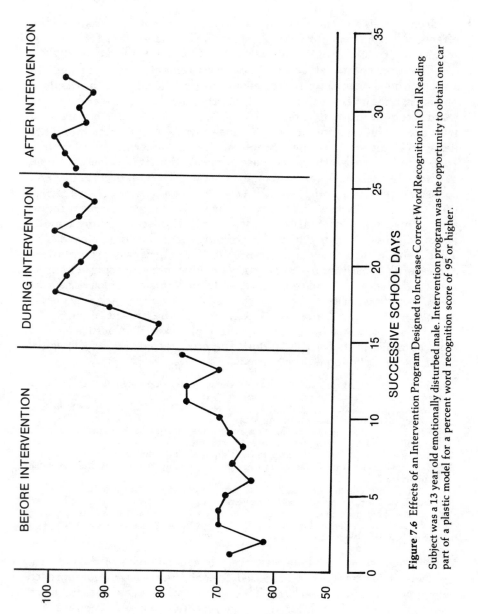

Figure 7.6 Effects of an Intervention Program Designed to Increase Correct Word Recognition in Oral Reading

Subject was a 13 year old emotionally disturbed male. Intervention program was the opportunity to obtain one car part of a plastic model for a percent word recognition score of 95 or higher.

emotionally disturbed children need experiences with external structure before they can develop the internal strengths to be successful as they function in a variety of environments.

Teachers of emotionally disturbed children must continually question their approaches to relationships and instruction and to follow through diligently to find answers. The questions and procedures listed in Figure 7.7 represent processes for solving the myriad of problems that arise. As such, they are not solutions, but if followed can lead to them. They include diagnosis, program planning, implementation and evaluation.

QUESTIONS	PROCEDURES
1. What behavior excesses and deficits are observed in the present learning environment and prior to entry into a changed learning environment?	1. Identification and analysis of behavior excesses and deficits observed in specific learning environments.
2. What are the specific terminal or target behaviors that will be acquired within, and upon departure from, a changed learning environment?	2. Specification of terminal behaviors that should be acquired to decrease the extent of excesses and deficits.
3. What are the systematic environmental transaction experiences that will be implemented to reduce discrepancies between behavior excesses/deficits and specified terminal behaviors?	3. Implementation of environmental transaction experiences in learning environments designed to reduce the discrepancies between behavior excesses/deficits and specified terminal behaviors.
4. What measurement and evaluation procedures can be applied to determine effectiveness of environmental transaction experiences implemented to reduce discrepancies between observed entry and departure behaviors?	4. Application of simultaneous measurement and evaluation procedures in order to assess the effectiveness of environmental transaction experiences in attaining specified terminal behaviors.
5. What measurement procedures can be utilized to assess the maintenance and generalization of acquired terminal behaviors after departure from a changed learning environment?	5. Initiation of systematic and periodic measurement to ascertain extent of maintenance and generalization of terminal behaviors in learning environments different from the one in which acquisition occurred.

Figure 7.7 Delineation of Behaviors that can be Designated for Application of Behavior Change Processes

Besides the basic instructional competencies involved in teaching subject matter, teachers need to know how to measure behavior, evaluate instructional effectiveness, prepare and organize learning environments, instruct with media, use differential instructional procedures based on children's needs, and apply principles of behavior in wise and productive ways. These skills and knowledge are not learned quickly or easily and must be constantly refined as teachers learn from and with children. Teachers also must learn how to help children develop self control over their lives (Fagan, Long, & Stevens, 1975), the ultimate goal of what we do for, to, and with them. Too, teachers must learn the techniques of smoothly changing classroom activities to reduce frustration encountered by emotionally disturbed children during periods of little external support (Kounin, 1977). The list of skills and understandings is endless, but important if emotionally disturbed children are to change their life pattern from one of predominant failure to one of earned success.

SUMMARY

Educational planning and programming for emotionally disturbed children have improved considerably over the years. The influences of diverse cultural, minority, and economic backgrounds are recognized as valued differences rather than undesirable deviance. Descriptions and definitions are becoming more educationally relevant rather than medically based. Various approaches to understanding child development have been combined, in some instances, to use as a foundation for planning academic and social behavior instructional strategies. Educators are becoming more aware of the role which children's language can play in self instruction procedures, a cognitive approach to behavior change (Meichenbaum, 1977). They are also learning how to enlist the assistance of children to help other children in need (Graubard & Rosenberg, 1974).

Although some progress has been made, much more remains to be accomplished in educational programming for emotionally disturbed children. Constant evaluation-research studies must be done to assess the effectiveness of educational efforts. The appropriate use of what is known is also a major challenge. Merely knowing what to do does not ensure that conditions are present to support the actual doing. Often, conditions are not present to sustain dedicated, professional educators. As a result, they may become discouraged and leave the field (Knoblock & Goldstein, 1971).

This discussion provides a spot-check, a still photograph, of a dynamic topic and field. Educators of emotionally disturbed children are still searching for more precise child behavior descriptions, for better understanding of how behavior develops and changes, for more functional approaches to help children acquire self control, and for better, more efficient and effective ways to ensure that the joys of successful learning are experienced frequently by the children for whom they are responsible. The ferment is still present, but it is now targeted toward helping children help themselves to become winners. And what happens when emotionally disturbed children become winners? They tell it best, because children know best what it is all about:

—Yep! She told me that I did good work today.
—Why can't I stay after school to finish this? It's fun.
—I like to be in your class.
—That tantrum is really crazy. Doesn't he know that won't get him any place?
—I'm tired of being so happy.

What better validation is there than from the children themselves? Indeed, children are the best evaluators of program effectiveness. Responsible educators must ensure that the evaluations reflect positive and successful, rather than negative and unsuccessful, programs for this country's most important resource—children.

REFERENCES

Bower, E.M. *Early identification of emotionally handicapped children in school* (2nd ed.). Springfield, IL: Charles C. Thomas, 1969.

Dodge, A.B. *National assessment of the supply and demand of personnel to work with the handicapped.* Unpublished master's thesis, University of Kansas, 1976.

Eysenck, H.J. (Ed.). *Handbook of Abnormal Psychology.* New York: Basic Books, 1961.

Fagan, S., Long, N.J., & Stevens, D.J. *Teaching children self control.* Columbus, OH: Charles E. Merrill Publishing Co., 1975.

Freud, S. Totem and Taboo (J. Strachey, Ed. and trans.). New York: W.W. Norton & Co., 1950. (Originally published 1913)

Gallagher, P.A. A synthesis of classroom scheduling techniques for emotionally disturbed children. *Focus on Exceptional Children,* 1970, 2 (5), 1-10.

Gallagher, P.A. Procedures for developing creativity in emotionally disturbed children. *Focus on Exceptional Children,* 1972, 4 (6), 1-9.

Goulder, R.J., & Trybus, R.J. *The classroom behavior of emotionally disturbed hearing impaired children* (Office of Demographic Studies, Series R, No. 3). Washington, DC: Gallaudet College, August, 1977.

Graubard, P., & Rosenberg, H. *Classrooms that work.* New York: E.P. Dutton & Co., 1974.

Haring, N.G., & Phillips, E.L. *Educating emotionally disturbed children,* New York: McGraw-Hill, 1962.

Haring, N.G., & Whelan, R.J. Experimental methods in education and management. In N. Long, W. Morse, & R. Newman (Eds.), *Conflict in the classroom* (1st ed.). Belmont, CA: Wadsworth Publishing Co. 1965.

Hewett, F.M. *The emotionally disturbed child in the classroom.* Boston: Allyn & Bacon, 1968.

Hobbs, N. *The futures of children.* Washington, DC: Jossey-Bass, 1975.

Johnson, J.L. Mainstreaming black children. In R.L. Jones (Ed.), *Mainstreaming and the minority child.* Reston, VA: The Council for Exceptional Children, 1976.

Jones, R.L. (Ed.). *Mainstreaming and the minority child.* Reston, VA: The Council for Exceptional Children, 1976.

Kanner, L. Autistic disturbances of affective contact. *Nervous Child,* 1943, *2,* 217-250.

Kauffman, J.M. *Characteristics of children's behavior disorders.* Columbus, OH: Charles E. Merrill Publishing Co., 1977.

Kelly, T.J., Bullock, L.M., & Dykes, M.K. Behavior disorders: Teachers' perceptions. *Exceptional Children,* 1977, *43,* 316-318.

Knoblock, P., & Goldstein, A. *The lonely teacher.* Boston: Allyn & Bacon, 1971.

Kounin, J.S. *Discipline and group management in classrooms.* Huntington, NY: Robert E. Krieger Publishing Co., 1977.

Long, N.J. In J.M. Kauffman & C.D. Lewis (Eds.), *Teaching children with behavior disorders; Personal perspectives.* Columbus, OH: Charles E. Merrill Publishing Co., 1974.

Meichenbaum, D. *Cognitive behavior modification.* New York: Plenum Press, 1977.

Morse, W.C. Worsheet on life-space interviewing for teachers. In N. Long, W. Morse, & R. Newman (Eds.), *Conflict in the classroom.* Belmont, CA: Wadsworth Publishing Co., 1976.

Morse, W.C., Serving the needs of children with behavior disorders. *Exceptional Children,* 1977, *44,* 158-164.

Morse, W.C., Cutler, R.L., & Fink, A.H. *Public school classes for the emotionally handicapped: A research analysis.* Washington, DC: The Council for Exceptional Children, 1964.

Pate, J.E., Emotionally disturbed and socially maladjusted children. In L. Dunn (Ed.), *Exceptional children in the schools.* New York: Holt, Rinehart & Winston, 1963.

Redl, F., & Wineman, D. *The aggressive child.* New York: The Free Press of Glencoe, 1957.

Rhodes, W.C. (Ed.). *A study of child variance* (Vol. 1). Ann Arbor, MI: The University of Michigan Press, 1972.

Rhodes, W.C. The illusion of normality. *Journal of the Council for Children with Behavior Disorders,* 1977, *2.* 122-129.

Rothman, E.P. *Troubled teachers.* New York: David McKay Co., 1977.

Szasz, T.S. *The myth of mental illness* (rev.). New York: Harper & Row, 1974.

Trieschman, A.E., Whittaker, J.K., & Brendtro, L.K. *The other 23 hours.* Chicago: Aldine Publishing Co., 1969.

Whelan, R.J., & Jackson, F.S. Labeling. In J. Cohen (Ed.), *Confrontation and change: Community problems of mental retardation and developmental disabilities.* Ann Arbor, MI: University of Michigan Publications, 1971.

Whelan, R.J., & Gallagher, P.A. Effective teaching of children with behavior disorders. In N.G. Haring & A.H. Hayden (Eds.), *The improvement of instruction.* Seattle, WA: Special Child Publications, Inc., 1972.

Whelan, R.J. What's in a label? A hell of a lot! In R. Harth, E. Meyen, & G.S. Nelson (Eds.), *The legal and educational consequences of the intelligence testing movement: Handicapped children and minority group children.* Columbia, MO: University of Missouri Extension Division, 1972.

Whelan, R.J., & Sontag, E. Prologue: Special education and the cities. In P. Mann (Ed.), *Mainstream special education.* Reston, VA: The Council for Exceptional Children, 1974.

Whelan, R.J. Human understanding of human behavior. In A.J. Pappanikou & J.L. Paul (Eds.), *Mainstreaming emotionally disturbed children.* Syracuse, NY: Syracuse University Press, 1977.

Wiener, N. The human use of human beings (2nd ed.). New York: Doubleday, 1954.

RESOURCE GUIDE

Historical Information

Berkowitz, P. H., & Rothman, E. P. *The disturbed child.* New York: New York University Press, 1962.

Bower, E. M., & Hollister, W. G. (Eds.). *Behavioral science frontiers in education.* New York: John Wiley & Sons, Inc., 1967.

Harth, R. (Ed.). *Issues in behavior disorders.* Springfield, IL: Charles C. Thomas, 1971.

Kauffman, J. M. Nineteenth century views of children's behavior disorders: Historical contributions and continuing issues. *Journal of Special Education,* 1976, *10,* 335-349.

Redl, F. *When we deal with children.* New York: The Free Press, 1966.

Family

Herzog, E., & Sudai, C. E. Children in fatherless families. In B. M. Caldwell & H. N. Ricciuti (Eds.), *Review of child development research* (Vol. 3). Chicago: University of Chicago Press, 1973.

Kroth, R. L. *Communicating with parents of exceptional children.* Denver: Love Publishing Co., 1975.

Kroth, R. L., & Simpson, R. L. *Parent conferences as a teaching strategy.* Denver: Love Publishing Co., 1977.

Lobitz, C. W., & Johnson, S. M. Parental manipulation of the behavior of normal and deviant children. *Child Development,* 1975, *46,* 719-726.

Misher, E. G., & Waxler, N. E. *Interaction in families: An experimental study of family processes in schizophrenia.* New York: John Wiley & Sons, 1968.

Patterns of Development

Johnson, J. L. Special education and the inner city: A challenge for the future or another means of cooling the mark out? *Journal of Special Education,* 1969, *3,* 241-251.

Kanner, L. Historical perspectives on developmental deviation. *Journal of Autism and Childhood Schizophrenia,* 1973, *3,* 187-198.

McClearn, G. E. Genetics and behavior development. In M. L. Hoffman & L. W. Hoffman (Eds.), *Review of child development research* (Vol. 1). New York: Russell Sage Foundation, 1964.

Payne, J. S., Kauffman, J. M., Bown, G. B., & DeMott, R. M., *Exceptional children in focus.* Columbus, OH: Charles E. Merrill, 1974.

Rubin, R., & Balow, B. Learning and behavior disorders: A longitudinal study. *Exceptional Children,* 1971, *38,* 293-299.

Treatment

Axline, V. *Play therapy.* Boston: Houghton-Mifflin, 1947.
Bettelheim, B. *The empty fortress.* New York: The Free Press, 1967.
Easson, W. M. *The severely disturbed adolescent.* New York: International Universities Press, Inc., 1969.
Glasser, W. *Reality therapy.* New York: Harper & Row, 1965.
Graziano, A. M. (Ed.). *Behavior therapy with children* (Vol. 2). Chicago, IL: Aldine Publishing Co., 1975.
Hobbs, N. How the Re-Ed plan developed. In N. J. Long, W. C. Morse, & R. G. Newman (Eds.), *Conflict in the classroom.* Belmont, CA: Wadsworth, 1965.
Robins, L. N. *Deviant children grown up.* Baltimore, MD: Williams & Wilkins Co., 1966.

Educational Programming

Ekstein, R., & Motto, R. L. (Eds.). *From learning to love to love of learning.* New York: Brunner/Mazel Publishers, 1969.
Knoblock, P. (Ed.). *Intervention approaches in educating emotionally disturbed children.* Syracuse, NY: Syracuse University Press, 1966.
Phillips, E. L., Wiener, D. N., & Haring, N. G. *Discipline, achievement and mental health.* Englewood Cliffs, NJ: Prentice-Hall, 1960.
Reinert, H. R. *Children in conflict.* St. Louis: C. V. Mosby Co., 1976.
Sulzer, B., & Mayer, G. R. *Behavior modification procedures for school personnel.* New York: Holt, Rinehart, & Winston, 1972.
Worell, J., & Nelson, C. M. *Managing instructional problems.* New York: McGraw-Hill, 1974.

8 The Physically Disabled

Barbara Sirvis
San Francisco State University

Who are the physically disabled, and what makes them exceptional children and youth? Unfortunately, any attempt at defining this group contributes to the stigma that may be attached to the condition. The term *crippled* has negative connotations for many people, as may the terms *physically handicapped, physically disabled,* and *physically impaired.* The terms *disability* and *handicap* also may be confusing since many people draw a distinction between the two concepts, referring to disability as a measurable, constant condition (e.g., loss of a leg below the knee), and to handicap as a consequence of disability for a given individual. Thus, the professional athlete who loses a leg can be expected to experience a greater handicap than a mathematics teacher with the same disability. In general, it is not the actual physical variation but, rather, the individual's attitude in relation to society's view of physical limitations that determines the extent of the handicap.

Essentially, the physically disabled population is comprised of individuals with *functional* limitations related to physical ability (e.g., hand use, trunk control, mobility) and *medical* conditions, such as strength and stamina. Some physically disabled individuals have multiple handicaps, with attendant emotional, social, and educational needs; in addition to their physical disability, they may have problems related to learning, social-emotional adjustment, developmental lags, speech and language development, vision or hearing impairments.

Wald (1971) summarized the physically disabled's situation as follows:

> The. . .population appears to be seen in three dimensions: physical definition, functional problems, and programmatic modifications. The population is comprised of those children and adults who as a result of permanent, temporary, or intermittent medical disabilities require modifications in curriculum and instructional strategies. Frequent separation from family and lack of adequate parental guidance contribute to secondary emotional problems. . . . The child's physical limitations are often the basis of functional retardation as well as sensory, perceptual, and conceptual deficits. The development of realistic expectation levels requires the identification of additional and unique instructional materials, equipment, and strategies for evaluation (p.95).

THE NATURE OF PHYSICAL DISABILITIES

Professional groups and individuals classify physical disabilities in various ways — e.g., etiology (cause), time of onset, functional effect. Others espouse noncategorical classification. Certain traditional categories remain, however, and will be used in the interest of clarity. The definitions and medical information included here are meant neither to

overgeneralize nor to label, but rather to provide a basis for understanding the nature of the physically disabled.

A typical inclusion in a discussion of this type—statistics and
incidence figures—will not be given, as their meaningfulness and accuracy are questionable. Fait (1972) stated:

> Because of the lack of uniformity in defining the conditions of crippling. . . statistics
> of incidence are neither very meaningful nor very accurate. . . . It is consequently not
> possible to determine how many cases of orthopedically handicapped youngsters. . .
> there are currently or how many of these may be expected to be found in the regular
> school, the special school, or the hospital (p. 98).

Etiological factors also are deemphasized in this discussion, since the
cause of many conditions is unknown and that specific knowledge is not
prerequisite to teaching the physically disabled. In brief, while the causes
of certain disabilities have been established (including some of genetic
origin), one should note prenatal care and nutrition, along with effects of
poverty-level living conditions and susceptibility to infection, as potential factors in physical disability.

To preface the following discussion of some specific, visible physical
disabilities often referred to as orthopedic and/or neurological impairments, the terminology explanation below may be helpful:

monoplegia: paralysis of one limb
paraplegia: paralysis of both lower extremities
hemiplegia: paralysis of both extremities on the same side
quadriplegia: paralysis of all four extremities
diplegia: paralysis of all four extremities, with greater involvement
in the lower limbs

Orthopedic and Neurological Impairments

Cerebral Palsy

Students with cerebral palsy comprise the largest number of
physically disabled children needing special education services. This
disability is the result of damage to, or maldevelopment of, the brain
before, during, or after birth. The term generally refers to a category of
motor disabilities entailing impairment of muscle coordination and
ability to perform normal motor patterns and skills. Cerebral palsy is the
disability most likely to have associated problems related to learning,
social-emotional growth, perception, vision, hearing, and intellectual

functioning. Causes of this disorder—anoxia (lack of oxygen), trauma, maternal infection, childhood trauma—are as varied as effects of the brain damage itself (Denhoff, 1976).

Several types of cerebral palsy exist, and each manifests itself in a slightly different manner. *Spasticity* refers to the condition of those who exhibit increased muscle tone in the form of overactive, tight muscles; *athetosis* refers to uncontrolled, jerky, and irregular movements due to fluctuating muscle tone; *ataxia* refers to a lack of coordination related to balance. *Mixed* cerebral palsy is also a common form, referring to various combinations of the above and other types.

Physical descriptions of a child's movements might be, for example: Bob has spastic cerebral palsy, which makes his muscles tight and resistant to movement; Susie has athetoid cerebral palsy, which causes difficulty in controlling her limbs for both gross and fine motor movements; John has ataxic cerebral palsy, so it is difficult for him to maintain his balance and produce steady movements.

Muscular Dystrophy

Muscular dystrophy has several adult forms but only one common fatal childhood form—Duchenne, or pseudohypertrophic muscular dystrophy. Characterized by increasing weakness of the skeletal muscles, the disease manifests initial symptoms which may hamper children when they run or climb stairs. Progressive muscle weakness, awkwardness, and slowness in movement eventually become so pronounced that the child will be confined to a wheelchair. Shoulder and arm weakness may appear at the same time or somewhat later. Duchenne is a hereditary disorder usually caused by a sex-linked recessive gene transmitted from mother to son. Consequently, this form of M.D. rarely is found in female children (Chutorian & Myers, 1974). The progression of muscular dystrophy is relatively rapid, with death usually occurring in the teen years. Students with M.D. will fatigue more easily as the disease progresses. Although they may be ambulatory in a typical school setting, a wheelchair may be needed for field trips and excursions.

Spina Bifida

A congenital disability, spina bifida takes several forms, each having its own name. Students with *myelomeningocele*, the most severe form, are more commonly found in special education classrooms because the disability is so complex. Essentially, spina bifida is caused by a defect in development of the vertebral column, which damages the spinal cord and nerve roots, causing related neurological deficits. The amount of damage to the cord affects the extent of neurological problems, which vary from minor sensory and ambulation problems in the milder form to paraplegia with lack of sensation and incontinence (lack of bladder control) in the more severe form. Urinary tract, orthopedic deformity, and skin sensitivity conditions also may occur. In addition, children with spina bifida seem to be susceptible to development of hydrocephalus (abnormal retention of cerebrospinal fluid in the cranial cavity) which may cause mental retardation if not corrected surgically (Swinyard, 1966).

Teachers need to be concerned about these students' practicing good personal hygiene, because odor and infection related to bladder and bowel control may be prevalent. Physical therapy for development of gait (walking) patterns or wheelchair use may be crucial.

Osteogenesis Imperfecta

Characterized by brittle bones, this disability involves defective development of both the quality and the quantity of bone. Bones do not grow normally in length and thickness, resulting in brittle composition. Dwarfism, resulting from multiple fractures, and deafness are possible secondary associated disabilities (Bleck, 1975). Individuals with osteogenesis imperfecta need to develop self-protective attitudes concerning their disability and, within school settings, exercise caution in even simple activities such as stapling.

Limb Deficiency

Absence of a limb may be either congenital or acquired after birth. Early intervention by rehabilitation personnel is crucial in some instances. The type and extent of rehabilitative aid may be governed by the location and severity of the limb deficiency. For example, loss of a leg below the knee allows near normal function, including sports and games, while loss of a leg above the knee creates greater disability. Acquisition of a prosthetic device (artificial limb) may be important to physical and psychological function for some, while others may choose to rely upon use of the remaining portion of the deficient limb. Full understanding of potential for functional use is critical in the later choice; motivation is likely to be a major determinant in the successful use of a prosthesis.

Spinal Cord Injury

Bicycle, automobile, and similar accidents are the most common childhood causes of this traumatic injury. Extent of the disability varies according to the level and type of lesion (injury) to the spinal cord. Generally, paralysis and lack of sensation occur below the level of the lesion. Treatment includes extensive medical and psychological rehabilitation to help newly disabled persons find ways to compensate for their physical disabilities in daily living activities. Potential related conditions include urinary tract infections, decubitus ulcers (pressure sores caused by sitting or lying too long in one position), contractures (muscle or joint tightening after being immobile for long periods of time), and mobility problems (Myers, 1974).

Legg-Calve-Perthes

This relatively temporary disability is sometimes referred to as Legg-Perthes or, more simply, Perthes disease. It involves degeneration of the growth center (epiphysis) of the femoral head (the round end of the long thigh bone which fits into the hip socket). Recovery depends upon the amount of damage that occurs to the femoral head during the course of the disease. With proper early medical intervention, good to adequate recovery is found in most cases. Treatment often includes use of a leg brace which prevents further insult to the bone tissue while it is healing (Nagel, 1975).

Other Health Impairments

The previous discussion focused on orthopedic/neurological impairments which often are more visible than other health impairments. The conditions described below present their own unique problems, in part because the general public may not be aware of specific behavior patterns required by the victim to adapt to these sometimes less obvious, but often equally severe, physical disabilities.

The discussion by no means includes all possible health impairments contributing to physical handicap, but gives a cross-section of some different types of conditions. The teacher should always be alert to possible physical reasons affecting a child's behavior and learning.

Epilepsy

Epilepsy is a seisure disorder commonly associated with other physically disabling conditions; it also occurs as a single problem. Seizures usually are characterized by abnormal, excessive electrical brain discharges, but not all are readily visible nor do they necessarily involve a change in state of consciousness. Seizures are organized into three basic categories: generalized, partial, and miscellaneous.

Generalized seizures include grand mal, petit mal, myoclonic, and akinetic seizures and are characterized by loss of consciousness. The *grand mal* involves extraneous, uncontrolled movement of the entire body, with increased salivation and possible loss of bladder and bowel control. Teachers should be prepared to act calmly and quickly when a student has a grand mal seizure, setting a good example for the students by remaining calm. The teacher should move furniture and other objects which the student might strike during the seizure. If possible, the student's head should be gently turned to the side, allowing saliva to drain to prevent choking and tongue biting. (Teachers should not be fearful that students will "swallow their tongue"; this cannot occur.) After the seizure, the child probably will be tired and should be allowed to sleep.

Petit mal seizures are less noticeable because behavior changes are minimal. The only clue may be a mild disorientation as the result of a short lapse of attention (e.g., the student may pause briefly in the middle of oral reading or miss a word in a dictation assignment). *Myoclonic* seizures involve an upward, or myoclonic, jerk of the arms and trunk flexion (bending) which may cause the student to fall. *Akinetic* seizures involve sudden loss of muscle tone and postural control, which affects the student's ability to protect himself or herself in falling. A helmet should be worn to prevent head injury (Bruya & Bolin, 1976).

Partial seizures sometimes are referred to as *psychomotor seizures*, because they may affect both motor function and behavior. Patterns vary, ranging from brief loss of consciousness to extended periods of purposeless activity. For example, the student may not be conscious of unusual behavior patterns which appear to the observer to be "acting out" behaviors.

Seizure disorders generally do not present major classroom problems because properly prescribed medication can control most seizures. Nevertheless, teachers should be prepared for seizures and should report them to medical personnel.

Juvenile Diabetes Mellitus

This metabolic disorder is caused by the body's inability to burn sugars and starches (carbohydrates) needed to create energy. Insulin is not adequately produced by the pancreas and, thus, glucose does not send energy to the cells. Without glucose, the body loses energy and functional capacity.

The major concern for the classroom teacher is to watch for signs of reaction to too much or too little insulin. Christiansen (1975) summarizes the symptoms and the necessary treatment: 1) An *insulin reaction* (too much insulin) is characterized by a rapid onset of symptoms which include headache, nausea, vomiting, irritability, shallow breathing, and/or cold, moist skin; the treatment is to give orange juice, a candy bar, sugar cube, or other sugar on which the insulin will react; 2) *Ketoacidosis* (too little insulin) is characterized by symptoms which begin gradually and may include fatigue, the child's drinking large amounts of water, production of large amounts of urine, excessive hunger, deep breathing, and/or warm, dry skin; the treatment is to give insulin. Teachers should be aware of these symptoms and report changes in behavior immediately to medical personnel.

Most diabetic children are largely self-sufficient and can administer their own medication, but they may need some assistance from medical personnel in monitoring dosage.

Cancer

The causes and cures of this irregular cell growth are still relatively unknown. The most common forms of cancer found in children and adolescents are leukemia and tumors of the eye, brain, bone, and kidney. Prognosis often depends upon early diagnosis and treatment. Side effects of the disease or the treatment may cause problems such as emotional imbalance, fatigue, extreme weight changes, nausea, and headaches. The major considerations for teachers involve understanding of the students' concern in dealing with the potentially terminal nature of their illness, as well as the need for rest. School work also may reflect the time lost due to physical problems and hospitalization.

Cardiac (Heart) Conditions

In the past, students with cardiac impairments often were placed in special education programs to assure minimum stress and maximum protection. Now, few students are placed in special education programs solely due to cardiac problems, because most of the necessary modifications can be made within regular education programming and settings. Minor program modifications may be necessary to accommodate a physician's order for limited physical activity.

Sickle Cell Anemia

A hereditary blood disorder, sickle cell anemia is more commonly found among, but not limited to, the black population. Hemoglobin in the red blood cells is distorted into a sickle, or crescent, shape which does not pass readily through the blood vessels. The resulting decrease of blood supply to some tissues causes severe pains, usually in the abdomen, legs, and arms. Additional symptoms may include swelling of the joints, fatigue, and high fever. Periods of difficulty are referred to as "crises" and are chronic at irregular intervals. For the longer term, degeneration of joints and related orthopedic problems may result from the poor blood supply to affected areas (Travis, 1976). The teacher's major concern will be the need for remediation due to frequent absences from school, which often affect academic performance.

Hemophilia

Hemophilia is often termed "bleeder's disease." Its major characteristic is poor blood clotting ability, because of the absence of a clotting factor in the blood. Although external bodily cuts and scrapes might appear to be the most dangerous, the greater danger is actually from internal bleeding which causes blood to accumulate in joints and surrounding tissues. Internal bleeding is potentially destructive to affected joints and tissues (McElfresh, 1974).

As with some other health impairments, the greatest effect on classroom performance may be from frequent, short absences from school for treatment. Also, a wheelchair may be needed for those with temporary or permanent involvement of their joints.

Cystic Fibrosis

A hereditary disorder, cystic fibrosis is found mostly in the Caucasian population. Characterized by chronic pulmonary (lung) involvement, and pancreatic deficiency, the major effects relate to respiratory tract involvement, including a dry cough, bronchial obstruction by abnormal secretions, and susceptibility to acute infections. Cystic fibrosis formerly had a generally poor prognosis, but recent medical advances have increased potential life-span (Travis, 1976).

The usual educational programming is appropriate for students with this disability, but teachers should be aware that strenuous exercise should be limited. In addition, coughing should be encouraged, to loosen the thick mucous coating on the bronchial passages.

EDUCATIONAL PROGRAMMING

Historically, treatment for the physically disabled evolved from a medical model. Most children with orthopedic or health impairments received medical treatment in hospitals or state institutions. Education received little consideration. While health problems gained maximum attention, the long-term needs of the "whole person" received little attention. Gradually, however, special classes developed and with them evolved home and hospital instruction for bedridden patients. As the importance and relevance of special education were realized, children with more severe physical problems—cerebral palsy, muscular dystrophy, spina bifida—were added to the educational group. Interdisciplinary teams began to work with the physically disabled in an effort to provide medical *and* educational services, recognizing the importance of each.

Educational programming for the physically disabled involves an interdisciplinary team approach to a number of problem areas. The team is comprised of professionals from a variety of disciplines including, but not limited to, physical and occupational therapy, social work, nursing, psychology, speech therapy, rehabilitation counseling, and recreation. In a hospital setting, these disciplines plus the medical team provide a full range of direct services, but in the school setting many disciplines provide only consultation services.

The team should work with the disabled person toward fulfillment of four basic developmental goals:

1. Physical independence, including mastery of daily living skills;
2. Self-awareness and social maturation;
3. Academic growth; and
4. Career education, including constructive leisure activities.

These goals create certain needs for curriculum planning: the needs for adaptive equipment, alternative communication systems, procedures for adequate assessment, and realistic goal planning.

Adaptive Equipment and Materials

The crux of programming and modification for the physically disabled lies in adapting tasks to allow the student to develop maximum independence. This often requires creating adaptive devices that facilitate or aid in completion of tasks. Often, a student can be independent with minimal adaptation of usual techniques or provision of an adaptive device. For example, students may be able to use a pencil if it is inserted through a rubber ball or lump of clay to provide a larger surface for grasping. Other students may not be able to use a pencil but may be able to complete assignments using a typewriter. For those who do not have good arm and hand control, a headwand (pointer stick fastened to headband) may be used to type out letters.

Daily living skills also may require adaptive methods and devices. A special nontippable cup may help to prevent spilling by a cerebral palsied youngster who has poor motor control. Another child may need a spoon with a special large handle that permits him or her to grasp it easily for feeding.

Federal laws now mandate removal of architectural barriers which present a hardship or deny equal access opportunity for disabled students. Classroom doors should be wide enough to accommodate wheelchairs. Blackboards and easels should be low enough—and desks and tables high enough—for those in wheelchairs. Bathroom stalls may need to be wider and deeper; bathroom sinks and water fountains may need to be higher so wheelchairs can fit underneath them.

Alternative Communication Systems

Some students with physical disabilities have accompanying difficulties related to communication. Many children with cerebral palsy have deficiencies in speech musculature control, making their speech difficult, if not impossible, to understand. Thus, they may choose to use an alternative form of expression and communication. Initially, the challenge is to find the most efficient and effective means for expression. Some students may use only yes/no responses; others may use picture or word communication boards; still others may use electronic devices. Even after the proper device is chosen, however, the student may have difficulty in attempting communication with others who are not familiar with that particular adaptive communication system. Nonhandicapped classmates should receive instruction in the use of alternate systems along with encouragement to communicate with the nonvocal student.

Development of even the simplest communication means for *yes* and *no* may open a new world to the previously noncommunicating student. Instruction in these two basic concepts introduces the student to choices and expression of desires. After the ability to use these concepts is developed effectively, the student may be motivated to expand communication ability through more complex systems.

Assessment

Because many students in the physically disabled population are multiply handicapped, they may have associated problems related to learning and intellectual function. Thus, use of an evaluation system may become necessary to assess specific problem areas. For those with no upper extremity involvement, standardized tests could be appropriate; but consider the pitfalls in giving an IQ test such as the WISC (Wechsler Intelligence Scale for Children) to a student with severe athetoid cerebral palsy. Because the child's lack of motor coordination would affect the results, a test having sections that require completion in a given time period would not produce a fair assessment. Many tests assume that a child has adequate hand use for manipulative tasks. Speech or some alternative communication system beyond yes/no responses usually is necessary. Many tests leave the physically disabled child at a cultural or experiential disadvantage because a physical problem may limit his or her ability to leave the confines of home or school to explore the world as his or her nondisabled peers have done since early childhood. This may be analogous to a situation in which a child from a cultural minority group is tested with tests using the majority language. With physically disabled students, criterion-referenced assessments are suggested. In this method the child's progress is compared only to his or her own earlier performance, rather than being forced into a standardized test framework.

Goal Planning

Proper assessment should reveal data that can assist in developing short- and long-term goals for the physically disabled student. The following are factors for consideration.

Physical Independence

Physical and occupational therapists are valuable resources in developing programs for maximum physical independence. Physical independence includes a number of skill areas related to physical function, including activities of daily living—toileting, bathing, eating, drinking, and moving from place to place. Adaptive equipment and methods are crucial in this area. Task analysis (Bigge & O'Donnell, 1977) may be a crucial evaluative tool in determining which skills have development potential. This is based on pinpointing task subskills, or components, to determine those subtasks the disabled person cannot do and devising adaptive means for independent completion.

Self-Awareness and Social Maturation

Blanket generalizations about the disabled, as convenient as they may be, are apt to be in error by virtue of their oversimplifications. Many people assume that the greater the physical disability, the greater the psychological consequences of the disability, or they are convinced that certain disabling conditions produce certain specific psychological results. These popular beliefs are not supported by the data presently available. The extent of the impact experienced by each individual is related to the significance of the disability for that person. This, in turn, will depend on the pattern of events in his or her life that have contributed to values, the way self-perception in relation to the rest of the world and the form which reactions to stress take (Levine, 1959, p. 1).

Although gross generalizations about socialization and maturation patterns are to be avoided, two general categories of reaction to one's own physical disability have been suggested: the *sense of loss* experienced by those with acquired disabilities, and the *sense of difference* experienced by those born with a physical handicap (Neff & Weiss, 1965).

People with physical disabilities have the same needs as their nondisabled peers to communicate with and relate to people. Their needs for love and understanding—as well as a feeling of personal acceptance, which allows them to live, love, and laugh fully—are crucial to the maturation process. Opportunities must be provided for social maturation, development of a positive, healthy self-concept, and fulfillment of needs for love, security, sense of belonging, and opportunities for self-expression.

Psychological problems potentially encountered by the physically disabled are not unique to them, but often may result from architectural and societal barriers which hinder emotional development. Some of these possible problem areas include:

1. Unresolved dependence feelings which may create an excessive need for affection and attention;
2. Excessive submissiveness which actually may be covering a deep-seated hostility toward physical dependence on others;
3. Extreme egocentrism and inability to deal with aloneness;
4. Fantasy as compensation for feelings of inferiority and/or inadequacy;
5. Resignation to, rather than recognition of, limits; and
6. Superficial conscious recognition of handicap, with a subconscious rejection of self.

Since concepts of ability and disability are integrated into self-image, a child's self-concept certainly may be affected by physical disability. Body image, life experiences, social relationships, emotions, and intellectual performance also affect sense of self. In addition, self-concept is derived from self-observations as we interact with others and compare ourselves with our peers. Parents, teachers, and significant others in the child's life without question must provide experiences which nurture the development of a positive self-concept (Sirvis, Carpignano, & Bigge, 1977).

In the classroom, physically disabled students will need encouragement to explore their attitudes toward themselves, including social, sexual, academic, and vocational potentials. They need to learn to express their true feelings of happiness, sadness, anger, and other emotions. Teachers and therapists must provide opportunities for physically disabled children to explore their feelings, including those related to family life, human sexuality, and death education. Disabled students need to know that to experience a wide range of feelings is normal. They need to learn to deal with constructive criticism in order to be better able to meet frustration and disappointment without experiencing fatal blows to their egos. They also need to learn to evaluate each experience and use information from these self-evaluations for future planning.

Along with traditional academic skills training, personal development and independence should be fostered throughout the school experience. Family life education, including human sexuality, should be part of that learning. Some physically disabled persons have neither the socialization experiences nor the information about social and sexual development they need; yet their physiological needs are the same as their nondisabled peers.

. . . . . sex education is more a social than an intellectual concern and is best accomplished as part of an approach treating all aspects of human development. It is based upon the further conviction that sex education should be a gradual, continuous and spontaneous process rather than a rigidly prescribed unit or series of units from a science or health manual, and that it should be introduced when the children indicate that they are ready, not when a curriculum guide indicates that they should be ready (Uslander, 1974, p. 35).

Death education also should be a part of one's personal development. Physically disabled students experience death more than their nondisabled peers; yet they have little or no preparation for dealing with it. Basic information about death and its part in the natural cycle of life provides students with factual knowledge to aid their understanding. The professional who deals with discussion of death and/or the terminally ill student must be willing to encourage honest expression of thoughts and feelings about death. This effort will provide the educator an opportunity to answer questions, correct misconceptions, and offer support.

Parents of physically disabled children may experience considerable difficulty in coping with their child's condition. Regardless of whether their child's disability is the result of genetic, traumatic, or unknown causes, parents often blame themselves and, as a result, experience considerable guilt. In addition, parents may overprotect their children. Although this may be done in a spirit of concern, extreme overprotection fosters dependence. Parents should be aware that the child will benefit from taking extra time to learn adaptive methods independently, rather than having parents intervene and complete tasks for them or offer too much help.

As disabled children reach an age at which they should be leaving home but still require an inordinate amount of physical care, feelings of resentment may arise on the part of either the child or the parents, or both. As parents grow older, such feelings of resentment may focus increasingly on their disabled child's continuing need for physical care and the accompanying decrease in the parents' ability to care for their adult child. Teachers, therapists, and other staff members can offer valuable assistance to parents by helping them develop a realistic attitude toward their child's physical problem—an attitude that fosters maximum physical and emotional independence.

Academic Growth

Because of the varied educational needs of the physically disabled, curricula must integrate adaptive techniques with a variety of educational materials, including those for regular education, learning disabilities, mental retardation, sensory handicapped, *and* gifted, in order to plan appropriate instructional materials. Emphasis should be on development of new and adaptation of existing materials from other areas to meet the needs of each youngster. Educational programming should be realistic, continually challenging, and should include development of competent daily living skills.

Early Childhood Education. An overview of long-range curriculum planning should note that infant stimulation and early childhood education programs emphasize developmental skills related to gross and fine motor development, as well as daily living skills and social interaction. Physical and occupational therapists should have a large role in development of programming for young children, because they have the major responsibility for physical development.

Although the emphasis may be on development of physical skills, coordination and readiness for academic work also should be developed at this time. Individualized instruction should provide for the beginning of criterion-referenced development. Environmental exploration and movement experiences should be encouraged. Wheelchairs can be too restrictive; children should be removed from them as often as feasible, to allow freedom of movement. Success in simple self-help skills such as dressing oneself will build motivation for learning.

Elementary Level. As physically disabled students begin elementary education, motor development continues to be a primary focus, but this emphasis should eventually peak and decrease as academic skills receive continually increasing attention. Academics may include some basic tracking, even at the elementary level, but overlap will occur in some skill areas. Basic skills in reading, arithmetic, language arts, and social studies are applicable for all students. Some students will need to continue readiness activities at the primary level. Educational programming should be differentiated and individualized but not separated.

Secondary Level. As students reach adolescence, and even before, they need to establish a relationship between academic skills and basic survival skills. Reading skills may include basic skills for information finding, and math skills may involve only basic computation. Language arts may be related only to those skills required for writing personal correspondence. These skills are basic to independent survival but, once learned, should not be considered as a limit. Many physically disabled students exceed these basic survival skills and seek completion of a general academic high school program.

Postsecondary Education. Although physically disabled students may need extensive adaptive methods and equipment to facilitate functional independence, their potential for successful completion of postsecondary education is not necessarily affected. Students with appropriate academic ability and perseverance should be encouraged to pursue high school academic programs in preparation for community college, university or other professional training.

For all physically disabled students, general educational goals involve developing their ability to think logically and express themselves effectively within their capabilities. In addition to basic survival skills and further academic knowledge, the curricula should incorporate understanding and evaluation of social and ethical responsibilities. Academic learning overlaps career education and life skills training.

Life Experience[1] Education

Educational goals for physically disabled students *must* include activities which prepare them for successful experiences in employment, recreation, social relationships, self-help skills, and constructive leisure activities. Suggested goals (Howard & Bigge, 1977) include:

1. Ability to obtain meaningful employment (whether it be homebound, sheltered workshop, or competitive);
2. Capacity for independent living appropriate to individual physical and mental capabilities;
3. Capacity for community involvement (including a variety of daily living skills);
4. Skills for participation in meaningful leisure time activities (a well-defined free time management system); the basic objectives here are recreational experiences for enjoyment, and meeting and retaining friends;
5. Development of reliable transportation means;
6. Mastery of self-care skills;
7. Ability to maintain residence away from parents, convalescent hospitals, or state institutions;
8. Development of a healthy self-concept (pp. 178-179).

Program needs related to most of these goals have been mentioned earlier in this chapter; however, two warrant further discussion.

Career Education

In its most generic definition, career education involves all those skills needed by a student after completing school. Included in career education should be the basic survival skills previously mentioned as related to academic growth and life experience education. Academics often provide the avenue for teaching these skills, including those necessary for job preparation—e.g., filling out an application form, reading and interpreting the want ads, using the telephone book. Arithmetic skills involve any computational tasks necessary to make change monetarily and to balance a checkbook. Social studies and science should focus on developing the students' good citizenship and hygiene skills. Adaptive techniques and equipment are likely to be important in teaching disabled students to complete at least some of these tasks with maximum independence.

With the establishment of the President's Committee on Employment of the Handicapped, a new era and a more positive vocational

---

1. This term adapted from *Life Experience Program: An Alternative Approach in Special Education.* San Jose, CA: Office of the Santa Clara County Superintendent of Schools, 1976.

outlook began to emerge for the physically disabled. Previously confined to sheltered workshops, many disabled people began to seek training for and employment in a variety of occupations within education, science, and industry. Receptivity to adaptive methods and equipment facilitated their successful acceptance in the "world of work." Not all physically disabled persons have been easily employable and, even with extreme adaptation, the more severely disabled will encounter difficulty in employment. This, however, should not suggest a limit to their employability.

In planning for vocational education, factors to consider include strength and stamina, mobility, independent toileting, communication skills, and potential for skill development. Students with limitations in these areas should not be regarded as unemployable, but these factors must be considered in selecting the most appropriate vocational training.

For some, there may be a choice of vocational training *or* other constructive use of time. Given appropriate counseling and adequate information about various prospects, the disabled young adult should be allowed to choose. The Puritan work ethic is so strongly ingrained in our society that statements which challenge it may bother both family and professionals, but there *is* an alternate way of examining the issue. Consider the concept of *quality of life*. If an individual is severely physically disabled, this condition should not automatically impose limits or boundaries on the quality of his or her life. That quality, however, may be interpreted in different ways. Unproductive days in front of a television set seem inappropriate and nonrewarding, but constructive leisure time education could teach the severely disabled student to use time wisely. Productive use of time is a key to quality of life.

Recreation and Leisure Time

> The primary function of the recreation program should be to stimulate physical and intellectual growth and to help each participant gain needed physical and social skills so that each can, in turn, become more acceptable as a member of a normal group of peers (Vannier, 1977, p. 49).

Recreation activities develop—in addition to physical, intellectual, and social growth—interests and hobbies which can be continued after the school years. Considerations in program planning include assessment of each child's controlled movements, strength, mobility, and balance (Sherrill, 1976). Given this general information, group activities should be planned which meet the unique interest needs of, and allow for active participation by, each child, regardless of disability and with or without the use of adaptive equipment. For individual activities, adaptive techniques and equipment again may be needed. For example, the child with limited hand use may need to have the checkerboard squares numbered in order to be able to tell his or her partner how to move the checkers.

Recreational activities should be included in the curriculum from the early years. Community recreation programs and public agencies have greatly expanded recreation programs for physically disabled children and adults. In addition, community college programs for the disabled learner may provide outlets for constructive use of time following completion of a regular public school program.

PRACTICAL SUGGESTIONS FOR THE REGULAR CLASSROOM TEACHER

The following considerations might serve as basic guidelines and suggestions for the teacher who has physically disabled students in class.

Physical Independence

The teacher should consult with health personnel (physical and occupational therapists, school nurse, etc.) to gain information about:

—Physical positions for optimal learning;
—Management of wheelchairs, braces, adaptive equipment;
—Self-help skills (feeding, dressing, mobility);
—Medication;
—Activity limitations (if any);
—Elimination of architectural barriers.

Academic Growth

The teacher should:

—Treat disabled students as normally as possible (e.g., no special considerations in grading);
—Establish the best communication system for nonvocal students;
—Find ways for nonvocal students to participate in class discussion;
—Identify necessary adaptive methods or equipment;
—Encourage disabled students to evaluate themselves and their work realistically (strengths, areas for improvement, limitations).

Self-Awareness and Socialization

Communication

—Identify students' optimal communication system if they cannot be understood because of unintelligible speech;

—Encourage interaction between physically disabled students and their nondisabled peers, including instruction in use of a communication board if necessary;

—Do not "talk down" to the child with unintelligible speech; assume that the child understands at age level unless the child indicates otherwise.

Attitudes

—Help nondisabled students develop positive attitudes rather than ridicule or permit ridicule of them;
—Establish with parents and physician the amount of medical information to be shared with students.

Life Experience Education

—Include recreation and leisure activities for all students;
—Encourage realistic assessment of abilities, noting strengths and limitations found in all people, regardless of disability;
—Encourage development of maximum independence in all activities.

SUMMARY

This chapter has focused on a general description of students with physical disabilities who might be enrolled in regular school or special education classrooms. Their needs—educational, social, and developmental—are as diverse as their disabilities, so individualized instruction is imperative for their instructional program.

The physically disabled are generally, but not always, a part of the multiply handicapped population, so curricula from other areas of education may be applicable in teaching. The essence of planning for the physically disabled student lies in the professional's ability to modify physical activities so students can complete them successfully and accurately.

Objectives for the physically disabled student should not be determined on the basis of physical diagnosis, but rather on the basis of educational needs which make the student unique. Often, this may involve mere adaptation of a writing implement or, even more basically, removal of an architectural barrier preventing the student from entering the school building.

Classroom teachers who have physically disabled students within their groups need support services from a number of ancillary personnel. Several interdisciplinary team members should be directly or indirectly involved. Physical and occupational therapists are important in the development of appropriate motor development programs, and adaptive equipment may be necessary for independent completion of skills. In addition, communication disorders specialists may play a large role in assessment and development of appropriate communication modes, especially with cerebral palsied students. Social workers and school psychologists trained in administration of adaptive tests which do not further handicap student responses also may provide support for the teacher, student, and family.

All those who work with the physically disabled student have a responsibility to become that student's advocate. In many cases, the students are best equipped to speak for themselves; in other cases, they may need the help of parents and professionals committed to removal of societal, architectural, and educational barriers to success.

REFERENCES

Bigge, J.L., & O'Donnell, P.A. *Teaching individuals with physical and multiple disabilities.* Columbus, OH: Charles Merrill, 1977.

Bleck, E.E. Osteogenesis imperfecta. In E.E. Bleck & D.A. Nagel (Eds.), *Physically handicapped children: A medical atlas for teachers.* New York: Grune & Stratton, 1975.

Bruya, M.A., & Bolin, R.H. Epilepsy: A controllable disease. *American Journal of Nursing,* 1976, *76* (3), 388-397.

Christiansen, R.O. Diabetes. In E.E. Bleck & D.A. Nagel (Eds.), *Physically handicapped children: A medical atlas for teachers.* New York: Grune & Stratton, 1975.

Chutorian, A.M., & Myers, S.J. Diseases of the muscle. In J.A. Downey & N.L. Low (Eds.), *The child with disabling illness: Principles of rehabilitation.* Philadelphia: W.B. Saunders, 1974.

Denhoff, E. Medical aspects. In W.M. Cruickshank (Ed.), *Cerebral palsy: A developmental disability* (3rd ed.). Syracuse, NY: Syracuse University Press, 1976.

Fait, H.F. *Special physical education.* Philadelphia: W.B. Saunders, 1972.

Howard, R., & Bigge, J.L. Life experience programming. In J.L. Bigge with P.A. O'Donnell, *Teaching individuals with physical and multiple disabilities.* Columbus, OH: Charles Merrill, 1977.

Levine, L.S. *The impact of disability.* Address presented to Oklahoma Rehabilitation Association Convention, Oklahoma City, October, 1959..

McElfresh, A.E. What is hemophilia? *The Journal of Pediatrics,* 1974, *84* (4), 623-624.

Myers, S.J. The spinal injury patient. In J. A. Downey & N. L. Low (Eds.), *The child with disabling illness: Principles of rehabilitation.* Philadelphia: W. B. Saunders, 1974.

Nagel, D.A. Temporary orthopedic disabilities in children. In E.E. Bleck & D.A. Nagel (Eds.), *Physically handicapped children: A medical atlas for teachers.* New York: Grune & Stratton, 1975.

Neff, W.S., & Weiss, S.A. Psychological aspects of disability. In B.B. Wolberg (Ed.), *Handbook of clinical psychology.* New York: McGraw-Hill, 1965.

Sherrill, C. *Adapted physical education and recreation: A multidisciplinary approach.* Dubuque, IA: W.C. Brown, 1976.

Sirvis, B., Carpignano, J., & Bigge, J.L. Psychosocial aspects of physical disability. In J. L. Bigge with P.A. O'Donnell, *Teaching individuals with physical and multiple disabilities.* Columbus, OH: Charles Merrill, 1977.

Swinyard, C.A. (Ed.). Comprehensive care of the child with spina bifida manifesta. *Rehabilitation Monographs,* 1966, *31,* 1-147.

Travis, G. *Chronic illness in children: Its impact on child and family.* Stanford, CA: Stanford University Press, 1976.

Uslander, A.S. Everything you always wanted to know about sex education. *Learning,* 1974, *3* (2), 34-41.

Vannier, M. *Physical activities for the handicapped.* Englewood Cliffs, NJ: Prentice-Hall, 1977.

Wald, J.R. Crippled and other health impaired and their education. In F.P. Connor, J.R. Wald, & M.J. Cohen (Eds.), *Professional preparation for educators of crippled children.* New York: Teachers College Press, 1971.

RESOURCE GUIDE

Historical Information

Connor, F. P. The education of children with crippling and chronic medical conditions. In W. M. Cruickshank & G. O. Johnson (Eds.), *Education of exceptional children and youth* (3rd ed.). Englewood Cliffs, NJ: Prentice-Hall, 1975.

Cruickshank, W. M. *Cerebral palsy: A developmental disability* (3rd ed.). Syracuse, NY: Syracuse University Press, 1976.

Family

Bigge, J. L., & O'Donnell, P. A. *Teaching physically and multiply handicapped individuals.* Columbus, OH: Charles E. Merrill, 1977.

Cruickshank, W. M. *Cerebral palsy: A developmental disability* (3rd ed.). Syracuse, NY: Syracuse University Press, 1976.

Fairchild, E. L., & Neal, L. L. (Eds.). *Common unity in the community: A forward looking program of recreation and leisure services for the handicapped.* Eugene, OR: Center for Leisure Studies, 1975.

Grollman, E. A. *Explaining death to children.* Boston: Beacon Press, 1967.

Killilea, M. *Karen.* New York: Dell Publishing Co., 1952.

Kubler-Ross, E. Facing up to death. *Today's Education,* 1972, *61* (1), 30-32.

Nagy, M. H. The child's theories concerning death. In H. Feifel (Ed.), *The meaning of death.* New York: McGraw-Hill, 1959.

Reynell, J. Children with physical handicaps. In V. P. Varma (Ed.), *Stresses in children.* London: University of London Press, Ltd., 1973.

Wright, B. A. *Physical disability: A psychological approach.* New York: Harper & Row, 1960.

Patterns of Development

Bleck, E. ., & Nagel, D. A. *Physically handicapped children: A medical atlas for teachers.* New York: Grune & Stratton, 1975.

Bobath, B., & Bobath, K. *Motor development in the different types of cerebral palsy.* London: William Heinemann, 1975.

Brocklehurst, G. (Ed.). *Spina bifida for the clinician* (Clinics in developmental medicine, No. 57). Philadelphia: J. B. Lippincott, 1976.

Connor, F. P. The education of children with crippling and chronic medical conditions. In W. M. Cruickshank & G. O. Johnson (Eds.), *Education of exceptional children and youth* (3rd ed.). Englewood Cliffs, NJ: Prentice-Hall, 1975.

Cruickshank, W. M. *Cerebral palsy: A developmental disability* (3rd ed.). Syracuse, NY: Syracuse University Press, 1976.

Downey, J. A., & Low, N. L. *The child with disabling illness: Principles of rehabilitation.* Philadelphia: W. B. Saunders, 1974.

Gordon, N. *Pediatric neurology for the clinician* (Clinics in developmental medicine, No. 59/60). Philadelphia: J. B. Lippincott, 1976.

Reynell, J. Children with physical handicaps. In V. P. Varma (Ed.), *Stresses in children.* London: University of London Press Ltd., 1973.

Wright, B. A. *Physical disability: A psychological approach.* New York: Harper & Row, 1960.

Treatment

Brocklehurst, G. (Ed.). *Spina bifida for the clinician* (Clinics in developmental medicine. No. 57). Philadelphia: J. B. Lippincott, 1976.

Bruya, M. A., & Bolin, R. H. Epilepsy: A controllable disease. *American Journal of Nursing,* 1976, *76* (3), 388-397.

Connor, F. P. The education of children with crippling and chronic medical conditions. In W. M. Cruickshank & G. O. Johnson (Eds.), *Education of exceptional children and youth* (3rd ed.). Englewood Cliffs, NJ: Prentice-Hall, 1975.

Cruickshank, W. M. *Cerebral palsy: A developmental disability* (3rd ed.). Syracuse, NY: Syracuse University Press, 1976.

Bigge, J. L., & O'Donnell, P. A. *Teaching physically and multiply handicapped individuals.* Columbus, OH: Charles E. Merrill, 1977.

Bleck, E. E., & Nagel, D. A. *Physically handicapped children: A medical atlas for teachers.* New York: Grune & Stratton, 1975.

Bobath, B., & Bobath, K. *Motor development in the different types of cerebral palsy.* London: William Heinemann, 1975.

Downey, J. A., & Low, N. L. *The child with disabling illness: Principles of rehabilitation.* Philadelphia: W. B. Saunders, 1974.

Fairchild, E. L., & Neal, L. L. (Eds.). *Common unity in the community: A forward looking program of recreation and leisure services for the handicapped.* Eugene, OR: Center for Leisure Studies, 1975.

Finnie, N. R. *Handling the young cerebral palsied child at home.* New York: E. P. Dutton, 1975.

Gordon, N. *Pediatric neurology for the clinician* (Clinics in developmental medicine. No. 59/60). Philadelphia: J. B. Lippincott, 1976.

McDonald, E. T., & Schultz, A. R. Communication boards for cerebral-palsied children. *Journal of Speech & Hearing Disorders, 38* (1), 73-88.

Pearson, P., & Williams, C. E. (Eds.). *Physical therapy services in the developmental disabilities.* Springfield, IL: Charles C. Thomas, 1972.

Robinault, I. P. (Ed.). *Functional aids for the multiply handicapped.* Baltimore: Harper & Row/Medical Dept., 1973.

Educational Programming

Bigge, J. L. The consultant in programs for the physically handicapped. In Kenneth Blessing (Ed.), *The role of the resource consultant in special education.* Reston, VA: Council for Exceptional Children, 1968.

Bigge, J. L., & O'Donnell, P. A. *Teaching physically and multiply handicapped individuals.* Columbus, OH: Charles E. Merrill, 1977.

Connor, F. P. The education of children with crippling and chronic medical conditions. In W. M. Cruickshank & G. O. Johnson (Eds.), *Education of exceptional children and youth* (3rd ed.). Englewood Cliffs, NJ: Prentice-Hall, 1975.

Cruickshank, W. M. *Cerebral palsy: A developmental disability* (3rd ed.). Syracuse, NY: Syracuse University Press, 1976.

Fairchild, E. L., & Neal, L. L. (Eds.). *Common unity in the community: A forward looking program of recreation and leisure services for the handicapped.* Eugene, OR: Center for Leisure Studies, 1975.

Grollman, E. A. *Explaining death to children.* Boston: Beacon Press, 1967.

McDonald, E. T., & Schultz, A. R. Communication boards for cerebral palsied children. *Journal of Speech & Hearing Disorders, 38* (1), 73-88.

Pomeroy, J. *Recreation for the physically handicapped.* New York: Macmillan, 1964.

Sherrill, C. *Adapted physical education and recreation.* Dubuque, IA: Wm. C. Brown Co., 1976.

Vanderheiden, G. C., & Grilley, K. (Eds.). *Nonvocal communication techniques and aids for the severely physically handicapped.* Baltimore: University Park Press, 1975.

9 The Speech and Language Impaired

Nicholas W. Bankson
Boston University

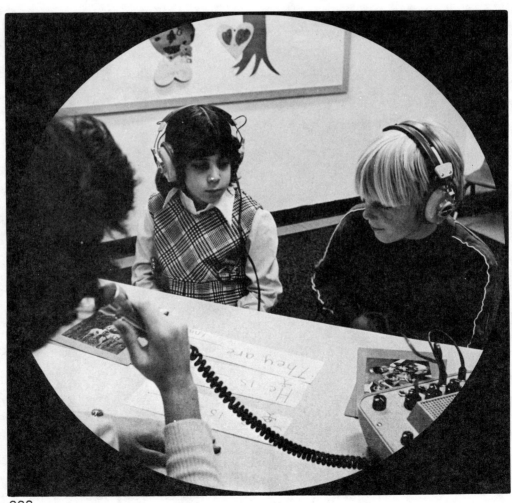

An area of exceptionality which classroom teachers frequently encounter is that of speech and language impairments. Prevalence studies indicate that one might expect between 1.5 percent and 12 percent of school-age children to have some sort of handicap in understanding or expressing oral language (Byrne & Shervanian, 1977). Although clinical speech instruction in the public school setting dates back to the 1920s, intervening years have witnessed a rapid proliferation of speech specialists in school systems. Originally, such specialists were called speech therapists, but the terminology presently advocated by the American Speech and Hearing Association is *speech clinician* or *speech pathologist.*

The addition of speech pathologists to school system staffs undoubtedly relates to the recognition that speech and language impairments pose a potential threat to social, emotional, and cognitive development, as well as to academic success. While speech clinicians possess the technical knowledge to evaluate, plan, and implement treatment programs for children with speech and language disorders, other professionals within a school have roles in helping children with communication problems. The classroom teacher often refers children for suspected problems, and he or she has the opportunity to play a critical role in remediation of speech and language disorders.

The term *speech impairment* is used in a generic sense to refer to disorders of articulation (speech sound production), voice, and fluency (rhythm). Each of these parameters relates to the mechanics of producing speech. *Language impairments*, as defined by speech pathologists, usually refer to disorders in comprehending or verbally expressing the symbols and grammatical rules of language. *Communication disorder* is an additional generic term referring, in the broadest sense, to any speech or language handicap singly or in combination.

A person's speech may be defined as impaired or defective if it is unintelligible, ungrammatical, culturally or personally unsatisfactory, or abusive of the speech mechanism (Perkins, 1976). To the extent that one's language, articulation, voice, or fluency fits one or more of these categories, a communication disorder is present. However, language which differs according to cultural patterns or norms (e.g., black English) is not considered defective. Since speech and language patterns are reflective of our linguistic community, a dialectal variation of standard English or a foreign dialect should not be identified as a communication disorder. In these cases, referral to a speech pathologist is advocated only if a disorder is suspected in addition to any "natural" language variations which may be present.

To determine the precipitating factors which may be associated with specific speech and language disorders is often difficult. Some speech problems are related to organic factors such as hearing loss, cleft palate, abnormal dentition, lesions of the vocal folds, or neurological disorders. Other problems may result from faulty learning, such as improper models in the family environment, or lack of reinforcement from parents and others for adequate speech patterns. Some disorders may result from inadequate environmental stimulation or inappropriate psychological development.

According to the *medical model* of human intervention, suspected causes of speech disorders should be diagnosed as inoperable before one attempts to change aberrant speech patterns. With many speech disorders, however, it is not always possible to determine obvious etiological (causal) variables. In such instances the clinician must operate from the *behavioral model* and plan the intervention program on the basis of observable communication deficits, recognizing that those factors maintaining the disorder remain unknown.

TYPES OF COMMUNICATION DISORDERS

Speech Disorders

Speech disorders are broadly classified into three primary areas — articulation disorders, fluency disorders, and voice disorders. Although these categories may overlap in some instances, they are discussed separately here.

Articulation Disorders

The most common speech disorder seen within the schools is in articulation. In the context of verbal communication, articulation refers to production of the sounds of language. Articulation is commonly considered defective if a child omits one or more sounds (e.g., *bu* for *bus,*), substitutes sounds for each other (e.g., *thoup* for *soup*), or distorts sounds (e.g., doesn't say *r* sounds correctly).

The English language utilizes approximately 45 sounds, or phonemes, which are divided into two major categories: vowels and consonants. There is no one-to-one correspondence between the alphabet of 26 letters and the spoken system of 45 sounds. To speak the letter *s*, for example, we must say two sounds, *eh* and *s*. On the other hand, the two letters *th* represent a single sound produced by placing the tongue under the upper teeth and blowing, as in *think*.

Research on the acquisition of speech sounds indicates that most children have developed adequate articulation of the majority of sounds by age four (Sander, 1972). A small percentage of children, however, is still in the process of mastering sounds through age seven or sometimes eight. Thus, it is not uncommon to find children in kindergarten and first grade who misarticulate certain sounds which are known to be late in developing, such as *sh, ch, j,* and *th.* Misarticulation of a single sound is not necessarily an articulation disorder. Rather, the number and nature of sounds in error must be compared with a child's age in determining whether or not the articulation errors are more properly considered within normal limits or do, in fact, reflect an articulation disorder. By the time a child reaches age nine, biological maturation alone will no longer result in improvements in sound production.

Articulation deficits usually are identified through two types of testing. The first consists of an articulation inventory which assesses a battery of consonant sounds in the initial, medial, and final positions of words (e.g., sun, bicycle, bus). Generally, a child is asked to name pictures or words containing certain phonemes in order to elicit production of these sounds. In addition to assessing consonants, inventories frequently assess consonant blends and sometimes vowels. Vowels are not included in many articulation inventories, however, because they usually are produced correctly by children before age three.

The second type of measure obtained with children suspected of articulation disorders is a sample of spontaneous or conversational speech. Generally, such a sample is tape-recorded, and the examiner replays the tape to analyze individual sounds. Sometimes children articulate sounds properly in the single word productions required in the initial inventory but revert to habitual errors when speaking in a conversational manner.

Other articulation measures are employed by speech clinicians in a complete diagnostic analysis of articulation, but the inventory and spontaneous sample usually are considered the basic tests. To determine prognosis for articulation improvement without treatment, clinicians frequently assess a child's ability to imitate the correct form of sounds produced in error. Results of all testing data then are reviewed relating the child's age to the number and type of sound errors, and the clinician makes a professional judgment regarding the need for articulation remediation.

Until the late 1960s, defective articulation cases frequently comprised as much as 85 percent of public school clinicians' case loads. Since then, the percentage of children with articulation disorders in case loads has decreased — not because fewer children are now exhibiting misarticulation but, rather, as a reflection of certain factors, namely: (1) Advancement in knowledge about communication disorders has led to increased concern about providing services for disorders of voice, rhythm, and especially language, along with the area of articulation; (2) Upgrading the level and quality of training required of clinicians has resulted in their increased competency to deal with a wider spectrum of communication impairments; and (3) Professionals have come to recognize that minor articulatory *differences* should be differentiated from articulatory *defectiveness*.

Fluency Disorders

Another type of speech disorder is evidenced when a child produces an excessive number of interruptions in the fluency of speech. Such disorders in speech flow are termed dysfluencies or, more commonly, stuttering and consist of one or more of the following characteristics:

1. Repetitions (e.g., "C-c-can you climb *the the the* tree?";
2. Prolongation of sounds (e.g., "I--------saw you ye--------sterday.");
3. Hesitations in the flow of speech (e.g., "Can (pause) you climb (pause) the (pause) tree?"); and
4. Interjections (e.g., "I *uh uh uh* saw you *uh uh uh* yesterday").

Since all speakers at one time or another produce interruptions in their speech flow similar to those just described, identification of stutterers is a somewhat difficult task, especially in children, for whom such speech attributes are more common than adults. According to Sheehan (1958), a stutterer may be defined as:

> . . . . a person who shows, to a degree that sets him off from the rest of the population, any one or more of the following groups of symptoms: (1) blockings, stickings, grimaces, forcings, repetitions, prolongations, or other rhythm breaks or interruptions in the forward flow of speech; (2) fear or anticipation of blockings, fear of inability to speak, or related symptoms prior to words or speaking situations; (3) a self-concept which includes a picture of himself as a stutterer, a stammerer, speech blocker, or a person lacking normal speech fluency.

Although evaluation of articulation disorders relies heavily on the use of formal tests, this is not true with evaluation of stuttering. Determining the presence of a fluency disorder usually is accomplished by the clinician's observing and recording a child's speech patterns, consulting with the child regarding self perceptions of his or her own speech patterns, and discussing with parents and teachers their perceptions of the child's speech fluency. In addition, the number of dysfluencies per minute may be counted and the nature of dysfluencies noted. Frequency and locus of a person's fluency failures may be made during oral reading, as well as conversational speech. And the speaker usually is asked to indicate situational contexts in which speaking behavior arouses negative emotional reactions. The evaluator, of course, is alert to situations during interaction with the child which may precipitate or intensify dysfluency on the part of the child.

Whether fluency or dysfluency is normal or abnormal is a matter of judgment, because the dividing line between stuttering and normal fluency is not clearly drawn. Further, as Sheehan's definition notes, identification of a stutterer is based not only upon observation of dysfluent speech, but also upon how the speaker views his or her own speech patterns and the self-concept tied to them.

One theory of stuttering as a speech disorder or clinical entity is that dysfluency is created when listeners, usually parents, encourage a young child to be overly aware of and concerned about his or her possible dysfluency or otherwise label the child as a stutterer (Johnson, 1959). Such a stigma attached to a speaker may generate further concern over his or her speech pattern and thus become a self-fulfilling prophecy.

Identification of children in school systems who need direct or indirect intervention in the area of speech fluency requires mutual cooperation among the speech pathologist, classroom teacher, and parents. The ultimate decision regarding the need for and type of intervention to be utilized rests with the speech clinician, but this decision cannot be made properly without input from parents, teachers, and other persons with whom the child is extensively involved.

Stuttering is a speech disorder that historically has plagued mankind and continues to be discussed widely to this day, but the actual percentage of persons identified as having such a problem is surprisingly low. Hull, Miekle, Timmons, and Willeford (1969) have estimated that approximately one percent of the general population has a fluency problem.

Voice Disorders

A third type of speech disorder is distinguished by highly unusual or defective voice characteristics. Adjectives such as hoarse, breathy, harsh, nasal, metallic, strident, strained, gutteral, and nasal have been used to describe such voice defects, but reaching agreement on the meaning and implication of the terms is another matter. These adjectives, moreover, primarily describe *quality* of voice only. *Pitch* and *volume* are additional characteristics of voice. A defect may occur on any of these parameters, but the most frequent occasion of voice disorder relates primarily to quality, less frequently to pitch, and seldom to loudness. Voice disorders also may combine all three or any two of these vocal dimensions.

Speech pathologists do not have formal tests of voice, per se, but rather rely on perceptual judgments made while speakers talk, read, display their pitch range, and perform other tasks designed to demonstrate the manner in which they customarily use their voice, as well as the vocal possibilities of which they are capable. The speech pathologist must determine, from observation, the presence or absence of a defect which should be treated, and the various possibilities and prognosis for changing the demonstrated voice pattern.

Before any type of therapy is prescribed for a person identified as having a voice disorder, he or she must be examined by a physician (preferably a nose and throat specialist) to establish any pathology of the larynx (voice box). If an organic pathology is present, the physician must determine whether voice therapy should be undertaken immediately or whether some type of medical intervention is necessary prior to speech treatment. No physiological basis for many voice disorders can be found, but some do have an organic basis. Of major concern among vocal pathologies is the possibility of some form of malignancy of the larynx.

An individual suggested as having an unusual voice quality indicating a possible communication disorder frequently exhibits one or more of the following characteristics:

1. An unusually hoarse voice;
2. An extremely breathy voice or sounding as if one has "lost" his or her voice;
3. A highly nasal voice quality.

The most frequent type of voice disorder among children and adolescents has the primary quality of excessive hoarseness. Many times such a condition is simply a result of misuse of the vocal mechanism — such as too much screaming or shouting over an excessive period of time. At other times, laryngeal pathology such as vocal nodules (small, benign growths on the vocal cords) may be associated with the voice disorder.

The prevalence of voice disorders is low — less than one percent of the total population. As with other communication disorders, prevalence figures are tentative, but we can state with some certainty that teachers will infrequently encounter a student having a voice disorder.

Language Disorders

A communication disorder with which clinicians and other professionals have become increasingly involved is of the type termed *language disorder*. This term refers to problems in comprehending, expressing, or otherwise functionally utilizing spoken language. Often, such difficulties portend or accompany academic difficulties in the areas of reading, writing, and mathematics.

Oral language is comprised of four components: phonemes, morphemes, syntax, and semantics. *Phoneme* is a linguistic term referring to a sound within a language (discussed earlier in this chapter). Since the field of speech pathology commonly includes the area of phonemics within the category of articulation, information presented under *Articulation Disorders* is applicable when considering disorders of the phoneme or sound system. One must remember, however, that sounds are part of the total language system and cannot be entirely separated from it.

A second component of language, the *morpheme*, can be defined as the minimal meaningful unit of language. Although the term may appear to be synonymous with "word," the two terms have different meanings. A word may be comprised of more than one morpheme (e.g., dogs, visited, rerun). Each of these single words is comprised of two meaningful units, or morphemes (e.g., dog-s, visit-ed, re-run). The joining of morphemes in a word unit is governed by *morphological rules*. Morphemes which can stand alone are called "free morphs" (e.g., dog), and those which must be used in combination with other morphemes are called "bound morphs" (e.g., dogs). The two major morphological categories are those for marking verb tense (e.g., visit-ed) and pluralization (dog-s).

A third component of language is *syntax* — referring to the rules for putting words together in sequences or sentences. Syntactic rules include, among other things, subject-verb agreement, use of the passive sentence form, negation, and appropriate question forms. Any linguistic rule which applies to more than a single word is regarded as syntactic. In practice, the rules of morphology and syntax are combined to form the *grammar* of a language. Thus, in discussing grammar, one would be referring to both morphology and syntax.

A final component of language is *semantics*—the meaning ascribed to the arbitrary linquistic symbols used in language. Behaviorally, a child's semantic knowledge is reflected in vocabulary, concepts, and word associations. As contrasted with phonology, morphology, and syntax, which constitute the structure of the language system, semantics refers to the meaning attached to those structures.

Standard language evaluations usually entail gathering behavioral estimates of both comprehension and expression of semantic knowledge, grammatical rules, and sentence forms. Such areas are assessed within the context of functional or pragmatic communication. Additional facets of assessment frequently include auditory memory, sequencing, and processing. From the ever-increasing assortment of available language tests, inventories, and informal assessment guidelines, the specific measures to be included in a language battery should be determined by: (1) the age of the child, (2) the specific areas in which the examiner wishes to concentrate, and (3) the purpose and uses for which the test data are intended (e.g., comparison with norms, establishing clinical instructional objectives).

Frequently, language tests assess only one aspect of linguistic functioning (e.g., receptive vocabulary; expressive syntax; auditory memory); therefore, the clinician must judiciously select a battery of measures which will allow him or her to best determine the nature and extent of language disorders. As with articulation testing, examiners are interested not only in language performance in response to structured test items (such as those found on language inventories) but also in how language is used in more informal situations where spontaneous functional language is required.

The number of children seen by clinicians for language therapy has increased rapidly in recent years. In fact, language disorders may have replaced articulation disorders as the type of communication problem most commonly observed in clinicians' case loads. Because knowledge and research in the area of language communication are interdisciplinary in origin and nature, the current interest in language disorders has stemmed not only from the field of speech pathology, but also from psychology, psycholinguistics, and special education. Society in general also has shown increased interest in children with reading and other learning disabilities, and this has sparked a deeper interest in oral language deficits which may underlie such disabilities. As a result of the above developments, children with language disorders commonly comprise up to 60 percent of a speech pathologist's case load.

INTERVENTION AND EDUCATIONAL PROGRAMMING

Once a child has been identified as having a speech disorder and an evaluation has been accomplished to identify specific areas of deficiency, as well as any potential etiological (causal) factors which may need to be considered, the speech pathologist is ready to develop a remediation program. The three stages through which clinical instruction progresses often are designated as establishment, transfer, and maintenance.

1. *Establishment* refers to the acquisition of a behavior in a person's repertoire, including the skill to produce that behavior spontaneously (e.g., say *s*; use appropriate subject-verb agreement in sentences; speak with a normal voice quality; talk without inordinate hesitations).
2. *Transfer* describes the process whereby an individual generalizes from training to nontraining items (e.g., words or sentences taught to those not taught, or from the training setting to a different setting, such as clinic to home).
3. *Maintenance* involves habituation, or making a habit of newly learned behavior so it will not disappear or revert to former behavior after training has ended.

Regardless of the communication skills to be acquired or modified, one must first teach or otherwise facilitate the person's ability to use the correct form rather than the deficient form, assist him or her to use this behavior in response to novel stimuli and situations and, through repeated practice, seek to automatize the proper communication skills.

Within this overall temporal sequence of clinical instruction, specific techniques and practices vary. Behavior modification procedures and techniques such as shaping and reinforcement are frequently used and often are incorporated into highly structured teaching procedures otherwise known as programmed instruction. The processes of imitation and delayed imitation are heavily relied upon in speech therapy. Emphasis also is placed upon the interpersonal dynamics between clinician and client and, therefore, clinicians must be sensitive to the influence of such factors on therapy. Utilization of specific instructional (including behavioral) techniques is predicated upon adequate technical knowledge of speech and language functioning which, together with interpersonal skills, have been regarded by Diedrich (1969) as essential elements of the clinical process.

Treatment of Articulation Disorders

Treatment approaches applied to articulation disorders utilize basic clinical procedures learned early in a clinician's professional training. These approaches, in a sense, constitute a prototype employed with other types of speech disorders. Misarticulation is a more explicit or defined type of communication disorder than is a problem associated with voice, language, or fluency, and thus is often perceived as lending itself more readily to a person's initial development of clinical skills.

In articulation therapy the practice of proceeding from part to whole (e.g., sound to syllable, word to sentence) is used widely. In addition, auditory discrimination training, either of someone else's speech or one's own speech, is frequently employed. Determining criterion levels of performance, obtaining repeated measures of sound productions, and assessing generalization or transfer of behavior are also facets of articulation remediation. Treatment strategies such as these are important not only in articulation remediation but also in the other areas of speech and language remediation.

During the establishment phase of articulation therapy, the child usually is taught first to produce the correct form of a misarticulated sound by itself (in isolation), then in syllables, words, and finally sentences. Frequently, "ear training" or auditory discrimination activities also are introduced at this level. Some clinicians prefer to work on more than one sound at a time and thus may use a multiple sound approach. The speed at which one can establish a new or corrected sound in a person's repertoire sometimes is facilitated by presence of the correct form of the misarticulated sound somewhere already within the persons's repertoire (e.g., even though the child cannot use *s* correctly in most instances, he or she may be able to say *s* by itself or in certain words).

During the transfer or "carryover" stage of therapy, the main objective is to facilitate production of a target sound in response to novel stimuli both within and outside the therapy setting. For example, new picture cards may be introduced in therapy, or the child may be required to use the target sound in sentences he or she creates. In addition, efforts are made to reinforce correct articulation in speaking situations other than the clinical setting.

During the maintenance phase, efforts are made to periodically monitor a person's speech to satisfy the objective of continuing correct articulation. Drill activities or structured reinforcement may need to be reinstated on occasion if correct articulation is not being maintained.

Variations and additions to the clinical procedures suggested above are numerous. Although the articulation remediation skills being used are considered sound, basic approaches, research developments and clinicians' desire to be more scientific and creative in therapy leads to constant changes and improvements in remediation approaches.

Treatment of Fluency Disorders

Treatment approaches employed with fluency disorders are of two major types: indirect and direct. In the *indirect therapy* process, the clinician counsels with parents, teachers, and other adults in a child's environment to enlist their support in helping the child become more fluent. Such counsel is predicated upon the theory that dysfluencies in the speech of young children may be decreased by proper attitudes and behaviors from significant others in the environment. Specifically, the significant others are asked to *not* show verbal or nonverbal reactions when dysfluencies occur in the child's speech, but are encouraged to allow the child to express himself or herself freely without fear of listener reaction or evaluation. Advice and counseling go beyond these suggestions, but these elements constitute the basic premises of an indirect approach.

In *direct therapy*, the establishment phase provides efforts to establish fluency during production of short segments of speech, gradually increasing to lengthier segments. Such efforts may consist of having the child count the number of dysfluencies produced in a given period of time, describe the way in which interruptions in the flow of speech are created (e.g., upper teeth held against lower lip for an inappropriate amount of time), and then modify in some way the types of inappropriate articulatory contacts made. In some instances, slowing down the rate of speech until fluency is achieved and then gradually increasing the rate is a successful means of establishing fluency.

During the transfer stage of stuttering therapy, the clinician attempts to facilitate use of the now-established fluency pattern in the presence of additional listeners and in new situations. The children are encouraged to use their newly-gained fluency at all times. The maintenance segment involves periodic monitoring of fluency patterns and reviewing the kinds of techniques that facilitated these fluency achievements.

The majority of younger children do not appear to have the same negative emotional reactions to stuttering that often are elicited by older adolescents and adults. Thus, an easy-going, direct approach to changing fluency patterns in young children is often successful. Counseling with parents and other teachers is usually a part of the direct approach to stuttering remediation, as it is with other speech disorders.

Treatment of Voice Disorders

The type of therapy used with children evidencing voice disorders is based upon the nature of the voice problem. The kinds of activities in which the child might engage during treatment are dependent upon, for example, whether there is too much (hyperfunction) or too little (hypofunction) activity of the vocal cords, or too much or too little nasal resonance. During the establishment phase of therapy, certain techniques are used to facilitate the occurrence of the desired voice quality. As with other speech disorders, the clinician may first work to establish adequate vocal production in small units of speech (e.g., vowel sounds) and gradually increase the length of the unit (e.g., syllables to words to phrases). The tape recorder may also be used, to facilitate external auditory discrimination; and, finally, self-monitoring is suggested as an integral part of this phase.

During the transfer stage of intervention, the objective is to use the modified voice quality attained during the establishment phase in situations other than the clinical setting. Often, success in this step requires the assistance of parents and teachers. The maintenance phase

of therapy calls for periodic reminders of the objectives that were sought during the transfer stage.

The most common type of voice disorder in young people has been described as hoarseness and is related to hyperfunctioning of the vocal cords, such as occurs with excessive shouting. This type of abuse can result in vocal nodules. Therapy consists of establishing and then transferring a relaxed, "easy" use of the voice, thus decreasing the amount of vocal abuse. To transfer the new "nonhoarse" voice quality to additional speaking situations, the individual must at the same time decrease the amount of shouting or vocal abuse which promoted the voice disorder. By helping a child self-monitor and subsequently decrease his or her abusive vocal activity, vocal nodules which may be developing may dissipate without the need for surgery or extended speech therapy.

Treatment of Language Disorders

While relatively little is known about the exact process by which normal children acquire language, the speech clinician is faced with the responsibility of teaching and correcting language skills in youngsters who are developing their language behavior in a slow or aberrant manner. Intervention is based on first identifying those aspects in need of remediation. Thus, morphological, syntactical, or semantic skills may constitute an area of concern. The presence or absence of such skills on a *receptive* or *expressive* level adds a further dimension. Depending upon the model of language from which one operates, auditory, visual, and gestural modalities, as well as automatic and representational levels of language, may constitute additional areas of concern. Instructional objectives are developed on the basis of those aspects of language functioning which are deficient, plus the level of development at which the client is operating in such areas.

During the establishment phase of therapy, the clinician emits many verbal models which reflect the language form being taught. Also, clinicians engage children in situations for which such models are meaningful. For example, if the clinician wants to teach the *agent-action* sentence form, he or she may structure the situation so that the child is playing with puppies, and then model such utterances as: "puppy sleeping," "puppy walking," "puppy yawn."

This phase relies upon both spontaneous and elicited imitations from the child. The sequence in which syntax, semantics, and other skills are taught usually is based upon a developmental hierarchy, to the extent that one is known. Approaches utilized by clinicians range from an informal language stimulation environment to formal, programmed instruction. Whether instruction is being provided on an individual or group basis further influences the extent of formality or structure incorporated into the therapy.

During the transfer stage of instruction, the child is encouraged to make use of the improved language skills in everyday functioning. Often, one must structure the environment to elicit these new skills and make certain that appropriate responses then are reinforced.

As transfer occurs from skills taught to those not taught, the maintenance process becomes relatively easy because of the positive natural reinforcement resulting from application of improved linguistic functioning.

The objective of most language therapy is verbal expression, but sometimes gestural systems or communication board type approaches to communication must be substituted, as in certain deaf children or some with severe handicaps. The pervasiveness of language handicaps requires singular attention in providing the type, quantity, and quality of therapy needed.

Role of the Classroom Teacher

The classroom teacher can do several things to facilitate speech and language development of children, especially for those in their classrooms who receive clinical speech instruction. Teacher efforts not only assist the speech pathologist, but allow teacher and clinician to work as part of a team for the good of their students.

A teacher's primary function is to be alert to students who may evidence speech disorders and to refer them to the proper specialists. Frequently, the classroom teacher is the first person to recognize a student's speech or language problem. Students who aren't understood clearly or produce their sounds incorrectly may have an articulation problem. Youngsters who are unusually quiet or seem to have difficulty comprehending what is said, don't follow directions well, or have difficulty putting sentences together may have a language problem. Although articulation and language disorders are the primary types of communication problems for which teachers can be most helpful in referral, school personnel should feel free, even obligated, to refer any child suspected of a communication disorder to the appropriate professional specialists.

Teachers certainly should set a good speech standard but, at the same time, must be tolerant and understanding of those who reflect less than desired speaking patterns. Teachers also may wish to conduct their own speech and language stimulation programs in the classroom, depending upon the students' needs. Commercially produced developmental language programs such as the Peabody Language Development Kits (Dunn, Smith, & Horton, 1965) and the Distar I and II Language Program (Engelmann, Osborn, & Engelmann, 1972) can be helpful in this regard. Emphasizing listening and speaking behavior and attempting to improve children's performance in these areas benefit a child in all aspects of daily living.

Related to teachers' personal understanding of speech variations in children is the role they can play in discouraging teasing, disparaging remarks, and negative attitudes toward those who have speech disorders. Teachers should be sensitive to the fact that children with speech and language problems often are embarrassed at their attempts in communication and should not have to endure the added burden of peer disapproval. In addition, sometimes the scheduling of a "speech class" creates a negative impression and can become a stigma. Careful planning by school personnel can not only reduce negative connotations but even make attendance of special classes something to be desired rather than avoided.

Depending upon the amount of time available (including whether or not the teacher has the services of a teaching aide), the teacher may be able to conduct certain drill activities associated with speech therapy. The specific need and nature of drills would be determined by the speech clinician; however, added classroom practice on a daily basis undoubtedly would be welcome and helpful.

One of the most valuable ways in which teachers can assist their pupils and the speech pathologist is to play a role in the process of facilitating transfer or carryover of newly acquired behaviors. Often, teachers can serve as reinforcing agents for children's use of new communication skills. Verbal praise, tangible reinforcement, or collecting data on improvements are possible forms of aid. The transfer process is of major concern to the speech pathologist. Since teachers have frequent contacts with students, they can provide valuable help in the clinical process.

SUMMARY

Speech and language disorders constitute a handicapping condition which can occur in isolation or in combination with other handicapping conditions such as mental retardation, cerebral palsy, emotional disturbances, and hearing impairments. Speech impairments can be broadly classified as disorders of articulation, fluency, and voice quality; and language disorders generally refer to problems associated with comprehending, expressing, or otherwise functionally using spoken language.

Intervention programs often utilize the three stages of establishment, transfer, and maintenance in therapy. The speech pathologist, or clinician, is a special educator responsible for directing such programs and whose skills are needed across a wide range of handicapping conditions. Because receptive and expressive communication skills are vital to a person's ability to function in society, every effort should be made to provide habilitative and rehabilitative services to persons with speech and language deficits.

Clinical speech services in the schools traditionally have been provided on an itinerant basis, with children typically receiving instruction twice weekly in half-hour lessons. More recently, speech therapy scheduling has been based on the extent of an individual's needs and, thus, a continuum of services is emerging. Some children now are seen daily for therapy, with session length determined by a student's needs in combination with availability of clinician time.

Classroom teachers may play a vital role in furthering their students' speech and language development as part of a team working to that end, as well as within the classroom by setting good speech standards, showing understanding and support to those indicating problems, and by being in the best position to identify and refer students needing special attention to the proper professional specialists.

REFERENCES

Byrne, M. C., & Shervanian, C. C. *Introduction to communicative disorders.* New York: Harper & Row, 1977.

Diedrich, W. M. Assessment of the clinical process. *Journal of Kansas Speech & Hearing Association,* 1969, *10,* 1-8.

Dunn, L. M., Smith, J., & Horton, K. *Peabody language development kits.* Circle Pines, MN: American Guidance Service, 1965.

Englemann, S., Osborn, J., & Engelmann, T. *Distar.* Chicago: Science Research Associates, 1972.

Hull, F. M., Miekle, P. W., Timmons, R. J., & Willeford, J. A. *National speech and hearing survey interim report* (Project No. 50978). Washington, DC: U.S. Office of Education/Bureau of Education for the Handicapped, 1969.

Johnson, W. *The onset of stuttering.* Minneapolis: University of Minnesota Press, 1959.

Perkins, W.H. *Speech pathology.* St. Louis: Mosby Publishing Co., 1976.

Sander, E. K. When are speech sounds learned? *Journal of Speech and Hearing Disorders,* 1972, 37, 55-63.

Sheehan, J. Projective studies of stuttering. *Journal of Speech and Hearing Disorders,* 1958, *23,* 18-25.

RESOURCE GUIDE

Historical Information

Boone, D. Our profession: Where are we? *Asha,* 1977, *19,* 3-6.
Paden, E. *History of the American Speech and Hearing Association: 1925-1958.* Washington, DC: American Speech & Hearing Assoc., 1972.
Winitz, H. Articulation disorders: From prescription to description. *Journal of Speech & Hearing Disorders,* 1977, *2,* 143-145.

Family

Baratz, J. Language in the economically disadvantaged child: A perspective. *Asha,* 1968, *10,* 143-145.
Olin, S., Hess, R., & Shipman, V. Role of mothers' language styles in mediating their pre-school children's cognitive development. *The School Review,* 1967, *75,* 414-424.

Patterns of Development

Brown, R. *A first language: The early stages.* Cambridge, MA: Harvard University Press, 1973.
Dale, P. *Language development.* New York: Holt, Rinehart & Winston, 1976.
Templin, M. *Certain language skills in children.* Minneapolis: University of Minnesota Press, 1957.
Trantham, C., & Pederson, J. *Normal language development.* Baltimore: Williams & Wilkins Co., 1976.

Treatment

Byrne, M. & Shervanian, C. *Introduction to communicative disorders.* New York: Harper & Row, 1977.
Emerick, L., & Hatten, J. *Diagnosis and evaluation in speech pathology.* Englewood Cliffs, NJ: Prentice-Hall, 1974.
Travis, E. (Ed.). *Handbook of speech pathology.* Englewood Cliffs, NJ: Prentice-Hall, 1971.
Winitz, H. *From syllable to conversation.* Baltimore: University Park Press, 1975.

Educational Programming

Lee, L. *Interactive language development teaching.* Evanston, IL: Northwestern University Press, 1975.

Rees, N. The speech pathologist and the reading process. *Asha,* 1974, *16,* 255-258.

Stark, J. Reading failure: A language based problem. *Asha,* 1975, *17,* 832-834.

Van Hattum, R. Services of the speech clinician in schools: Progress and prospects. *Asha,* 1976, *18,* 59-63.

10 The Visually Impaired

Carson Y. Nolan
American Printing House for the Blind

Formal education of visually impaired children in this country began in 1829, with incorporation of the New England Asylum for the Blind (now Perkins School for the Blind) in Watertown, Massachusetts. Successful education of the first deaf-blind child, Laura Bridgeman, was undertaken by Samuel Howe in 1837. In 1858 the American Printing House for the Blind was chartered, and in 1879 Congress passed *The Act to Promote the Education of the Blind*. This act, administered by the American Printing House for the Blind, provided free educational materials to legally blind children and was among the first (if not *the* first) federal laws for special education.

The first public school class for braille readers opened in Chicago in 1900, and in 1913 the first public school program for partially seeing children opened in Boston. The adoption of Standard English Braille (Grade 2) in 1932 ended a 100-year controversy over the mode of tactile printing for the blind.

Educationally, visually impaired children and youth are now defined as those whose visual condition is such that special provisions are necessary for their successful education. Many are impaired enough to come under the legal definition of blindness—central visual acuity of 20/200 or less in the better eye with correcting glasses, or central visual acuity of more than 20/200 if there is a field defect in which the peripheral field has contracted to such an extent that the widest diameter of visual field subtends an angular distance no greater than 20 degrees.

This legal definition is used to qualify individuals for a variety of state, federal, and other services. In addition, children whose corrected visual acuity in the better eye ranges from 20/200 to 20/70 often require special educational services.

Visually impaired children often are classified functionally into two groups: those who use their fingers to read and those who use their eyes to read. Members of the first group are referred to as "blind" or "braille readers"; members of the second group are referred to as "partially seeing" and, in some cases, "large-type readers." A frequent, confusing practice is to use the term "blind" to refer to all children who fall within the legal definition of blindness, although this group includes both braille readers and large-type readers. In terms of educational practice, it is important to determine as early as possible whether legally blind children will function as visual readers or as tactile readers.

Further, many visually impaired children have one or more additional handicaps. These multihandicapped children may have other sensory deficits, orthopedic handicaps, mental retardation, emotional disturbances, or learning disabilities.

The total number of visually impaired children requiring special education is not clearly known. A recent estimate (National Advisory Committee on Education of the Handicapped, 1976) suggests a figure of 66,000 visually impaired children in the age group 0-19. This estimate is probably low. The number of legally blind children enrolled in formal education programs through grade 12 is determined by a census conducted annually by the American Printing House for the Blind. In 1976 this organization identified 28,995 legally blind children. Of these, 6,200 read braille, 12,426 read large type, 1,104 read both media, and 9,265 read neither. This total group included 1,234 children classified as deaf-blind.

CAUSES OF VISUAL IMPAIRMENT

Visual impairments stem from varied sources. Causes may include prenatal development deficits, disease, injury, or poisoning. Onset of impairment may be before or at birth, or any time subsequent to birth. Visual impairments occur because of problems with the surrounding protective structures of the eye, problems with light-transmitting and light-focusing parts, problems with muscles which move the eyes, and problems with the eye's neural components.

Among specific causes of visual impairment is *trachoma*, a severe infection of the eyelid and the outer covering of the eye. *Myopia* (nearsightedness) occurs when the eye is too long from front to back and light from distant objects focuses in front of the light-sensitive rear lining (retina) of the eye. *Astigmatism* is an irregularity in the light-focusing element of the eye (lens), resulting in a blurred visual image. *Cataract* (clouding of the lens) interferes with light transmission.

Defective muscle functioning can cause *strabismus* (crossed eyes or squint), which often results in suppression of use of the weaker eye— *amblyopia ex anopsia*. Use of excessive amounts of oxygen in incubation of premature infants causes *retrolental fibroplasia* (deterioration of the retina). In later years, the retina may become loose and fall away from the rear of the eye, a condition called *retinal detachment*. Many other known causes of impairment to the eye have been identified.

IMPLICATIONS OF VISUAL IMPAIRMENT FOR EDUCATIONAL PRACTICE

Effects of visual impairment on child development vary depending on severity of the impairment, age of onset of impairment, developmental opportunities, and the type and degree of any associated handicap.

The primary effects of visual impairment have been described by Lowenfeld (1962, p. 90) as restrictions imposed on the individual in (1) the range and variety of possible experiences, (2) the ability to move about the environment, and (3) control of the environment and of the self in relation to it.

Visually impaired children rely more than nonimpaired individuals on their remaining senses (touch, audition, kinesthesis, smell, and taste) to build up their conception of the world. As information-gathering sources, however, these senses are inferior to vision. They have a lesser degree and range of sensitivity than vision, and opportunities for vicarious experience are greatly restricted.

Restriction in opportunities to move about the environment inhibits the child in voluntarily changing the environment to provide new opportunities for observation and experience. Opportunities for the visually impaired to move about are largely dependent upon the assistance of others, a consequence which seriously affects the child's relationships and attitudes.

Lack of control of the environment in relation to the self has far-reaching effects which can be subtle. Visual impairment lessens the opportunity to determine the qualities of things at a distance and to acquire information about relationships of form, size, and position. Likewise, visual impairment limits the opportunity to orient oneself to the environment while remaining stationary. From the social standpoint, visual impairment denies the opportunity to communicate through facial expression or bodily gesture.

In terms of educational practice, the heterogeneity of effects of visual impairment on students makes the individualization of their educational programming imperative. The greatly reduced opportunities for actual experiences, vicarious experiences, and experiences at a distance compel the use of concrete, as opposed to abstract, teaching methods. Instruction must stress the relationship among things in the environment, since they are not readily discernible. Because many common experiences are lacking, deliberate planning is required to provide sources of stimulation. Since passivity may result from environmental restrictions, the child must be taught to actively engage in the world. Thus, a teacher must thoughtfully plan to maximize participation of the visually impaired student in all phases of the school program.

EDUCATIONAL PROGRAMMING

Types of Educational Program

In a review of educational programming for the visually impaired, Taylor (1976) quotes herself regarding "the need for flexibility in selecting facilities. That facility should be selected which fulfills a particular need, at the time of the need, and for only as long as—in light of the total situation—it is fulfilling this need. Switching from one facility to another should not necessarily be considered as a failure of the first facility but rather as a success in having solved the problem for which it was selected, or as an outgrowth of new developments" (p.18).

Initially, visually impaired children were educated in residential schools. Today, however, most visually impaired children are educated in public school programs in their own communities. Fifty-two residential schools in this country still serve children from areas without local services, children from broken homes, multihandicapped children, and those whose parents prefer this educational solution.

Public school programs for the visually impaired vary widely in design. Special classes, in which children were taught by a special teacher in a self-contained classroom, are infrequently found today. The resource room approach, where students attend regular classes but report to a specially trained resource teacher for instruction and materials as necessary, is frequently used.

The least restrictive alternative, the itinerant teacher, and teacher-consultant plans are the most recently evolved approaches. In these plans, the child is enrolled in regular classes in his or her neighborhood school and given direct instruction or indirect services by specially trained teachers as required. The teachers also provide consultation and support to neighborhood school administrators and regular classroom teachers.

All educational programs require the services of a variety of supporting personnel. Through diagnosis, the opthalmologist provides basic data for educational programming as well as prescriptive visual aids. The orientation and mobility specialist provides information to teachers and instruction to students. School psychologists provide assessment services through adaptations of standard measures. Students may have problems in addition to vision which require the services of such specialists as speech clinicians, physical therapists, social workers, and others.

Educational Goals

Educators of visually impaired children set the same academic goals for them as for other children, but a number of additional educational goals are stressed. These include educational readiness, sight utilization, braille reading, print reading, listening, orientation and mobility, and daily living skills. If visually impaired students have one or more additional handicaps, pursuit of these goals must be augmented or modified to accommodate other goals or limitations associated with the added handicap.

Readiness

Because of the restrictions imposed by visual impairment, many children require extensive and formal readiness programs to prepare them for a successful school experience. Training may need to emphasize both gross and fine motor skills; sensory skills, including use of remaining vision; cognitive development; language skills; self-concept and body image; social skills; and self-help skills. Readiness training can be carried out in the home or in any of the wide variety of preschool and kindergarten programs in the community — provided that persons responsible for the training understand the visually impaired child's needs and how to serve them. The extent of readiness training required depends upon the severity and type of visual handicap, other associated handicaps, and opportunities open to the child to interact with various physical and social environments during the earliest years.

Braille Reading and Writing

Braille is a system of printing and writing which consists of tactually distinguishable raised-dot patterns which represent elements of the language. The characters which comprise braille are made up of the 63 possible combinations of one to six dots within an array of six equally spaced positions, three high by two wide, called the *braille cell*. Standard English Braille (grade 2) is a highly contracted system in which 263 elements or meanings are assigned to the 63 characters. These elements include the letters of the alphabet, letter sequences, words, numbers, punctuation, and pronunciation and composition signs.

Braille reading differs from print reading in that the braille character, rather than the whole word, appears to be the perceptual unit

(Nolan & Kederis, 1969). In addition, braille is a more complex and ambiguous code than is print. The effect of these factors is that children often learn to read braille more slowly than print, and their ultimate reading speeds are much slower. For example, high school seniors read braille at an average of 90 words per minute as compared to about 250 words per minute for those who read print (Myers, Ethington, & Ashcroft, 1958). Teaching braille reading requires a thorough knowledge of the braille code, as well as knowledge of how the braille and print reading processes differ.

a	b	c	d	e	f	g	h	i	j

k	l	m	n	o	p	q	r	s	t

u	v	w	x	y	z

Figure 10.1 Alphabet in Braille

Each letter is indicated by the raised dot pattern within the 6-dot braille cell. In Standard English Braille, additional combinations include numbers, punctuation, pronunciation, letter sequences, and words.

Children write braille using the braillewriter or the braille slate and stylus. Because of its greater ease of operation, students usually learn to write using the braillewriter. This analog of a typewriter is activated by six keys (one for each dot position) and a space bar. Students form the 63 combinations of braille dots by depressing appropriate key combinations.

Later, the student learns to use the braille slate and stylus. The slate is a hinged frame into which paper is clamped. The front of the slate has rows of openings shaped in outline like the braille cell. Under each opening, the back of the slate contains six depressions arranged like the dots in a braille cell. Using an awl-like device, the stylus, the writer presses the paper down into the depressions, forming the combinations of dots required. Since the writing is done upside down and in reverse, it must start at the right and proceed to the left.

The braillewriter is a basic tool in written communication.

Reading and Writing by the Partially Seeing

Many factors affect seeing efficiency. Levels of illumination must be controlled to fit the child's visual problem; glare and shadows should be avoided. Sharpness in contrast is important between print or objects and the background against which they are viewed. Greater time may be necessary for viewing, and images must be larger. The latter can be achieved, in part, by seating a student in the front of the classroom or close to the chalkboard.

In reading, the size of the print image must be increased. For some students, the simplest way to do this is to hold the reading material closer to the eyes. Also, special textbooks with enlarged type (18- or 24-point size) are available. Optical aids such as spectacles and hand magnifiers can be used to enlarge images, as well as to compensate for other visual deficiencies. Closed-circuit television equipment also can be used to benefit the visually impaired. Learning to read takes longer for many visually impaired children, and ultimate reading speeds often are much slower than for normally seeing children (Nolan, 1968).

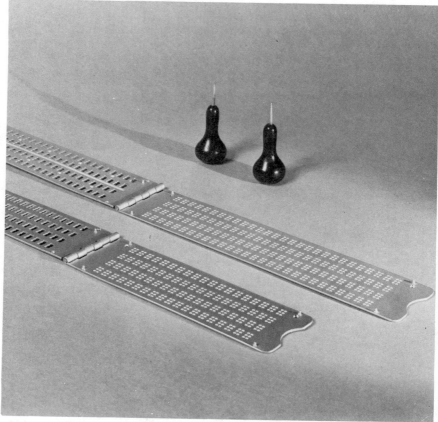

The slate and stylus is an alternate method for writing braille. Paper is clamped between the hinged sections, and the stylus is used to make indentations, forming the dot combinations desired.

Partially seeing children learn to write similarly to other children. The pen or pencil should produce a clear bold line which contrasts sharply with the writing paper. Many varieties of slightly tinted, nonglare writing paper are available which are ruled in bold, wide lines.

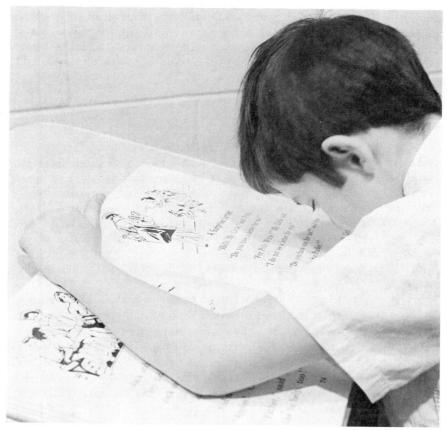

Large-type books are useful aids for the partially seeing.

Sight Utilization

Most visually impaired children have some degree of vision remaining. The amount of vision and its quality, however, can vary greatly because of the wide differences in causes and degrees of visual impairment. Children without visual handicaps learn to use their vision routinely and to perceive their world accurately at an early age. However, visually impaired children, because of the restrictions previously discussed, may not learn to use their vision to its maximum functional level. Nevertheless, the use of special evaluative procedures and special training techniques can help to increase, sometimes dramatically, the child's ability to perceive features of his or her environment accurately (Barraga, 1964). Some visually impaired children are enabled to read print as a consequence of such training. Basically, this training consists of a variety of activities which require the child to make visual recognitions and discriminations at increasing levels of difficulty and complexity.

Listening

Since not all subject matter is available in braille or large type, students sometimes must use recorded textbooks or have their materials read by a live reader. Many ordinary classroom activities depend upon listening for successful participation. For many visually impaired children who read slowly, listening is often a more efficient way to learn than is reading.

Listening skills can be improved through appropriate training and practice. Training materials for listening are available for use with all children, and some have been adapted especially for use with the visually impaired.

A number of practices can enhance learning through listening. Having a quiet, organized listening environment helps. Active listening by stopping a recording to mentally review material or to take notes has been shown to increase comprehension (Nolan & Morris, 1969). Taking well-organized notes for subsequent review also is helpful. As students gain in listening skills, they can increase the rates at which they listen, through playing the recording at faster-than-normal speeds. Special playback equipment is available for this purpose.

Orientation and Mobility

Because severely visually impaired children are restricted in their interaction with the environment, they need specific help in developing realistic environmental concepts and in learning techniques to move safely through it. Specially trained teachers called orientation and mobility instructors usually provide this training.

Developing realistic concepts must come first through concrete, direct experience with the immediate environment. In the home the child should be taught such things as floor plans, that rooms have ceilings, and the relationship of lower and upper floors of houses. These concrete relational experiences then should be continued to teach the layout of the yard, the block, and the neighborhood.

Body orientation, use of the senses to relate to the environment, environmental concepts and language, correct posture, and the gaits necessary to move through different environments often must be taught directly. Basic mobility skills such as using the forearm as a bumper, trailing the fingertips along a vertical surface to maintain direction of movement, and using the edges of things such as sidewalks as guides need to be learned.

As the student matures, he or she can learn how to interact unobtrusively with a sighted guide, to use the long cane as a mobility aid, or eventually to acquire and learn the use of a guide dog. Proper use of the long cane requires formal instruction by a trained orientation and mobility instructor. Students must go to special training sites to be instructed in the use of guide dogs. Only older, mature students in the upper high school grades or beyond are encouraged to seek use of a guide dog.

Daily Living Skills

Severely visually impaired children are unable to observe others and imitate their activities. Consequently, many simple, everyday self-care activities must be taught directly. At early ages, such things as eating, dressing, and bathing may require special attention. As the child grows older, personal grooming and identification, care and location of clothing must be taught. Simple and complex household activities and chores must be explained explicitly.

The child should be taught to use the phone, to identify money and make change, to purchase in stores, and to use community services. He or she needs direct instruction in simple cooking. Ultimately, instruction should extend to interpersonal relations and self-management.

Curriculum Considerations

Because of deficits in educational readiness, slow reading speeds, and associated handicaps, the visually impaired child may progress slowly in education. Typically, visually impaired students may be older chronologically than sighted children in the same grade (Birch, Tisdall, Peabody, & Sterrett, 1966). Many visually impaired children, however, complete the regular academic curriculum and pursue goals in higher education within reasonable and even typical time spans.

The restrictions imposed by visual impairment, described earlier, have implications for educational progress which vary directly with the severity of the impairment. The many experiences that fully seeing children encounter incidently, vicariously through pictures or television, or at a distance must be compensated for and substituted by methods that purposely provide real, concrete, immediate experiences. Carefully planned encounters with objects in the home, in the classroom, in the school, and in neighborhood environments must replace the experiences of nonimpaired children. Well thought-out field trips to a wide variety of locales such as stores, transportation facilities, public services, museums, zoos, and natural environments (gardens, parks, forests) are essential.

Because visually impaired children require special materials, particularly books, a critical part of educational programming is determining the child's material needs early enough in the programming effort to assure that the necessary materials are available to the student when needed.

When provided with an adequate background of valid concepts, the visually impaired child has the potential to master the verbal content of his or her curriculum. When educational content is presented nonverbally, however, students may encounter problems. The braille reader is denied access to the many visual aids employed today. To present the pictures, charts, and diagrams in textbooks in a form understandable to the tactual sense often is not possible.

The large-type reader is less restricted in access to these forms of information but, depending on the severity of the impairment, he or she still may have difficulty. When textbooks printed in color are reproduced in black and white large-type form, legibility of pictures, charts, and diagrams can be seriously impaired. In addition, the large-type reader may experience considerable difficulty in viewing the projected visual materials which are frequently used in the classroom. Progress in the social sciences often is impeded because of problems encountered in these areas.

Mathematics is another area in which visually impaired children may be hampered in rate of progress (Nolan, 1959). Lack of adequate readiness is often a factor critical to achievement. A special braille code (Nemeth Code) is used for math. Writing out problems in braille can be a slow and tedious process. Long formulas, graphs, charts, and diagrams pose special problems for the braille reader. These problems are not as serious for the large-type reader. Special aids for calculating are available for use by these students.

Science instruction presents similar hurdles for the visually impaired. The use of a wide variety of pictures, diagrams, and graphs often cause problems. Use of measuring devices and experimental apparatus may be difficult. In many cases, however, special materials are available for use by these students. Pairing the visually impaired student with a normally seeing lab partner for experiments and demonstrations is a good means to help in overcoming impediments to successful learning.

Because many activities in physical education rely on imitation, adequate geographical orientation, and interacting with others and the environment at a distance, the visually impaired may be unable to participate easily. Their need for physical activities, however, is usually greater than that of normally seeing children. Pairing visually impaired children with normally seeing children can enable the former to participate in many physical activities. Some activities such as hiking, swimming, wrestling, calisthenics, roller skating, and bowling can be taught with little or no adaptation.

Since some of the arts are highly visual in nature, many visually impaired individuals are not able to participate. Manual arts such as sculpting offer opportunities, and many children with less severe visual impairments can successfully engage in drawing and painting. Music is an art form in which visually impaired students may participate freely. Modification of standard instructional approaches may include special braille music codes, large-type musical scores, and rote aural learning.

Typing is a skill that should be mastered by visually impaired students in academic and other programs. Use of typing enables the braille reader to complete lessons in a form more easily read by a sighted teacher. Typing allows large-type readers to prepare neater and more legible papers and present more written information in less space.

Adequate educational programming for visually impaired children requires a clear understanding of the problems they encounter in learning, anticipating these problems through the timely provision of special materials and environments, and modifying standard educational techniques to accommodate special needs.

Special Educational Materials

Visually impaired children require a variety of special educational materials. These include texts and other books, especially developed or adapted tools, educational aids, and school supplies. The primary source for such educational materials is the American Printing House for the

Blind. The Printing House administers the federal *Act to Promote the Education of the Blind,* which provides free educational materials to legally blind students enrolled in formal educational programs in the United States and its possessions.

Special books are a critical need. Blind children require texts and other books in braille, and many (but not all) partially seeing students require books in large type. Both these groups can use recorded books. In addition to the Printing House, many volunteer workers throughout the country produce single copies of books in braille, large type, or recorded form, upon request. The Printing House maintains a *Central Catalogue of Volunteer Transcribed Textbooks* as a national reference service for volunteer-produced books.

The APH Speech Plus calculator gives results in both visual and auditory form (through an earphone).

Several special tools are available to provide access to text material. The thermoform machine makes copies of braille pages through vacuum-forming thin sheets of plastic. The Optacon is a device which converts print directly to a tactile form that is readable by the blind. Various closed-circuit television systems also are available; they permit the reader to display print on a television screen in almost any size.

Braillewriters or braille slates and stylus are required to write braille. Special paper is needed for this purpose. For young, partially seeing children, bold-line paper is available.

In mathematics the abacus may be one solution for use in calculations. Recently, the hand-held electronic APH Speech Plus calculator has become available; this device gives results of the calculation process in both visual and auditory form. Other special tactile and visual aids have been and are being developed to help the visually impaired learn and use mathematical concepts.

For social studies, tactile and large-type maps and map training materials are available. Special science materials include a variety of tools, tactile and visual aids. Individualized science experiments and demonstrations are becoming available for use in the lower grades.

In the preschool and readiness area, increasing numbers of aids are becoming available, including materials for basic sensory stimulation, communication skills, and sensory-motor training.

For braille reading instruction, several sets of reading readiness materials have been developed. A primary braille reading program, correlating the use of these with a specially designed primary braille reading series, will be available.

Sources of special materials for visually impaired children are:

American Printing House for the Blind
1839 Frankfort Avenue
Louisville, KY 40206

Howe Press of Perkins School for the Blind
175 North Beacon Street
Watertown, MA 02172

Sources of volunteer-produced textbooks are:

National Association for the Visually Handicapped, Inc.
3201 Balboa Street
San Francisco, CA 94121

National Braille Association
85 Godwin Avenue
Midland Park, NJ 07432

Recording for the Blind, Inc.
125 East 58th Street
New York, NY 10022

A source of recorded and braille library materials is:

Division for the Blind and Physically Handicapped
1291 Taylor Street, NW
Washington, DC 20542

Research and Development

Education of the blind is in a constant state of evolution through research. A continuing strong program for research on behaviors basic to education and for development of educational materials in a broad range of curricular areas is carried out by the American Printing House for the Blind. In many parts of the world, technological developments are under way—devices that optically scan printed material and reproduce it in synthetic spoken form, highly indexible tape-recording systems, systems that store braille on magnetic tape and display it on demand, and a variety of calculators with braille or spoken outputs.

SUMMARY

Visually impaired children were among the first to receive special education services. For almost 100 years federal legislation has provided many free school materials to children classified as legally blind. About 29,000 children are classified as legally blind, and many more children are visually handicapped to the point of needing special educational services.

These children represent an extremely heterogeneous group for educational purposes. Factors such as degree of visual handicap, cause of visual handicap, age of onset, and inclusion of handicaps other than visual contribute to this heterogeneity. Visual impairment may result in developmental deficits because it restricts the range and variety of environmental experiences open to the growing child.

Types of educational programs for visually impaired children include regular classroom enrollment with itinerant teacher service, resource rooms with regular class participation, special classes, and residential schools. The educational goals set for many of these children correspond to those set for all children, but additional special educational goals may be inserted. Where handicaps in addition to visual impairment are present, special goals identified with these handicaps also must be pursued.

Other goals that need emphasis for visually impaired children may include educational readiness, braille reading, reading by partially seeing children, sight utilization, listening, orientation and mobility, and daily living skills. Instruction of visually impaired children may require modifications of common teaching techniques. Many special educational materials and aids are available for instruction of these students.

REFERENCES

Barraga, N. *Increased visual behavior in low vision children* (Research Series #13). New York: American Foundation for the Blind, 1964.

Birch, J.W., Tisdall, W., Peabody, R., & Sterrett, R. *School achievement and effect of type size on reading in visually handicapped children* (Cooperative Research Project No. 1766, Contract No. OEC-4-10-028). Pittsburgh: University of Pittsburgh, 1966.

Lowenfeld, B. Psychological foundations of special methods of teaching blind children. In P.A. Zahl (Ed.), *Blindness*. New York: Hafner, 1962.

Myers, E., Ethington, D., & Ashcroft, S. Readability of braille as a function of three spacing variables. *Journal of Applied Psychology*, 1958, *42*, 163-165.

National Advisory Committee on Education of the Handicapped. Education of the handicapped today. *American Education*, 1976, *12*, 6-10.

Nolan, C. Y. Achievement in arithmetic computation. *International Journal for Education of the Blind*, 1959, 8, 125-128.

Nolan, C.Y. *Reading and listening in learning by the blind: Terminal progress report* (PHS Grant No. NB-04870). Louisville, KY: American Printing House for the Blind, 1968.

Nolan, C.Y., & Kederis, C.J. *Perceptual factors in braille word recognition* (Research Series #20). New York: American Foundation for the Blind, 1969.

Nolan, C.Y., & Morris, J.E. Learning by blind students through active and passive listening. *Exceptional Children*, 1969, *36*, 173-181.

Taylor, J. L. Mainstreaming visually handicapped children and youth: Yesterday, today, and tomorrow. In Association for Education of the Visually Handicapped, *Selected papers from the fifty-third biennial conference*. Philadelphia, PA: Association for Education of the Visually Handicapped, 1976.

Photographs in this chapter (with the exception of the title page) were provided by and reprinted with the approval of the American Printing House for the Blind, Louisville, Kentucky.

RESOURCE GUIDE

Historical Information

Buell, C. E. *Physical education for blind children.* Springfield, IL: Charles C. Thomas, 1971.

Harley, R. K., Jr. Children with visual disabilities. In L. M. Dunn (Ed.), *Exceptional children in the schools.* New York: Holt, Rinehart & Winston, 1973.

Hathaway, W. *Education and health of the partially seeing child.* New York: Columbia University Press, 1959.

Lowenfeld, B. (Ed.). *The visually handicapped child in school.* New York: John Day, 1973.

Family

Halliday, C., & Kurzhals, I. W. Stimulating environments for children who are visually impaired. Springfield, IL: Charles C. Thomas, 1976.

Harley, R. K., Jr. Children with visual disabilities. In L. M. Dunn (Ed.), *Exceptional children in the schools.* New York: Holt, Rinehart & Winston, 1973.

Lowenfeld, B. Psychological problems of children with impaired vision. In W. M. Cruickshank (Ed.), *Psychology of exceptional children and youth.* Englewood Cliffs, NJ: Prentice-Hall, 1971.

Patterns of Development

Barraga, N. C. *Visual handicaps and learning.* Belmont, CA: Wadsworth Publishing Co., Inc., 1976.

Bishop, V. E. *Teaching the visually limited child.* Springfield, IL: Charles C. Thomas, 1977.

Bluhm, D. L. *Teaching the retarded visually handicapped.* Philadelphia, PA: W. B. Saunders, 1968.

Cratty, B. J. *Movement and spatial awareness in blind children and youth.* Springfield, IL: Charles C. Thomas, 1971.

Davidow, M. E. *Social Competency.* Louisville, KY: American Printing House for the Blind, 1974.

Halliday, C. *The visually impaired child: Growth, learning, and development; infancy to school age.* Louisville, KY: American Printing House for the Blind, 1970.

Halliday, C., & Kurzhals, I. W. *Stimulating environments for children who are visually impaired.* Springfield, IL: Charles C. Thomas, 1976.

Treatment

Bishop, V. E. *Teaching the visually limited child.* Springfield, IL: Charles C. Thomas, 1977.

Cratty, B. J. *Movement and spatial awareness in blind children and youth.* Springfield, IL: Charles C. Thomas, 1971.

Harley, R. K., Jr. Children with visual disabilities. In L. M. Dunn (Ed.), *Exceptional children in the schools.* New York: Holt, Rinehart & Winston, 1973.

Harley, R. K., & Lawrence, G. A. *Visual impairment in the schools.* Springfield, IL: Charles C. Thomas, 1977.

Hathaway, W. *Education and health of the partially seeing child.* New York: Columbia University Press, 1959.

Lowenfeld, B. Psychological problems of children with impaired vision. In W. M. Cruickshank (Ed.), *Psychology of exceptional children and youth.* Englewood Cliffs, NJ: Prentice-Hall, 1971.

Educational Programming

Barraga, N. C. *Visual handicaps and learning.* Belmont, CA: Wadsworth Publishing Co., Inc., 1976.

Bishop, V. E. *Teaching the visually limited child.* Springfield, IL: Charles C. Thomas, 1977.

Bluhm, D. L. *Teaching the retarded visually handicapped.* Philadelphia, PA: W. B. Saunders, 1968.

Buell, C. E. *Physical education for blind children.* Springfield, IL: Charles C. Thomas, 1971.

Cratty, B. J. *Movement and spatial awareness in blind children and youth.* Springfield, IL: Charles C. Thomas, 1971.

Davidow, M. E. *Social Competency.* Louisville, KY: American Printing House for the Blind, 1974.

Fulker, W. H., & Fulker, M. *Techniques with tangibles.* Springfield, IL: Charles C. Thomas, 1968.

Halliday, C. *The visually impaired child: Growth, learning, and development; infancy to school age.* Louisville, KY: American Printing House for the Blind, 1970.

11 The Hearing Impaired

Alfred D. Larson and June B. Miller
University of Kansas Medical Center

430

Some children and youth require special educational attention because of hearing impairments. Although hearing deficiencies are readily described, the handicapping condition is not as easily defined—in fact, the number of definitions of hearing impairments may approach the number of hearing impaired individuals. In any case, general and specific terminology is needed so these students can be identified, referred, and treated within the context of school and learning.

In a study to assess effects of 11 labels commonly used in conjunction with hearing impaired individuals, Wilson, Ross, and Calvert (1974) reported that the label "hearing impaired" evoked fewer negative semantic associations than any of the other common terms and phrases used to denote hearing deficiencies. Since this term generates fewer negative expectations, it consequently may elicit better performance from children to whom the label is applied.

Two primary classifications have emerged within the hearing impaired condition: (1) A *deaf* person is one whose auditory channel cannot and *does not* serve as the primary sensory means by which speech and language are received and developed; this classification of hearing impairment usually is based upon the amount of hearing loss, as well as age of onset and ability to communicate; (2) A *hard of hearing* person is one whose auditory channel can and *does* serve as the primary sensory means by which speech and language are received and developed; this classification of hearing impairment is based upon the amount of hearing loss. Wilson et al. summarize these classifications and their implications as follows:

> The point is not the labeling itself, but how appropriately it is applied in a particular case. Certainly there are "deaf" children, who should be labeled and treated as such. But since the category is a more functional than physiological one, and since differentiation between a "deaf" child and a "hard of hearing" child is quite difficult with very young children, we need and can properly apply the generic term "hearing impaired" until we have some assurance of the particular category to which a child belongs. Then too, when referring to groups of children with auditory deficiencies, it is necessary to invoke a general term to avoid misapplying the labels "deaf" and "hard of hearing" to particular children in the group. Referring to a "deaf" child as "hard of hearing" may do him an injustice; but it is equally damaging to misapply the label "deaf"to a "hard of hearing" child (p. 413).

The following definitions were adopted by the Conference of Executives of American Schools for the Deaf during its annual meeting in Greensboro, North Carolina, June 22, 1975.

> A deaf person is one whose hearing disability precludes successful processing of linguistic information through audition, with or without a hearing aid.
> A hard of hearing person is one who, generally with the use of a hearing aid, has residual hearing sufficient to enable successful processing of linguistic information through audition.

Hearing Impairment: A generic term indicating a hearing disability which may range in severity from mild to profound; it includes the subsets of deaf and hard of hearing.

PREVALENCE

Davis and Silverman (1970) reported that 5 percent of school children have hearing impairments, and 5 in 1,000 of this group will require special education attention. The Illinois Commission on Children (1968) reported that 1-3 percent of all school children have a hearing impairment severe enough for medical or special education attention. Thus, prevalence of hearing impairment in the United States may approach nearly four million people.

The Bureau of Education for the Handicapped, U.S. Office of Education, cites the figure of .75 percent (3 in 4000) as the prevalence of school-aged children in the United States who are considered deaf, and .5 percent (1 in 200) who are hard of hearing. According to the National Advisory Committee on the Handicapped, in 1975-76 approximately 45,000 *deaf* children were being served, and 4,000 were not being served. (In terms of percentages, 92 percent were being served and 8 percent were not being served.) The reverse was true regarding the *hard of hearing*, in which data showed 66,000 being served and 262,000 not being served (or 20 percent being served and 80 percent not being served).

The Office of Demographic Studies (ODS) conducts an Annual Survey of Hearing Impaired Children and Youth, in which all programs known by the Office to be offering special services to hearing impaired students are invited to participate. In 1973, of the 1,050 programs contacted, approximately 68 percent responded. The Annual Survey reported that during the 1972-1973 school year, approximately 21,000 hearing impaired students were attending residential schools for the deaf, 9,000 were attending 105 day schools for the deaf, and 24,000 were receiving other special educational services in more than 3,000 regular schools and clinics with special programs. Services ranged from full-time special classes to resource rooms and itinerant programs in regular schools and clinics. The total of 54,000 students in programs responding to the Annual Survey included 81 percent of the estimated 54,000 students receiving special educational services throughout the country.

The Annual Survey reports information on the following topics: ethnic background of hearing impaired students; regional and state distribution for age and sex, degree of hearing loss, age of onset of hearing loss, cause of hearing loss, additional handicapping conditions, and hearing status of parents; also, data are presented on the degree of integration of ethnic groups receiving special educational services. Table 11.1 shows the type of special education program attended by hearing impaired individuals by ethnic classification.

DESCRIPTION AND CLASSIFICATION OF HEARING IMPAIRMENTS

Certain variables are of paramount importance in classifying hearing impaired individuals. These variables include: degree of hearing loss, usually reported in reference to an audiogram, in decibels (dB) or in percentages; age of onset of the hearing loss; and the type of loss (conductive, sensorineural, mixed, or other). As a preface to discussion of these variables, the reader should have a basic understanding of the physical hearing mechanism.

The Ear

The hearing mechanism, for practical purposes, consists of three parts: the *outer ear*, the *middle ear*, and the *inner ear*. The outer ear consists of the auricle and the external auditory canal. The auricle collects sound waves and passes them into the ear canal. At the end of the ear canal is the tympanic membrane, or ear drum.

The middle ear contains the ossicular chain, which consists of three tiny bones: the malleus (hammer), which is connected to the tympanic membrane; the incus (anvil), which is connected to the malleus; and to the stapes (stirrup). The stapes separates the middle from the inner ear and rests on a body wall that has two membranous windows, the oval window and the round window. The footplate of the stapes rests on the oval window.

In the process of hearing, sound waves are collected by the auricle and passed down the auditory canal, striking the eardrum and setting the ossicular chain in motion. The footplate of the stapes pushes on the oval window, which is in the inner ear. Another important mechanism, the Eustachian tube, provides drainage as well as equalizing pressure in the middle ear.

Table 11.1

Type of Special Educational Programs, By Ethnic Group

Type of Educational Program	Total		White		Black		Spanish American		Other		Not Reported	
	No.	%	No.	%	No.	%	No.	%	No.	%	No.	%
All Programs	43,946	100.0	28,672	100.0	5,671	100.0	2,650	100.0	670	100.0	6,283	100.0
Residential	19,232	43.8	12,971	45.2	2,404	42.4	710	26.8	323	48.2	2,824	44.9
Day	24,714	56.2	15,701	54.8	3,267	57.6	1,940	73.2	347	51.8	3,459	55.1
Total Specified Programs	43,946	100.0	28,672	100.0	5,671	100.0	2,650	100.0	670	100.0	6,283	100.0
Residential School for Multiply Handicapped	717	1.6	456	1.6	68	1.2	24	0.9	4	0.6	165	2.6
Residential School for Deaf	18,515	42.1	12,515	43.6	2,336	41.2	686	25.9	319	47.6	2,659	42.3
Day School for Deaf	4,965	11.3	2,424	8.4	902	15.9	815	30.8	40	6.0	784	12.5
Full-Time Special Education Classes	11,368	25.9	7,244	25.3	1,415	25.0	799	30.2	218	32.5	1,692	26.9
Part-Time Special Education Classes	2,590	5.9	1,866	6.5	287	5.1	146	5.5	48	7.2	243	3.9
Itinerant Program	3,305	7.5	2,279	7.9	361	6.4	114	4.3	19	2.8	532	8.5
Resource Room	117	0.3	82	0.3	10	0.2	4	0.2	--	--	21	0.3
Speech & Hearing Clinic	973	2.2	789	2.8	93	1.6	23	0.9	13	1.9	55	0.9
Other Special Services	1,396	3.2	1,017	3.5	199	3.5	39	1.5	9	1.3	132	2.1

ETHNIC CLASSIFICATION

From: *Ethnic Background in Relation to Other Characteristics of Hearing Impaired Students in the United States,* Office of Demographic Studies, Washington, D.C., 1975.

The inner ear is complicated but basically serves two major functions: The semicircular canals control the *balance* of the individual, and the cochlea (cone-shaped tube) is the organ of *hearing*. The cochlear branch of the eighth cranial nerve sends the impulses to the temporal lobe of the brain. Figure 11.1 provides a graphic depiction of the major elements of the hearing mechanism.

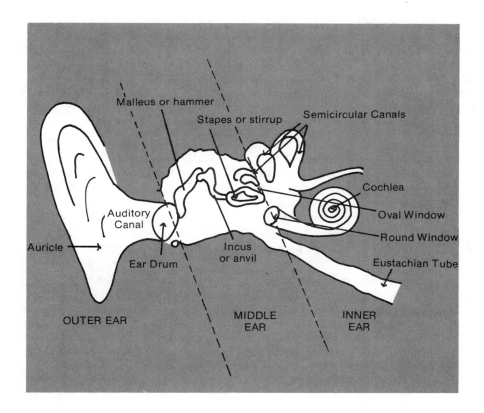

Figure 11.1   Cross-Section of Auditory Mechanism

Measurement of Hearing Loss

Hearing levels are recorded on an audiogram via pure tone hearing testing using an *audiometer*. An audiometer is an electronic device that generates, both in frequency and in sound pressure level, pure tones that cover most of the human auditory range. The *audiogram* is a graph depicting hearing threshold levels. It shows frequency in Hertz, or Hz (cycles per second) across the top (abscissa), and intensity (loudness) in decibels down the side (ordinate).

The graph depicts the least intensity at the top to the greatest intensity at the bottom. It expresses logarithmic ratios of intensity, power, and pressure. The hearing threshold is the faintest sound of a given frequency that a person can detect 50 percent of the time on a number of trials. Each ear is tested separately and the responses recorded on the audiogram. The right ear air conduction threshold usually is recorded by a red circle, and the left ear air conduction threshold by a blue X. *Air conduction* means that the sound is traveling (via earphones) through the outer and middle ear to the sensory end organ and to the auditory nerve in the inner ear.

Bone conduction thresholds are recorded for the right ear as >, and < for the left ear. *Bone conduction* may be defined as sound transmission through the bones of the skull to the neural pathways of the inner ear. In this way the outer and middle ear are bypassed and the inner ear stimulated directly, via a bone oscillator placed behind the ear on the mastoid bone or on the forehead.

The degree of handicap can be estimated by averaging the decibel notations at 250, 500, and 1000 Hz (cps) in the better ear. The degree of handicap also may be labeled as slight (25-40), mild (40-55), marked (56-70), severe (70-90), or profound (+90). "ISO" recorded on the audiogram refers to the International Standards Organization, which formulated audiometric standards; these standards were adopted in the United States in 1964. Figures 11 2 and 11.3 are audiograms illustrating degrees of handicap.

Types of Hearing Loss

Conductive Hearing Loss

Conductive hearing loss is caused by interference with the transmission of sound from the external auditory canal to the inner ear. In such cases the inner ear is capable of normal function, but sound vibration cannot stimulate the cochlea via the normal air conduction pathway. The condition is characterized by loss of air-conducted sounds. However, sounds conducted to the inner ear directly by bone conduction of the skull are heard normally. The maximum air conduction hearing loss is 60 dB. Many conductive hearing losses can be corrected through medical treatment or surgery. A person with a conductive hearing loss is a good candidate for amplification, because cochlear damage generally is not involved: *If the sound is made loud enough*, it reaches the ear relatively undistorted. Figures 11.4 and 11.5 illustrate conductive hearing loss.

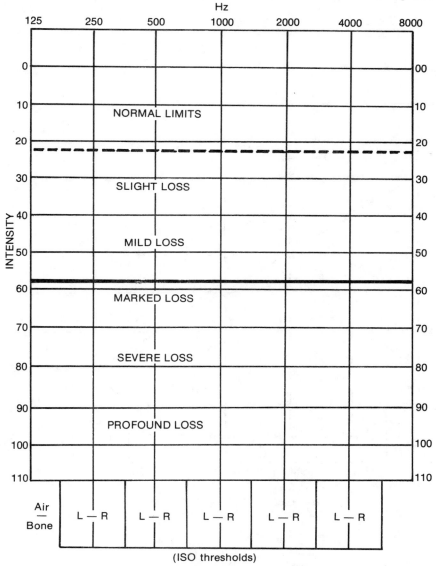

Figure 11.2 Unplotted Audiogram showing degree of handicap ranges

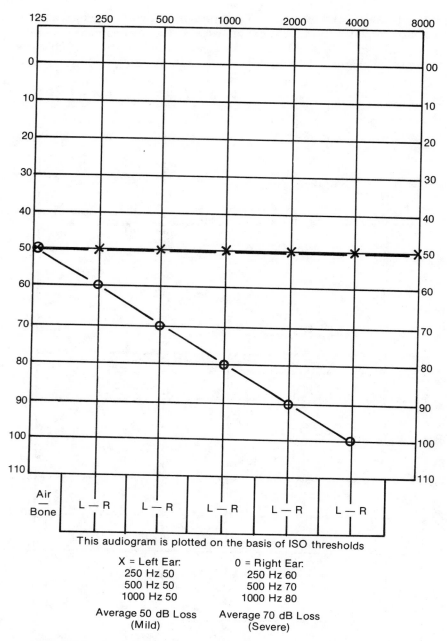

Figure 11.3　Audiogram showing degree of hearing loss in left and right ears

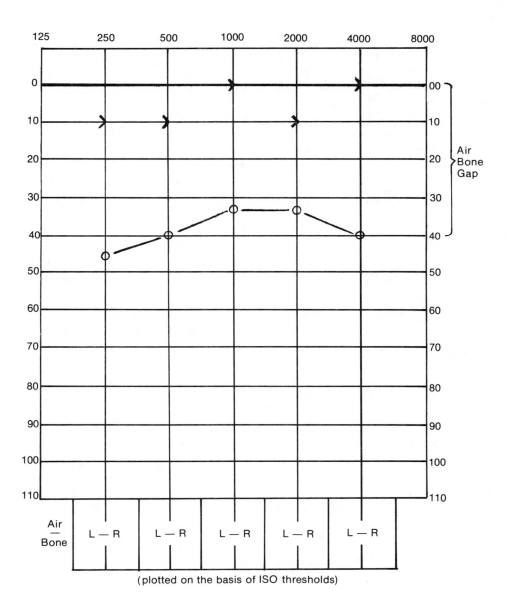

Figure 11.4   Audiogram showing slight conductive hearing loss, right ear/ normal bone conduction

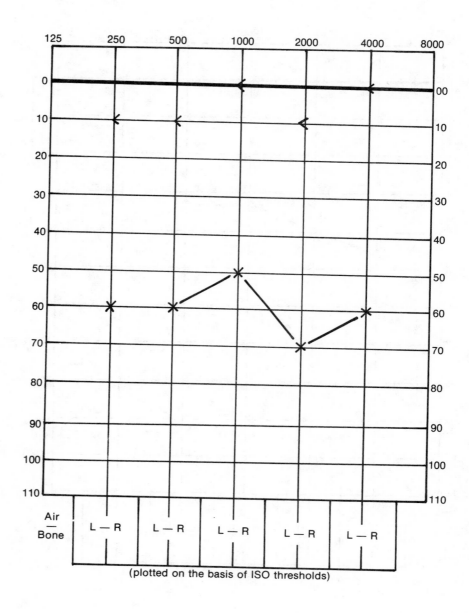

Figure 11.5 Audiogram showing marked conductive hearing loss, left ear/
normal bone conduction

Sensorineural Hearing Loss

Sensorineural hearing loss is associated with damage to the sensory end organ or cochlear hair cells, or a dysfunction caused by the auditory nerve. Differentiating between damage to the auditory nerve and to the end organ is difficult without special tests, so the resultant hearing loss has been lumped under the single category of "sensorineural." Air and bone conduction thresholds in both cases are nearly identical. This indicates that the loss is either in the inner ear or in the eighth nerve (auditory nerve). Sensorineural losses cannot be corrected surgically or medically. The external and middle ear appear to be normal in sensorineural hearing losses. Candidacy for amplification is not as promising as with a conductive loss. Although sounds can be delivered to the brain in an amplified form, they are still *distorted*, because of the response of the end organ, the result of nerve damage, or, in numerous cases, an inability to tolerate amplification. Even though the sound can be amplified, it remains *unclear* or *distorted*. Figures 11.6 and 11.7 represent sensorineural hearing losses.

Mixed Hearing Loss

When both conductive and sensorineural losses are present, the result is categorized as a mixed loss. A significant air conduction/bone conduction gap (commonly known as air/bone gap) may exist; this disappears if the air conduction component is resolved. When the conductive component is stabilized and medical diagnosis is obtained, a hearing aid may be fitted. Candidacy for amplification is generally good, and conditions are similar to those described for conductive losses. However, individuals with mixed hearing loss may share the same problems as those with sensorineural loss. Figure 11.8 represents a mixed hearing loss.

Configuration

The configuration (shape of the curve) and number of frequency responses recorded on the audiogram are additional important factors in identifying hearing loss, and especially in determining the potential for amplification. If responses are made across the frequency spectrum on a relatively flat configuration, this individual will benefit greatly from amplification. Usually, the flatter the responses and the more responses an individual exhibits, the more usable the existing residual hearing.

If hearing exists through the speech frequency range (500-2000 Hz), the individual usually can benefit from amplification and the

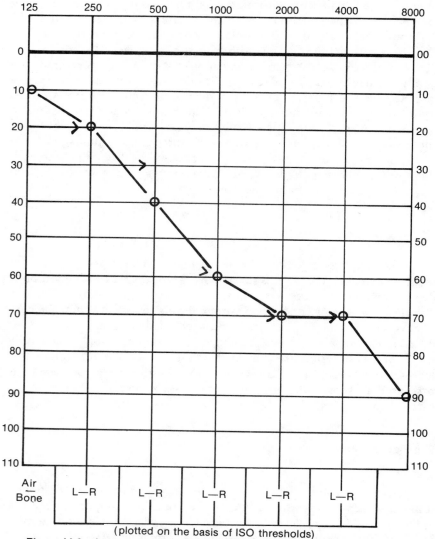

Figure 11.6   Audiogram showing marked sensorineural hearing loss, right ear/bone conduction nearly the same

handicap is less devastating. If few responses are made at a high decibel notation and not within the speech frequency range, much less amplification can be utilized and the hearing handicap is more severe. Pre-

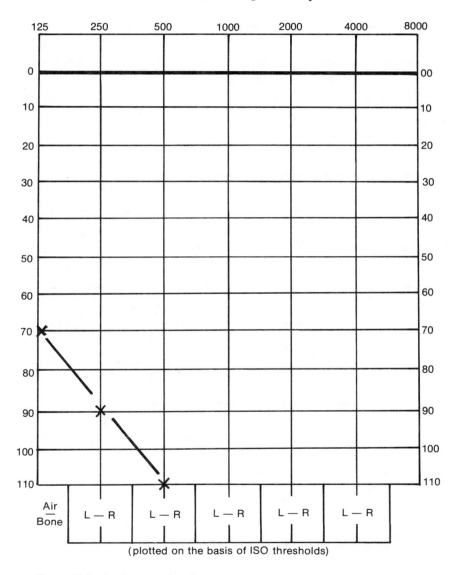

Figure 11.7 Audiogram showing extreme sensorineural hearing loss, left ear, bone conduction - no response

dictions based on the audiogram alone, however, are misleading and ill advised, as *each child functions as an individual, and each utilizes residual hearing in a different way.*

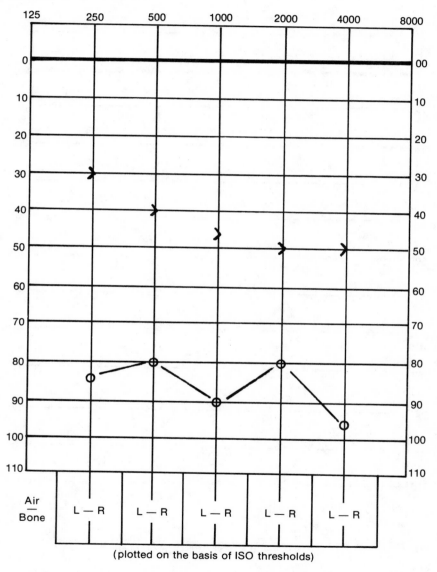

(plotted on the basis of ISO thresholds)

Figure 11.8   Audiogram showing mixed hearing loss, right ear/difference between air and bone

Amplification

Hearing aids are common and often helpful appliances, but a misconception is that these amplifying devices, when utilized correctly, will always make the individual a hearing person. This is not true, of course, since the amount of benefit derived from amplification depends upon the type of hearing loss (conductive or sensorineural) and the configuration.

A hearing aid is an amplifying system with the primary function of making sounds louder. Hundreds of types and arrangements of hearing aids are available, but, basically, each is made up of three parts: an amplifier, a microphone, and a receiver. The microphone collects the sound; it is amplified; and then it is transmitted to the ear. Hearing aids differ in the size of the system, the distance from sound source to the microphone, and capacity to amplify sounds. Hearing aids are essentially of two types: the body aid, and the over-the-ear or ear-level hearing aid. Both types contain the three essential parts of any amplifying system. (See Figure 11.9.)

Audiologists recommend the type of hearing aid most suitable for the individual. Batteries supply the energy for the amplifiers; they should be checked daily. The amplifying system is connected to the ear by the earmold. The earmold should be kept clean; it usually is washed with soap and water after being disconnected from the aid. If the earmold does not fit properly, one will hear a squeal (feedback). If the mold is too tight, it can cause physical discomfort to the wearer. One should check with the audiologist or hearing aid dealer if problems occur.

The auditory information is collected by the microphone, converted to electrical energy, and amplified and transmitted to the receiver by means of a cord. The cord is probably the most delicate part of the hearing aid. It also should be checked daily. The receiver converts electrical impulses generated from the amplifier and changes them into sound waves to be transmitted to the ear canal via the earmold.

Age of Onset

The time in life at which an individual becomes hearing impaired is especially relevant to the degree of expected language handicap. If the hearing loss is before or at birth, there is no chance for language to be heard normally nor for incidental learning to occur. This constitutes a serious handicapping condition. If the hearing loss occurs during the prime language acquisition years of 1-5, the child develops some

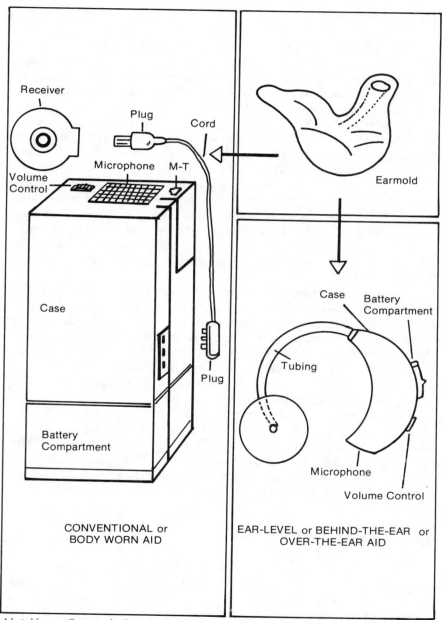

Adapted from an illustration by the Auditory Services Program, Montgomery County Public Schools, Maryland, and the Alexander Graham Bell Associates for the Deaf, Washington, DC. Used by permission.

Figure 11.9   Types of Amplifying Devices (Hearing Aids)

language, according to the specific age at which the hearing loss occurs. The handicap understandably is lessened if the child has acquired some language.

If the hearing loss occurs during school years, the handicap is lessened significantly, since the child has acquired most of the language structures; emotional adjustment, however, may be greater. In any case, an unrecognized hearing loss will seriously affect the child's social and educational progress. Depending upon the amount of loss, speech may deteriorate. If the loss is acquired after school years and into adult life, the language handicap is less severe, but psychological and emotional problems may still manifest themselves.

CAUSES OF HEARING IMPAIRMENT

Causes of hearing impairment may be grouped into the two major areas of endogenous (genetic) conditions and exogenous (external agent) conditions, each of which contains the sub-classifications of *congenital* or *acquired*.

Endogenous Conditions

Endogenous refers to conditions which originate in the *genetic* characteristics of an individual and are transmitted from parent to child as an inherited trait. Genetic factors have been the leading cause of deafness throughout this century, except during certain epidemic periods of rubella (German measles). Approximately 50 to 60 percent of all deafness is attributed to genetic factors. Children deafened through hereditary causes are less likely to have ancillary defects than are children deafened through nonhereditary causes, except in certain conditions which entail visual problems.

For some conditions deafness may be acquired (e.g., progressive deafness, otosclerosis), although most endogenous conditions are congenital. If genetic deafness is suspected or established, one should seek competent genetic counseling concerning the probabilities of deafness in future offspring. Also, regular, complete ophthalmological examinations should be conducted because, of the 57 identified forms of genetic deafness, 10 involve both hearing and vision.

Exogenous Conditions

Exogenous refers to external agents which cause conditions of deafness and are acquired by other than genetic factors. These conditions may be either congenital or acquired, and are grouped into three major categories, as follows:

1. Disease

   Maternal rubella may affect the unborn child's hearing system; therefore, hearing loss is congenital (present at birth), but exogenous.

2. Toxicity

   Toxicity is drug-induced, either on the part of a pregnant mother who is taking medication, which classifies the condition as *congenital exogenous;* or on the part of a child taking a drug, which describes the condition as *acquired exogenous.* Kanamycin, Neomycin, and Gentamycin are three drugs which may cause hearing losses. Aspirin, quinine, and diuretics may produce temporary hearing loss, often recoverable after patients discontinue use of the drug.

3. Physical Injuries and Accidents

   Accidents and injuries are other agents which may be responsible for hearing impairment. Medical skull fractures might produce middle ear bleeding or disruption of the ossicular chain, creating a maximal 60 dB hearing loss. Trauma to the side of the head may cause a sensorineural hearing loss on the opposite side, taking the form of a 4000-Hz dip in the audiogram. Hearing loss due to fracture of the cochlea is irreversible.

Causes of hearing loss may be organized within another framework, such as that used by the Office of Demographic Studies (Gentile, A., & Rambin, J., 1973). Causes of impairment of hearing impaired students enrolled in special classes in 1970-71 were reported according to prenatal factors, factors in early childhood, and other causes as follows.

Prenatal Factors

1. Virus infection of the mother during early pregnancy. Among the prenatal causes of deafness, rubella ranked first, according to the census, although chicken pox and other viral infections also may result in prenatal deafness.

2. Family history of deafness ranked second in terms of prevalence.

3. Blood incompatibility. (One such incompatibility occurs when Rh negative mothers have Rh positive fetuses.)
4. Maternal bleeding, especially during the first trimester of pregnancy.
5. Medication, notably any one of the mycin groups or quinine.
6. Complications of labor:
   a. Premature delivery: Four times as many deaf children as non-deaf children are born prematurely. Prematurity ranks third among the causes of deafness revealed by the survey.
   b. Fetal distress due to maternal shock.
   c. Prolonged or precipitous labor.

Factors in Early Childhood

1. Infection
   a. Meningitis: This condition involves inflammation of the menge protective covering of the brain and the spinal cord. It deafens an estimated 3 to 5 percent of the children who contract it and ranks first among postnatal causes.
   b. Measles: Deafness resulting from measles is caused by damage to the inner ear due to direct infiltration of the internal meatus. It ranks second among postnatal causes.
   c. Other viral infections: Mumps, chicken pox, influenza, and viruses of the common cold are included in this group.
2. Chronic respiratory infection, cold, and/or allergy: This type of condition often results in *otitis media*, or common middle ear infection, and ranks third in the order of incidence. The condition usually develops from a head cold in which the infection travels from the nasal passage along the Eustachian tube to the middle ear. Otitis media can be *serous, acute* or *chronic;* the labels refer to various conditions of fluid in the middle ear space. Chronic otitis media is recurrent; serous and acute types may invoke temporary conductive hearing losses. The danger of sensorineural hearing loss is present in chronic otitis media if toxic material passes through the round window of the inner ear. Otitis media also may cause a perforation in the ear drum.
3. Injuries:
   A blow to the side of the head, a water-skiing fall, diving injury, or sudden changes in air pressure may perforate the ear drum, causing a sudden hearing loss. If the blow to the head is intense, it may create a sensorineural loss on the opposite side.

Other Causal Factors

1. Cleft Palate: There is a high incidence of recurrent otitis media among young children having cleft palates. Frequency of this condition decreases as children with cleft palates grow older.
2. Noise induced or noise trauma hearing loss: Loud sounds may produce destruction of the hair cells in the Organ of Corti. The most common exposure in childhood is related to a single identifiable noise experience such as a firecracker. Generally, the loss consists of sensorineural impairment at 4000 Hz, regardless of the type of noise exposure.

EDUCATIONAL PROGRAMMING APPROACHES

For hundreds of years, educators of hearing impaired individuals have differed in their teaching approaches. The oralist uses an oral/aural approach—teaching the individual to listen, speak, and speechread as the mode of communication. The manualist teaches the individual to fingerspell and sign as the mode of communication. The total communication approach stresses a combination of methods to fit the appropriate communication system to the child. The focus of this discussion is not to try to resolve the educational issues of hearing impairments, but rather to present some of the philosophies, methods, and approaches to the education of hearing impaired individuals.

Oral/Aural Method

The oral/aural method usually is considered a "natural" method. It makes use of auditory training (learning to listen), oral training (learning to speak), and speechreading (learning to read lips). The child also is taught to use hearing as a supplement to language development. With moderate hearing impairment, attempts are made to train subjects to auditorially discriminate words and sentences. Severely to profoundly hearing impaired students are taught to discriminate gross sounds, intonation, rhythmic speech patterns, and appropriate vocabulary. Speech training, or the development of articulation production, is emphasized. The two common approaches to speech are:

1. The *analytic approach,* which uses practice in producing phonemes (sounds of letters) in isolation, in syllable drills, and in words and sentences; and

2. The *whole word method*, in which phonemes are never taught in isolation, but always in the context of words.

Other emphases are in rhythm, intonation, pitch, and voice quality. Usually, speech work is emphasized during content lessons and during specified individual tutoring time. Numerous mechanical devices include pitch indicators (meters that record pitch levels), visible speech translators, electronic displays of speech sounds, and mechanisms that provide a more visible approach to teaching speech.

Speechreading, or lipreading, is a visual interpretation of the lip movement of an individual and is based on standard American English. It is a modality system and, in the oral/aural method, is sometimes almost synonymous with language development.

Difficulties which may be encountered in the oral/aural method include the following:

1. Not all children appear to have the necessary skills to learn by the oral/aural method, and some cannot make the necessary auditory and visual discrimination.
2. A student sees less than one-half of all the necessary cues. Many phonemes are not visible on the lips or do not look the same on the lips (*p-b, t-d*).
3. Although emphasis is placed on some degree of hearing, such hearing may not permit word discrimination. Often, the hearing is extremely poor or lack of training has made it nonfunctional and the student may reject amplification.
4. Because of the lack of auditory feedback, speech production is laborious and unnatural.
5. Some groups of deaf persons think that oral/aural communication is an unnatural means and reject it completely.

Manual Method

The manual method makes use of one or all of the following: fingerspelling (a series of finger positions to represent the individual letters of the alphabet, and to spell out words); and American Sign Language, which is a system of ideagraphic gestures representing words or concepts and is used by most deaf people. The American Sign Language possesses a structure unlike English. Attempts are being made to increase signing vocabulary and to make the system conform to English in terms of structure and word endings. Examples of these recent efforts are: Seeing Essential English, Signing Exact English, and Linguistics of Visible English.

Some past and potential problems of the manual method are that:

1. Fingerspelling is basically a reading process and may not be a viable method of teaching language to preschoolers who have not learned to read. If this were the only modality used during the first three or four years of learning, language would not be developed.
2. With regard to the actual signs—
   a. There is no one-to-one relationship between sign language and English.
   b. Semantic differences exist between the signed word and its English equivalent.
   c. Structurally, sign language is an entirely different language from American English.
   d. Reading and signs have no correlation, since reading is a phonemic system based on oral language, and signs are ideagraphic.
   e. Although attempts are being made to bring signs closer to English, confusion is still widespread with the various systems, and they are still inexact.

Total Communication

Theoretical and semantic differences are apparent among advocates of total communication, but Garretson (1976) says: (1) The total communication concept is a philosophy rather than a method; (2) It combines the oral/aural and manual modes according to the communicative needs and the expressive-receptive threshold of the individual; and (3) It is the moral right of the hearing impaired, as with normally hearing bilinguals, to receive and give maximal input to reach optimal comprehension or total understanding in a communication situation.

Several difficulties are inherent in the total communication concept, as it now is used, including the following considerations:

1. Agreement has not been reached on the definitions being used.
2. In combining the methods, some introduce oral/aural first, then

fingerspelling and signs, and others the reverse, so the process is not standardized.

3. Some professionals attempt to use American Sign Language in conjunction with speechreading and use of residual hearing, but syntax and sentence structure are different between the two methods.

4. Research has indicated that many persons cannot process two different visual stimuli simultaneously.

5. Auditory training units or hearing aids are not being used in this process, nor is residual hearing being educated.

6. The most appropriate age to introduce the system has not been determined, and varies.

The Methods Controversy

Educators of the deaf differ on the most useful method of communication for the deaf—the oral/aural, the manual, or the total communication system.

Some advocates of the purely oral/aural instruction method concede that speech and speechreading, aided by auditory training to utilize any residual hearing, may be more difficult and take longer to learn than do manual methods. They maintain, however, that this method prepares the deaf child for wider horizons and greater opportunities in the world, culturally, socially, and economically. It prepares the child to take advantage of a wider range of educational opportunities than are likely to be offered by special programs for those who can communicate only manually. They believe that this method makes possible a fuller, more satisfying life. They also discourage initial teaching by the manual communication method, pointing out that since manual communication is more easily acquired, a child is less likely to put forth the extra effort required to achieve success in speech and speechreading.

Those who favor the manual methods, however, feel that few hearing impaired individuals can learn to speak intelligibly. They may agree with most professionals, though, on the desirability of oral/aural instruction for young deaf children. The difference in philosophy appears to hinge on how readily one should give up on oral/aural instruction and replace it with another method, or on the age of introduction of manual communication. Advocates of manual methods emphasize that some children will be unable to acquire usable speech or speechreading well enough to communicate effectively. They maintain that a child should not be denied the opportunity to learn a form of communication within his or her capabilities. They also contend that it is easier to communicate subject matter in the classroom by manual methods.

Some professionals advocate combining oral methods with finger-spelling—a combination that retains the English language as the symbol system of instruction and communication. Others favor employing all methods—aural, fingerspelling, and the language of signs—in an effort to simplify the learning process. They also believe that less strain on the deaf person occurs with manual communication, and they point to the fact that most deaf adults prefer to use manual communication among people—deaf or hearing—who know it (Babbidge, 1965).

EFFECTS OF HEARING IMPAIRMENT

Regardless of the method of communication used, individuals with impaired hearing have developmental and adjustment problems, to varying degrees. Obviously, the more damage to the auditory senses, the more devastating the handicap. If a child possesses some hearing, it may or may not be usable for learning speech and language. The most obvious handicap pertains to speech intelligibility and understanding language concepts. An individual who is deficient in language and speech development is handicapped in all communication abilities. Hearing impairment also may manifest itself in feelings of insecurity and frustration.

Effects on Language

Learning language is most difficult for hearing impaired individuals. Even though early training may have been established, much of our language is learned incidentally. Vocabulary acquisition is a lifelong process and depends upon a number of exposures to words before they become part of one's repertoire. To develop vocabulary related to concrete items is relatively simple. A horse is a horse. It may be brown, tan, or gray, but it is easily represented pictorially. But consider trying to explain *kindness, am, is, was,* or *were.* Multiple meanings of words to express different ideas become areas of confusion. For example:

A river *runs.*
I have a *run* in my stocking.

Did you *run* up the hill?
Don't *run* down your neighbor.

A hearing impaired individual is further confused by the fundamentals of sentence structure, since the natural order has not been developed through auditory channels. "Garden plant me" from a hearing impaired child might mean, "I planted a garden."

Among speech impairments, word endings often are omitted. Maybe the child cannot hear the *ed, ing* — and especially the *s* — endings of words. "He go Phyl hou" might mean, "He is going to Phyllis' house."

Also, shades of meaning can be misinterpreted from change in intonation:

I KNOW I saw him yesterday.
I know I saw HIM yesterday.
I know I SAW him yesterday.
I know I saw him YESTERDAY.

Effects on Speech

The speech of hearing impaired individuals has been described as breathy, nasal, and "different" in every respect from normal hearing, but the task of acquiring and maintaining good speech habits is of great importance. One learns to listen to one's own voice and compare it to the speech of others, but hearing impaired individuals must rely on visual feedback or their use of small amounts of hearing to make adjustments and/or corrections.

Voiced and voiceless consonants for which visual clues are nonexistent are often troublesome (*p-b, t-d, f-v*). *Mat, pat, bat* all look alike on the lips when spoken, so they provide no clue other than from context. Other sounds are difficult to see—sounds made at the back of the throat (for example, *k* and *g* and several vowels).

A hearing impaired child must learn the differences between and among sounds before he or she can learn to use them correctly. On a positive note, great numbers of hearing impaired individuals can be understood by hearing individuals.

Effects on Academic Areas

Hearing impairment affects learning in all academic areas. Areas that rely upon reading skills and language concepts are the most severely affected. Reading entails the association of written symbols with meaning, based on sounds. Hearing loss restricts acquisition of associations, and the lack of language, or vocabulary, seriously retards reading achievement. Understanding science, social studies, and even mathematics, depends upon reading skills and comprehension.

Reading aloud is one way of helping to identify reading problems in hearing children; the hearing impaired, however, can often read aloud quite well, using their background in speech training, but they may be unable to comprehend the meaning.

Effects on Emotions/Behavior

During the 1972-73 school year, demographic data were collected on 43,946 students in special education programs for the hearing impaired, and reported in the *Annual Survey of Hearing Impaired Children and Youth* (Jensema & Trybus, 1975). Of those students, 3,438 were reported as having educationally significant emotional/behavioral problems. The student's sex and the presence or absence of additional handicapping conditions were two important variables. These factors produced the greatest differences in rates of reporting of emotional behavior problems. Rates were higher among males than females, and in those with additional handicapping conditions. Little relationship was shown between the frequency of reported emotional behavior problems and the age of onset of the hearing loss or the degree of hearing loss.

Sociological Effects

From a research point of view, little is known about the sociological aspects of a hearing impaired child. In terms of social maturity, the ability to take care of oneself, the ability to assist in the care of others, or in becoming independent and self sufficient, the hearing impaired child appears to be at par with hearing peers. During the elementary years, hearing impaired children have been observed to have minimal difficulty socializing with hearing siblings or neighbors but, as they get older, socialization and interaction decrease. This is particularly true if a child is the only hearing impaired child in a family or neighborhood, and/or in a day school. Because of the communication barrier, all deaf children tend to be isolated in one form or another within the family and hearing world. Nonhearing children in residential schools have the advantage of close contact with each other, but this may be offset by a lack of a continued close familial relationship.

Behavior Within the Classroom

A student with a *slight* hearing loss (25 to 40dB) may have difficulty hearing faint and distant speech, but this student usually will not experience difficulty in most school situations. He or she might benefit from a hearing aid as the loss approaches 40 dB. The teacher should be aware that the student might need favorable seating and lighting and some assistance in speechreading and/or speech correction.

A student with a *mild* hearing loss (41 to 55 dB) understands conversational speech at a distance of only 3-5 feet. This child may miss as much as half of the class discussion if he or she is in a crowded classroom, if voices are faint, not in line of vision, or if noise level is unusually high. The child possibly could benefit from a hearing aid and should be referred to the proper specialist, who would also supervise training in the use of the aid. The teacher should be aware that the student will need favorable seating and lighting; and careful monitoring should be sustained regarding vocabulary development and reading comprehension. The child also will probably need instruction in speech-reading, language, and speech.

A student with a *marked* hearing loss (56-70 dB) understands only loud conversation. This child will encounter much difficulty in school situations, especially those requiring participation in group discussions or activities. The individual evidences limited vocabulary, as well as deficiency in language usage and reading comprehension. He or she most likely has defective speech. This student probably will need a resource teacher or special class, at least during early training. The child will need special assistance in developing language, speech, speechreading, and reading skills. The teacher should be particularly aware that this child must rely heavily on vision to learn effectively.

A student with a *severe* hearing loss (71 to 90 dB) may be able to hear loud voices about one foot from the ear. This child possibly can identify some environmental sounds, but speech and language are defective. The student will require a full-time special program for the hearing impaired during early training and supportive services thereafter. Emphasis should be on all language skills, concept development, speechreading, and speech.

A student with a *profound* hearing loss (91 dB or more) may appear to hear some loud sounds, but this actually is an awareness of vibrations rather than tonal patterns. This student relies on vision rather than hearing as a primary avenue of communication. Speech and language do not develop spontaneously and are defective. The student will need full-time special programs for hearing impaired children, with emphasis on all language skills, concept development, speechreading, and speech, at least in earlier years.

PROGRAMS AND SERVICES

Early Intervention

Of utmost importance is the initiation of training hearing impaired children at an early age. Hearing children develop language auditorially from many sources; they are exposed to language from all areas of their environment. Hearing impaired children, however, must rely on their families to set the stage for language development.

Realizing the importance of early training, educators of the hearing impaired first began establishing preschool public school programs on a widespread basis over 30 years ago. Various programs for hearing impaired and youngsters below the age of three have been set up in the United States, with varying philosophies and formats. In some cases, parents bring the child to a special facility for training; in others, the parent educator goes to the home. The main impetus has been to train parents to *promote language development*, regardless of the method used. Usually, the parent-home or parent-infant training program develops its philosophy in three main areas.

1. *Amplification:* The program provides avenues to assess the hearing of young children and to select appropriate amplification (hearing aid), if warranted. Personnel also assist parents in helping the child use the hearing aid appropriately. A hearing aid is of little value unless a person is properly trained to use it.
2. *Training:* The program guides parents, grandparents, babysitters, and other helpers in establishing a working relationship with their child. Emphasis is placed upon training the parent to utilize everyday situations, such as washing dishes, to develop language concepts. In making the bed, for example:

   > Let's make Sam's bed.
   > Pull up the sheet.
   > Pull up the blanket.
   > Pull up the bedspread.
   > Fluff the pillows.
   > Etc.

3. *Support:* The program establishes an information-giving service. What is hearing loss? What is a hearing aid? Why did we have a hearing impaired child? These and other questions are answered. The program may represent parents' first source in assisting them to understand, accept, and help train their hearing impaired child.

Types of Programs

Various types of programs for hearing impaired individuals are available throughout the country. Even though terminology may vary, seven basic classifications can be delineated as follows.

1. *Residential Schools for Deaf Students.* A residential school is a facility in which hearing impaired students are educated and housed. Schools may be either public (usually state) or private. Various programs serve the hearing impaired in an age range from 3- and 4-year-olds to 21-year-olds. Such programs may be divided into a nursery unit, preparatory unit, lower school, middle school, and upper school; the upper school may be further divided into academic and vocational departments. These schools usually are relatively large, with 300 or more students. Some state schools use oral methods up to the middle grades and then provide either a manual or total communication method of instruction. (This general pattern is changing, however, as many schools are adopting a total communication orientation.) Many private residential schools employ the oral/aural philosophy.

2. *Day Schools for Deaf Students.* A day school is a facility in which all classes are held in a single building, and deaf students reside at home. This type of facility usually is located in the larger metropolitan areas.

3. *Self-Contained Classes.* Classes are located in regular elementary or secondary buildings. Although hearing children are also taught in the building, they remain separate from the self-contained classes for hearing impaired students.

4. *Part-time or Integrated Programs.* In these programs, students are assigned to a special class for the hearing impaired but spend part of the day with hearing children in regular classes. The

ratio of regular/special time and the subject areas which are integrated or segregated are determined on an individual basis.

5. *Resource Rooms.* These programs set apart a room in the regular school for the purpose of serving the varying needs of exceptional students. Often, hearing impaired students are assigned to the resource room for study halls or time blocks for special tutorial assistance.

6. *Itinerant Programs.* These programs are set up to assist students enrolled in regular classes. A specialized teacher assists students on a scheduled basis, with the amount of time varying from once a day to once a week. Numerous junior and senior high school programs are organized in this manner.

7. *Postsecondary Education.* Education after high school for the hearing impaired falls into three main categories:

a. Enrollment in colleges designed primarily for hearing students;
b. Enrollment in colleges designed primarily for hearing impaired students—Gallaudet College for the Deaf; the National Technical Institute for the Deaf;
c. Enrollment in junior college programs or vocational technical programs.

Approximately 1.5 percent of the total hearing impaired population (as opposed to 45 to 50 percent of the hearing population) is enrolled in some form of postsecondary education.

Gallaudet College, in Washington, D.C., is the world's only liberal arts and sciences college for the deaf. Admission to the college is based upon an entrance test, which is basically an achievement test developed by the college, along with reports from the student's school including results of achievement testing, an audiological evaluation, and a psychological evaluation. Vocational rehabilitation programs often assist in admissions and/or expenses. The college is funded by the United States government.

The National Technical Institute for the Deaf (NTID) is located at the Rochester Institute of Technology, Rochester, New York. The purpose of NTID is to give deaf students an opportunity to pursue a vocational technical program in science, business technology, or the applied arts. Admission is based upon an entrance test similar to that of Gallaudet College, as well as reports from the sending schools, which include academic achievement scores and audiological and psychological information. NTID employs three levels of programming: certificate, diploma, and degree. Gallaudet enrolls only hearing impaired students, but NTID students take courses along with hearing peers, with the aid of notetakers and/or interpreters. This institute, too, is funded by the United States government.

Junior college and vocational technical programs for the hearing impaired are becoming numerous. Such programs provide services to the hearing impaired at the postsecondary level at existing vocational technical and junior colleges. These programs retain hearing impaired students in the mainstream of general education by supplying them with some or numerous required special services. A complete resource of postsecondary programs is available in *A Guide to College/Career Programs for Deaf Students* (Rawlings, Trybus, Delgado, & Stuckless, 1975).

LEAST RESTRICTIVE ENVIRONMENT

Public Law 94-142 sets forth statements concerning the least restrictive environment. For some children, the least restrictive environment will and should be in the regular public school with appropriate supportive personnel. For others, the least restrictive environment will be residential placement, with staff available to provide an intensified program. The degree of hearing loss may not influence placement success as much as quality of the program, ability and interest of the parents to be supportive, and the social and emotional adjustment of each child.

As published research of the Office of Demographic Studies (Jensema, 1975) has demonstrated, academic achievement of severely hearing impaired children may reveal drastic differences from that of the normal hearing population in the regular public school, and yet the child may be succeeding. Evaluation of academic achievement should not be the only variable considered. Social and emotional adjustment is crucial, along with physical development, plus the understanding and acceptance of teachers, children in the classroom, and the public in general. Achievement in school, moreover, often depends upon the leadership of the supervisor and building principal.

Karchmer and Trybus (1977) have reported that of 49,427 hearing impaired children attending school in 1975-76, 47 percent were in residential schools, 23 percent in day schools, 18 percent in full-time classes, and 36 percent in integrated classes. In the residential schools, 63 percent had profound losses, 27 percent had severe losses, and 9 percent had moderate losses. In the integrated classes, 18 percent had profound losses, 20 percent had severe losses, 40 percent had moderate losses, and 22 percent had mild losses. Day schools and full-time classes fell in between these two extremes. For postlingually deaf children, 4 percent were in residential schools, and 13 percent of those found in the integrated programs were postlingually deaf. The percentages of hearing impaired children who never wear hearing aids are: residential schools, 30 percent; day schools, 10 percent; full-time classes, 7 percent; integrated, 17 percent. Percentages of children with intelligible speech were: residential schools, 31 percent; day schools, 43 percent; full-time classes, 52 percent; and integrated, 74 percent.

Day schools serve predominantly nonwhite populations and have the lowest income proportionately (Ries, Bateman, & Schildroth, 1975). Percentages of fathers who are college educated, by types and programs, are: residential schools, 21 percent; day schools, 19 percent; full-time classes, 34 percent; and integrated, 36 percent. A reassessment of the population within the next five years should prove interesting as it relates to the number of children who are integrated into local school districts. Being mainstreamed without necessary supportive personnel could doom the child to failure rather than success.

The appropriate Individualized Education Program (IEP) and its *impact* will and should be a determining factor in the success of a hearing impaired child. Professionals must learn about, cooperate with, and build upon the concepts presented by least restrictive environment and the Individualized Education Program.

SPECIFIC PROGRAMMING SUGGESTIONS FOR THE CLASSROOM TEACHER

The teacher who hopes to help a hearing impaired child must not feel sorry for the student but, rather, must attempt to show understanding, be willing to spend a little more time in meeting individual needs, and help other children in the group or class understand and accept the handicap of a person with hearing loss.

Whenever possible, the child should have assistance from an itinerant teacher who has been well trained in hearing rehabilitation and speech correction.

In the regular classroom, however, the teacher should be aware of many small things that can be done to assist the child along the road to success. Among them:

1. Give the child favorable seating in the classroom and allow him or her to move to the source of speech within the room; let the child turn around or have speakers turn toward the child, to allow visual contact with anyone who is speaking.
2. Encourage the student to look at the speaker's lips, mouth, and face. Speechreading should help clarify many of the sounds the child cannot hear.
3. Speak naturally—neither mumbling nor overarticulating. Speak neither too fast nor too slow, too loud or too soft.
4. Keep hands away from the mouth when speaking, and make sure that books, papers, glasses, pencils, and other objects do not obstruct the visual contact.
5. Take note of the light within the room so that the overhead light or window light is not at the speaker's back. Speechreading is

difficult when light shines in the speechreader's eyes. Try to prevent shadows from falling on the speaker's mouth.

6. Stand in one place while dictating spelling words or arithmetic problems to the group, allowing the hard of hearing child to see better, as well as to give a sense of security that the teacher will be there when he or she looks up.

7. Speak in complete sentences. Single words are more difficult to speechread than are complete thoughts. Approximately 50 percent of the words in the English language look alike on the lips. Such groups of words are termed *homophenous*. (Example: man, pan, ban, band, mat, pat, bat, mad, pad, bad.) Phrases and sentences placing the word in context help promote visual differentiation among homophenous words.

8. Give the student assignments in advance, or give the topic which will be discussed. A list of new vocabulary to be used in an assignment also assists the student. Because the family may help the child understand these words in speechreading practice, send the vocabulary home prior to the time it will be used in class.

9. Occasionally, have the hearing impaired child repeat the assignment to some other child so you are sure the assignment has been understood.

10. Remember at all times that this is a normal child with a hearing handicap; never single out a hearing impaired child in front of the group or in any other manner encourage an attitude of being "different."

11. Understand that the child with a hearing loss may tire faster than a child with normal hearing. The demands placed upon a child in speechreading and listening are greater than for hearing people. (Recall how tired an audience becomes when trying to listen to a speaker in a noisy hall.)

12. Take into consideration that many children hear better on some days than they do on others. Also, children may suffer from tinnitus (hearing noises within the head) which may make them nervous and irritable.

13. Restate a sentence, using other words that have the same meaning, when the hearing impaired individual does not understand what has been said. The reworded sentence might be more visible. (Example: Change, "Close your book," to "Shut the book," or "Please put your book away now." Look in a mirror and observe the difference.)

14. Encourage the hearing impaired child to participate in all school and community activities. This child is just as much a part of the environment as any other child.
15. Help the child to accept mistakes humorously. The deaf and the hard of hearing resent being the target of laughter just as much as anyone else. Laugh with them, not at them.
16. Encourage an understanding of and interest in the handicap of a hearing impaired child by the entire group. (A 12-year-old boy who had recently received a hearing aid refused to wear it to a Boy Scout meeting. His parents discussed it with the scoutmaster. The scoutmaster, in turn, was able to develop an interest by the group in radios and walkie-talkies, and eventually the hard of hearing boy agreed to bring his own walkie-talkie (hearing aid) and demonstrate it to the group.)

The path to success and the broadening of tomorrow's horizons for the child with a hearing loss depend upon coordination and teamwork on the part of the school, otologist, psychologist, audiologist, parents, and teacher. Many times, the teacher becomes the key to the lock of an otherwise lonely world.

SUMMARY

The term *hearing impaired* is most often used to describe individuals who are deaf or hard of hearing. In schools, hearing impaired students usually require special education to compensate for the accompanying difficulties in emotional adjustment and in social and academic development, primarily in the speech and language areas, which are essential to communication.

Measurement of hearing loss, primarily through use of the audiometer, pinpoints degree of loss and type of loss, which is categorized into the three major classifications of *conductive, sensorineural,* and *mixed.* The configuration of an audiogram, in conjunction with other information, may be used to predict success through amplification by hearing aids.

Hearing loss may occur before, at, or any time after birth, and in all cases, specialized training in language skills should be initiated as soon as possible. Causes of loss are either *endogenous* (genetic) or *exogenous* (produced by external agents such as disease, toxicity, or accident/ injury). From 50 to 60 percent of all deafness is attributed to genetic

4

factors; and of the 57 identified forms of genetic deafness, 10 involve both hearing and vision.

Some specific causal factors are maternal viral infection, such as German measles; medication or drugs taken by the individual or the mother of an unborn child; childhood infection, such as meningitis; respiratory infections; accidents or injury to the head and ear; and noise trauma.

Professionals have developed educational programming along three different lines of thought—the oral/aural approach, emphasizing listening, speaking, and speechreading (lipreading); the manual method, teaching fingerspelling or some form of sign language as the primary mode of communication; and the total communication approach, incorporating a combination of methods which are individually developed to meet the needs of the specific person.

Programs and services utilized by the hearing impaired include residential schools, day schools, self-contained classes, part-time or integrated programs, resource rooms, itinerant programs, and specialized post secondary education. The two postsecondary institutions designed primarily for the hearing impaired are Gallaudet College and the National Technical Institute for the Deaf.

Hearing impairments may affect the individual's family situation, language and speech communication, academic achievement, and emotions/behavior. The teacher should be attuned to programming considerations for hearing impaired students and should also feel comfortable in requesting additional help in making the learning experience more pleasant and successful for children and youth within the school setting.

REFERENCES

Babbidge, H.D. *Education of the deaf.* Washington, DC: Department of Health, Education and Welfare, 1965.

Davis, H., & Silverman, S. R. (Eds.). *Hearing and deafness.* New York: Holt, Rinehart & Winston, 1970.

Garretson, M.D. Total communication. *The Volta Review.* 1976 78(4), 88-95.

Gentile, A., & Rambin, J. *Reported causes of hearing loss for hearing impaired students: United States, 1970-71.* Washington, DC: Office of Demographic Studies, July 1973.

Illinois Commission on Children. Program for hearing impaired children in the state of Illinois. *Illinois Journal of Education,* 1968, 40-48.

Jensema, C. *The relationship between academic achievement and the demographic characteristics of hearing impaired children and youth.* (Series R, No. 2). Washington, DC: Office of Demographic Studies, 1975.

Jensema, C., & Trybus, R. *Reported emotional/behavioral problems among hearing impaired children in special educational programs: United States, 1972-73.* (Series R, No. 1). Washington, DC: Office of Demographic Studies, 1975. (Abstract) in special educational programs: United States, 1972-73. Washington, DC; Office of Demographic Studies, 1975. (Abstract)

Karchmer, M.A., & Trybus, R. *Who are the deaf children in "mainstream" programs?* Washington, DC: Office of Demographic Studies, 1977. (Abstract)

Office of Demographic Studies. *Reported causes of hearing loss for hearing impaired students.* Washington, DC: Author, 1970-71.

Office of Demographic Studies. *Ethnic background in relation to other characteristics of hearing impaired students in the United States.* Washington, DC: Author, 1975.

Rawlings, B.W., Trybus, R.J., Delgado, G.L. & Stuckless, E.R. (Eds.). *A guide to college career programs for deaf students.* Washington, DC & Rochester, NY: Gallaudet College & The National Technical Institute for the Deaf, 1975.

Ries, P., Bateman, D., & Schildroth, A. *Ethnic background in relation to other characteristics of hearing impaired students in the United States.* Washington, DC: Office of Demographic Studies, 1975.

Wilson, G.B., Ross, M., & Calvert, D.R. An experimental study of the semantics of deafness. *The Volta Review,* 1974, *76* (7), 408-414.

RESOURCE GUIDE

Historical Information

Babbidge, H. D. *Education of the deaf* (A report to the Secretary of Health, Education & Welfare by his Advisory Committee on the Education of the Deaf). Washington, DC: U.S. Government Printing Office, 1965.

Bender, R. *The conquest of deafness.* Cleveland, OH: Western Reserve University Press, 1960.

Davis, J. (Ed.). *Our forgotten children: Hard-of-hearing pupils in the schools.* Minneapolis: National Support Systems Project, 1977.

Davis, H., & Silverman, S. R. *Hearing and deafness.* New York: Holt, Rinehart & Winston, 1970.

Schein, J. D., & Delk, T. *The deaf population of the United States.* Silver Spring, MD: National Association of the Deaf, 1974.

Parent/Family

John Tracy Clinic. *Correspondence course for parents of little deaf children,* Los Angeles.

Northcott, W. H. *Curriculum guide: Hearing-impaired children, birth to three years, and their parents.* Washington, DC: The Alexander Graham Bell Association for the Deaf, Inc., 1972.

Simmons-Martin, A. *Chats with Johnny's parents.* Washington, DC: The Alexander Graham Bell Association for the Deaf, Inc., 1975.

Sitnick, V., Rushmer, N., & Arpan, R. *Parent-infant communication.* Beaverton, OR: Dormac, Inc., 1977.

Patterns of Development

Furth, H. G. *Thinking without language.* New York: Free Press, 1966.

Levine, E. *The psychology of deafness.* New York: Columbia University Press, 1960.

Myklebust, H. R. The psychological effects of deafness. *American Annals of the Deaf,* 1969, 105.

Quigley, S. *The relationship of hearing to learning: Some effects of hearing impairment upon school performance.* Springfield, IL: Illinois Office of the Superintendent of Public Instruction & University of Illinois, 1968.

Treatment

English, G. M. *Otolaryngology.* Hagerstown, MD: Harper & Row, 1976.
Gallaudet College. *What every person should know about heredity and deafness.* Washington, DC: Author, 1975.
Jeffers, J., & Barley, M. *Speechreading (Lipreading).* Springfield, IL: Charles C. Thomas, 1975.
O'Rourke, T. A basic course in manual communication. Silver Spring, MD: National Association of the Deaf, 1970.
Sanders, D. A. *Aural rehabilitation.* Englewood Cliffs, NJ: Prentice-Hall, 1971.

Educational Programming

Frisna, R. (Ed.). A bicentennial monograph on hearing impairment: Trends in the USA. *The Volta Review,* 1976, *78*(4).
Hart, B. O. *Teaching reading to the deaf.* Washington, DC: The Alexander Graham Bell Association for the Deaf, Inc., 1963.
Ling, D. *Speech and the hearing-impaired child: Theory and practice.* Washington, DC: The Alexander Graham Bell Association for the Deaf, Inc., 1976.
Northcott, W. H. *The hearing impaired child in a regular classroom: Preschool, elementary, and secondary years.* Washington, DC: The Alexander Graham Bell Association for the Deaf, Inc., 1973.
Streng, A. *Syntax, speech and hearing.* New York: Grune & Stratton, 1972.
Vorce, E. *Teaching speech to deaf children.* Washington, DC: The Alexander Graham Bell Association for the Deaf, Inc., 1974.

12 The Gifted and Talented

Joseph J. Walker
Georgia State University

The regular classroom teacher traditionally has had direct responsibility for educating the gifted child. During the 1950s and 1960s, when public schools were investing major resources to establish special programs for exceptional children, little was being done for gifted and talented children. Today, in many parts of the country, the gifted still are not being given special help through differentiated curricula suited to their needs. The age-old fallacy that "the gifted will achieve under any conditions" continues to be held by some as a universal truth, even though sufficient evidence exists to show otherwise.

For every John F. Kennedy, Albert Einstein, Martin Luther King, Eleanor Roosevelt, or Thomas Edison who do succeed, countless others with similar abilities do not reach their potential levels of achievement. Unfortunately, schools sometimes are to blame for this failure. Many school administrators and teachers throughout the country fail to recognize the gifted and talented students in their school rooms, or they do not attempt to provide special programs for students they *do* recognize as being talented and gifted. Compounding this situation is the widespread thinking that equates giftedness with super intelligence or genius. A student who is a genius is definitely highly gifted, but other students who are not geniuses also may be gifted.

DEFINING GIFTEDNESS

No consensus has been reached on a definition of giftedness, but if we accept the idea that a wide array of human abilities can be possessed to a greater or lesser degree, we can begin to comprehend giftedness. The statement by Witty (1972, p. 167) that the gifted are those *whose performance in any valuable line of human activity is consistently or repeatedly remarkable* is widely accepted, because it is broad enough to include the kinds and degrees of superiority that an individual may display.

In agreement with this general philosophy, Public Law 91-230, Section 806, states:

> . . . Gifted and talented children are those identified by professionally qualified persons who, by virtue of outstanding abilities, are capable of high performance. These children require differentiated educational programs and/or services beyond those normally provided by the regular school program in order to realize their contribution to self and society.
>
> Children capable of high performance include those with demonstrated achievement and/or potential ability in any one of the following areas, singly or in combination:
> 1. general intellectual ability
> 2. specific academic aptitude

3. creative and productive thinking
4. leadership ability
5. visual and performing arts
6. psychomotor ability

It can be assumed that utilization of these criteria for identification of the gifted and talented will encompass a minimum of 3 to 5 percent of the school population (Marland, 1972).

CLASSIFICATIONS

Until recently, most school programs developed for the gifted have concentrated only on the academically gifted student. Group IQ scores, group achievement scores, teacher recommendations, and grade-point averages have been used commonly by school systems to identify this population. However, each of these methods alone or in combination potentially overlooks or misidentifies children. In addition to the academically gifted, students may be creatively gifted, psychosocially gifted, or kinesthetically gifted. Although a student may possess any combination of these gifts, they will be discussed separately here, for better understanding.

The Academically Gifted

Individuals possessing superior general intellectual ability or specific academic aptitude are referred to as the academically gifted. IQ scores often are the major determinant in identifying academically gifted students.

Gallagher (1960) identifies three general levels of academic aptitude according to standard deviation above the mean, using the Stanford-Binet instrument as a measure. The lowest level is referred to as academically *talented* and is comprised of approximately 15-20 percent of the general school population. This group, one standard deviation above the mean, is represented by the Stanford-Binet reference point of IQ 116 as the lowest level. The second group exhibiting academic aptitude is termed *gifted*. This group is represented by a Stanford-Binet reference point of 132, two standard deviations above the mean, comprising 2-4 percent of the general school population. Gallagher refers to the third group as *highly gifted*. This segment is represented by a Stanford-Binet score of IQ 148 and above, and constitutes about .1 percent of the general population. Gallagher asserts that the highly gifted have unlimited intellectual achievement potential. The above described groups, then, are delineated as follows:

Talented	IQ 116+	15-20 percent of school population
Gifted	IQ 132+	2-4 percent of school population
Highly Gifted	IQ 148+	.1 percent of school population

Pegnato and Birch (1959) conducted a study involving over 1,000 junior high school students, to determine the most feasible method for identifying intellectually (academically) gifted children. They concluded that, when individual intelligence tests are unavailable, the most appropriate screening device for most school systems is a combination of group intelligence scores and group achievement scores.

In 1921 Terman and Oden (1959) began a longitudinal investigation of academically gifted children, extending from the 1920s into the 1950s. Approximately 1,000 children with Stanford-Binet IQ scores of 140 and above were selected, and a study was made of their development from childhood into adulthood. According to teacher ratings of these children as compared to a population of control children identified as typical for their grade level, the study group excelled in subjects requiring abstract thought. The smallest differences between the gifted and control samples were in subject areas requiring motor ability or some specialized skill such as penmanship, sports, and manual training. Stanford Achievement Tests administered to these gifted children indicated a consistently superior performance over that of their "average" chronological age group peers.

The Terman and Oden study found that, in general, bright children become bright adults; they enjoyed better health and adjusted better to the problems of life than average children. They also were more productive than their "average" colleagues. The Terman and Oden work concluded with this statement:

We would agree with the subjects that vocational achievement is not the only—perhaps not even the most important—aspect in life success. To many, the most important achievement in life is happiness, contentment, emotional maturity, and integrity. Even failure to rise above the lowest rungs of the occupational ladder does not necessarily mean that success in the truest sense has been trivial. There may have been heroic sacrifices, uncommon judgment in handling the little things of daily life, countless acts of kindness, loyal friendships won, and conscientious discharge of social and civic responsibilities. If we sometimes get discouraged at the rate society progresses, we might take comfort in the thought that some of the small jobs, as well as the larger ones, are being done by gifted people.

To demonstrate and stimulate the rapid mental skills of academically gifted students, and to promote understanding between gifted and typical students, appropriate classroom activities may be introduced. One such example is *Lutts and Mipps* (Pfeiffer & Jones, 1971), a problem solving activity requiring high levels of cognitive performance; participants include one or more groups including both typical and gifted students. The activity consists of translating nonsense words into distance, time, and rate, and although the solution relies on a simple arithmetic formula (rate x time = distance), it becomes much more analytically complicated due to the game structure. Each member of a group of 6 to 12 participants is randomly assigned several cards having printed selections from the 26 statements necessary to solve the problem. (For instance, "It is 8 lutts from A to B"; or "A wor is 5 mirs.") No one member of the group has sufficient information to solve the problem alone. Participants may share information verbally, but they may not exchange or give away their cards to other group members.

After solving the problem, discussion ensues. Participants discuss the frustration they may have felt at not finding the solution, their feelings toward the person in the group who contributed most to solving the problem, their feelings toward another group which arrived at the solution first, the feelings of those faster problem solvers toward those who were slower in finding the solution, and an explanation of the process used to arrive at the solution. By dealing with these and other questions, participants can better understand the feelings of both the academically gifted and their peers who are not capable of as high a level of intellectual performance (Johnson & Johnson, 1975).

The Creatively Gifted

Individuals who exhibit superior ability in creative or productive thinking often are referred to as creatively gifted. Although depth of intellect generally is associated with creative thought, and creative individuals may be high academic achievers, their ability to think divergently and develop new, unique, and original ideas sets them apart in this category (Martinson, 1974). An example of the creatively gifted is described by Arthur C. Clarke (1973) in *Profiles of the Future*. He mentions that not necessarily the scientist forecasts the future best, but rather the person with sound scientific knowledge or a "feel" for science plus a flexible imagination.

This kind of flexibility, divergence, and freedom of thought prevents the imagination from being clogged. Flexibility and freedom of thought allowed the Wright brothers to fly at Kitty Hawk, even though a leading astronomer "proved" aviation impossible just a few months before their flight.

What is creativity? According to Torrance (1970), creativity is "the process of sensing gaps or disturbing, missing elements; forming ideas or hypotheses concerning them; testing these hypotheses; and communicating the results, possibly modifying and retesting the hypothesis." Osborn (1967) defines creative thinking as the "imaginatively gifted recombination of known elements into something new." And Hammer's (1967) definition is that of "the unique innovation, the unique configuration, whether it be artistic, philosophical, or scientific. It must be new, fresh, and original, and it must be worthwhile, important, or highly valued. If it is creativity in the arts as opposed to creativity in the sciences, it must have richness of communicated emotion."

Gallagher (1975) states that a person evidences different activities during various stages of the creative process. He cites four major *creative process stages*:

- preparation
- incubation
- illumination
- verification.

During the preparation stage, the individual is studious and gives sustained attention to the problem; the predominant thinking operation is cognitive memory. The second stage, incubation, often is confused or jumbled. The individual must be intellectually free to partake in divergent thinking. The third stage, illumination, often is referred to as the "A-ha!" stage—when the individual, through a high tolerance for failure and ambiguity, breaks through to a creative solution to a problem, moving him or her to verification or proof that the solution is sufficiently pleasing, successful, and unique.

Four major *cognitive behaviors* form the creative process:

- fluency
- flexibility
- originality
- elaboration.

Fluency is the total number of responses given to a cue, excluding those which are irrelevant or repeated; sheer quantity is important. Flexibility is the number of category changes or shifts in thinking taking place as the response ideas develop and change. Originality refers to infrequent, unusual, or remote responses. Elaboration includes the embellishments, details, or complexity added to a basic idea.

The following activity demonstrates the difference between convergent thinking (arriving at a commonly accepted correct response) and divergent thinking (generating a number of alternatives and arriving at a unique solution to a problem). It is based on Frank Williams' (1973) model for encouraging creativity in the classroom.

Before the activity is introduced, the dialogue of a newspaper comic strip is covered with construction paper, exposing the pictures only. Participants, in groups, are asked to generate as many ideas as possible relative to the pictures. During this activity phase, brainstorming rules are in effect—no judgments may be made; quantity of ideas is important; and "wild" ideas are encouraged. After completing this phase, participants decide which of the ideas best relates to the pictures. They then develop the cleverest or most humorous dialogue to support the depicted situation.

This activity is designed to cue participant performance in the four major areas of creative cognitive behavior. During the first phase, the number of group responses (excluding duplicative ideas) would produce the fluency count. The number of different categories in the first phase would comprise the group's flexibility score. Originality is determined by deciding upon the most clever and humorously unique captions for the comic strip. Elaboration would include the amount of detail added to the basic idea to make it more clever and humorous (Walker, 1975).

These cognitive areas combine to give experts an indication of creative ability in children, and serve as the basis for such tests of creativity as the Torrance Tests of Creative Thinking.

The Psychosocially Gifted

Psychosocial giftedness includes superiority in political and social leadership and consists of an ability to facilitate attainment of group goals and to improve interpersonal relations within the group. Leaders and leadership have been defined in many ways. Perhaps one of the simplest yet most comprehensive definition is that of Wayman Crowe (1967): "A leader is defined as a person who influences the thoughts and actions of at least one other person . . . leadership may be described as the activity of producing change in the thoughts and actions of individuals in interaction." Children possessing psychosocial ability have the potential to be our future governmental, church, and social leaders.

These may be the people to whom we look to guide our moral and ethical destinies and future national development.

Children with psychosocial ability often serve as behavior models for their peers. They generally are liked and respected by their classmates. Their ideas and suggestions often are sought by others when a decision must be made. They generally can take responsibility and direct a group toward an established goal, either as elected or appointed leaders. They can find better ways of accomplishing objectives than ways previously established.

An excellent activity to employ in leadership training ability is the simulation game *Score as Much as Possible*. Four dyads (pairs) play the game. During the 10 rounds of play, each team bids an X or Y to accumulate points. Points won or lost by a team are tabulated according to the established scoring system. For instance, if one team bids an X and the other three teams bid Ys, the team bidding an X would win 3 points and the teams bidding Ys would each lose 1 point. Or, if each team bids a Y, each would win 1 point. At intervals throughout the game, teams are allowed to consult with the other teams to decide how they all might better score points. At no time before or during the game are the groups instructed to either cooperate or compete. The game, however, inevitably becomes cutthroat competition involving cheating, deceit, and lying by participants.

This activity can lead to discussions about leadership and examples of how negative characteristics have been exhibited by leaders throughout history, and their effects on humanity. The discussion then may proceed to one of future leadership and the necessity for leaders to have honesty and integrity. The students may wish to predict how they would function as leaders under various simulated conditions. They might ask the questions: Is attainment of a goal worth the sacrifice of personal integrity? Does the end always justify the means? (Schrank, 1972).

Through activities of this kind, our future leaders hopefully will develop a well-ordered set of personal values and a sound set of ethics to employ in leading others to a positive and productive future.

The Kinesthetically Gifted

A high level of visual, performing arts, or psychomotor skills often is referred to as kinesthetic giftedness. Included in this group are the talented artist, dancer, actor, and musician. Because sharing one's artistic ability with others in performance or receiving positive reactions from one's creations are emotionally rewarding experiences, kinesthetic

giftedness has both individual and social values. The most commonly used identification method for kinesthetic giftedness is that of expert recommendation. Identification of kinesthetically gifted children and youth, along with encouragement and support of this manner of talent, is valuable both for the individual and for the people to whom the talent will bring pleasure.

IDENTIFICATION

Because identification of gifted and talented children in all of the above areas is not an easy task but the human loss resulting from not identifying this population is costly, schools should take specific measures to seek out these students. Such measures may include professional, parent, peer, and self nominations, along with use of checklists and applicable testing instruments, to reveal skills and strengths.

The State of Florida *Resource Manual for Gifted Education* (Runyon, 1973) describes a suggested sequence for identifying the academically and creatively gifted, as well as (to a lesser degree) those with kinesthetic and psychosocial abilities.

First, schools should solicit nominations for possible participants in the gifted education program from persons including classroom teachers, principals, educational specialists, guidance counselors, parents, peers, and self-referrals. Parent and student interviews should not be bypassed, as they are valuable sources of information. In screening possible participants, weighted checklists might be used to insure that the student showing abilities other than a high IQ score has an opportunity for admission into the program. The Renzulli-Hartman checklist (1971) has been helpful in assisting teachers in selecting potential candidates. Also, a case study should be prepared, consisting of information about the candidate. (An official transcript can provide the candidate's academic history.) A committee comprised of teachers, psychologists, and administrators can then study and evaluate all available information to reach a decision concerning a child's acceptance and placement into the program.

As part of the identification and screening processes, testing information should be sought from different sources, including *cognitive tests* for measuring thinking, and *affective tests* for measuring feeling.

Cognitive Tests

Cognitive tests include *convergent* tests (having a commonly accepted correct response) for measuring *aptitude*, such as the California Achievement Tests (grades 1-8), Metropolitan Achievement Tests (grades 1-12), Stanford Achievement Tests (grades 1-9), and SRA Achievement Tests (grades 1-9). Or convergent tests may measure *intelligence*. Such tests include the Stanford-Binet Intelligence Scale (grades K-10), the Wechsler Intelligence Scale for Children (WISC), the California Tests of Mental Maturity (grades 4-12), and the Peabody Picture Vocabulary Test (grades K-12).

Tests to measure *divergent* thinking (generating a number of alternatives to arrive at a unique solution) fall into two major categories—*creativity* tests and tests of *intellectual maturity*. The Torrance Tests of Creative Thinking, both verbal and figural tests of creativity, are primary examples of creativity tests; the Goodenough Draw-A-Man Test is a test of intellectual maturity.

Affective Tests

Affective tests, for measuring feelings, include those on self-concept, such as both the elementary and secondary scales of *Self-Concept as a Learner,* and the *How Do You Really Feel About Yourself?* inventory (grades 4-12). Character and personality tests include the Children's Personality instrument (grades K-12).

The testing dimensions are summarized as follows:

Cognitive Tests —Convergent:	Aptitude Intelligence	
— Divergent:	Creativity Intellectual Maturity	
Affective Tests —	Self-Concept Character and Personality	

The Culturally Different Gifted

Irving Sato (1975) says:

> The culturally different gifted comprise one segment of a larger subpopulation called the educationally disadvantaged. This latter, broader category includes not only the culturally different, but also such groups as the economically deprived, female, handicapped, rural, and underachieving. The major refining factor in the definition of the culturally different is membership in a culture other than the dominant culture in society.

Sato has compiled information based on the work of Fitzgerald, Renzulli, Martinson, Gallagher, and others of the myriad ways currently being used to identify culturally different gifted pupils. Included in this list are various psychometric instruments such as the WISC Performance Scale, Goodenough Draw-a-Man Test, Peabody Picture Vocabulary Test, Torrance Tests of Creative Thinking, Raven Progressive Matrices, nonverbal sections of group and individual IQ tests, and portions of other existing performance tests. Other sources of information include planned student and parent interviews, local checklists for student, teacher, counselor, or parent use, the Alpha Biographical Inventory developed by the Institute for Behavioral Research in Creativity, and peer nominations.

Interviews and teacher and peer nominations were the primary methods for selecting members of a special class grouping for gifted children as reported by Baldwin (1977). She states that in the longitudinal study of 24 black children selected for the special grouping, only one of the students would have qualified if conventional IQ and achievement measures had been the only selection criteria.

Fitz-Gibbon (1974) proposed a method for identifying disadvantaged gifted children, stemming from a research project which had as its objective the development of a fair and practical method for identifying the top 2 percent of an inner-city eighth grade. Four hundred students in a predominantly black school were participants. Fitz-Gibbon concluded that when discriminant function analysis is not feasible, a simpler method is available.

The procedure has three primary steps:

1. In the screening stage, administer the Raven Standard Progressive Matrices to all students as a 30-minute classroom test.
2. In the selection stage, administer the Advanced Progressive Matrices as a power test to the top 6 percent on the Raven Standard Progressive Matrices and to any students strongly recommended by teachers or parents.
3. In the identification stage, administer the WISC to students whose Advanced Progressive Matrices scores were in the top half of the sample and also to students who were in the top 2 percent on the Standard Progressive Matrices.

The top students on the WISC, says Fitz-Gibbon, comprise the gifted group.

Numerous other means currently are being used to identify the culturally different gifted. The most important consideration, regardless of the specific procedure, is that the most appropriate method(s) available be used to locate students among the culturally disadvantaged group who will benefit from encouragement of their particular talents.

On the basis of experience and a great deal of related research, Torrance (1969) has identified 18 creative characteristics that occur frequently and to a high degree among culturally disadvantaged young people. These characteristics include an ability to express feelings and emotions, an ability to improvise with commonplace materials, an ability in and enjoyment of creative movement, dramatics, dance, etc., expressiveness in speech, enjoyment of and skills in group learning and problem solving, problem-centeredness, originality of ideas in problem solving, and humor.

Substantial progress is being realized, through the work of Torrance, Stallings, Bernal, Bruch, Renzulli, and others, toward identification of the culturally different gifted. Efforts must continue in that direction, not only for the benefit of individual children, but for those who will benefit from the discovery and nurture of their talents.

CHARACTERISTICS

May Seagoe (1976) presents a list of characteristics of the gifted and talented that has been extremely helpful to teachers of the gifted, regular classroom teachers, administrators, parents, and other interested citizens. Seagoe's list deals not only with characteristics present in a majority of gifted children, but also prepares one for concomitant difficulties sometimes encountered in associations with the gifted. Understanding these characteristics allows one to develop strategies to help alleviate possible distress on the part of the student.

Some Learning Characteristics of Gifted Children

Characteristics	Concomitant Problems
1. Keen power of observation; naive receptivity; sense of the significant; willingness to examine the unusual.	1. Possible gullibility; social rejection; defense of value system.
2. Powers of abstraction/conceptualization, synthesis; interest in inductive learning and problem solving; pleasure in intellectual activity.	2. Occasional resistance to direction; rejection or omission of detail.
3. Interest in cause-effect relationships; ability to comprehend relationships; interest in applying concepts; love of truth.	3. Difficulty in accepting the illogical.

Characteristics	Concomitant Problems
4. Liking for structure and order; liking for consistency, as in value systems, number systems, clocks, calendars.	4. Invention of own systems, sometimes conflicting.
5. Retentiveness.	5. Dislike for routine and drill; need for early mastery of foundation skills.
6. Verbal proficiency; large vocabulary; facility in expression; interest in reading; breadth of information in advanced areas.	6. Need for early specialized reading vocabulary; parent resistance to reading; escape into verbalism.
7. Questioning attitude; intellectual curiosity; inquisitive mind; intrinsic motivation.	7. Lack of early home or school stimulation.
8. Power of critical thinking; skepticism; evaluative testing; self-criticism and self-checking.	8. Critical attitude toward others; discouragement resulting from self-criticism.
9. Creativeness and inventiveness; liking new ways of doing things; interest in creating; brainstorming, freewheeling.	9. Rejection of the known; need to invent for oneself.
10. Power of concentration; intense attention that excludes all else; long attention span.	10. Resistance to interruption.
11. Persistent, goal-directed behavior.	11. Stubborness.

12. Sensitivity, intuitiveness; empathy for others; need for emotional support, a sympathetic attitude.

12. Need for success and recognition; sensitivity to criticism; vulnerability to peer group rejection.

13. High energy, alertness, eagerness; periods of intense voluntary effort preceding invention.

13. Frustration with inactivity and absence of progress.

14. Independence in work and study; preference for individualized work; self-reliance; need for freedom of movement and action; need to live with aloneness.

14. Parent and peer group pressures because of inherent nonconformity; problems of rejection and rebellion.

15. Versatility and virtuosity; diversity of interests and abilities; many hobbies; proficiency in art forms such as music and drawing.

15. Lack of homogeneity in group work; need for flexibility and individualization; need for help in exploring and developing interests; need to build basic competencies in major interests.

16. Friendliness and outgoingness.

16. Need for peer group relations in many types of group situations, to develop social leadership.

"Some Learning Characteristics of Gifted Children" appears in *The Identification of the Gifted and Talented* and has been published by the N/S LTI and by The Council for Exceptional Children, Reston, VA (1976). Reprinted by permission of May V. Seagoe and Irving Sato.

The listing provides brief descriptions of some of the superior abilities included in the six major areas covered in PL 91-230, Section 806. The gifts represented are found among all socio-economic groups, races, creeds, and cultures. As educators, our responsibility is to recognize them and provide differential educational opportunities for these students.

EDUCATIONAL PROGRAMMING

Program design for the gifted should add depth and breadth to a child's present knowledge. It must raise the child's conceptual level and provide opportunities to deal with high-level abstractions. Programs should offer opportunities for the students to engage in creative problem solving, decision making, predicting and forecasting, communicating, and gathering information. Several models exist as guides to ensure that programs for the gifted incorporate the above-mentioned areas. One of the most useful is Bloom's (1972) *Taxonomy of Educational Objectives*, which gives six types of intellectual activity that develop as a hierarchy in the cognitive domain:

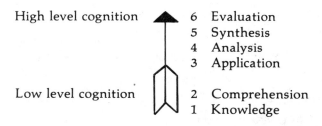

High level cognition		6	Evaluation
		5	Synthesis
		4	Analysis
		3	Application
Low level cognition		2	Comprehension
		1	Knowledge

Knowledge refers to the ability to recognize or recall information. This is typically the teacher-dominant, student-passive role relationship and involves transmission of factual information from teacher to student. *Comprehension* involves the student's understanding of knowledge gained. *Application* is the ability to use abstractions in concrete situations. *Analysis* is the breaking down of a complex problem into its component parts; it seeks to discover relationships between problem components. *Synthesis* is the joining together of elements not previously joined, to produce a new, unique whole. Evaluation is the judgment stage, at which decisions are made about the value of what has been cognitively generated.

Research conducted in Illinois (Steele, House, Lapan, & Kerins, 1970) indicated significant differences between average classes and gifted classes. These differences essentially were in degree of emphasis on higher thought processes, classroom focus, classroom climate, enthusiasm, independence, memory, and test/grade stress. These differences are delineated in the following listing.

Differences Between Average and Gifted Classes in Illinois

Average Classes | **Gifted Classes**

1. Most classes emphasize few (two or less) thought processes.

1. Most classes emphasize many (three or more) thought processes.

2. Most classes emphasize only one (if any) of the higher thought processes.

2. Most classes emphasize two or more of the higher thought processes.

3. A high level of teacher talk occurs.

3. A moderate level of teacher talk occurs.

4. Classes have *little* opportunity for or involvement in discussion.

4. Classes have *much* opportunity for and involvement in discussion.

5. Test/grade stress is characteristic of average classes as a group.

5. Test/grade stress is not characteristic of gifted classes as a group.

6. An absence of enthusiasm is the general climate in a majority of the classes.

6. A presence of enthusiasm characterizes almost all classes.

7. Little opportunity for independence is afforded.

7. Much opportunity for independence is offered.

8. Focus is on the teacher as information-giver, with students in a passive role.

8. Focus is on the student assuming an active role in the class.

The Illinois Gifted Program (Hardy, 1972) presents a set of 20 questions helpful in establishing a viable gifted program in our schools.

1. What are the needs of your school district?
2. What is your district's definition of giftedness?

3. What type of talent do you want to encourage?
   a. How will this talent be identified?
   b. How many students do you want to reach?
   c. What kind of minimum standards do you expect to set?
   d. What characteristics will the students demonstrate before and after the program?
4. What will happen differently to the students identified than would normally happen?
5. Does the present teaching and course offering provide for all the talents you want to encourage?
6. What content areas need the most change?
7. What student materials need to be changed?
8. Do you plan to change anything other than the materials?
9. How will the training of teachers differ?
   a. Will they need specialized training?
   b. What type of inservice education will be needed?
   c. How will inservice education be implemented?
10. What human and other resources are already available in your district?
11. What role will this project assume in the total school program?
12. Should special classes, times, or teachers be used for this project?
13. How will this project change the present pattern of the system?
14. How will you develop policy regarding various aspects of the projects?
15. How does the school district as a whole feel about this project?
16. What funds and expertise are needed for the project?
17. To what extent is the school district supporting this project?
18. How does the cost of this program compare with other special programs in the district, such as athletics, bands, educable mentally handicapped, dramatics?
19. What barriers do you expect to encounter while putting this program into effect?
20. How will your program and its impact be evaluated?

House, Steele, and Kerins (1970) indicated in their report regarding development of new quality gifted programs in Illinois that the success of such programs depends upon a small number of powerful variables; namely:

— *Size of the developing unit*—Larger developing units typically have available the necessary personnel, resources, and facilities to better provide quality gifted programs for their students than do smaller individual units.

— *Norms of the unit toward the innovation*—The philosophy and values of the school and community reflect the nature of the local school program and the support it receives.

— *Optimal leadership exerted within the district in behalf of the innovation*—Administrative and other school leadership support is imperative to the successful development of a quality gifted program.

— *Status of advocates within the system*—The perceived status of the gifted program coordinator and other program advocates by the administrators, other school faculty members, and the community can affect the reception, support, and sustenance of a quality gifted program. The highest quality programs are those with a program coordinator who is functioning in a staff position and devotes full time to developing and furthering the gifted program.

— *Contact of the system with the outside world*—The highest quality programs had contact and interaction with other school systems, state coordinators, university personnel, and others interested in development of quality programs for the gifted.

If these variables are considered in developing a gifted program, schools may be able to avoid some of the problems they might otherwise encounter in developing a quality program.

In developing an educational program, the gifted and talented among disadvantaged and minority groups pose a particular challenge and opportunity to educators. Passow (1972) believes that particular attention must be directed to the special problems of program development for the disadvantaged. Identification procedures that search for talent must be stressed, rather than those that screen out or bar minority group participation. The school staff must master teaching strategies and ways of using learning school and community resources, as well as altering any negative attitudes they may harbor toward the culturally different. By attending to students' affective as well as cognitive development, combined with an achievement rather than failure orientation, schools are capable of providing exemplary gifted programs for disadvantaged children.

Passow concludes that the entire community must become the classroom, and better strategies are needed to recognize language needs and the richness of differences among cultures. The culturally different gifted may need special guidance, and financial assistance may be essential to allow the economically disadvantaged gifted an opportunity to truly develop their abilities.

Delivery Systems

The most common delivery systems for providing programs for the gifted are:

Ability Grouping

This administrative delivery system is used widely in educating the gifted. Students are divided into homogeneous groups, based upon student performance in meeting set criteria necessary for participation in a particular group.

Acceleration

This type of program emphasizes advanced content. Priority generally is given to mastery of the subject matter. The most successful forms of acceleration build in enrichment or advanced placement features. Grade-skipping is a form of acceleration which is not as commonly used today as in the past.

Enrichment

This delivery system typically is a supplement to regular school curriculum offerings and includes honors courses, independent study programs, summer school programs, electives, and special co-curricular projects.

Special Classes

This "school within a school" concept may provide resource classes for the gifted, enrollment in regular college program courses while attending high school, Saturday sessions, and special summer programs.

In most instances, special classes include provision of instruction for gifted children by temporarily removing them from their regular classes for a given amount of time prescribed by a planned schedule.

Each of the above-mentioned delivery systems is used with varying degrees of success throughout the country. The school structure generally determines which delivery system will work best for its gifted students. As a result of his research, Julian Stanley (1976) believes that the better the enrichment program for gifted students, the greater the need for acceleration of subject matter or grade placement later. If this type of followup does not occur, boredom will almost certainly set in and will be severe in nature.

Curriculum

Curriculum and its adaptations should be considered as the means through which teachers and students achieve educational goals. Philosophically, the goals are the same for all students, but the ways in which students reach them must be individually determined. For gifted students, curriculum and its adaptations should be developed in accord with individualized aims and objectives to parallel the mental abilities and talents of students, and in accord with the role these students can be expected to play in society. The curriculum should differ in degree of quality and excellence from that planned for intellectually normal or slow learners. According to Bynum (1976a), curricula activities should provide opportunities for students to:

1. Add breadth and depth to present knowledge;
2. Utilize many instructional media, especially those which free the student from limited content bounds;
3. Develop efficient reading and study skills;
4. Raise the conceptual level on which they function, and to think conceptually;
5. Utilize problem solving techniques;
6. Develop and utilize critical thinking skills;
7. Develop and utilize creative abilities;
8. Do independent work;
9. Explore under guidance and independently many fields of interest;
10. Deal with high level abstractions;
11. Converse with students of like abilities;
12. Participate in planning learning experiences;
13. Apply theory and principles to solving life problems;

14. Develop leadership abilities or to become effective followers;
15. Develop a personal set of values;
16. Set and reach immediate and ultimate goals;
17. Develop self-discipline and a sense of social responsibility.

Leonard Lucito[1] describes his concept of curriculum, ideally, for the intellectually gifted as:

Pre-School   —Children should be independent readers.

—Children should deal with quantitative ideas (e.g., symmetry, positive and negative).

—Children should begin approach behavior to calculators and computers (logic).

—Children's programs should be mostly exploratory and should build on explorations.

Intermediate   —Children should learn models of how information has been organized—teaching disciplines, content, facts, structure of content.

—Children should learn processes used in a given field (natural science, mathematics, social science, communicative arts) and how these processes are applicable and relevant to the child.

—Curriculum should emphasize interdisciplinary study.

High School   —Curriculum should stress interdisciplinary study and specialization.

Basically, then, the curriculum should be flexible enough to allow independent and guided explorations into many fields of interest and, when the child is ready, large amounts of independent work. The curriculum should provide opportunities for children to develop and utilize critical thinking skills, problem solving techniques, and creative abilities. Gifted children should be provided opportunities to develop

---

[1] Personal verbal communication with author, 1977.

leadership abilities based on their personal set of values. The curriculum should provide an environment unique to a democracy in which everyone has the right to progress as far as his or her abilities allow.

Teacher Qualifications

An evaluation of the Illinois Gifted Program (Steele, House, Lapan, & Kerins, 1970) conducted by the Center for Instructional Research and Curriculum Evaluation at the University of Illinois drew as one of its conclusions that in the better local school gifted programs, the director selects teachers who are *change-minded*. Further, some types of training can increase the possibility of success in the classroom, and self-assessment procedures seem to be particularly effective in this regard.

The following teacher characteristics list compiled and distributed by the State of Georgia Gifted Program (Bynum, 1976b) gives a number of skills and characteristics necessary to experience success as a teacher of the gifted:

1. The ability to utilize research-type teaching when working with gifted students, and the ability to teach students to use research-type approaches to learning.
2. The ability to recognize a gifted student and to accept that student for him or herself.
3. A high degree of general intelligence and an in-depth knowledge of the academic area being taught.
4. A thorough understanding of the nature of giftedness and its relationship to developmental patterns of growth.
5. The ability to recognize and manipulate ideas, and the ability to translate ideas into learning situations that enable the student to gain knowledge and understanding of his or her responsibility to self and to society.
6. Recognition of learning processes and the ability to assist students becoming involved in processes of learning.
7. The ability to teach with enthusiasm and to transmit this enthusiasm to students in such a way that a love of learning develops.
8. A willingness to become a learner along with students.
9. The ability to create a classroom atmosphere that allows the student to become responsible for his or her own learning and one that is conducive to good mental health.
10. The ability to create and implement a flexible, enriched, challenging, and individualized curriculum which is suited to each student's needs and avoids quantity without quality.
11. An understanding of the social and emotional problems that may be created for the gifted student because of his or her accelerated mental development.
12. A positive attitude toward teaching the gifted.
13. The ability to create an environment in which the gifted learn to participate effectively in small-group and large-group situations and in which students learn to work independently.
14. A willingness to become a facilitator of learning.

An activity for reproducing the behaviors some teachers exhibit toward the gifted as well as other children is found in *The Behaviors of Acceptance* (Edwards, 1971). In this activity, the leader is asked to head a group discussion on any assigned topic and to accept the ideas of some individuals and reject the ideas of other individuals. Those whose ideas are accepted and those whose ideas are rejected are determined in advance by the color name card they were randomly assigned. (Those wearing green and blue name cards have their ideas accepted, and those with red and orange cards have their ideas rejected.)

After allowing the activity to proceed for an appropriate time period, the leader calls a halt to the activity. Discussion ensues about how those whose ideas were accepted felt toward the leader, toward others whose ideas were accepted, and toward those whose ideas were not. The group whose ideas were rejected reacts to the same questions. Group members discuss how they feel about "typical" teacher behavior — calling on the bright student when you want the correct answer or intellectually stimulating conversation at the expense of the other students.

To answer a question foremost in the minds of many potential teachers of the gifted: Many teachers of the gifted may not be as bright as some of the students with whom they work, but they cannot be dullards. The teacher, even though not as talented as the students he or she may be teaching, can serve as a model and friend whom the child will cherish long after the student has moved on in the development of his or her abilities.

One of the most succinct assessments of the characteristics of a good teacher of the gifted was generated by a group of gifted high school students who summarized a good teacher of the gifted as "someone who knows what they're talking about and listens when I talk."

SUMMARY

It might be said that every parent's child is gifted—at least to them. Still, the gifted are thought by some to be the most disadvantaged of our school children. For years they have been ignored by school systems, and the talents of many have been lost because of unconcern. Even when they have been recognized, only the *academically* gifted have received the bulk of attention.

Today's direction is to seek, along with the academically gifted, other students who may possess abilities in the creative, psychosocial, or kinesthetic areas, or combinations thereof. A focus also is directed at seeking out the culturally different talented, who formerly were placed in a position of disadvantage because of failure to recognize and appreciate talents among this population. This combined effort appears to be a sound approach to encouraging the positive growth of not only the individual students, but all of us as total human beings and a total society.

Perhaps C. F. Kettering, famed engineer, had this concept in mind when he said, "My interest is in the future, for it is there I will spend the rest of my life." If we are interested in our future, we must be interested in those who have the potential to make our future better. We can begin to achieve this by providing a school environment in which gifted, talented children and youth are identified and encouraged to achieve.

SELECTED TESTS AND MEASURES

The following are by no means a thorough representation of the many instruments which may aid in identification of this population; however, the listing serves to show that such measures are available and appropriate, with some adaptation to age and grade levels. Suggested age and grade levels given below are for "typical" children and are given merely for general perspective.

For measuring intelligence:

Draw-A-Man Test (ages 3-13)	Goodenough, F. *The Measurement of Intelligence by Drawings.* Yonkers on Hudson, NY: World Book Co., 1962
Peabody Picture Vocabulary Test (PPVT) (ages 2-5 to 18)	Dunn, L. M. American Guidance Service, 2106 Pierce Ave. Nashville, TN
Raven Progressive Matrices (ages 5-11)	Raven, J. C. Psychological Corp., 304 E. 45th St., New York, NY

For measuring divergent thinking:

Torrance Tests of Creative Thinking (with Words) (grades 4-12)	E. P. Torrance. Personnel Press, Inc., Div. of Ginn & Co., 20 Nassau St., Princeton, NJ
Torrance Tests of Creative Thinking (with Pictures) (grades 1-12)	E. P. Torrance. Personnel Press, Inc., Div. of Ginn & Co., 20 Nassau St., Princeton, NJ

For measuring feelings:

Self Concept as a Learner (grades 3-12)	Waetjen, W. University of Maryland, College Park, MD
How Do You Really Feel About Yourself? (grades 4-12)	Educational Technology Publications, Inc., 140 Sylvan Ave., Englewood Cliffs, NJ

REFERENCES

Baldwin, A. Y. Tests can unpredict: A case study. *Phi Delta Kappan,* 1977, *58*(8), 620-621.

Bloom, B. S. Taxonomy of educational objectives. In Syphers, D. F., *Gifted and talented children: Practical programming for exceptional children.* Reston, VA: Council for Exceptional Children, 1972.

Bynum, M. *Curriculum for gifted students.* Atlanta: State Department of Education, 1976.(a)

Bynum, M. *Teachers of the gifted.* Atlanta: State Department of Education, 1976. (b)

Clarke, A. C. *Profiles of the future.* New York: Harper & Row, 1973.

Crowe, W. In Jacobson, D. (Ed.), *Handbook on inservice education.* Springfield, IL: Superintendent of Public Instruction, 1967.

Edwards, D. *The behaviors of acceptance.* Oak Lawn, IL: Contemporary Curriculums, 1971.

Fitz-Gibbon, C. T. The identification of mentally gifted, disadvantaged students at the eighth grade level. *Journal of Negro Education,* 1974, *43*(1), 53-66.

Gallagher, J. J. *Analysis of research on the education of gifted children.* Springfield, IL: Superintendent of Public Instruction, 1960.

Gallagher, J. J. *Teaching the gifted child* (2nd ed.). Boston: Allyn & Bacon, 1975.

Hammer, E. F. In Jacobson, D. (Ed.), *Handbook on inservice education.* Springfield, IL: Superintendent of Public Instruction, 1967.

Hardy, R. *Twenty questions to aid in program development for gifted children.* Springfield, IL: Illinois Department of Program Development for Gifted Children, 1972.

House, E. R., Steele, J. M., & Kerins, T. *Advocacy in a non-rational system.* Springfield, IL: Illinois Department of Program Development for Gifted Children, 1970.

Jacobson, D. (Ed.). *Handbook on inservice education.* Springfield, IL: Superintendent of Public Instruction, 1967.

Johnson, D. W., & Johnson, T. P. *Joining together group theory and group skills.* Englewood Cliffs, NJ: Prentice-Hall, 1975.

Marland, S. P., Jr. (Submittor). *Education of the gifted and talented* (Vol. 2). Report to US Congress by U.S. Commissioner of Education. Washington, DC: U.S. Government Printing Office, 1972.

Martinson, R. A. *The identification of the gifted and talented.* Ventura, CA: Office of the Ventura County Superintendent of Schools, 1974.

Osborn, A. In Jacobson, D. (Ed.), *Handbook on inservice education.* Springfield, IL: Superintendent of Public Instruction, 1967.

Passow, H. A. The gifted and the disadvantaged. *The National Elementary Principal,* Feb. 1972, 22-31.

Pegnato, C., & Birch, J. In Gallagher, J. J. *Analysis of research on the education of gifted children.* Springfield, IL: Superintendent of Public Instruction, 1959.

Pfeiffer, J. W., & Jones, J. E. Lutts and Mipps. In *A handbook of structured experiences for human relations training* (Vol. 2). Iowa City, IA: University Associate Press, 1971.

Renzulli, J., Hartman, R. K., & Callahan, C. M. Teacher identification of superior students. *Exceptional Children,* November, 1971.

Runyon, J. *Florida state resource manual for gifted child education.* Tallahassee: State of Florida Department of Education, 1973.

Sato, I. In Miley, J., Sato, I., Luche, W. J., Weaver, P. W., Curry, J. A., & Ponce, R. H. *Promising practices: Teaching the disadvantaged gifted.* Ventura, CA: Ventura County Superintendent of Schools, 1975.

Schrank, J. *Teaching human beings.* Boston: Beacon Press, 1972.

Stanley, J. C. Identifying and nurturing the intellectually gifted. *Phi Delta Kappan,* 1976, *58*(3), 234-238.

Steele, J. M., House, E. R., Lapan, S., & Kerins, T. *Instructional climate in Illinois gifted classes.* Urbana: University of Illinois, 1970.

Terman, L. M., & Oden, M. H. The gifted group at mid-life: Thirty-five years' follow-up of the superior child. In *Genetic studies of genius* (Vol. 5). Stanford, CA: Stanford University Press, 1959.

Torrance, E. P. Creative positives of disadvantaged children and youth. *Gifted Child Quarterly,* 1969, *13,* 71-81.

Torrance, E. P. *Encouraging creativity in the classroom.* Dubuque, IA: William C. Brown, 1970.

Walker, J. J. Developing values in gifted children. *Teaching Exceptional Children,* 1975, *7*(3), 98-100.

Williams, F. E. *A total curriculum program for individualizing and humanizing the learning process.* Englewood Cliffs, NJ: Educational Technology Publications, 1973.

Witty, P. In Syphers, D. F., *Gifted and talented children: Practical programming for exceptional children.* Reston, VA: Council for Exceptional Children, 1972.

RESOURCE GUIDE

Historical Information

Barbe, W., & Renzulli, J. *Psychology and education of the gifted.* New York: Irvington, 1975.

Gallagher, J. *Teaching the gifted child.* Boston: Allyn & Bacon, 1975.

Gallagher, J. *Research summary on gifted child education.* Springfield, IL: Department of Program Development for Gifted Children, OSPI, 196.

Hildreth, G. *Introduction to the gifted.* New York: McGraw-Hill, 1966.

Newland, T. E. *The gifted in socio-educational perspective.* Englewood Cliffs, NJ: Prentice-Hall, 1976.

Rice, J. P. *The gifted: Developing total talent.* Springfield, IL: Charles C. Thomas, 1970.

Family

Coffey, K., & Ginsberg, G. *Parents speak on gifted and talented children.* Ventura, CA: Office of the Ventura County Superintendent of Schools, 1977.

Delp, J. L., & Martinson, R. A. *A handbook for parents of gifted and talented.* Ventura, CA: Office of the Ventura County Superintendent of Schools, 1974.

Ginsberg, G., & Harrison, C. *How to help your gifted child: A handbook for parents and teachers.* New York: Monarch Press, 1977.

Goertzel, V. *Cradles of eminence.* Boston: Little, Brown & Co., 1962.

Hersey, J., *The child buyer.* New York: Knopf Publishers, 1960.

Kanigher, H. *Everyday enrichment for gifted children at home and school.* Ventura, CA: Office of the Ventura County Superintendent of Schools, 1977.

Patterns of Development

Barbe, W., & Renzulli, J. Psychology and education of the gifted. New York: Irvington, 1975.

Rice, J. P. The gifted developing total talent. Springfield, IL: Charles C. Thomas, 1970.

Treatment

Gowan, J. C., & Bruch, C. B. *The academically talented student and guidance.* Boston: Houghton Mifflin, 1971.

Hauck, B. B., & Freehill, M. F. *The gifted — Case studies.* Dubuque, IA: William C. Brown Co., 1972.

Hoyt, K. B., & Hebeler, J. R. *Career education for gifted and talented students.* Salt Lake City: Olympus, 1974.

Torrance, E. P., & Myers, R, E. *Creative learning and teaching.* New York: Dodd, Mead, 1970.

Williams, F. E. *A total creativity program for individualizing and humanizing the learning process.* Englewood Cliffs, NJ: Educational Technology Publications, 1972.

Educational Programming

Kaplan, S. N. *Providing programs for the gifted and talented: A handbook.* Ventura, CA: Office of the Ventura County Superintendent of Schools, 1974.

Newland, T. E. *The gifted in socio-educational perspective.* Englewood Cliffs, NJ: Prentice Hall, 1976.

Renzulli, J. *A guidebook for evaluating programs for the gifted and talented* (workshop draft). Ventura, CA: Office of the Ventura County Superintendent of Schools, 1975.

SELECTED NATIONAL ORGANIZATIONS AND AGENCIES CONCERNED WITH EXCEPTIONAL CHILDREN AND YOUTH

ACLU Juvenile Rights Project
22 East 40th Street
New York, NY 10016

Alexander Graham Bell Association
  for the Deaf, Inc.
3417 Volta Place NW
Washington, DC 20007

American Academy for Cerebral Palsy
University Hospital School
Iowa City, IA 52240

American Academy of Pediatrics
1801 Hinman Avenue
Evanston, IL 60204

American Association for the Education
  of Severely and Profoundly
  Handicapped
1600 West Armory Way
Garden View Suite
Seattle, WA 98119

American Association for Gifted
  Children
15 Gramercy Park
New York, NY 10003

American Association for Health,
  Physical Education, and Recreation
1201 16th Street NW
Washington, DC 20036

American Association on
  Mental Deficiency
5201 Connecticut Avenue NW
Washington, DC 20015

American Association of Psychiatric
  Clinics for Children
250 W. 57th Street
Room 1032, Fish Building
New York, NY 10019

American Association for
  Rehabilitation Therapy
P.O. Box 93
North Little Rock, AR 72116

American Corrective Therapy
  Association, Inc.
811 Street Margaret's Road
Chillicothe, OH 45601

American Diabetes Association
18 E. 48th Street
New York, NY 10017

American Epilepsy Society
Department of Neurology
University of Minnesota
Box 341, Mayo Building
Minneapolis, MN 55455

American Foundation for the Blind
15 W. 16th Street
New York, NY 10011

American Heart Association
44 E. 23rd Street
New York, NY 10016

American Lung Association
1790 Broadway
New York, NY 10019

American Medical Association
535 N. Dearborn Street
Chicago, IL 60610

American Occupational Therapy
  Association
6000 Executive Blvd.
Rockville, MD 20852

American Orthopsychiatric
  Association, Inc.
1790 Broadway
New York, NY 10019

American Physical Therapy
  Association
1156 15th Street NW
Washington, DC 20005

American Printing House for the Blind
1839 Frankfort Avenue
Louisville, KY 40206

American Psychological Association
1200 17th Street NW
Washington, DC 20036

American Rehabilitation Counseling
  Association of the American
  Personnel and Guidance Association
1607 New Hampshire Avenue NW
Washington, DC 20009

American Rheumatism Association
1212 Avenue of the Americas
New York, NY 10036

American Speech and Hearing
  Association
9030 Old Georgetown Road
Washington, DC 20014

Arthritis Foundation
1212 Avenue of the Americas
New York, NY 10036

Association for Children with
  Learning Disabilities
2200 Brownsville Road
Pittsburgh, PA 16210

Association for the Aid of
  Crippled Children
345 E. 46th Street
New York, NY 10017

Association for Education of the
  Visually Handicapped
919 Walnut
Philadelphia, PA 19107

Association for the Help of
  Retarded Children
200 Park Avenue South
New York, NY 10003

Association of Rehabilitation
  Centers, Inc.
7979 Old Georgetown Road
Washington, DC 20014

Association for the Visually
  Handicapped
1839 Frankfort Avenue
Louisville, KY 40206

Bureau for Education of the
  Handicapped
400 6th Street
Donohoe Building
Washington, DC 20202

Center on Human Policy
Division of Special Education and
  Rehabilitation
Syracuse University
Syracuse, NY 13210

Center for Sickle Cell Anemia
College of Medicine
Howard University
520 "W" Street NW
Washington, DC 20001

Child Welfare League of America, Inc.
44 East 23rd Street
New York, NY 10010

Children's Defense Fund
1520 New Hampshire Avenue NW
Washington, DC 20036

Closer Look
National Information Center for
  the Handicapped
1201 16th Street, NW
Washington, DC 20036

Council for Exceptional Children
1920 Association Drive
Reston, VA 22091

Epilepsy Foundation of America
1828 "L" Street, NW
Washington, DC 20036

Foundation for Child Development
345 E. 46th Street
New York, NY 10017

Goodwill Industries of America, Inc.
9200 Wisconsin Avenue
Washington, DC 20014

Hemophilia Research, Inc.
30 Broad Street
New York, NY 10004

Institute for the Study of Mental
Retardation and Related Disabilities
130 South First
University of Michigan
Ann Arbor, MI 48108

International Association for the
Scientific Study of Mental Deficiency
Ellen Horn, AAMD
5201 Connecticut Avenue, NW
Washington, Dc 20015

International League of Societies for
the Mentally Handicapped
12, Rue Forestiere,
Brussels -5, Belgium

International Society for Rehabilitation
of the Disabled
219 E. 44th Street
New York, NY 10017

Mental Health Law Project
1220 19th Street NW
Washington, DC 20036

Muscular Dystrophy Association
of America
810 7th Avenue
New York, NY 10019

National Aid to the Visually
Handicapped
3201 Balboa Street
San Francisco, CA 94121

National Amputee Foundation
12-45 150th Street
Whitestone, NY 11357

National Association of the Deaf
2025 Eye Street, NW
Suite 321
Washington, DC 20006

National Association for Gifted
Children
8080 Spring Valley Drive
Cincinnati, OH 45236

National Association for Mental
Health, Inc.
Suite 1300
10 Columbus Circle
New York, NY 10019

National Association for Music
Therapy, Inc.
Box 610
Lawrence, KS 66044

National Association for Retarded
Citizens
2709 Avenue E, East
P.O. Box 6109
Arlington, TX 76011

National Association of Sheltered
Workshops and Homebound
Programs
1522 "K" Street NW
Washington, DC 20005

National Association of Social Workers
2 Park Avenue
New York, NY 10016

National Association of State Directors
of Special Education
1201 16th Street NW
Washington, DC 20036

National Association for the
Visually Handicapped
3201 Balboa Street
San Francisco, CA 94121

National Cancer Foundation
1 Park Avenue
New York, NY 10016

National Center for Law and the
Handicapped, Inc.
1235 N. Eddy Street
South Bend, IN 46617

National Committee for Multi-
Handicapped Children
239 14th Street
Niagara Falls, NY 14303

National Council for the Gifted
700 Prospect Avenue
West Orange, NJ 07052

National Cystic Fibrosis Research
Foundation
3379 Peachtree Road NE
Atlanta, GA 30326

National Easter Seal Society for
Crippled Children and Adults
2023 West Ogden Avenue
Chicago, IL 60612

National Epilepsy League, Inc.
116 S. Michigan Avenue
Chicago, IL 60603

National Federation of the Blind
218 Randolph Hotel
Des Moines, IA 50309

National Foundation for Infantile
Paralysis
Box 2000
White Plains, NY 10602

National Foundation—March of Dimes
800 2nd Avenue
New York, NY 10017

National Heart Institute
9600 Rockville Pike
Building 31, Room 5A50
Bethesda, MD 20014

National Hemophilia Foundation
25 W. 39th Street
New York, NY 10018

National Institute of Arthritis
and Metabolic Disease
Bethesda, MD 20014

National Institute of Health
United States Department of Health,
Education and Welfare
Washington, DC 20014

National Kidney Foundation
116 E. 27th Street
New York, NY 10016

National Multiple Sclerosis Society
257 Park Avenue, South
New York, NY 10010

National Paraplegia Foundation
333 N. Michigan Avenue
Chicago, IL 60601

National Rehabilitation Association
1522 "K" Street NW
Washington, DC 20005

National Therapeutic Recreation
Society
1700 Pennsylvania Avenue NW
Washington, DC 20006

National Society for Autistic Children
621 Central Avenue
Albany, NY 12206

National Society for Prevention of
Blindness, Inc.
79 Madison Avenue
New York, NY 10016

Orton Society, Inc.
8415 Bellona Lane
Baltimore, MD 21204

President's Committee on Employment
of the Handicapped
U.S. Department of Labor
Washington, DC 20210

President's Committee on Mental
Retardation
Regional Office Building #3
7th and D Streets SW
Room 2614
Washington, DC 20201

Society for the Rehabilitation of the
Facially Disfigured
550 1st Avenue
New York, NY 10016

United Cerebral Palsy Association
66 E. 34th Street
New York, NY 10016

United Epilepsy Association
111 W. 57th Street
New York, NY 10019

Volta Speech Association for the Deaf
1537 35th Street, NW
Washington, DC 20007

LITERATURE ON EXCEPTIONAL CHILDREN
Selected Periodicals

AAESPH Review (American Association for the Education of the
    Severely and Profoundly Handicapped)
American Educational Research Journal
American Journal of Art Therapy
American Journal of Mental Deficiency
American Journal of Occupational Therapy
American Journal of Psychology
American Sociological Review
Archives of Otolaryngology
Arithmetic Teacher
Asha (American Speech and Hearing Association journal)
Assignment Children
Aviso (Journal of Special Education)
Behavior Therapy
Behavorial Science
British Journal of Mental Subnormality
Bulletin of the National Association of Secondary School Principals
Bulletin of the Orton Society
Bulletin of Prosthetics Research
Career Education Quarterly
Child and Family
Child Care Quarterly
Child Psychiatry and Human Development
Child Welfare
Childhood Education
Children Today
Day Care and Early Education
The Deaf American
Developmental Psychology
Devereaux Schools Forum
Early Years
Education Forum
Educational Leadership
Educational Medicine
Educational Researcher
Elementary School Journal
Exceptional Children
Exceptional Parent
Family Coordinator
Focus on Exceptional Children
Generic Psychology Monographs
Gifted Child Quarterly
Harvard Educational Review
Health Service Reports
Hearing
Insight (a publication of the Council for Exceptional Children)
Instructor
Journal of Abnormal Child Psychology
Journal of Abnormal Pyschology
Journal of Applied Behavior Analysis

Journal of the Association for the Study of Perception
Journal of Career Development
Journal of Career Education
Journal of Child Psychology and Psychiatry
Journal of Consulting and Clinical Psychology
Journal of Creative Behavior
Journal of Education
Journal of Experimental Education
Journal of Language, Speech, and Hearing
Journal of Learning Disabilities
Journal of Music Therapy
Journal of Negro Education
Journal of Nervous and Mental Disease
Journal of Pediatrics
Journal of Personality Assessment
Journal of Personality and Social Psychology
Journal of Psychology
Journal of Social Issues
Journal of Social Psychology
Journal of Special Education
Journal of Speech and Hearing Disorders
Journal of Teacher Education
Language, Speech and Hearing Services in School
National Elementary Principal
Perceptual and Motor Skills
Personnel and Guidance Journal
Phi Delta Kappan
Physical Therapy (Journal of the American Physical Therapy
    Association)
Psychology in the Schools
Reading Research Quarterly
Rehabilitation Digest
Rehabilitation Research and Practice Review
Rehabilitation Teacher
Research in Education
Review of Educational Research
School Psychology Digest
Social Work
Speech Monographs
Teacher of the Deaf
Today's Education
Vocational Guidance Quarterly

GLOSSARY OF SELECTED TERMS

This glossary is not intended to be exhaustive. The terms were selected because of their current implications for the broad area of special education, and are included in this separate section because of their particular importance to beginning students in interpreting new legislation and practices. The definitions are general and are not intended as authoritative references. More technical terms specific to areas of exceptionality have not been included here; they are explained within the chapter context in which they are used. The reader also is encouraged to refer to the index as a reference leading to further understanding of specific terms and their application.

Adaptive Behavior Generally used in referring to an individual's ability to meet standards set by society for his/her cultural group. The American Association on Mental Deficiency considers three areas of performance in assessing adaptive behavior — maturation, learning, and social adjustment.

Adaptive Physical Education Physical education programs designed to meet the specific needs of handicapped children and youth.

Annual Goals Activities or achievements to be completed or attained within a year. Annual goals are required to be stated for handicapped children when writing individualized education programs (IEPs), as directed in Public Law 94-142.

Average Daily Attendance In this context, the number of students in attendance per day is totaled and divided by the respective number of days. Unless there are no absentees, the average daily attendance is less than the average daily membership.

Average Daily Membership The number of children assigned to a class or school district totaled and divided by the respective number of days. Unless there are no absentees, the average daily membership always is larger than the average daily attendance.

BEH An abbreviation for the *Bureau of Education for the Handicapped*. This is the major unit within the federal government responsible for administration and educational policies affecting handicapped children and youth.

Behavior Modification A technique used to change behavior; it applies principles of reinforcement learning.

Bilingual Proficiency in two languages. Frequently used in describing children for whom a non-English language is spoken in the home but who attend schools in which English is the standard language.

CEC Abbreviation for the *Council for Exceptional Children.*

Compulsory Attendance A provision of federal and state laws requiring children to enroll for and attend school.

Congenital Present at birth, as differentiated from acquired after birth. The term is used frequently in referring to handicapping conditions.

Consent Used in reference to obtaining permission from parents to evaluate a child or to place a child in a program. PL 94-142 contains specific provisions regarding consent. The reader is referred to Section 121a.500, *Federal Register*, August 23, 1977, Vol. 42, No. 163.

Consulting Teachers Specially trained teachers who provide consultation to teachers and other instructional personnel involved in educational programs for exceptional children. Their roles differ from those of itinerant teachers in that consulting teachers do not provide direct services to handicapped children and youth except for purposes of demonstrating a technique as part of their consulting role.

Deficit A term used to describe a level of performance that is less than expected for an individual.

Developmental Disabilities Conditions which originate in childhood and which result in a significant handicap for the individual. These include conditions such as mental retardation, cerebral palsy, epilepsy, and conditions associated with neurological damage.

Due Process Used in an educational context, the term refers to procedures and policies established to ensure equal educational opportunities for all children. PL 94-142 contains due process procedures specific to handicapped children.

Endogenous Originating from within.

Etiology Refers to the cause of a disorder or disease; e.g., the cause of a handicapping condition.

Exceptional Children Children whose performance in school-related behaviors varies from the norm to the extent that special instruction, assistance, and/or equipment are required. Children may be classified as exceptional because of intellectual, physical, and/or behavioral and/or sensory reasons. The term also is used in referring to gifted children.

Excess Costs A term frequently used to denote the extra costs incurred in educating a handicapped child. For example, if the average pupil cost for educating a nonhandicapping child is $1,800 per year and the average per-pupil cost for educating a handicapped child is $2,800 per year, the excess cost would be $1,000.

Exogenous Pertaining to external causes.

Flow Through Funds Some federal laws allocate funds to local districts but require them to be distributed by the state educational agency. Federal funds that are distributed by the state educational agency directly to local districts are referred to as flow through funds. Also called *pass through funds.*

Free Appropriate Public Education (FAPE) Used in PL 94-142 to mean special education and related services which are provided at public expense, which meet requirements of the state educational agency, and which conform to the individualized education program (IEP) requirement of PL 94-142.

Habilitation A process of improving an individual's performance. It could apply to a broad range of skills and abilities. Often used in referring to services provided to severely handicapped individuals in the process of preparing them for employment opportunities.

Handicapped (Also see *Exceptional Children*) The term *handicapped* is more restrictive than the term *exceptional* in that it does not include the gifted. When the gifted are to be included in referring to a population of students requiring special instruction, assistance, or equipment, the term *exceptional* is generally applied.

Homebound Instruction Teaching provided by specially trained instructors to students who are unable to attend school. Homebound instruction generally is provided on a short-term basis; under some circumstances, however, instruction is provided through this method over an extended period of time. Teachers of the homebound work closely with the student's regular teachers in coordinating the tutorial program.

IEU An abbreviation for *Intermediate Educational Unit.* Several states have educational units which comprise several districts or counties. These units may also be referred to as intermediate districts, cooperative, multi community, or county units.

IHE An abbreviation for Institutions of Higher Education. Frequently used when referring to private or public colleges and universities.

Incidence As applied to exceptional children, incidence refers to the number of individuals who at some time in their life might be considered exceptional.

Individualized Education Program (IEP) A requirement of PL 94-142 which specifies that an educational plan must be developed in writing and maintained for each handicapped child. The IEP must include a statement of the child's current level of educational performance, annual goals, short-term instructional objectives, specific services to be provided, information and dates services are to be provided, and criteria for evaluation.

Integration Used in the context of special education, this term refers to the placement of handicapped children in educational programs also serving nonhandicapped children.

Itinerant Teachers Teachers who are trained to provide direct services to handicapped children and youth. Such teachers do not operate a classroom; instead, they assist handicapped children and youth who are assigned to regular classes. They also may consult with regular classroom teachers.

LEA An abbreviation for *Local Education Agency.* Often used in referring to public school districts.

Least Restrictive Environment When applied to the education of exceptional children, the term refers to the principle that handicapped children should be educated with nonhandicapped peers in regular educational settings whenever possible. Allowances are made for placement in special classes or other settings when they are the least restrictive based on needs of the individual involved.

Mainstreaming The practice of educating handicapped children in regular educational settings. This generally involves the placement of handicapped children in regular classrooms and the provision of support services when necessary. The practice is gaining wide popularity in meeting educational needs of the mildly handicapped.

Mandate A requirement that specific tasks or steps are to be carried out; i.e., federal and state laws exist which mandate that educational services be provided to all handicapped children and youth.

Mental Age A level of intellectual functioning based on the average for individuals of the same chronological age.

Monitoring Activities conducted to ensure that particular requirements or procedures are being carried out. For example, states may establish monitoring procedures to determine the degree to which local districts are carrying out the IEP requirements of PL 94-142.

Native Language The language normally used by an individual.

Neonatal Pertaining to newborn children. Generally refers to the time between the onset of labor and six weeks following birth.

Nondiscriminatory Testing Refers to the use of instruments for assessing performance of individuals which allow for the individual being tested to perform maximally on those skills or behaviors being assessed. Tests discriminate against individuals when the norms are inappropriate, the content of the items does not relate to the individual's cultural background, the examinee does not understand the language of the items or of the person administering the test, or when sensory problems interfere with performance on the test.

Normalization An ideology that has been emphasized as a principle of human service; addresses the provisions of patterns of life for the handicapped which are as close as possible to those of members of society in general. This principle has received particular support in reference to improving services for the mentally retarded.

Occupational Therapy Involves engaging individuals or groups in activities designed to enhance their physical, social, psychological, and cognitive development. Occupational therapy is a major service provided by most rehabilitation centers.

Organic As used in referring to etiology of a handicapping condition, it means the cause is due to factors within the body, particularly the central nervous system.

Paralysis Impairment or loss of voluntary movement or sensation.

Paraprofessional A person trained as an assistant to a professionally qualified teacher. Some states have certification requirements for paraprofessionals.

Physical Therapy Services provided by trained physical therapists in the general area of motor performance. Physical therapy is provided upon prescription by a physician. Services focus on correction, development, and prevention.

Postnatal Following birth.

Prenatal Prior to birth. Frequently used in referring to the medical care received by women during pregnancy, e.g., prenatal care.

Prevalence When applied to exceptional children, it refers to the number of exceptional children who exist at the present time.

Protective Safeguards Procedures established to ensure that the rights of the individual are protected.

Prosthesis An artificial body part.

Public Law 93-380   Educational Amendments of 1974 passed August 21, 1974.

Public Law 93-516   An amendment passed by Congress broadening the application of Section 504 of the Rehabilitation Act of 1973 to include educational services among those services covered by the Act.

Public Law 94-142   The Education For all Handicapped Children Act of 1975. (See the *Federal Register*, August 23, 1977, Vol. 42, No. 163, for details on the rules governing this Act.

Rehabilitation   Restoration; for example, a child may suffer an injury that results in damage to a limb and, through therapy, the limb may be restored to good condition. The term frequently is applied to a variety of services designed to assist individuals in overcoming handicaps, especially in preparation for vocational employment. Such services are referred to as *vocational rehabilitation services.*

Remediation   Correction of a deficiency. Often used in referring to correction of academic deficits; e.g., problems in reading.

Resource Room   A program option involving placement of a student in a regular class plus assignment to a special teacher for remedial or supplemental instruction. The special teacher may be referred to as a resource teacher, and the room in which special instruction is offered is referred to as a resource room.

SEA   An abbreviation for *State Education Agency.* Commonly used in referring to the department in state government with primary responsibility for public school education.

School Social Work Services   School social workers provide a major communication link between the school staff and the family, and a variety of case work services including assistance in interpreting evaluation reports and making recommendations. In some districts they chair child study committees. They also provide a major resource to special educators in working with community agencies.

Section 504   Refers to Section 504 of the Rehabilitation Act of 1973. This section contains requirements designed to guarantee the civil rights of the handicapped. (See the *Federal Register*, May 4, 1977, Vol. 2, No. 86.

Special Class   A program option for exceptional children involving the assignment of children with similar instructional needs to a class taught by a certified special teacher. Special classes sometimes are referred to as *self-contained classes.*

Special Purpose School   This term frequently is applied to schools that serve only exceptional children. Such schools may offer programs for one or more types of exceptional children. They sometimes are referred to as *special schools.*

Special Teacher   Refers to a teacher certified to teach exceptional children. Historically, the term has been applied primarily to teachers of self-contained classes for exceptional children. Currently, the term is applied to certified teachers who are assigned to teach exceptional children.

Speech Clinician   A trained specialist who works with students having articulation or language problems, as well as children with more serious speech disorders. Speech therapy services may be provided in individual therapy sessions, group therapy sessions, or, in many cases, through consultations with the student's teacher.

State Aid   Funds allocated from the state treasury to local districts. Most states provide extra funds to local districts to assist in covering the additional costs incurred in educating exceptional children.

State Institutions   A term used to identify residential programs supported by public tax sources. Most states operate institutions for the mentally retarded and mentally ill.

State Plan   Public Law 94-142 requires each state department of education to submit to the U.S. Office of Education a plan for implementation and administration of the law. The Public Act Regulation for PL 94-142 contains guidelines for the content and structure of state plans.

Support Services   Special services provided to exceptional children beyond their basic educational program. Such services may include speech therapy, occupational therapy, physical therapy, music therapy, tutoring, and psychological services.

Surrogate Parent   A person other than an individual's natural parent who has legal responsibility for the individual's welfare.

Therapy/Treatment Examples of therapies often provided to exceptional children include speech therapy, occupational therapy, physical therapy, and music therapy.

Trauma Generally used in referring to a physical injury. However, the term is also used in referring to the harmful effects of a psychological experience.

USOE The *United States Office of Eduction*. Sometimes abbreviated further to OE (Office of Education).

Underachiever Based on expected levels of performance, an underachiever is an individual who does not achieve at a level expected for his or her age and ability level. The term generally is applied in reference to academic performance in school.

Vocational Education Educational programs designed to prepare individuals for employment.

AUTHOR INDEX

SUBJECT INDEX

Date Due

NO 30 '98			